The Best AMERICAN SPORTS WRITING 2000

The Best AMERICAN SPORTS WRITING 2000

Edited and with an Introduction
by Dick Schaap

Glenn Stout, *Series Editor*

HOUGHTON MIFFLIN COMPANY
BOSTON · NEW YORK   2000

Visit our Web site: www.houghtonmifflinbooks.com.

ISSN 1056-8034
ISBN 0-618-09394-X
ISBN 0-618-01209-5 (pbk.)

Printed in the United States of America

QUM 10 9 8 7 6 5 4 3 2 1

Contents

Foreword

THIS IS ONE of the best jobs I've ever had.

That may say as much about some of my previous stints in the working world as anything else, but even if I'd spent my early years, oh, I don't know, monitoring water temperature off Caribbean beaches instead of pouring concrete, it would be hard to match this task on the monitor of accumulated pleasure. Not many people do for a living what many others do purely for pleasure, but sometimes I'm one of them. In the decade I've served as series editor for *The Best American Sports Writing* I have had to learn to respond to the question "What did you do today?" by shaking my head grimly back and forth and responding with a well-timed sigh, "I worked all day."

This ensures a more sympathetic response than the truth, which is usually some variation of "I sat around reading."

"More fun at the incinerating plant," as Ring Lardner once wrote.

Ten years ago, when I was first approached to serve as series editor for the idea of a book to be called *The Best American Sports Writing*, I knew it was one of those rare moments when your life can be divided into "before" and "after." I'd been chipping away at the fringes of the sports writing world for several years, writing articles and trying to hustle — er, obtain — a book contract for any number of projects, with some success; I was quickly accumulating a world-class collection of rejection letters. Still working at a job every day, I was not doing much that I wanted to. But from the instant this book was mentioned to me, I could envision the entire shelf stretched out before me. Somehow, I was meant to do this. I was familiar with the old *Best Sports Stories* series, which had recently deteriorated into a contest with a panel of judges and, unbeknownst to us all, had just ceased publication. This series, I was convinced, could be both different and better. The genre had evolved and changed.

That is one reason why my first suggestion was to title the series *The Best American Sports Writing* rather than *The Best American Sportswriting*. I thought that "Best Sportswriting" indicated a narrow view of what writing about sports could be and that the reader would expect a book with clear and predictable boundaries. *Best American Sports Writing* seemed more open and more reflective of what was going on. I thought it was important that each selection succeed as an independent piece of writing first and felt that the effect of the adjective *sports* could change and evolve year by year.

My role in the series would be to read as much as I could and cull a more manageable assortment of material from which a guest editor would make the final selections. Not knowing who this would be from year to year gave me another reason to use the widest possible definition of sport, not trying to decide "what is sport" as much as just trying to be aware of "what most certainly is not sport." By my count, over the last ten years we've published stories on nearly forty different sports, among them such familiar pursuits as auto racing, baseball, basketball, billiards, boxing, diving, figure skating, fishing, football, golf, hockey, horse racing, hunting, mountaineering, pool, rodeo, rowing, running, soccer, tennis, and volleyball. Nothing too surprising there. But we've also used stories on arm wrestling, beagling, bird-watching, bodybuilding, bullfighting, cheerleading, curling, dog sledding, handball, pigeon racing, rock lifting, skateboarding, surfing, and wire walking. In fact, we've used *two* bullfighting stories. We've even selected stories that aren't about a particular sport at all per se, but about something that stands alongside sports — broadcasting, exercise, gambling, spectators, and so on. And on a couple of occasions we've reprinted a story or two that, well, as one guest editor said, "I don't know if it's about sports or not, but it's so damn good it has to be in the book." I agree.

When asked how many stories I read each year, I usually say, "Ten thousand." This is admittedly a kind of guess, for I've never been quite sure of what really counts as reading. I mean, some magazines and newspapers may publish only one or two pieces of writing in a particular issue, if that, while others have a dozen or more. Most pages are filled with words that often announce quite loudly: Not Writing. After only a sentence or two (thankfully), they reject me, usually relieving me of making that determination myself and providing an answer when people comment, "You must read a lot of really bad stuff." Well, not really, because it usually doesn't get that far.

But when I find Writing, it grabs me by the throat and pulls me close, whether it is disguised as a daily column, a large "take-out," a game story, a magazine feature, or a personal essay, in sources that have ranged from daily newspapers, the alternative weekly press, general interest magazines, sports magazines, academic journals, and, increasingly, online publications. The best always stands out, and sometimes I feel as if I've developed the sensitivity of the old baseball scout for whom a single pitch or swing tells him all he needs to know. Some of the stories I've forwarded to the guest editor were later selected for the book, and I never read them in their entirety until the galleys showed up. Sometimes, you just *know.* I see myself first as a reader of this book, then as its editor. It is a book I too look forward to reading each year, and I reserve the pleasure of flipping at least a few of its pages to read something for the first time.

Over the last decade I've probably read more sports writing than anyone else I know. On most days I spend several hours on this project, although I spend more time than that in December and January, when submissions start arriving in bulk. Over the years this book has become so much a part of my life that the line between working and not working on it is wonderfully blurred. As with any other writer, reading is most of what I do, and I don't know any of us who think most of that is work.

Early on, one colleague wondered whether my most difficult task would be to write a foreword each year to what is, in some sense anyway, the same book. That has been a bit of a challenge, but even so, I was looking forward to this edition of the book, the tenth in the series (not including last year's companion volume *The Best Sports Writing of the Century*). This being a book about sports, I knew that edition number ten would provide a great excuse to roll out the numbers. So the career averages follow.

In the ten years since the first *Best American Sports Writing* was published, we have reprinted 240 stories, by 177 writers, and nearly 1,000 more have been listed in the annual selection of "Notable Sports Writing" that appears in the back of the book. Of the writers who have appeared in the book more than once, Gary Smith of *Sports Illustrated,* Roger Angell of *The New Yorker,* and Charles P. Pierce, lately of *Esquire,* have each appeared in the book six times.

Stories have been chosen from more than 150 publications, and of those 240 stories, 87 have been from newspapers, and 152 from magazines. For the first time this year, one was selected from an on-line publication (Pat Toomay's "Clotheslined" from *SportsJones*). An index to the series from 1991 to 2000 is available at www.glenn stout.net.

One of the best things about doing this book each year is watching the changes in the landscape of sports writing. Ten years ago, for example, there was simply no such thing as an online publication. Ten years from now stories from online publications will make up a significant portion of the book.

I've also noted the proliferation of stories about and interest in alternative and lesser-known sports. It's not all baseball, football, and basketball anymore, spiced occasionally by boxing, horse racing, golf, and tennis. People have more options now, and it sometimes seems to me that no matter what sport someone is participating in, at virtually any level there's a writer just a step or two behind, taking notes and learning.

Another change I've noted is the growing number of stories written by women, 21 of which have made it into the book; more than 100 others have been listed as "Notable Sports Writing."

From where we are now, it is difficult to believe that prior to Title IX legislation, women's participation in sports was practically nil. On the sports page it was even worse. Not until 1978 did a woman earn a living as a sports columnist for a major daily newspaper, and female sports reporters were extraordinarily rare, as were bylines by female writers covering sports for magazines. On the few occasions when women were allowed to "write sports," editors tended to be seeking, with an almost audible chuckle, a stereotypically "female" perspective.

That, thankfully, and to everyone's benefit, has changed. Female sports reporters are now commonplace, as are the bylines of female sports writers in magazines. But women still don't come close to producing half of the annual output of either "sportswriting" or "sports writing." Despite the changes that have taken place, the sportswriting profession remains overwhelmingly male — look on the masthead of any major sports magazine, or compare the number of inches newspapers give to male and female writers, and you'll see what I mean. This is reflected in what I read each year, far less than 10 percent of which is written by female writers. But the number is rising. We've never picked a story just to get a woman in the book — it hasn't been necessary. Every writer has appeared in here on her or his own merit.

Perhaps the most significant change in sports over the last decade has been the increase in female participation in sports. Except at the professional level, it is nearly equal to that of men. My daughter, who has grown to age four while surrounded by the detritus of this project, is just as serious about being a soccer player as she is about the other goals on her "What I Want to Be" list: a teacher, an artist, a musician, a chef, a waiter, a writer, and a fire truck driver.

But from where I sit reading every day, it seems to me that female subjects are rarely given the same attentiveness — or space — that male subjects are, whether the writer is male or female. As a subject, female athletes, teams, and sports are still marginalized.

There are undoubtedly "sound business reasons" for this. Markets and demographics seem to drive everything, and the few subjects the pollsters have identified as of interest to a larger audience tend to be written about again and again. The sports publishing machine is inclined to repeat itself, writing the same about the similar over and over again.

But I don't think there are any sound *writing* reasons this is so. As writers we all know the difficulty — and delight — of finding stories untold. It seems to me, as this book moves into its second decade and this society into a new century, that there is much left to be discovered, by writers both male and female, among women athletes, who compete and play in ways both different from and the same as men. Whatever changes take place in sports, I am confident that it is the writers who will lead us there.

Which brings me around to my colleague's warning about the challenge of writing this foreword year after year. It is no more a challenge than reading those ten thousand stories each year — the writing and the writers change and grow, as do I and the readers of this series. My hope since its inception has been that *The Best American Sports Writing* would grow and evolve as a collection. That is what makes my role in this book such a great job — from one story to the next, one edition to the next, the book changes even as it stays the same. That adjective *best* is both demanding and elusive, and, I hope, never arbitrary. The pursuit of the "best" — by myself, by the readers of this series, and, most important, by the writers whose words have earned them a place in this company — makes editing the series both a continuing pleasure and one hell of a way to earn part of my living. My many thanks to both the writers who have appeared in this book and its readers, for any pleasure this book has given cannot approach the pleasure I've had in putting it together each year.

Even after ten years I'm often asked, "How do you get in the book?" Well, I have to see a story before I can pick it, and any way a story ends up in my hands is fine with me. To help that process along, I ask for and receive complimentary subscriptions to hundreds of general interest and sports magazines. I also send a letter to the editors of several hundred magazines asking for submissions. I do the same with the sports editors of newspapers.

But if I had to depend on these two sources alone, I don't think this book would ever be published. Writers are also more than welcome to submit stories on their own, because editors sometimes either forget to submit materials (gasp!) or ignore my requests (can you believe it?).

So I also ask that writers submit their own material, or the work of others that they admire. Believe me, I don't think less of any writer who personally sends me a story he or she has written. Readers are also welcome to send me stories they've read that they think should make the book. Writers' girlfriends, boyfriends, spouses, parents, siblings, and second cousins are likewise encouraged to submit material.

Be aware, however, that every story submitted has to meet the same basic criteria. For the next edition of this book, each story:

- must have been published in a newspaper, magazine, or online publication in the calendar year 2000, in the United States or Canada;
- must be column-length or longer;
- must not be a reprint from a book (but serial excerpts are eligible); and
- must be received by me before February 1, 2001.

Please send subscriptions or submissions to this address:

Glenn Stout
Series Editor
The Best American Sports Writing
PO Box 381
Uxbridge, MA 01569

I may also be contacted by e-mail at GSchinmusic@cs.com. But no submissions will be accepted electronically, as there is no way to confirm publication, so please respect this request. All submissions must be made in hard copy. Photocopies, tear sheets, and clear copies are all acceptable. Reductions to 8½ by 11 inches are best. Please be sure to include the author's name, the publication title and address, and the date published for each story. This information should be attached or written on the individual story rather than in a cover letter, which tends to get separated over time.

Submissions cannot be acknowledged or returned, nor is it appropriate for me to comment on or critique a submission. There is no limit to the number of submissions I'll accept from either individuals or publications, but please be realistic.

Each year, I submit seventy-five or so stories to our guest editor. This year Dick Schaap, who made the final selection of the stories that appear in this edition, masterfully manned that post. My thanks also go out to Eamon Dolan and Emily Little of Houghton Mifflin, and to David Halberstam for his generosity toward this series from its first edition and for suggesting that we ask Dick Schaap to serve as guest editor. Siobhan and Saorla have proven once again to be the best at what they do while I do this. But any success this series has enjoyed is due the writers, who turn working with words into something else again.

GLENN STOUT

Introduction

I BRING certain credentials to this guest editorship.

I always had an eye for athletic talent, and I knew from an early age that I did not have that talent. I did not have the speed, strength, or hand-and-eye coordination I needed to be a great baseball, basketball, or football player, or a good one. I decided I wanted to be a sportswriter.

When I was fourteen, I began writing a sports column for a weekly newspaper called the *Freeport* (New York) *Leader.* I think I was paid five dollars a column. I have recently reread some of those pieces. I think I was overpaid. My column was called "Spanning the Sports Scene" — alliteration was my strong suit — and one of my early efforts began (typically, I'm afraid), "The local football season is about to open with a bang! Two of the local titans, Hempstead and Freeport, clash . . ." In subsequent columns, the prose did not markedly improve.

When I was fifteen, I went to work for a daily newspaper, the *Nassau Daily Review-Star.* I was in high school. My boss was Jimmy Breslin, who became a Pultizer Prize–winning columnist. Jimmy was the night sports editor, and he was twenty years old. He was in college. You can imagine how good a newspaper it was.

At first I covered only my own high school's games. I started by phoning in results. Then I began going to the office and writing the game stories. My weaknesses included an inability to type. I hunted and pecked with one finger. I took hours to write a story two or three paragraphs long.

As my typing improved, I was given more responsibility. I wrote about other high schools' games. I worked four nights a week, four hours a night, for a dollar an hour. I became the paper's resident horse-racing handicapper, even though I was not old enough to go to the track. I picked five winners one day.

One night, in the infancy of my career, I went to work, and Breslin had written a script for me. He told me I was to call Fred McMorrow at the *Long Island Press,* which was then a sister paper to the *Review-Star,* and I was to repeat his words to McMorrow with feeling and precisely as he had written them.

I did as I was told. "Mr. McMorrow," I said when I reached him on the phone, "my name is Dick Schaap and I am fifteen years old and I am working in the sports department at the *Nassau Daily Review-Star,* and when Mr. Breslin came in to work tonight, he took one look at the layouts Mr. Stirrat [the sports editor] had left for him and said they were a bunch of shit and threw them in the wastepaper basket and walked out, and I'm here all alone, trying to put out the sports section."

"Oh, you poor kid," McMorrow said, and then he cursed Breslin for his character flaws.

"Mr. McMorrow, I've written a headline that says, 'Brooklyn Baseball Club Defeats Pittsburgh Baseball Club by Score of Three to One,'" I said, resuming Breslin's script. "And I have another one that says, 'Giants One Helluva Ball Club.' Is that okay, Mr. McMorrow?"

"Oh, you poor kid," McMorrow said again. "I'm gonna get you some help."

McMorrow then called the city desk at the *Review-Star* and asked them to assign someone to help me. Breslin, the possessor of a very good if warped mind, had thought ahead and informed the city desk of what he was doing to McMorrow. "We can't spare anyone," the desk told McMorrow.

He called me back and told me to do my best. "You poor kid," he said.

Meanwhile, of course, Breslin was putting out the sports section as well as could be expected on a paper with a twenty-year-old assistant sports editor and a fifteen-year-old reporter.

McMorrow called me again. "I've called every bar in Queens and Nassau," he said, mentioning the two neighboring counties that were home to the *Press* and the *Review-Star,* "and I can't find the bastard anywhere."

"I will do my best," I promised.

Finally, after the section closed, McMorrow called once more, and this time Breslin answered the phone. Breslin was sober, but his voice did not give it away. "Where have you been?" McMorrow shouted. "I've called every joint I know."

Breslin muttered an expletive, hung up the phone, and congratulated me on a job well done. Mr. McMorrow did not speak to me for several years.

As little as I knew at the time, I knew Breslin was good. I knew I wanted to be like him. There were laws, however, against drinking at my age.

After the apprenticeship under Breslin, I went to college and became a journalistic schizophrenic. I started as a sportswriter on the *Cornell Daily Sun* and ended up editor-in-chief. In my sophomore year, I covered the Cornell-Penn football game. In my senior year, I defended a zoology professor against the House Un-American Activities Committee.

The summer between my sophomore and junior years, I worked in Pittsburgh for a steel company on weekdays and at a drive-in diner on weekends. When the Brooklyn Dodgers came to Pittsburgh, Roger Kahn of the *New York Herald-Tribune,* whom I had met when I was in high school, invited me to dinner with Jackie Robinson, Joe Black, and Jim Gilliam. I thought I was in heaven, which is not easy to think when you are in Pittsburgh. At dinner the conversation turned to the young star of the New York Yankees, Mickey Mantle, and Kahn told a story he had heard about how dumb Mantle was. "Shit," said Jackie Robinson, "we got plenty of guys that dumb, but we don't have anybody that good."

I went from Cornell to the Columbia University Graduate School of Journalism. I won a Grantland Rice fellowship, and at the luncheon announcing the award, my father sat between Jimmy Cannon, the great sports columnist, and Willard Mullin, the great sports cartoonist. Cannon told my father that if I was going to school on a Grantland Rice fellowship, I would have to major in martinis.

At Columbia, I wrote my major paper on the recruiting of New York City high school basketball players. My professor sold my story to *Sports Illustrated.* They edited me drastically. They buried my lead. They inserted a word I had never seen or heard before.

After Columbia, I became assistant sports editor of *Newsweek*

magazine. I worked for Roger Kahn, who wrote *The Boys of Summer.*
Kahn was a good mentor but not a good person. He told me to cut
down my adjectives. He also told me to add up his earnings. He rat-
tled off his freelance sales, and I calculated he was making $30,000
a year. I was making $67.50 a week.

When Kahn left *Newsweek*, I got his job but not his income. I was
twenty-five years old. A few weeks after I took the job, I met an eighteen-year-old fighter named Cassius Clay and took him to dinner at
Sugar Ray Robinson's restaurant in Harlem. A few weeks later I met
a comic named Lenny Bruce and took him to the seventh game of
the 1960 World Series. They both became my friends for life. Unfortunately, Bruce's life lasted only seven more years. "One last
four-letter word for Lenny Bruce," I said in the obituary I wrote for
Playboy. "Dead. At forty. That's obscene."

On November 22, 1963, after a one-year tour as *Newsweek*'s youngest senior editor, I accepted an offer, at only a slight cut in pay, to
become the *Herald-Tribune*'s youngest city editor. The paper's editor, Jim Bellows, made the offer over lunch at an excellent French
restaurant. The owner of the restaurant interrupted our meal. "Excuse me, gentlemen," he said, "but your president has been shot."
We both went back to work.

I spent ten months as city editor of the *Tribune* and then, just as
I was learning how to do the job, I became, at my own request, a
general three-times-a-week columnist. I covered the murder of
Malcolm X, the riots in Watts, the civil-rights murders in Missis-
sippi, and politics in New York City. I invented the nickname "Fun
City" for New York.

When the *Herald-Tribune* and its ill-conceived successor, the *World
Journal Tribune,* both folded, I went home and wrote books for a few
years. In the mid-1960s, I wrote *Turned On,* about a young woman
who died of a drug overdose; *RFK*, about a young man who wanted
to be president; and *Instant Replay,* the diary of a Green Bay Packer
named Jerry Kramer. At the time, *Instant Replay* was the best-selling
sports book ever, and its success prompted a variety of publishers to
offer me contracts. I said yes to all of them. I wrote seven books in
sixteen months, some of them utterly forgettable.

Among the books was *I Can't Wait Until Tomorrow . . .'Cause I
Get Better-Looking Every Day,* the ghostwritten story of Joe Namath's
life. The book led to a television program called *The Joe Namath*

Show, and I cohosted and booked the guests. One week I booked Rocky Graziano and Truman Capote together. Capote began talking about what a great athlete he had been as a youngster, and Graziano interrupted him and said, "Didn't I fight you a four-rounder in Cleveland once?"

In 1971, I accepted a full-time television job as the sports anchor for WNBC-TV in New York. The first day I went to work, I went on the air. I had very little idea of what I was doing. The *New York Daily News* critic reviewed my debut. "He sounded like he wasn't going to get through it," she wrote. "Unfortunately, he did."

While I worked for WNBC, I also spent five years as editor of *Sport* magazine. I worked on the magazine in the morning, at the television station in the afternoon, and on both at night. At *Sport,* I served as the host of our annual athlete-of-the-year dinner. One year we honored Muhammad Ali, the former Cassius Clay, and I wanted a comedian to be part of the program. I wanted Robert Klein, but he was busy, and his agent offered an alternate. "Who?" I said.

"Billy Crystal," she said.

"Who?" I said.

"He's funny," she said. "Trust me."

She was an agent. How could I trust her? But she was right, he was funny, and since the night of the dinner, Billy and I and our extended families have been friends. When he and I collaborated on a book called *Absolutely Mahvelous,* Billy inscribed a copy to me and my wife "I'm glad Klein was busy."

I spent the seventies at NBC, the eighties and nineties at ABC and ESPN, always managing to find time to write magazine articles and books. "How do you do it?" I was often asked. "Alimony," I usually explained. I collaborated with Bo Jackson on a book called *Bo Knows Bo,* which, like *Instant Replay* more than twenty years earlier, rose to number two on the *New York Times* bestseller list. It was the best-selling sports autobiography ever, until Dennis Rodman decided to become an author. Rodman shattered all of sports' literary records.

At the turn of the century, I remained schizophrenic. I hosted *The Sports Reporters* for ESPN and reviewed the Broadway theater for ABC's *World News Now.* I was the only person who voted for the Heisman Trophy and for the Tony Awards. I also hosted a weekly two-hour radio program and an interview show, *Schaap One on One,* on ESPN Classic, and still made time for magazine articles, books, and speaking engagements. I still paid alimony.

I have been a journalist for half a century. I have been a reporter, a writer, an editor, and a broadcaster, using the same basic techniques to cover the Son of Sam or the San Francisco 49ers. I have played golf with Bill Clinton, tennis with Johnny Carson, and tonk with Wilt Chamberlain. I have been to the Olympics, the Super Bowl, the World Series, the Final Four, the Masters, Wimbledon, the Kentucky Derby, the Thrilla in Manila, and the World Chess Championships.

In other words, I have never worked a day in my life.

I know that stories that deserve to be in this collection have been omitted. I know that stories that do not deserve to be in this collection have been included. I know because in years past, in this series and others, I have had some of my better stories omitted and some of my lesser ones collected. *They* were wrong. *I* could be wrong.

(Now that I've covered myself, I hope, with friends whose work is *not* represented . . .) My errors, of omission and inclusion, are, I hope, honest errors, based purely on what I like to read and what I don't like to read. I like to read stories that have a beginning, a middle, and an end, that tell a story, that lead somewhere. I like to read stories that provoke a response, anger or sadness or terror or joy or, best of all in the case of sports stories, laughter. I think sports, at its best, is entertainment, and sports writing, at its best, is entertaining. I guess I don't want sports to be a microcosm of life, even though it too often is. I want it to be an escape, a diversion, a pleasure.

In assembling this collection, I was struck by how many of the articles I chose are about so-called minor or fringe sports, especially X-sports, as they are now called, and how few are really funny. Garrison Keillor's bogus ghostwritten autobiography of a wrestler who becomes governor of Minnesota is the only determinedly humorous work in the book — humor in the vein, though not quite of the stature, of Ring Lardner's classic epistolary novel, *You Know Me, Al.* The story about the Kentucky shooting party, "Blown Away," is comic but chilling. Several of the other stories have witty passages, amusing anecdotes, clever turns of phrase — words and sentences and paragraphs that made me smile or laugh — but they are not, essentially, funny.

There is nothing funny about my favorite piece in the package, "Storm Warning," a suspenseful article about the perilous 1998 Sydney-to-Hobart yacht race that arrived on my desk without a by-line, an article whose author, as I write this introduction, I still do not know by name, age, nationality, or gender. The first faintly humorous passage in the (to me) anonymous article refers to Rupert Murdoch, whom I refer to as America's loss, Australia's gain, losing "a fingertip to a screaming rope in Sydney Harbor," forcing him to be replaced in the race by his son, "because his father ran out of fingertips." I presume that was intended to be lighthearted. Personally, I cringed. To my amazement, I shared Murdoch's pain.

While I am quibbling, let me go back to the lead to "Storm Warning": "Booom!"

I liked the directness of it — I am partial to short sentences, as you may have noticed — but I was irritated by the spelling. "Booom," so far as I can tell, is pronounced exactly the same as "Boom," so why not use the correct spelling? I inherited this prejudice from my former associate and hero, John Lardner, the son of the aforementioned Ring. John could never understand why any writer would quote the less articulate as saying "wuz" instead of "was," since the two words are identical when they reach the ear.

John wrote my all-time favorite lead for a magazine article about sports: "Stanley Ketchel was only twenty-four years old when he was fatally shot in the back by the common-law husband of the lady who was cooking his breakfast."

Boom! That tells you a story, doesn't it?

Boxing, historically, has inspired masterful sports writing, fiction and nonfiction, from the Lardners to Hemingway to Mailer and Schulberg and Bill Heinz and Joyce Carol Oates, but I've never felt that the quality of the literature justified the brutality of the sport. Boxing, strangely enough, is missing from this collection, not because of my feelings about the sport but because no boxing story measured up to the selections celebrating yachting, skiing, skateboarding, ultra-marathoning, shooting, curling, bull-riding, free-falling, distance swimming, bass fishing, motorcycle jumping, bowling, cockfighting, and poker playing, some of which are considerably more lethal than boxing. Horse racing, which was as big as boxing in the days of Dempsey and Man o' War, Ali and Secretariat, does not get a mention. Football, baseball, basketball, and hockey, the meat-and-potatoes sports, do, but none of those selections deals with the Super Bowl, the World Series, the Final Four, the NBA championships, or the Stanley Cup playoffs. This confirms my theory that the larger the event and the more sports reporters in attendance, the less the likelihood that the event will generate exceptional stories.

I am delighted by the number of writers represented whom I had never read before, whom I had never heard of, gifted men and, impressively, women, some contributing to obscure journals, some to popular publications. I am disappointed by the fact that I didn't see a single newspaper sports column as good as the ones Red Smith used to write regularly, perhaps because the columnists today have such varied interests — half of them, it seems, with their own radio shows, half of them appearing on television as often as Regis Philbin (who used to cover sports) — that they feel no urgency to make certain that the best of their written works are considered in an annual competition.

When I was a magazine and newspaper editor, when I wrote a weekly column about books and authors, I read much more than I read now. Helping to assemble this collection forced me back into reading, and for that I am grateful.

I hope you will be, too.

DICK SCHAAP

The Best
AMERICAN
SPORTS
WRITING 2000

BRYAN BURROUGH

Storm Warning

FROM VANITY FAIR

Booom!

The little black-powder cannon's powerful report, signaling five
minutes till the start of the race, could barely be heard over the ca-
cophonous chopping of helicopters hovering above the sailboats
in Sydney Harbor. It was a glorious, sun-washed Saturday afternoon, the December 26 Boxing Day holiday in Australia, and all
around the harbor — from the black-wire uprights of the Sydney
Harbor Bridge, which locals call "the Coat Hanger," to the scal-
loped hood of the famed opera house, to the multimillion-dollar
mansions blanketing the hillsides above Rushcutters Bay — more
than 300,000 people had gathered to watch the start of this, the
54th Sydney-to-Hobart yacht race, one of the three jewels in the
crown of international ocean sailing.

As they inched toward the starting line, out by Shark Island, the
115 boats appeared from the air to be a swarm of vibrating gypsy
moths. Down on the water, chaos reigned. Officials of the Cruising
Yacht Club of Australia had elected to kick off the 630-mile run
down the coast of New South Wales to Tasmania by starting all sizes
of boats at once — which is not how it's done with many other
ocean races. This irked Larry Ellison, who surveyed the scene from
the cockpit of his gargantuan, 80-foot-long *Sayonara*, hands down
the world's fastest and most advanced racing yacht; *Sayonara* was so
vast that Ellison had hired the cream of New Zealand's national
racing team to crew it for him. Ellison, who as the playboy chairman of the American software giant Oracle Corporation is worth
more than $7 billion, was the odds-on favorite to win the multi-day

race, barring a collision or other unforeseen disaster. And that was what bothered him. Looming over the 40- and 50-foot boats clogging the starting line, *Sayonara* was a great white shark hemmed in by dozens of pesky pilot fish.

Ellison had mixed feelings about the race. His arch-rival, the German software magnate Hasso Plattner, had kept his yacht, *Morning Glory*, out of the race, which took some of the fun out of things; now Ellison could only hope to beat *Morning Glory*'s race record (set in 1996), not the boat itself. His girlfriend, who had flown into Sydney with Ellison on his Gulfstream V jet the previous Thursday, had begged him not to go. Everyone knew the Sydney-Hobart was a rough race; Bass Strait, the shallow channel that separates Tasmania from the Australian mainland, is a notoriously treacherous swath of ocean, renowned for its steep waves and unpredictable storms. In his only other Hobart race, in 1995, Ellison had brought along News Corp. chairman Rupert Murdoch, who promptly lost a fingertip to a screaming rope in Sydney Harbor. This year Ellison had invited Murdoch's reserved 27-year-old son, Lachlan, a rising star in his father's media empire, to come along. "Lachlan came with us," Ellison said, "because his father ran out of fingertips."

Ellison ignored his girlfriend's warnings about the race, he said, because he wanted to see how good a sailor he had become. At 52, the lean, garrulous executive was popular with his crew, but like most rich yachtsmen, he was nowhere near their equal on the ocean. After 1995 he had frankly grown leery of the Hobart. "The Sydney-Hobart is a little like childbirth," Ellison liked to say. "It takes a while to suppress the pain, and then you're ready to do it again." Like Ellison, many of the other captains in the harbor that afternoon were wealthy men, some out to prove their manhood, others just hoping for a good time. Securely in the latter camp was Richard Winning, a bearded 48-year-old Sydney executive who ran his family's appliance company. Two years earlier Winning had bought a vintage wooden yacht named *Winston Churchill* and poured a quarter of a million dollars into updating it with the latest technology. Neither Winning nor any of the eight chums he invited aboard for the race, however, had any illusions about their intentions. "Gentlemen's ocean racing — that's our game," Winning told a Sydney reporter that winter.

*

Australians like to believe theirs is a classless society, and indeed, for a nation where more than half the population lives near the ocean, big-time yacht sailing has little of the snootiness that clings to the sport in America and the United Kingdom. The 1,000 or so sailors that day came from every walk of life, from the slim British Olympian Glyn Charles to schoolgirls who had won their way aboard boats in an essay contest. For every Ellison or Winning there was a bloke like 43-year-old Tony Mowbray. Mowbray was a stout, balding laborer from the coastal Australian coal-mining town of Newcastle, and he had mortgaged his modest house to buy and outfit a 43-foot sailboat he hoped to take around the world. He had spent much of his savings, about $50,000, on a sparkling aluminum mast, bright new sails, and shelves of electronic equipment for his boat, which he grandly named *Solo Globe Challenger.* For Mowbray, the Hobart race was a test run, a chance to see if his boat was ready for the big water. His crew was a collection of pals, several of whom worked in the mines.

Like golf, sailing is run on a handicap system, so while everyone knew Ellison's *Sayonara* would be first to Hobart, the harbor was full of Australian captains who thought they might win the handicapped race. Groups of friends from yacht clubs all across the country, from Adelaide, Melbourne, Brisbane, Townsville, even as far as Perth, had pooled their money to prepare their boats and buy bus tickets to Sydney. The nine Tasmanian sailors aboard the 40-foot *Business Post Naiad* were typical. The boat's skipper, a meticulous 51-year-old plant manager named Bruce Guy, had won a regatta in Bass Strait earlier in the year and thought he might have the stuff to win a big race. He had gathered pals from across the island's northern coast — Steve Walker, a sailmaker, Rob Matthews, a public-housing inspector, even his back-fence neighbor, a gentle locksmith named Phil Skeggs — who had pitched in $500 apiece to get the boat ready.

As the final seconds ticked away before the one-o'clock starting time, Ellison gripped *Sayonara*'s wheel and mentally went through the race's first minutes. It would be a difficult upwind start, forcing him to tack back and forth several times within the narrow confines of the harbor. With luck no one would hit them.

Booom!

The little cannon rang out again, and across the water hundreds of men, and a scattering of women, lunged forward on their boats.

There were screams and curses as some of the lesser boats banged hulls, but for the most part it was a clean start beneath a brilliant blue sky. As they furiously cranked their winches and raced to and fro, no one had any idea that several of their number would not live to see Monday morning.

Just after eight o'clock on Saturday morning, Peter Dunda, a 33-year-old forecaster in the Australian Bureau of Meteorology's New South Wales regional office, sat at his low-slung, L-shaped desk overlooking the busy tracks of Sydney's Central Railway Station, 16 floors below. Before him, on the wide screen of his IBM workstation, were the latest satellite photos, taken the previous night, and a computerized model of the weekend's weather generated by an NEC supercomputer at the bureau's headquarters in Melbourne. One photo showed a giant cold-air mass, a fluffy pancake of bright-white speckled clouds, moving northeast along the western shore of Tasmania toward Bass Strait. It was a classic "southerly buster," the kind that had buffeted the last several Sydney-Hobart races, a whirring system of winds and waves that regularly shot up the coast of New South Wales. It would make for rough sailing, but nothing most skippers in the fleet hadn't encountered many times before.

What interested Dunda wasn't the front itself — forecasters had seen it coming all week — but a development in the computerized model on his screen, called the Meso Limited Area Prediction System (LAPS), which generated weather maps at three-hour intervals over the course of 36 hours. In the corner of his computer screen the model indicated a strong low-pressure system, a swirling knot of gray-white cumulus, forming by Sunday afternoon about 400 miles east of Tasmania. While it looked as if the low would be safely out of the Sydney-Hobart fleet's path, it would mean higher winds along the system's western edges.

At 9:04, Dunda issued what the bureau called a "priority gale warning" to race organizers, posted it on a special Web site for race participants, and made it available to the bureau's weather-by-fax system. In the warning he predicted winds of 30 to 40 knots off Australia's southeast coast by Sunday night. (A knot is about 1.15 miles an hour; a 40-knot wind blows about 46 miles an hour.) Down at the yacht club's modern brick building on the harbor, where the bureau had set up a booth to hand out packets of meteorological charts and predictions, a forecaster named Kenn Batt, who had given the fleet's weather briefing on Christmas Eve wearing a jaunty Santa's cap, quickly photocopied Dunda's alert and jammed it into his packets.

Three hours later, as the boats spent their final hour in Sydney Harbor, Dunda received his next set of satellite photos and LAPS models. What he saw took his breath away. In the year or so since the bureau had begun working with the new, detailed computer models, he had never encountered anything like the picture that now appeared on his screen. It showed an unusually strong low-pressure system forming not safely east of Tasmania but at the eastern mouth of Bass Strait, directly in the fleet's path. The system looked like a boxer's left hook, a forearm of white clouds jutting from the vast empty spaces of the Southern Ocean northeast into the strait, its northern end a curled fist of thunderheads. The model predicted winds of 30 to 40 knots in the area by nightfall, rising to 55 knots by Sunday afternoon, with gusts as high as 70 knots — more than 80 miles an hour.

Dunda's phone rang. It was Melbourne.

"Have you seen this?" his counterpart there asked, the alarm clear in his voice. "It certainly looks like a storm warning."

"Yes."

A storm warning was highly unusual for Australia's southeast coast; the bureau had issued only one all year, on August 7, in the depths of the Australian winter. Still, at 1:58, with the fleet just clearing Sydney Harbor, the Melbourne office issued the warning. Sixteen minutes later Dunda did the same. In it he predicted that waves off Gabo Island, at the continent's southeastern tip, would average 15 to 20 feet by Sunday afternoon, with the highest waves reaching perhaps 40 feet.

Returning from the harbor, Kenn Batt, who had dozens of friends sailing in the race, grew emotional as the enormity of the situation sank in. "Those poor people are heading into a massacre," he said, taking a deep breath. After a moment he walked out onto an adjoining terrace and began to cry. Down at the yacht club, a private meteorological consultant named Roger "Clouds" Badham, who was supplying forecasts to *Sayonara* and more than a dozen other big boats, looked over his own new set of computer models in amazement.

"Oh, shit," he said to no one in particular. "This is Armageddon."

The entrance to Sydney Harbor is barely 1,500 yards wide, flanked by high basalt cliffs. Shaking free its lesser brethren, *Sayonara* was the first to burst through the gap, followed immediately by George Snow's streaking *Brindabella*. As the yachts wheeled to the south, surfing by the crowds baking on Sydney's famed Bondi Beach, a strong northeasterly wind billowed their sails. Aboard *Sayonara*, Ellison ordered the spinnaker hoisted, and set a course due south. A spreading host of smaller boats helmed by well-known Aussie captains soon followed, led by Martin James's *Team Jaguar,* Rob Kothe's *Sword of Orion,* the mammoth 70-footer *Wild Thing,* and the Queensland yacht *B-52.* Thanks to the strong winds, by midafternoon much of the fleet was on a record pace — with the gentlemen's boats, such as Richard Winning's striking *Winston Churchill* and Tony Mowbray's beloved *Solo Globe Challenger,* in the rear.

Few in the fleet were alarmed by Peter Dunda's storm warning, which was broadcast at three P.M. by the *Young Endeavour,* an Australian Navy brigantine whose radio was staffed by race volunteers. Sailing off Australia means an occasional blow of 50 knots or more, especially in Bass Strait, and few in the race expected to finish without encountering such winds. "The warning on Saturday didn't say anything more than what you could expect in any Hobart," recalls Rod Hunter, navigator on the Adelaide yacht *VC Offshore Stand Aside.* "It was for the 40s and 50s, a southerly buster. We sail in 40s and 50s all the time. It's normal. It's just a fact of life." Recalls Ellison, "There was a sense of 'Storm? Piece of cake!' Of course, no one said anything about a hurricane."

Back in the pack, the nine veteran Tasmanian sailors aboard *Business Post Naiad* greeted news of the storm warning with hearty laughter. Almost all had been sailing Bass Strait since they were boys, and they were accustomed to fighting the strait's steep, choppy waves and 50- and 60-knot winds. The skipper, Bruce Guy, speculated that the coming blow might actually give them an advantage the next day. "The guys from behind, who haven't been in Bass Strait before, they're going to get a bit of a dustup," observed Rob Matthews, the housing inspector.

*

The powerful wind at their backs, Ellison would later say, should have been a warning. It was "explosive, gusty," he notes, and it quickly began to take a toll on *Sayonara*. By late afternoon, as *Sayonara* and *Brindabella* left the rest of the fleet miles behind, the gusts had blown out three different spinnaker sails aboard Ellison's boat and had snapped the brass fitting of one of the spinnaker poles, damage Ellison had never seen before. But the boat was simply going too fast for this to worry anyone. That afternoon *Sayonara* hit a boat record, 26.1 knots, and was already on pace to break *Morning Glory*'s 1996 record time.

As darkness fell around nine, the wind swung around, as predicted, and began blowing hard out of the south. Raindrops pelted *Sayonara* as the boat crossed the incoming front, and the crew of 23 slipped into their bright-red heavy-weather gear. By 11, *Sayonara* was plowing into a 40-knot head wind. Waves grew to 15, then 20 feet, and almost everyone on board began to experience seasickness. "Anyone that said he didn't get sick out there is lying," recalls Ellison. "We had guys who've sailed the Whitbread [round-the-world race] puking their guts out, like five times in the first 12 hours. We were on the Jenny Craig plan — a great weight-loss experience."

By the time *Sayonara* entered Bass Strait after midnight, Ellison was having difficulty driving the boat. Heavy, dark clouds hung down, obscuring the horizon, and the flying spume and rain stung his face. A small rip developed in the mainsail, and when crewmen went to fix it they found the giant sail was tearing out the metal track that fastened it to the mast. Around three Ellison realized he couldn't take it anymore.

"You take over," he yelled to Brad Butterworth, a veteran New Zealand sailor standing to his side in the cockpit. "Get me outta here!"

Ellison went belowdecks to check the weather forecasts with his navigator, Mark Rudiger. Just as he walked up to the nav station, Ellison saw a new satellite photo downloading onto one of Rudiger's laptops. Stunned, both men looked for several seconds at the ominous doughnut of white clouds forming above Bass Strait.

"Mark," Ellison finally said, "have you ever seen anything like that before?"

Rudiger slowly shook his head. "Well, I have," Ellison said. "It was on the Weather Channel. And it was called a hurricane. What the fuck is that thing doing out here?"

Will Oxley, a strapping 33-year-old marine biologist, crouched on the deck of *B-52* and watched the front move in. Lightning zig-zagged across the horizon to the south, and as the first raindrops wet his face, Oxley felt satisfied. He glanced at his watch. It was 12:15. As the boat's navigator, Oxley had worked with "Clouds" Badham to predict that the front would hit them at midnight.

For *B-52*, like many of the 114 boats trailing *Sayonara*, the night passed uneventfully. At 8:30 the next morning, as winds continued gusting up toward 50 miles an hour, Oxley stepped down the companionway to check the latest weather reports. He faxed the weather bureau in Melbourne for a coastal update and was surprised to see that winds off Wilson's Promontory, the southernmost point in Australia, had registered 71 knots — over 80 mph — two hours earlier. While the peninsula was well west of the racecourse, it served as an early indicator of the winds Oxley expected to blow through the strait. He guessed they might hit a 60-knot blow, which worried him. He listened to an oil-rig weather forecast and heard the same. Oxley caucused with skipper Wayne Millar, and the two men agreed that by later that day they would be in "survival mode" for several hours but should be able to begin racing again by the evening. "Looks like it's going to be a bit bouncy, mates," Oxley told the crew.

All that morning as the fleet moved briskly south, the winds picked up to 30, 40, then 50 knots. By noon some boats were already retiring from the race. At 10:30 the race's first major casualty occurred when the mast broke aboard *Team Jaguar*, a sleek 65-footer owned by the prominent Sydney attorney Martin James, forcing the boat to wait nearly 18 hours for rescue by a fishing trawler.

2:30 P.M.

Simon Clark sat on the starboard bow of *Stand Aside* and dangled his legs into the booming waves. Clark, a 28-year-old who had sailed since he was a boy, and three friends had joined up with Adelaide businessman James Hallion's eight-man crew, and Clark thought Hallion had driven a bit conservatively early in the race. Nevertheless, they had busted down the coast at an average speed of 15 knots, even hitting 18 and 19 at times.

Around noon, as winds continued to pick up, they had taken down the mainsail and put up a storm jib, expecting heavy weather. Clark wasn't too worried, nor was anyone on board. By two, winds were hitting just 35 or 40 knots, while Clark had seen only one "green wave" — that was what he called it — a rogue wall of water that looked as if it had risen straight from the mossy bottom of Bass Strait.

Suddenly he saw another. As the wave rose up before him, Clark thought it looked like a tennis court standing on end.

"Bear away!" he shouted.

Hallion was unable to steer down the wave. The boat rode high on the wave and slithered to the left. Just then the wave crested and crashed onto the deck, rolling the boat hard to port. As *Stand Aside* fell down the face of the wave, its roll continued. For a fleeting second it felt as if they were airborne. Then they landed, upside down.

Slammed facedown into the roiling ocean, Clark felt a terrific pain in his left knee; his anterior cruciate ligament had snapped like a rubber band. Underwater, he unhooked his safety harness and floated to the surface just as the boat righted itself. Pulling himself back on board, Clark was stunned to see a seven-foot gash in the cabin; the mast lay draped over the side, broken. His crewmates were no better off. His friend Mike Marshman had somehow lost a chunk of his finger. Another man had broken ribs, still another a nasty cut across his forehead. Within minutes *Stand Aside* began sending out the first of what would be many Maydays that afternoon.

3:00 P.M.

As the storm system intensified, the first to encounter the full force of its lashing winds was a group of a half-dozen yachts led by *Sword of Orion*, which was running seventh overall as the afternoon began. Like so many others, Rob Kothe, the boat's 52-year-old skipper, had shrugged off the storm warnings, but as he staggered down the companionway to call in *Sword*'s position at the 2:05 radio check, he realized conditions were growing far worse than anything they had been warned of. Now about 100 miles south of the sleepy port of Eden, Kothe's boat began to experience winds above 90 miles an hour. The sharp, spiking green waves towered 40 and 50 feet over the boat, crashing into the cockpit, churning his crew's bodies like laundry and stretching their safety lines to the breaking point.

In a race, weather data is a jealously guarded secret, something boats rarely share. As Kothe sat at his radio console belowdecks wiping seawater from his face, he tuned his HF dial to the race frequency and listened as boat after boat, going in alphabetical order, radioed in its position and nothing more. When it came to the S's, Kothe listened to Sayonara's position report, then made a decision that probably saved many lives: he gave a weather report. "The forecast is for 40 to 55 knots [of wind]," Kothe announced to the fleet. "We are experiencing between 65 and 82. The weather is much stronger than forecast."

Kothe listened as the radio operator aboard Young Endeavour, obviously struck by news of winds approaching 100 miles an hour, repeated the warning to the fleet. Back in the pack, about two dozen boats, including the Queensland yacht Midnight Special, decided to quit the race and head for the port of Eden.

3:15 P.M.

Tucked away on an inland plateau two hours from the sea, the drowsy Australian city of Canberra is one of those kit-designed capitals where office workers and diplomats brown-bag their lunches around concrete fountains and sterile, man-made lakes. Downtown, the airy, third-floor war room of the Australian Maritime Safety Authority, lined with purring Compaq desktops and sprawling maps of the continent, could pass for the office of almost any government bureaucracy, a geological survey maybe, or a census bureau. But the tiny red target symbols that began popping up on Rupert Lamming's screen that afternoon weren't minerals or voters. They were distress calls.

When Lamming, a sober 41-year-old with 15 years in the merchant marine behind him, arrived for his shift at three, there was just a single target in Bass Strait, and it appeared to be a false alarm. A Thai-registered freighter, Thor Sky, had radioed in that it had accidentally activated its forearm-size emergency beacon, known as an Emergency Position Indicating Radio Beacon (EPIRB). Every hour, one of seven satellites in polar orbit — three Russian, four American — tracks across Bass Strait; the EPIRB's signal bounces off these satellites, then ricochets down through ground stations in Queensland, Western Australia, and New Zealand to the computers on Lamming's pristine white countertop.

Trouble was, *Thor Sky*'s beacon broadcast at 406 megahertz; clicking his mouse on the red target on his computer screen, Lamming saw that the beacon emanated from an older, smaller model, broadcasting at 121.5 megahertz. Aware that the Hobart fleet was sailing into treacherous weather, Lamming decided to take no chances. He had a colleague dial a charter air service in Mallacoota, a tiny beach town near the continent's southeastern tip. A half-hour later the plane radioed back: it had a Mayday from a yacht named *Stand Aside*.

3:35 P.M.

After finishing his impromptu weather report, Rob Kothe emerged onto the deck of *Sword of Orion* to find that the winds had suddenly fallen to 50 knots — "a walk in the park," as he later put it. Had the storm passed? Or were they merely in its eye? At 3:35 — he looked at his watch — Kothe got his answer. As if a door had swung open, the winds slammed back hard, spiking up above 80 miles an hour. Kothe gave orders for everyone but two crewmen, a young bowman named Darren Senogles and the 33-year-old Olympic yacht racer Glyn Charles, to remain below. Kothe ran down the companionway, then radioed the *Young Endeavour* that *Sword of Orion* was quitting the race and heading back north, toward Eden.

Sword's decision to turn north, however, sent it back into the strongest winds wrapped around the eye of the storm. "The storm," Kothe later observed, "didn't give a rat's ass whether we were still racing or heading to port." After 15 minutes, as Kothe hunched over the radio, he felt the boat rising up an especially steep wave. Suddenly *Sword* rolled upside down and they were airborne, falling down the face of the wave for a full two seconds, until Kothe felt his boat hit the ocean with a sickening crack. Seconds later the boat rolled back over, righting itself, and he found himself facedown on the floor of the cabin, bound up with ropes and shattered equipment as if he were a broken marionette. As Kothe struggled to regain his footing, he heard Darren Senogles's waterlogged screams from above deck: "Man overboard! Man overboard! Man overboard!"

It was Glyn Charles. When the wave hit, Charles had been at the helm, attempting to muscle the seven-foot-wide wheel through oncoming waves. The force of the wave apparently swung the boom around like a baseball bat into a fastball; it struck Charles in the midsection, driving him against the spokes of the wheel and snapping his safety harness. As everyone else scrambled up onto the broken deck, Charles could be seen in the water, about 30 yards away.

"Swim! Swim!" people began shouting as Senogles frantically wrapped himself in a long rope and prepared to dive in after his friend. Charles, obviously stunned, raised a single arm, as if the other was injured. Someone threw a life ring toward him, but Charles was upwind, and the ring sailed helplessly back onto the deck.

Just then another huge wave broke and boiled onto the deck, knocking people and equipment about. By the time Kothe regained his feet, Charles was 150 yards off. The roll had actually torn the deck loose from the cabin below, and the men on deck, crouching unsteadily, were powerless to retrieve the struggling Brit. In the roiling seas Charles could be seen only when he crested a wave. Everyone watched in agony for a seemingly endless five minutes as he floated farther and farther from the boat. And then he was gone.

Kothe had already raced to the radio and began sending out an urgent Mayday. But the boat's mainmast lay broken in five places and had lost its aerial. Kothe broadcast Maydays for a solid two hours, but no one in a position to help Glyn Charles heard a word Kothe said.

4:00 P.M.

The storm system's hurricane-force winds and steep black waves had begun to engulf the rest of the fleet. Aboard *Solo Globe Chal-*

lenger, Tony Mowbray thought he was handling the mountainous seas well. In 32 years of sailing, he had never seen such conditions. The waves weren't normal waves. He thought of them as cliffs — cliffs of water — that rose to impossible heights and suddenly fell onto his boat, one after another, with a stultifyingly rhythmic *Bang! . . . BANG! . . . Bang!* When a large wave landed atop you, all you could do was hold on to something and twist your body away as the boat shuddered with the impact: if it struck you square in the ribs, it felt like a Mike Tyson body shot. Mowbray had pulled down all his sails a bit early, at noon, just to be safe. He had heard *Sword of Orion's* weather warning, but thought he could still make it across the strait.

But *Solo* couldn't survive the marine equivalent of a one-two punch. Mowbray was below when the first wave socked it in the bow, swinging it around for the enormous 65-foot wave that suddenly reared up behind the boat and fell on top of it. The gleaming white yacht lurched to port and fell sideways. Then it rolled to 145 degrees and seemed to dig in as the mighty wave shoved it through the ocean, not quite facedown in the water, for what Mowbray later estimated was a full 20 seconds. The force of the "shove" shattered the interior cabin's seven-foot skylight. Seawater poured in.

When the boat finally righted itself, Mowbray charged up on deck to see what fate had befallen the four crewmen there. Glen Picasso, a 40-year-old coal miner, was in the water clinging to the stern; he had been pulled behind the boat by his safety line and had sustained broken ribs. Tony Purkiss lay on the floor of the cockpit, his head drenched in blood from a deep cut. But it was 45-year-old Keir Enderby who was in the worst shape. The mast and rigging, broken into pieces by the force of the wave, had fallen across his legs. He was screaming, "Get it off me!" Hurriedly Mowbray and others shoved the mast into the sea, then took Enderby below and tucked him into a bunk. Picasso soon followed, overcome by shock. The emergency beacon was activated.

Those uninjured bailed out the cabin, stuffed sleeping bags into the gaping hole where the skylight had been, and prayed. Mowbray spent the next few hours staring at the waves and hoping his crippled boat wouldn't founder. "I'll never look at waves the same again," he says. "Those waves were out to kill you. That was our attitude. You could see death working in that water."

5:00 P.M.

As her medevac helicopter struggled to maintain its position in the shrieking winds 50 feet above *Stand Aside,* Kristy McAlister leaned far out its right-hand door and gulped. McAlister, a trim, girlish 30-year-old paramedic with Canberra's SouthCare helicopter-ambulance service, had been working on choppers for only two months, and this was her first ocean rescue. Below was a scene unlike any she had dreamed of: evil black waves, as blocky and stout as apartment buildings, crashing this way and that. The helicopter's altimeter swung wildly, registering 60 feet one moment, 10 feet the next, as a dark wave swept up beneath its underbelly. The winds hit McAlister's face with a force she knew only from sticking her head out the window of a car speeding down the highway at 80 miles an hour. One thought crossed her mind: Oh, God . . .

Another helicopter had already winched eight sailors out of a life raft beside the boat and then, running low on fuel, had wheeled about and headed back toward land. Below, a man was in the water, floating briskly away from the raft. McAlister, wearing a black wet suit, a navy-blue life vest, and a lightweight helmet, had no time to waste. Grabbing an oval rescue strop, she held her breath — and jumped.

The water felt like concrete as she hit it, and a wave immediately drove her under, down, down, forcing seawater into her mouth and down her throat. She fought her way to the surface, coughing and hacking, and found herself barely 10 feet from the man loose in the ocean.

"I'm going to put this over your head and under your armpits!" she shouted, indicating the strop. "You must keep your arms down or you will fall out!"

The man nodded just as a wave drove both of them underwater for several seconds. When they returned to the surface, the helicopter winched them both skyward.

Within minutes McAlister had returned to the roiling ocean, this time landing beside the life raft, where two shivering sailors awaited rescue. When the last man was safely aboard, McAlister rolled to one side and began vomiting seawater. Ten minutes later she was still retching.

5:15 P.M.

As the winds swirled and howled around them, the nine Tasmanian sailors aboard *Business Post Naiad* remained in high spirits. Roughly 10 miles east of *Sword of Orion,* they had listened to Rob Kothe's weather report, but had decided to press on. Rob Matthews, like almost everyone else on board, had survived winds of more than 70 knots in Bass Strait, and had been forced down to "bare poles," with all sails lowered. A few minutes past five, Matthews was behind the wheel, attempting to drive the boat's bow through the incoming waves, when he heard Tony Guy, Bruce's nephew, pipe up behind him. "I've lit a fag, Robbie," said Guy, proudly displaying a cigarette.

"Tony reckons he's going to have a smoke in 70-knot winds," Matthews yelled to Steve Walker, the boat's helmsman. Walker grinned.

Moments later, as Matthews attempted to maneuver the boat up the face of a 50-foot wave, the boat slid sideways just as the wave crested. To the dismay of Matthews and the four other sailors on deck, *Business Post Naiad* rolled to its left and plummeted down the wave's face, then rolled still further as it fell. It landed upside down in the trough of the wave with a thunderous crack. All five men were plunged facedown into the raging sea. Then, almost before anyone had a chance to realize what had happened, the boat righted itself. The five men, thrown over the starboard side to the end of their safety lines, popped to the surface to find the deck suddenly awash.

"Fuck, the mast is over the side!" someone yelled.

It was true. The mast had broken in half and was lying across the starboard side, its top buried in the waves. "That wasn't in the bloody brochure," Phil Skeggs said, trying to make a joke. But as the full crew of nine men struggled to pull the broken mast back on deck, their mood turned somber. For *Business Post Naiad,* the race was over. Grudgingly the crew agreed to rev up the motor and set a course toward Eden.

5:30 P.M.

"Mayday! Mayday! Mayday! Here is *Winston Churchill, Winston Churchill.* We are taking water rapidly! We can't get the motor started to start the pumps! We are getting the life rafts on deck!"

His mast and long-range aerials still intact, Richard Winning broadcast a furious Mayday even as seawater lapped onto the deck and the rest of the crew dropped the boat's life rafts over the side. Winning had been at the helm a half-hour before when a sneering green wave had slapped the old wooden yacht, knocking it flat on its side. Below, John Stanley, a taciturn 51-year-old Sydney marina manager, had been thrown into a wall as the three starboard windows imploded and foamy saltwater sprayed across the cabin. When the boat righted itself, Stanley noted with horror that a full six feet of *Churchill*'s inner bulwarks was gone. "Must've sprung a plank!" Stanley yelled to Winning.

They were going down fast. As seawater began sloshing across the deck, Winning and his eight crewmates, ranging from a Sydney merchant banker to a friend's 19-year-old son, scrambled into the life rafts — Winning, the boy, and two others in one, Stanley and four friends in the other. The inflatable black rubber rafts were both topped with bright-orange canopies, which could be tied shut, though seawater still poured in, forcing the men to bail constantly. As *Churchill* sank, Winning managed to tie the two life rafts together, but the waves tore them apart barely 10 minutes later. The two boats, climbing, then falling down the faces of 50-foot waves, lost sight of each other soon after. Winning could only hope his Mayday would be answered.

6:15 P.M.

On the deck of *B-52*, Mark Vickers, a 32-year-old ceramic-tile layer, was standing at the giant, seven-foot wheel when he caught a glimpse of a mammoth wave rising up behind the boat. A wall of bluish-green water that towered over the boat's mast — Vickers later estimated its height at 60 feet or more — the wave began to crest and fall forward just as he called out to his friend Russell Kingston, who was crouched forward.

"Oh, shit, Russell!" Vickers called out. "This one's gonna hurt!"

With that the massive wave came crashing down directly onto the boat. *B-52* half rolled, half pitchpoled — an end-over-end flip — and landed upside down. The wave had hit with such force that Vickers was driven through the wheel's spokes, breaking them and badly denting the wheel. For several seconds he felt as if he were inside a blender as the sea furiously tossed him about. Coming to his senses, he opened his eyes and at first saw only blackness. Disoriented, he glanced upward and saw light flashing through portals in the ship's hull. Only then did he realize the boat was upside down and he was beneath it.

He couldn't swim free. The rope to his safety harness was wrapped twice around the wheel. He unhooked the harness but still couldn't find a way clear of the lines and equipment swirling around him. Eventually, with his breath running out, he kicked down and swam out, coming to the surface about 10 feet from the boat's stern. He saw Kingston clinging to ropes at the overturned boat's edge.

The boat was drifting away from Vickers, and quickly. Exhausted, he began dog-paddling faster and faster, but the boat seemed only to be pulling away, eventually reaching a distance of about 100 feet. Somehow, with a helpful wave or two and the last of his energy, he reached a rope leading to the boat just as it righted itself.

The rest of the crew scrambled up the companionway to find the mast broken and deep cracks zigzagging through the deck. They activated an emergency beacon, began bailing, and prayed they could make it through what promised to be a long night.

7:00 P.M.

Peter Joubert, a wry 74-year-old engineering professor at the University of Melbourne, had quickly grown tired of fighting the waves in this, his 27th Hobart. The spume blasting his 43-foot *Kingurra* felt like a pitchfork jabbing into his face; the only way he could steer was to wear goggles. Around six he curled up in a bunk and fell into a deep sleep, leaving the driving to the group of younger men who had the energy to fight the waves.

At seven Joubert woke with a start to the sound of a "horrific crash like none I'd ever heard before." The boat pitched hard to port, and he felt a massive pain spread across his chest: a slumbering crewman in another bunk had flown across the cabin, slamming into his ribs, breaking several and rupturing his spleen, Joubert later learned. As seawater gushed into the cabin, he lurched out of the bunk and crawled to the nav station, where his 22-year-old grandson helped him flip on the pumps. Glancing up the companionway, he saw three crewmen, including his friend Peter Meikle, lifting an American named John Campbell, 32, back on deck.

Just then Joubert heard someone cry, "Man overboard!" It was Campbell. Halfway back onto the boat, he had slipped out of his jacket and safety harness and slid back into the ocean, wearing nothing but long underwear.

Joubert grabbed the radio. "Mayday! Mayday! Mayday! We have a man overboard!" he shouted.

As Joubert began to go into shock, Campbell floated swiftly away from the boat. *Kingurra*'s motor wouldn't start; the storm jib was shredded. There was no way to retrieve him.

"Mayday! Mayday!" Joubert repeated. "We need a helicopter!"

ABOUT 7:20 P.M.

Barry Barclay, the 37-year-old winch operator on a Dauphin SA 365 helicopter operated by the Victoria Police air wing, had just finished refueling at his base in Melbourne when the call came in that racers were in trouble. Scrambling east over the mountains known as the Great Dividing Range, Barclay and his two crewmates stopped to refuel once again, at the dirt airstrip in Mallacoota, before heading out into the howling winds in Bass Strait. First ordered by the Maritime Safety Authority's war room to rescue sailors off *Stand Aside*, Barclay's crew detoured en route when word came of a man overboard off *Kingurra*. Cutting through the swirling clouds at speeds topping 200 miles an hour, the helicopter reached *Kingurra*'s last reported position in 10 minutes — only to find nothing there. "I think we've overshot them!" pilot Daryl Jones shouted. "I'm heading back!"

Just then Barclay spotted a red flare arcing into the sky. Jones made for it. It was from *Kingurra*. Barclay hailed the boat on his radio. In a shaky voice Joubert told him Campbell had last been seen about 300 yards off the port bow. Jones wheeled the copter around as Barclay scanned the seas below. It was almost impossible to see. Even at an altitude of 300 feet, the waves seemed to be reaching for them, trying to suck them into the sea.

"Got something!" yelled Dave Key, another crew member. Barclay hung out of the copter's left-hand door and saw a white life ring winking among the waves; he thought he saw someone waving from inside it. But as they neared its position, the ring shot high in the air and flew off, tumbling crazily over the wave tops. There was no one inside.

Just then, out of the corner of his eye, Barclay caught a flash of movement. Peering down through the spume, he could just make out a man in the water, clad in blue long johns, waving. It was Campbell.

"I've got him! I've got him!" Barclay shouted.

Hovering above him, Barclay played out a hundred feet of wire cable and slowly lowered Key into the ocean. Three times he raised and lowered Key, like a tea bag, as the waves engulfed him and drove him under. When Key finally reached Campbell he was limp, at the edge of consciousness, and unable to help as the paramedic tried to slip the strop over his head. Eventually Key got him into the strop, and Barclay began winching them toward the helicopter.

Just as the two men were about to reach the open doorway, the winch froze. Barclay hurriedly cycled through a series of switches, trying to unlock it. It was no use. Campbell and Key hung two feet below the doorway, Campbell too exhausted to pull himself into the copter. Finally, giving up on the winch, Barclay reached down, grabbed Campbell by his underwear, and yanked him into the aircraft. Key soon followed. Campbell lay on his back, saying over and over, "Thank you thank you thank you thank you."

8:00 P.M.

By late Sunday afternoon *Sayonara* had been pushed well east of the cyclonic winds that were smashing the rest of the fleet. Eighty miles northeast of Tasmania, however, Ellison's boat suddenly began to encounter conditions worse than anything it had seen so far.

A high-pressure system had developed east of Hobart, and where it brushed against the raging low the seas had taken on the character of an industrial clothes washer. *Sayonara* would surge to the top of a wave, then free-fall three, four, sometimes five seconds before landing in the trough behind it. On deck, this sent men flying up toward the rigging, then slammed them down hard each time the boat landed.

When Phil Kiely, the 44-year-old head of Oracle's Australian operation, shattered his ankle and had to be tucked into a bunk writhing in pain, Ellison began to grow worried. It wasn't just bones breaking that concerned Ellison; it was the boat. At least one of the titanium rope connectors on deck had exploded. The port-side jib winch, made of carbon fiber and titanium, had simply levitated from the deck.

Ellison had just gone belowdecks and climbed into a bunk when he noticed Mark Turner, whom everyone called Tugboat, tapping the carbon-fiber hull inside the bow.

"Tuggsy, whaddya doing?" Ellison asked.

"Trying to make sure the boat's OK."

Ellison pulled himself out of the bunk and lurched over to where Turner stood. The constant crash of the waves, Turner discovered, had caused a section of the hull to begin delaminating, or wearing through: it was the worst thing that could happen on a carbon-hulled vessel. Turner took out a Magic Marker and drew a circle around the weakened area. There was no telling how long they had before it gave way.

"This is wacko!" Ellison shouted at Mark Rudiger, the serene navigator. "I'm not sure how much more of this the boat can take." Maybe, Ellison suggested, it was time to tack upwind, toward the shelter of the Tasmanian coastline.

"I'm not sure that's the right race decision," Rudiger averred. The move would give *Brindabella* a chance to catch them.

"Well, we can't win the race if the boat sinks," Ellison shot back. The two men talked it over with skipper Chris Dickson, who like Rudiger was reluctant to give *Brindabella* an opening. But in the end it was Ellison's boat — and Ellison's life. "Tack the fucking boat!" he ordered.

11:00 P.M.

By the time Brian Willey began his shift in the Canberra war room at 11, chaos reigned. Fifteen blinking EPIRB beacons pleaded for help on his computer screen, but there was no way to tell who was who, or who needed rescue the most. Almost every yacht in distress had lost its mast, and with it its radio aerials, leaving Willey and his dozen co-workers fumbling in the dark, confused and depressed. At nightfall four Australian Navy Sea King and Seahawk helicopters had flown toward the racecourse, but while the navy helicopters had night-auto-hover capabilities, they had no night-vision equipment. Willey was reduced to gathering scattershot and unreliable reports from the helicopters. The crews were so busy battling hurricane-force winds, normal conversation was all but impossible.

At one point Steve Francis, the 56-year-old former air-traffic controller in overall charge of rescue efforts that Sunday night, was in contact with one of the helicopters when he heard the pilot shout, "Look out for that wave!"

Francis thought the helicopter had gone down. Then the pilot came back on for a moment before shouting again, "Look out for that fucking wave!"

A burst of static came through the phone. Again Francis feared the worst. But the pilot came back on again. "Sorry, mate, had a bit of a problem there," he reported. "Trying to stay between the waves and the clouds, you know."

Precious hours were wasted looking for boats that no longer needed rescue. At one point Francis discovered that several yachts on his search list had been sighted, safely at anchor in the harbor at Eden. "They musta run outta beer," he grimly cracked.

When Rob Matthews emerged from belowdecks to take his turn behind the wheel of *Business Post Naiad,* the Tasmanian boat was a wreck. The splintered mast lay roped to the deck. Below, the contents of the refrigerator had spilled out and were sloshing about in eight inches of water along with shattered plates and cups; the stove had broken free of its mounting and was careening about with every wave. Bruce Guy, the boat's owner, flipped on the pumps, but they jammed with debris within minutes and failed. Reluctantly, the crew had activated an EPIRB and, after rigging a new aerial, had radioed in a request for a helicopter evacuation.

As Matthews took the helm, flying spume sandblasted his face. Phil Skeggs, the easygoing locksmith and the boat's least-experienced sailor, stood beside him in the cockpit, shouting out compass readings, as Matthews attempted to ram the boat through waves he could barely see. At one point the moon broke through the clouds, giving Matthews a view of the enormous waves just as they crashed onto the deck. He decided he liked it better in the dark.

Just past 11, after the moon disappeared, leaving them once more wrapped in darkness, Matthews felt the familiar sensation as they began to creep up the face of what seemed like an especially large wave. Then, suddenly, the boat was on its port side and they were airborne once again, falling down the face of the wave. In midair the boat overturned, landing upside down in the trough. Plunged underwater, tangled in a morass of ropes and broken equipment, Matthews held his breath. He tried to remain calm as he waited for the boat to stabilize, as it had before. When it didn't, he attempted to shed his safety harness so he could swim out from beneath the boat. But he couldn't unfasten the hook. Just as he was running out of breath, a wave tossed the boat to one side, allowing a shaft of air into the cockpit, then slammed the boat down on his head yet again.

Coughing and sputtering, Matthews was driven underwater once more. The cockpit walls jackhammered his head and shoulders. Now convinced that the boat would not right itself, he struggled again to get out of the safety harness. Finally managing to undo it, he kicked free of the boat and surfaced at the stern, where he grabbed a mass of floating ropes, "hanging on like grim death," as he later put it. There was no sign of Skeggs. "Phil! Phil!" he began shouting.

The scene belowdecks was bedlam. Water began gushing into the cabin from the companionway as the six men, trapped upside down, struggled to find their footing on the ceiling. The only light came from headlamps two of the crew had thought to grab, which now, as they lurched about, filled the cabin with a crazy, strobe-like effect. Bruce Guy and Steve Walker, fearful that the boat was sinking, rushed to clear the companionway of debris, then kicked out two boards that blocked their exit to the sea below. In a minute the water level stabilized as the trapped air prevented more seawater from entering, leaving the men up to their waists in water. Guy began trying to muscle one of the black life rafts out the companionway.

"Bruce, wait," Walker said. "We're not taking on any more water. You're going to get another wave shortly. I reckon it'll flip us back over." Just then, the sound of a waterfall, the next giant wave, filled their ears. "We're goin' over!" someone shouted.

The boat flipped once more, sending everyone in the cabin toppling. As the boat righted itself, seawater began cascading over the cockpit into the cabin. Now Walker was certain they were about to sink. As others leapt by him to wade up on deck, Guy suddenly slumped into the water. Walker grabbed him before he went under. He held his friend's head and watched as his eyes rolled back, then shut. Guy, Walker realized, was having a massive heart attack; before he could do anything, Bruce Guy died in his arms. Walker dragged him to a bunk, where he cradled his head and attempted to clear his mouth, but it was too late.

Meanwhile, in the moments before *Business Post Naiad* righted itself, Rob Matthews had clung to the side of the boat, sitting on the broken mast in neck-deep water. As the waves tore at him, he saw he would need to raise himself onto the keel or risk being sucked into the sea. Exhausted, he was just about to set his feet on the submerged mast when the boat began to right itself. To his dismay, the mast beneath him shot upward, flipping him into the air like a flapjack. Matthews landed with a crunch in the cockpit just as the boat finished rolling over. He looked down and saw Phil Skeggs's motionless body, wrapped in a spaghetti of ropes on the floor of the cockpit. As his crewmates hustled up the companionway and administered CPR, Matthews was too exhausted to do anything but watch. Their efforts were in vain. Skeggs, the gentle locksmith, had drowned.

ABOUT 4:00 A.M.

The orange-canopied life raft holding John Stanley and his four friends from *Winston Churchill* began to disintegrate sometime after three that morning. By then everyone aboard was fighting hypothermia and injuries. An outgoing Sydney attorney, John Gibson

— "Gibbo" to his mates — had cut two of his fingers down to the bone trying to manhandle a rope during their rushed exit from *Churchill* 12 hours before. Stanley had broken his ankle and torn a net of ligaments in his hip when a wave had tumbled the raft, wildly throwing the five men together. There was no first-aid kit, nor, aside from the biscuit Stanley had stashed in his jacket, any food.

The real problems had arisen after midnight. An unusually large wave — Stanley could often identify the big ones because they sounded like freight trains — had tossed the raft upside down, leaving all five men up to their necks in the water, their feet resting on the submerged canopy, the bottom of the raft inches above their heads. It was impossible to right the raft from inside. Someone would have to swim out through the submerged canopy opening, with no lifeline, and try to pull them upright. Jimmy Lawler, the Australian representative for the American Bureau of Shipping, said it wasn't possible. He couldn't get through the opening wearing a life vest, and wasn't willing to shed his vest.

In 20 minutes they began to run out of air. Stanley found himself gasping for breath. To get air, they agreed Lawler would use his knife to cut a four-inch hole in the bottom of the raft. He did so, and for a time they were actually comfortable. But then it happened: another wave flipped the raft upright again. Suddenly the five men found themselves sitting in a life raft with a constantly growing tear in its bottom. The weight of their bodies gradually ripped apart the underpinnings of the raft. In a half-hour they were forced back into the water, this time clinging to the insides of their now doughnut-shaped raft. They tried to maintain their spirits, but it was difficult. Other than Gibson, who kept up a steady patter of jokes, the men were too tired to talk much.

In the darkness before dawn no one heard the black wave that finally got them. One moment they were inside the raft, shoulder to shoulder, breathing hard. The next they were airborne, hurtling down the face of the gigantic unseen wave. Stanley was driven deep beneath the raft, but somehow managed to keep his hold on it. Fighting to the surface, he looked all around and saw nothing but blackness. "Is everyone here?" he shouted.

"Yeah!" he heard a sputtering voice answer to one side. It was Gibson, the only one of the five who had worn a safety harness he had clipped to the raft.

Stanley craned his head, looking for the others. His heart sank: about 300 yards back he could see two of the three men. He was never sure whom he missed: Lawler, John Dean, a Sydney attorney, or Mike Bannister. All three men were gone.

"We can't do anything for them," Stanley said. "It's impossible."

"Just hang on," Gibson said. "For ourselves."

DAWN, MONDAY

As the eastern horizon reddened around 4:30, the scene at the small airport in the resort town of Merimbula resembled something out of China Beach. At first light 17 aircraft were sent searching for *Winston Churchill*. The second priority, curiously, was finding Glyn Charles, who, in the unlikely event he was still alive, would have been in the water more than 12 hours.

Around six, David Dutton, a paramedic aboard one of the South-Care helicopters flying out of Canberra, spotted a dismasted yacht southeast of Eden. Below him, *Midnight Special*, a 40-foot Queensland boat, was rolling violently. The boat had taken on the solemn air of a floating hospital. The crew, nine longtime friends who sailed out of the Mooloolaba Yacht Club, near the resort city of Brisbane, were older men, most in their 50s, with a variety of occupations and an even wider range of injuries. Ian Griffiths, a lawyer, had a broken leg and crushed cartilage in his back. Neil Dickson, a veteran ocean sailor who at 49 was the youngest crew member, had hit his head against the cabin ceiling during a rollover, which had knocked him momentarily unconscious and left him with a concussion. Peter Carter had crushed vertebrae in his lower back. The others had collected an assortment of cracked ribs and gashed foreheads.

On Sunday the crew had surprised themselves by surfing into Bass Strait in 18th place. Had they not ranked so high, Roger Barnett, the yacht club's commodore, felt, they might have headed back earlier. As it was, *Midnight Special* had plunged south through the mountainous waves until injuries incapacitated much of the crew. Around three P.M. the five men who jointly owned the boat had gathered belowdecks and engaged in a lively debate about whether to forge on. Dickson recalls that in the middle of this discussion, a gigantic wave struck the boat, flinging Griffiths across the cabin, breaking his leg and a large part of the ship's cupboard. That ended the debate. *Sword of Orion*'s three-o'clock report of 75-knot winds ahead of them in Bass Strait silenced any doubters.

A little after three the crew started the engine and began plowing back the 40 miles northwest toward Gabo Island. Conditions worsened as the boat fought heavy seas. Twice *Midnight Special* was slammed on its side, tossing the crew belowdecks, breaking noses and cracking ribs. Then, later that night, a giant wave crashed out of the darkness directly into the cockpit, rolling the three-year-old boat through a 360-degree arc. Windows smashed everywhere, and as water began pouring into the crushed cabin below, large cracks began to appear in the deck. Frantically, Neil Dickson began stuffing sleeping bags into the widening cracks in a vain attempt to maintain the integrity of the hull. When waves tore the sleeping bags out, the crew resorted to cramming spinnaker sails into the openings. The sails did the trick, but their trailing ropes fouled the boat's propeller, leaving *Midnight Special* dead in the water. The radios were destroyed, and an EPIRB was activated. As red flares from other boats lit the sky all around them, those who could spent the rest of the night bailing.

At dawn the crew spotted a P3C Orion flying overhead; it wagged its wings, buoying their spirits. Not long after, Dutton's chopper arrived, and he motioned for crew members to jump into the waves and begin swimming toward the dangling rescue strop. It was decided that David Leslie should go first. He was their doctor — well, a dermatologist — and could brief the rescuers on their injuries. Leslie plunged into the sea, swam toward Dutton, and slipped his upper body into the strop. Trevor McDonough, a 60-year-old bricklayer, and Bill Butler, a nursery owner, stood on deck and watched as Leslie was slowly lifted up toward the helicopter. The other six crew members stood safely belowdecks, at the bottom of the companionway, swapping smiles. "We're outta here!" someone said joyfully.

No one saw the wave. It hit without warning and, as Dutton and the helicopter crew looked on helplessly, rolled the boat upside down. The first thing Dickson knew, he was on his hands and knees in the pitch-dark cabin, with water inching up his thighs. This time Dickson wanted no part of any of his partners' debate; he just wanted out. Without a word he plunged headfirst into the flooded companionway. The exit was blocked by boards and debris, but he found an opening about two feet in diameter and managed to get his shoulders, then his waist through and into the swirling ocean outside. But then, as he fought to get his thighs through the hole, he became stuck. A rope had looped around his midsection and was holding him tight against the boat. Dickson frantically kicked his legs, trying to get loose.

Trapped beneath the boat, both McDonough and Butler fought to free themselves from entangling ropes; neither was able to do so. In fact, all three men — Dickson, McDonough, and Butler — were as good as dead. And then, with a vicious jerk, the boat swung around and righted itself. After several moments spent gasping for breath Dickson ripped himself free and charged up onto the deck, where he was met by this seriocomic image: Butler standing perfectly upright, mummylike, still trapped in ropes. McDonough lay in the cockpit, seawater streaming from his nose.

As the three men recovered, they were met by a sight that left no one laughing: Dutton's helicopter, low on fuel, was forced to head for land. As the helicopter flew off, Dickson and his crewmates could do nothing but watch, dumbfounded. The boat beneath was sinking slowly by the stern, and every wave threatened to roll it over once more. It took another unnerving half-hour before a second helicopter finally rescued the men on *Midnight Special.*

All down the east coast of New South Wales and out past Gabo Island, the rescues continued in the first hours after dawn. The remaining sailors aboard *Sword of Orion* scrambled aboard a hovering Seahawk, while a medevac out of Canberra winched the seven survivors off *Business Post Naiad,* leaving the bodies of Phil Skeggs and Bruce Guy to be picked up later. *B-52* struggled under its own power into Eden Harbor just after lunchtime. In the hour before dawn the yacht's port-side windows had imploded, sending gushers of seawater below; the crew had somehow managed to nail wooden planks over the windows and had spent the rest of the morning bailing with buckets. Tony Mowbray's *Solo Globe Challenger* would be one of the last to reach port, limping into Eden on Wednesday morning.

Late Monday afternoon the lifeboat carrying Richard Winning

and three other survivors from *Winston Churchill* was spotted, and everyone was winched aboard a waiting helicopter. Like those aboard *Churchill*'s other raft, Winning's group had capsized twice during the night. Unlike the occupants of the other raft, however, Winning had bravely swum outside and forcibly righted the rubber inflatable, which had then survived the night intact.

9:00 P.M.

Night began to fall with no sign of *Churchill*'s second life raft. At the rescue center in Canberra, hope was dwindling that the men would be found. At Merimbula the civilian aircraft — those without any night-rescue capabilities — began landing, one by one. None had seen anything that looked remotely like a life raft. Then, just after nine, a P3C Orion on its way back to Merimbula saw a light flashing in the darkening ocean below. Descending to 500 feet, the pilot spied two men clinging to a shredded orange life raft. It was John Stanley and "Gibbo" Gibson, still alive after 28 hours in the water.

"Gibbo!" Stanley rasped, swinging a handheld strobe, "I think they've seen us!"

Within minutes, during which the sun set, Lieutenant Commander Rick Neville had his Navy Seahawk hovering 70 feet above Stanley and Gibson. Petty Officer Shane Pashley winched down a wire into the waves below and, as Neville fought to maintain position in the gusting winds, managed to get a rescue strop around Gibson. As the two men were lifted skyward, a terrific gust blew the Seahawk sideways, dumping the pair back into the waves. Neville swung the chopper around once more, and this time the two water-logged men were successfully winched aboard.

It was too much for Neville. His Radalt auto-hover system was being overtaxed by the winds, and he was unwilling to send Pashley back into the ocean. Stanley, he decided, would have to make it into the rescue strop on his own. As Neville maneuvered the Seahawk back over the raft, Pashley dangled the strop down into the sea, and Stanley somehow grabbed it and hoisted his upper body into it. The winch lifted him into the air, but when he was 20 feet above the waves, Stanley felt a weight around his ankles and realized, to his dismay, that he was still hooked to his life raft, which was sagging in midair below him. Reluctantly he shrugged himself out of the strop and dropped like a stone back into the sea, where he managed to unhook the raft. Once again the strop was dangled to him, and once again he got into it. This time everything worked. After more than a day in the ocean, Stanley and Gibson were on their way home.

8:00 A.M., TUESDAY

As *Sayonara* tacked the last mile up the Derwent River toward the Hobart docks, a small launch with a bagpiper aboard swung alongside. It was the most stunning sunrise Ellison had ever seen, splashes of rose and pink and five different hues of blue, and as the pipes played a mournful tune, the enormity of what the fleet had endured hit all 23 men aboard the winning yacht. *Sayonara*'s sideband radio had shorted out, and it hadn't been until late Monday afternoon that the crew learned of the tragedies in their wake. As they reached the dock and piled out to hug their loved ones, Ellison was overwhelmed. "It was an incredible moment of clarity, the beauty and fragility of life, the preciousness of it all; that's when people appreciated what we had been through," he recalls. "Having said that, if I live to be a thousand years old, I'll never do it again. Never."

Amid all-too-predictable recriminations, Hugo van Kretschmar, commodore of the Cruising Yacht Club of Australia, stoutly defended the club's decision to continue the race despite warnings of bad weather. Even as he announced an internal investigation, van Kretschmar pointed out, correctly, that the decision whether to race is traditionally left up to the skipper of each boat. Yacht-club officials, after all, had the same forecasts that every skipper had. As a result, few of the sailors who survived the race were willing to attack the organizers. One exception was Peter Joubert of *Kingurra,* who emerged from several weeks in the hospital sharply critical of race management. "The race organizers weren't properly in touch with what was going on out there — they just didn't know enough," Joubert says. "It's only a yacht race. It's not a race to the death." Outside Australia, the judgment was just as harsh. "They should have waited; there is ample precedent for waiting," notes Gary Jobson, the ESPN sailing analyst. "But race officials were under a lot of pressure. Live TV, all these people, a major holiday."

Three days after *Sayonara* crossed the finish line more than 5,000 people gathered on Hobart's Constitution Dock for a memorial service for the six men who died in the race. The funerals of Bruce Guy, Phil Skeggs, James Lawler, and Mike Bannister were to follow shortly; the bodies of John Dean and Glyn Charles have never been found. "We will miss you always; we will remember you always; we will learn from the tragic circumstances of your passing," van Kretschmar said as the muted bells of St. David's Cathedral rang out. "May the everlasting voyage you have now embarked on be blessed with calm seas and gentle breezes. May you never have to reef or change a headsail in the night. May your bunk always be warm and dry."

BURKHARD BILGER

Enter the Chicken

FROM HARPER'S MAGAZINE

> Suddenly we noticed barnyard cocks beginning a bitter fight just in
> front of the door. We chose to watch.
>   — St. Augustine, *De Ordine*

THE ROAD from Baton Rouge to Lafayette snakes through the
heart of Louisiana's Cajun country, and is barely elevated, at times,
above the swamp's reach. On the night I traveled it, floodwaters
from the north had already strained the levees to bursting, threatening to capsize chemical barges along the Mississippi; now a thun-
derstorm swept in to finish the job. My plane had spent hours in a
holding pattern above this storm, and the *kerschlick* of my tires
ticked off every second of delay: midnight in the bayou seemed an
inauspicious setting for a cockfight.

I was looking for a club called the Red Rooster, near the town of
Maurice. A cockfighter named Jim Demoruelle had promised to
meet me there, though I was three hours late. Ours would be a perfectly legal meeting — cockfighting has never been outlawed in
Louisiana — yet I felt like I was going undercover. Cockfighters are
strange attractors of vice, I'd been told, conduits for drugs and
gambling and episodes of violence. They shun publicity and hide
their meetings as assiduously as any drug cartel or pornography
ring. A few weeks earlier, I'd tracked down the editor of a cockfighting magazine at an unlisted number in rural Arkansas. When I
called, she barked into the phone, "You sound like one of them animal lovers to me," and hung up.

If Demoruelle had agreed to meet me, I thought, it was because he was a little desperate. As president of the Louisiana Gamefowl Breeders' Association, Demoruelle had managed to fight off "the humaniacs" for years, but history seemed to be turning against him. Once a sport of kings and country gentlemen, cockfighting was a misdemeanor in twenty-nine states and a felony in sixteen. Arizona, Louisiana, Missouri, New Mexico, and Oklahoma still allowed it, but in Louisiana some of the sport's biggest boosters had been swept out of office, and in Arizona and Missouri animal-rights groups were mounting state referendums on the sport. "It's the beginning of the end," a spokeswoman for the Humane Society of the United States said. "When it's so few states left, you get a kind of landslide effect."

And yet, at the same time, cockfighting has never been more popular. There are at least 500,000 cockfighters in the United States, and due to immigration of Asians and Latin Americans, the number grows every year. There are three national cockfighting magazines — Feathered Warrior, Gamecock, and Grit and Steel — and there are cockpits in even the most tranquil, law-abiding communities. When I told the name of my hometown in Oklahoma to a criminologist who specializes in cockfighting, he laughed. "Oh yeah. I know that place. There's a pit just outside of the city limits."

Part of me wanted to go back and see that side of small-town life, to rattle my memories like the false fronts of a Hollywood set. But another part, Demoruelle must have known, was just looking for a thrill. When he wasn't fighting chickens, Demoruelle worked in a drug-rehab center, and he knew all about forbidden pleasure. "Be careful," he'd told me, only half joking. "If you get into this thing, you might really like it. I can get somebody off drugs or alcohol better than I can off of chickens."

Beyond my headlights, the night was nearly absolute, the skeletal landscape exposed by lightning now and then, as if by X-ray. I was almost to the next town by the time a low, rickety building swam into view. Turning in, I saw a few dozen pickup trucks scattered across the mud and gravel, as if flung there by the storm. Off to the side, perched on the embankment, a portable neon sign flickered and buzzed in the rain: R D R OST R.

Demoruelle was standing on the top rung of the bleachers across the room, arms folded over his beefy chest. Although I'd only heard his voice, I picked him out of the crowd right away: silver hair, bullish features, melancholy eyes. Even at that distance, he radiated a kind of sullen power, surveying the scene like Henry VIII inspecting his troops. A few eyes locked on to mine as I came in, but when Demoruelle raised his hand and called me over, they drifted back to the fight. A moment later I was standing within his protective circle, shaking hands with two men who flanked him like lieutenants.

It was then that I began to notice an odd thing: the Red Rooster was a fairly cozy place. Warm and brightly lit, high-ceilinged and amiably sloppy in its construction, it seemed better suited to a Boy Scout jamboree than a cockfight. Over in the central tier of bleachers a mother was tickling her toddler into ecstatic peals of laughter. A few rows down, a woman was nursing her baby within touching distance of the cocks, cupping her hands over the child's ears when their squabbling grew too loud. There were crawfish farmers in overalls and old-timers trading gossip, a woman hawking cockfighting T-shirts, and teenagers loitering in the aisles, flirting between sips of Dr. Pepper. It was 2:00 A.M. by now, and the Red Rooster looked as harmless as a bingo parlor.

Where were all the drunks and scofflaws, dope fiends and edgy hustlers? Where were the "vain, idle, and wanton minds," as William Penn wrote in 1682, who "gratify their own sensualities and raise the like wicked curiosity in others"? I felt like some South Sea explorer, making my way past spooky totems and grim palisades only to find a few peaceable villagers inside, eating roots and swatting at flies. "It's almost like a demographic frozen in time," sociologist Clifton Bryant later told me. "The country changed, but cockfighters didn't." In 1974 and again in 1991, Bryant conducted national surveys of cockfighters. "They're mostly middle-class, from small towns or the country, more likely to be married, more likely to stay married, more likely to go to church, to be veterans," he says. "In fact, if you tried to go back and put together a typical American of the 1940s or '50s, that would be a cockfighter."

Demoruelle's friends were typical cockers. Sonny Wabinga, to his left, was an Army ranger on his third tour of duty. He had a moon-shaped face, wide, dreaming eyes, and a body as compact and lethal as any gamecock's. I'd once seen film clips of rangers on patrol so sleep-deprived they mistook tree branches for telephones and tried to call home. Surviving that sort of thing, and raising chickens, had given Sonny an oddly upbeat Darwinian outlook. "My wife's German and I'm Filipino, so my boys have the power and the speed." John Hickerson, to Demoruelle's right, was lanky and gray-haired, with the loose, loquacious manner of a cowboy poet. He is from Michigan, but had to come south to do his cockfighting. "Where I come from," he said, "it's a felony just to own cockfighting *equipment.*"

They made a strange threesome, standing on that bench together, calling out their bets: a St. Bernard, a pit bull, and a bloodhound all howling at the same moon. As Sonny put it, "If you have chickens, great, we can talk. Otherwise . . ." He smiled his strange smile and turned to the fight.

The cockpit rose from the center of the room like a miniature thunderdome: an octagonal cage, eight feet high and more than twenty feet across, surrounded on three sides by bleachers. The cage was meant to protect the audience, not to confine the birds, Demoruelle told me. "They say we're cruel, that we're making them fight. But I guarantee, if you put those chickens on either end of a football field, they'd crow and charge and end up fighting at the fifty-yard line." He spoke in a flat, faintly Gallic grumble, with flashes of local color but not much music — the voice of a man who'd never gotten used to defending himself. But I believed him. The two men entering the pit just then were cradling their birds like jars of nitroglycerin. The cocks' heads jutted from their owners' arms, wild-eyed and quivering, desperate for release. From where I sat, they looked less like farm animals than birds of prey, barely a chromosome removed from gyrfalcons.

If cockfighting is still legal in Louisiana, if calling it immoral can still get your nose broken, this is why: most blood sports are merely cruel; no bear or badger is willingly baited, and dogs rarely fight to the death. But chickens are different. Egg factories can lose as much as 80 percent of their layers to cannibalism, unless they cut off the birds' beaks; and even on a free range, roosters are seized by blood lust now and then. "We call it comin' into their pride," one chicken breeder told me. "After a storm sometimes, you'll go out into the yard and it'll be littered with dead birds."

Still, a good gamecock, like a good roaster, is largely a human invention. Three thousand years ago, Asian cockfighters took the most unfriendly birds on the planet — jungle fowl, *Gallus gallus* — and proceeded to make them even meaner. Over the years, cockfighters crossed them with Himalayan Bankivas for speed and flying kicks, and with Malay birds for stamina and wallop. They taught them to punch and feint and roll. They marched them through gamecock calisthenics, trimmed their wattles and combs, and stuffed red pepper up their anuses. A few thousand generations later, this was the result: two birds programmed to kill each other, each a glimmering alloy of instinct, training, and breeding.

Below us in the pit, the two men were standing side by side now, swaying toward each other like dancers bumping hips, holding their birds at waist-level and letting them peck at each other. "Gamecocks are meant to fight," Demoruelle said, finally. "Anyway, they were doing it when Christ walked the earth, and he never said a word about it." Then he held up a roll of $10 bills and hollered, "Fifteen on the gray!"

Two rows down, a hairless old man with ears like flügelhorns turned and nodded.

The art of cockfighting, the Kama Sutra tells us, is one of the sixty-four things that every sophisticated woman should know. The rules are simple: two roosters are matched by weight and given identical weapons (wild cocks use their bony back spurs to fight, but cockfighters cut these off and strap knives or gaffs, like curved ice picks, onto the stumps). Once armed, the birds are placed in a ring and launched at each other like self-guided missiles, exploding in a flurry of beaks and feet. The fight is no-holds-barred, but it's a controlled sort of mayhem, full of stops and starts and odd points of etiquette. When a cock stops fighting, the referee counts to twenty and then calls a twenty-second break. (In Bali, they drop a pierced coconut into a pail full of water; when the coconut sinks, the birds fight.) If a cock goes down for three counts of ten and one count of twenty, or if he runs away or simply dies, the fight is over.

The whole thing can look a lot like a boxing match, but with one essential difference: "gameness" matters more here than landing punches. Your bird may be mortally wounded, he may even drop dead while chasing the other bird, but if he's the last one to show some fight, he wins.

Those are the basics, and any young adept could learn them in a day. But in a cockpit everything bristles with hidden meanings. Before a cock steps into the pit, for instance, the owner may lick his bird's weapons, or the referee may swab them with wet cotton and squeeze the water into the bird's beak. Both acts have a certain strange sensuality, a symbolic aptness, but the reason behind them is prosaic: some cockfighters have a fondness for poison. On the Venezuelan island of Margarita, for example, the locals like to coat their knives with sting-ray venom before a fight, or they may spread a foul-smelling ointment beneath the bird's wings: when the opponent runs to escape the odor, the referee will disqualify him. Some cockfighters have been known to poison the other bird's food, or else reach over and snap a small bone in his back when no one's looking.

To protect their birds, most cockfighters keep them hidden until just before a fight and sometimes put them under guard. Still, nothing can thwart the most determined cheater. In one famous case, in the Philippines, a local mayor was at a cockpit when his bird began to lose. Rather than wait for a decision, the man pulled out a .45 and blew the other bird away. All bets were off, he declared, since the fight never officially ended. His armed bodyguards made sure everyone agreed.

At the Red Rooster, the betting was more casual — Demoruelle was the highest roller here, and he was sticking to twenties — and cheating was a rarity. Once the voices died down, the handlers set their birds behind lines of white cornmeal, eight feet apart in the dirt, and waited for the referee to shout "Pit!" To the left was a "gray," in cockfighters' terms: a tall, lean bird with creamy hackles, gray-green legs, and auburn wings. To the right was a stockier "red," with crimson hackles, yellow legs, and dark wings, his tail iridescent with ruby and turquoise. Like warrior monks preparing for an ordeal, they'd both spent two days fasting, in darkness and isolation, preserving their strength and stoking their frustrations. Depending on their owners, they might be fueled by injections of testosterone, vitamin K to clot their wounds more quickly, and digitalis to speed up their already racing hearts. Now the bright lights and shouting faces were sending them into overdrive. "A bird should have a little nervousness to him right before a fight," Demoruelle said, watching them squirm, "a tremble, a twitch to him, like a boxer."

What came next, to my eyes, was an almost meaningless blur. But to Demoruelle it unspooled in slow motion, every frame distinct:

the referee's hoarse shout, unnaturally drawn out in the sudden quiet; the handlers watching his mouth, pulling back their hands as his lips pursed to speak; the cocks gathering themselves to leap, unfolding their wings as their necks strained upward; their legs driving toward each other, at the top of their arcs, talons spinning like teeth on a chain saw. And then the tumble, the scramble for footing, and another rattling clash.

"Oh, that was a good hit," Demoruelle said, when the red connected with a kick to the head. "The gray's hurt." Although most hits with a gaff aren't fatal, a good cock can do plenty of damage with it. "Oh hell, yes," Hickerson said. "If you hold a plastic milk jug up to them, they can punch eight holes in it before you can pull it away."

It was all a matter of opposing forces, Demoruelle explained. "When a rooster has his wings back, he brings his feet forward and his tail down like an air brake." He raised his hands and made a few quick jabs in the air. In his twenties, he went on, he was expert at the martial arts — "135 pounds and greased-chicken-shit fast" — and I could almost see the young fighter moving beneath his middle-aged bulk. "When you're watching a cockfight," he said, "you're watching pure karate."

Both roosters were striking home now, spraying the referee with blood and bits of down. They hurled themselves at each other in weary spasms, biting each other's necks and windmilling their feet, until their gaffs snagged and the handlers rushed in to separate them. Demoruelle had hoped the gray would gradually gain the upper hand — green-legged birds have more "bottom" than yellow-legged birds, he explained — but that didn't seem to be happening. After five minutes of fighting, both birds were wounded, though the gray looked worse: one eye dim, the other destroyed, pale feathers matted with blood, beak trembling with every breath. Between rounds, his handler held him close, swabbed his head with a wet sponge, and whispered to him urgently. When that didn't work, he put the bird's whole head in his mouth, sucked the blood from his throat, and then spat saliva into his beak. Little by little, the gray revived, twisting his head to glare across the ring.

A rooster's rage is a simple-minded thing. His courage is more complicated, and only certain weapons truly test it. So some cockfighters say, at least, and their choices divide them into camps as ardent and contrary as religious sects. In the Pacific islands and most of North America, cockfighters prefer the clean, quick kill of a knife fight. (Filipinos, who like their knives especially long, sometimes forge them from armor-piercing bullets.) In India and Pakistan, they breed huge, powerful Asile birds, wrap their feet to form miniature boxing gloves, and fight them for days on end. In the Caribbean and Louisiana, cockfighters tend to prefer gaffs, but even gaff fighters split into factions. Puerto Ricans cut off a bird's spur, scrape and varnish it until it's needle sharp, and strap it back on. Most Cajuns prefer their gaffs made of surgical steel, with a pointy end, but others favor a blunt gaff known as a peg awl.

Like a bullfight without a matador to finish the job, a gaff fight can go on for more than an hour, the cocks goring each other again and again until one surrenders from blood loss, exhaustion, or fear. On this night, the gray and the red were soon lying side by side in the sand, chests heaving. But even then the fight was far from over. After a moment, the gray staggered to his feet and flailed about blindly, delirious with anger and pain.

"Now that's heart," Hickerson murmured next to me. I looked over at him: shoulders hunched tight, eyes squinting slightly, a twinge of pleasure to his lips. Like most gaff fighters, Hickerson was a throwback, a believer in the ancient, primal meaning of the fight. Gaff fights are long and brutal, he admitted, but the anguish was worth it, if only for that one moment when two hearts are put to the test. "At least with the gaffs, you're really only replacing their natural spurs," he told me later. "And a gaff fight doesn't rely on a few good kicks, it relies on this." He pointed to his chest.

Demoruelle started to chuckle when the red dashed away from the gray. "Did you see that guy's butt start to pucker?" he said, jerking his head toward the red's embarrassed owner. Gamecocks, for Demoruelle, were more than symbols of courage; they were stand-ins for their owners ("detachable, self-operating penises," in anthropologist Clifford Geertz's great phrase, "ambulant genitals with a life of their own"). And when they collided, he didn't just see windmilling feet; he saw converging plotlines, intersecting histories crystallized in a moment.

The gray eventually won his match, and died in doing so. But the crowd barely seemed to notice. Most of them weren't here for the gambling, or the spectacle, or some terrible communion. They

were here for something more mundane: a sense of community —
one drawn all the tighter by secrecy and persecution. "So what do
you think?" Hickerson turned and asked. I shrugged. "If you think
it's hard for you to watch, think how it is for me. I've raised chickens from birth, and they're damn cute when they're little." He
paused for a second, then added, "I'm a compassionate man. I
have a lot of crippled roosters running around my yard that I
should have gotten rid of a long time ago. It's bad business, really."
Then he turned to watch the next fight, the same hungry look in
his eyes.

Driving around Louisiana with Demoruelle and talking to him over
the following months, I began to fill in the outlines of his double
life. It had started, oddly enough, overseas. Although he grew up in
the mecca of American cockfighting, he discovered the sport in
1960, as a nineteen-year-old Navy corpsman stationed in the Philippines. "There was this beautiful girl," he told me. "I wanted to
date her, but when I finally worked my way around to asking, she
said I had to meet her family first." The visit wasn't quite what
he had expected. "I walked out into the courtyard and there all the
men were," he remembered, "a beer in one hand, a rooster in the
other."

He forgot about the girl eventually, but he fell in love with the
birds. "Gamecocks will fight for their territory and defend it to the
end," he told me. "They have a spirit about them that's very gal-
lant." American men have very little of that spirit left in them,
he said, but wherever he was stationed, he found it among cockfighters. He could stand on a hill in Borneo and listen to a rooster
crow on another hill. If it was a gamecock — and he could always
tell — he would knock on its owner's door, knowing he would not
be refused. "I used to go out to the jungle to see fights between operations in Vietnam," he said. "I never worried about being kid-
napped by the Viet Cong, though I'm sure they were there. I was a
cockfighter like them."

It was back in the States, between tours, that he had to be careful.
During the day he worked at Camp Pendleton in California, but
evenings and weekends he gave to gamecocks, training them in secret for airline executives and others with a taste for the trans-
gressive. Real cockpits were hard to hide from the authorities, so he

would set up in local hotels. "We used to go up the service elevators real early on Sunday morning," he remembered. "We'd fight them in a suite with a tarp thrown over the floor, a few inches of dirt on top. By noon, we'd be out." Some say that cockfighting is more orderly where it's illegal, that codes of honor are more binding when they're a fighter's only guarantee. But Demoruelle disagreed. "In illegal states," he told me, "a lot of the people who do it are bad apples." Finally, in 1980, he went home to Louisiana, where he thought he had nothing to hide.

He lives and works back in Ville Platte now, not far from where he was born, and directs 156 employees at Evangeline Psychiatric Care. On the surface, he could be a poster boy for the Louisiana tourist board: farm owner, Cajun song composer, consumer of vast racks of baby-back ribs — *Laissez les bon temps roulez!* Yet his double life continues. Demoruelle's posh suburban house feels barely inhabited, its rooms oversized and echoey beneath their cathedral ceilings. His wife and children sometimes seem to float through the house like extras on a set. "Cockfighting wives tend to be either supporters or tolerators," he said. "Mine's a tolerator — and not much of one at that."

Standing in his driveway one morning after a cockfight, I felt oddly at home. The trim lawns and quiet neighbors, the sense of local culture pushed to the far edges of consciousness, could have placed me in any suburb in America. But fifteen minutes away, among rolling hills blanketed with pine, white oak, and magnolia trees, lay Demoruelle's game farm. And it was unlike anything I had ever seen.

When we stopped by, it was still early morning. A-frame huts, fashioned from cement or corrugated metal, marched across the weed-choked yard like miniature missile silos, their launching strips stretched out in front. Near each one a lone rooster kept vigil, often from the top of its hut, bound by one leg and screaming out challenges in ragged counterpoint to the others. "The crowing?" Demoruelle said. "That's all day. I don't even hear it anymore."

Although the farm looked like a bivouac in miniature, these birds were more pampered than any soldier. The average broiler chicken lives for six weeks, wing-to-wing with tens of thousands of others. These gamecocks, by contrast, typically lived for two to three years. And they lived like pashas. Every day, from 5:30 in the morning till sundown, three employees tended to their every need. They fed, trained, and vaccinated the birds; trimmed their feathers and searched their droppings for worms; put them on trapezes to strengthen their legs and slowly stroked the twitches out of them. If the birds still went a little stir-crazy, the trainers might even bring around some nice, plump pullets to calm them down. "The prisons could learn something from us about conjugal visits," Demoruelle said. "The cocks won't fight as much if they get to see a female occasionally."

We walked around to his training room, crudely built of fiberglass and steel. An adolescent bird, or stag, begins its schooling at around nine months, he said, when he grows his spurs and starts to show some fight. He grabbed a scruffy red bird from one of the cages lining the wall. "First we'll put sparring muffs on 'em and let 'em hit each other once or twice," he said. "Then, about six weeks before their first fight, we'll start tamin' 'em and workin' 'em on the bench." He walked over to a table the size of an executive's desk, padded with foam and carpet, and ran the stag through a series of drills. He shoved the stag back and forth between his hands, making him sidestep as delicately as a dancer, pressed him down to strengthen his legs, then rolled him on his back ("that's not a natural position for a rooster") and flipped him backward through the air in a fluttering pinwheel; the bird landed deftly on his feet. "You can't train a rooster to fight," Demoruelle said. "But you're always looking for that little edge."

Every culture has its cockfighting secrets. In Louisiana old-timers feed their birds sulfur and gunpowder. In Martinique they rub them with rum and herbs every morning. In Brittany they give them a sugar cube soaked in cognac before a fight. In Argentina, when a bird is wounded, the gauchos will rub his testicles until he ejaculates; if the sperm contains blood, the bird is retired. The one tradition that seems to cut across cultures — the one downside of training from the cock's perspective — is celibacy. Sex before a fight, cockers universally believe, will sap a bird of its fighting spirit. In the Philippines the mere touch of a menstruating woman is said to spell doom.

Demoruelle had his share of tricks: to increase his birds' appetite, for instance, he gave them a little strychnine. But for the most part he put his money on exercise, nutrition, and breeding. (Like most American cockfighters, he could talk genetics like a postdoc.) If a stag showed promise, Demoruelle would start fighting him at around eighteen months and keep on doing it for another two or three years. Then, if the bird was very lucky and survived, he would come back to the farm to stud.

Demoruelle had a few chickens in his yard that were more than six years old. One of them, a dark red bird with green legs known as Crooked Toe, was nine years old and had won seven fights. "I'd love to have 500 like him," Demoruelle said. "If I did, I'd have a Cadillac in every garage." As it was, he just about broke even, selling birds to Hawaiian businessmen at prices ranging from $75 to $500, though champion birds have been known to fetch $25,000. "If I quit everything else I could make a living at it — an old man's living," he said, "but I wouldn't get fat."

John Hickerson, walking next to me as we entered the feed shed, glanced around with unvarnished envy. "You have to understand that for 90 percent of cockfighters it's a losing proposition," he said. He scooped up a handful of greenish feed — a mixture of Canadian peas, corn, milo, oats, red wheat, and soybeans — from a drum the size of an oil barrel. "Look at this: nutrients. Not cheap." (Last year alone, Demoruelle's 300 gamecocks and chicks went through some 7,000 pounds of feed.) Hickerson went over to another drum, this one filled with a pink powder. "Oyster shell and granite for their beaks and gizzards. Not cheap." Then he swept his arm in a circle, pointing to the farm, the training rooms, the cages, and the surgery rooms. "Look around here and see the amount of work that goes into this each and every day, and you'll realize that the cockfight's only the culmination," he said. "It's only the last of things."

Hickerson had left behind his family, his job, and his roots in Michigan just to live in a house next to Demoruelle's farm and raise birds. More than for any of the others, cockfighting was a way of life for him — one he had been denied up North. In the battle over legal cockfighting in Louisiana, he was in this for the long haul. "We are the keepers of the chickens' genetic pool," he declared, as we climbed in the van and headed for another cockpit. "We can't afford to lose this stock." Wabinga nodded quietly in the front seat. "We are the keepers of the flame."

Outside our windows, beneath a lowering sky, the swamp forest was luminous green, its trunks and branches still black from recent rain. Hickerson popped in a tape by Woody Guthrie and told me about the Calumet copper strike of 1913. When the next song came on, he stopped in mid-sentence and began to sing along, half-smiling at the melodrama of it: *I ain't got no home, I'm just rambling 'round. Just a wand'rin' worker, I go from town to town. The police make it hard wherever I may go. And I ain't got no home in this world anymore.*

If ever there was a home for cockfighters, the cockpit we were visiting was it. Known as Sunrise, it was tucked along the border between Louisiana and Mississippi, and drew cockfighters from the entire region. Other pits were larger: Texoma, on the southern Oklahoma border, had given away $150,000 at a single fight the previous year, along with a new truck for the "Cock of the Year"; Sunset, in western Louisiana, had air-conditioning, plush seats, and a history of hosting the most famous cockfighters in the country. But as a symbol of big-time cockfighting — of what the sport might look like if it were widely accepted — Sunrise would do.

"From the sandlots of Florida to the bayous of Louisiana to the cotton rows of Mississippi and Georgia," Hickerson was saying as we passed some trailers in the parking lot, "these are some well-traveled chickens." Those at the Red Rooster, Demoruelle added, were a kind of avian underclass, poorly conditioned and sloppy in their attacks. These birds were in a different league. Each owner had paid $300 for the right to enter six of them in the derby. Because 150 owners were signed up in all, that came to 900 chickens fighting for one $45,000 pot. Demoruelle pointed to a middle-aged man in jeans and a sport shirt. "That guy over there? He's the largest fish wholesaler in Mississippi."

But all I could think about were those 900 chickens. A cockfight, as I understood it, was a single combat between lone fighters. But this sounded more like a mass slaughter, a battle royal. True, not all 900 birds would fight: a cockfighter would stay in the contest only as long as his birds were undefeated, or were slated to fight an undefeated fighter's birds. (In Martinique the list of matched roosters is called a *tableau de marriage*.) Still, a good half of the birds would enter the pit tonight, and half of them might die.

Sunrise, at first glance, hardly seemed the place for such epic carnage. Slapped together of corrugated steel, painted sky blue, and thrust into a patch of scrub oak, it had an almost deliberate impermanence about it, as if it could be disassembled with a moment's warning and spirited into the woods. As we shouldered our way through the front door, one of the men we passed shook his head and said, "It's a madhouse in there. You can't even get a seat." But we pushed ahead anyway, past concession stands, surgery rooms, and bloody drag pits where the endgames of the longest fights were played out, past walls of raw particle board, and through leaning, unsquare spaces. Although we never descended any stairs, we seemed to be tunneling underground, the heat pipes like earthworms glistening in the walls. When a long corridor opened at last onto the cockpit, it felt like an animal's burrow, spacious yet claustrophobic.

The bleachers rose in a steep-sided bowl around us, two stories high and bristling with spectators. This was no neighborhood social club, like the Red Rooster. These people had paid $16 a seat and traveled hundreds of miles to be here, and they focused on the pit below with clenched jaws and avid eyes. There was a sense of volatility in the air, of minds at the edge of ignition, and I kept imagining the chaos if a grease fire erupted in a concession stand and we had to claw our way back through those tunnels.

The pit itself, by contrast, was a model of neatness and grim good order. Most of the birds wore one-inch Spanish knives or three-inch Filipino knives on their heels, and their bouts were often over within seconds. A Filipino knife, driven by a powerful gamecock, can split a bird's head in a single stroke, and Spanish knives are nearly as deadly. ("I know a thoracic surgeon who handles his own chickens in the ring," Hickerson had said on the ride over. "Now how can you be that smart and that dumb at the same time?") The referee would cry "Handle!", the birds would flurry in the air a few times, and then one or both of them would lie dead. No bludgeoning brawl, no show of courage or fear, surprisingly little blood.

Should cockfighting ever make it on *ABC's Wide World of Sports,* I thought, this is how it would be: a little trash-talking between the handlers, a little fancy footwork by the birds, and then the knockout blow. Watching a gaff fight required a nearly religious devotion, a hard slog toward an uneasy enlightenment. But a knife fight offered instant gratification. It was all highlight film and no story.

Throw in a few bets, to give yourself a stake in the outcome, and you had the ultimate in guilty pleasures.

Now I could see why Demoruelle had thought cockfighting might seduce me. If he preferred knives to gaffs, it was partly because the fights were shorter and they gave him more chances to gamble. But part of him, too, had come here to see something killed. "Man is born a warrior," he told me later, "and the more we constrict his natural tendency to hunt and to kill, the crazier the world seems to become." After ten or fifteen bouts, though, Hickerson began to fidget. "Knives are going to kill this sport," he muttered. These cocks weren't bred for courage, they were bred for speed and power. Knife fights were mostly about luck and getting in the first punch, Hickerson said. Knife fights were a crapshoot.

But then a crapshoot was exactly what this crowd wanted. Whenever a gaff fight began, their attention went slack and they drifted into small talk. But as soon as two knife fighters came out, the crowd seemed to catch its breath. Soon the bets began to ring out, shyly at first, then with more urgency as some failed to find takers: "Ten on the red!" "I'll take twenty on the white shirt's bird!" A few rows over, a man handed a few bills to his skinny boy and whispered some instructions in his ear. The boy jumped on his seat, screwed up his face, and screamed an octave above the rest of the crowd: "Twenty on the red! Twenty on the red!"

This was where things get interesting at many Asian cockpits. Small-time fights are merely about money, but bigger ones are about status and kinship — you always bet on your kin group's cock, and you do so for prestige, not winnings. But these bets, unlike those at the Red Rooster, are as impersonal as coins tossed into a slot machine — six roosters in a row and you hit a jackpot. Hickerson, for his part, hardly bothered to assess the birds. When knife fighters came into the pit, he almost always stood up and yelled, "25–20! 25–20!" meaning, "You choose the bird, but I get $25 if mine wins, and you get $20 if yours wins." As long as a cockfight is just a game of chance, he said, you might as well play the odds.

The fights would go on like this till dawn; there were a lot of chickens to get through. At one point, I stepped into the bathroom and found a referee scrubbing the blood from his face while a line formed behind him. He kept squinting into the mirror, face sop-

ping wet, and then bending down to scrub some more. Finally, he
glanced at my reflection in the mirror and laughed.

"Stuff still isn't comin' off!"

"Must get pretty thick by the end of the night."

"Heck yeah. I'll be covered in it head to foot. These white stripes
won't be white no more."

The owners were honor-bound to stay till the end, but we were
only spectators, and so we slipped out before midnight. By then,
there were dead cocks lying in the hallways and heaped in trash
barrels, their bodies twisted and brittle, their once-brilliant feathers dimmed by dried blood. "We used to eat the losers after a fight,"
Demoruelle said in passing, "but the dewormer some people use
now makes the meat carcinogenic."

Surreal as it was, the scene made a certain sense. At pits like Sunrise, cockfighting was big business — less folk tradition than mass-
market entertainment — and the audiences were hardly different
from those at riverboat casinos in Baton Rouge. The cocks we had
seen, impeccably trained though they were, had lost much of their
glamour to commerce. Elsewhere, they might be symbols of sin or
sexuality, courage or betrayal, stand-ins for their owners, or for the
devil himself. But at Sunrise, a gamecock was just another form of
disposable culture.

In Bali, Clifford Geertz once wrote, a cockfight is a story that people tell themselves about themselves. For more than a century, the
same was true in this country. Long before the Revolution, George
Washington loved a cockfight for the spirit of anarchy it embodied,
and he once invited Thomas Jefferson to Mount Vernon to see his
"yellow pile" gamecocks. By the 1830s, Andrew Jackson was fighting cocks on the White House carpet and cockfighting was a national pastime — an embodiment of the country's new arrogance.
Three decades after that, Abraham Lincoln, a former cockfighting
referee, saw something darker and more ambivalent in it: "As long
as the Almighty permits intelligent man created in His image and
likeness to fight in public and kill each other while the world looks
on approvingly," he is reported to have said, "it is not for me to de-
prive the chicken of the same privilege."

But nowadays blood sports are a story we would rather forget.
Last fall, volunteers with anti-cockfighting groups in Missouri and
Arizona managed to gather 136,000 and 189,000 signatures, re-

spectively, forcing state referendums on the sport. In early polls, 88 percent of Missourians said they were against cockfighting, and 87 percent of Arizonians, but in the privacy of the voting booth many must have had second thoughts: only 63 percent voted against the sport in Missouri, and 68 percent in Arizona. Still, today, hosting a cockfight is illegal in both those states, and Oklahomans are said to be planning a referendum of their own.

Only in Louisiana, where they once seemed most vulnerable, do cockfighters feel a measure of security. Twenty years ago, when Louisiana passed a new set of animal-rights laws, cockfighters had to dabble in taxonomy to avoid them: chickens are not animals, they declared in an amendment pushed through at the eleventh hour; they are birds. But a 1997 anti-cockfighting bill that Demoruelle had feared would pass never even made it past committee. And last year, when an anti-cockfighting amendment reached the floor of the State Senate, it was defeated by a vote of 22 to 5.

Nevertheless, most observers say that legal cockfighting will be gone within the next ten years. Even in Louisiana, a single election and a new crop of legislators could consign cockfighting to the chopping block. "I think the forces of modernity and New South boosterism are just going to do it in," says Frederick Hawley, a criminologist at Western Carolina University who wrote his Ph.D. thesis on cockfighting. "And if I'm wrong now, it won't be long before I'm right."

Animal activists will tell you this fight is all about morality. Cockfighters will tell you it's about individual liberty. Most legislators, if you catch them in an honest moment, will tell you it's about economics — about the South reinventing itself to attract investors. But mostly it's a matter of appearances. Demographics, more than animal advocacy, have doomed legal cockfighting — the more urban an area was, the quicker it banned the sport. And although country values have given way to city values, cockpits to KFCs, the sum total of bloodshed has hardly been diminished, only swept out of sight.

Not long after I left Louisiana, I went to visit a chicken factory an hour south of Little Rock, Arkansas. One of forty-one "vertically integrated" operations owned by Tyson Foods, this one slaughtered 1.3 million birds a week and spat out an endless stream of chicken parts and precooked wings. A mill, a hatchery, and dozens of henhouses lay around it like spokes on a wheel, and most of the work was automated. (When a chicken laid an egg, a tiny conveyor belt beneath the roost trundled the egg off for incubation.) Thanks to such efficiencies, American factories slaughter some 7 billion chickens a year, and chicken meat, once more expensive than filet mignon, has become blandly ubiquitous — poor man's fare. Breeders, meanwhile, keep picking up the pace: a century ago, a broiler needed sixteen weeks to reach two pounds; today chicks reach four pounds in six weeks.

My guide at the factory, a man named Archie Schaffer III, was a rare believer in full disclosure. (The public-relations people at Perdue wouldn't let me near their factories.) "Nobody has any idea in America where their food comes from," he told me, "and the reason is people like me." Schaffer was more than happy to show me the hatchery where 85,000 chicks tumble down chutes every hour like cotton balls at a cotton-ball factory; the vast hangers where the chicks grow into broilers; the trucks that haul the broilers to the factory 7,000 at a time. And yet, when I asked to see the killing floor, he nearly refused.

I could see why. If a broiler's life sometimes looked like a trip to the amusement park — shuttling down roller coasters, standing in crowds, watching gizmos pop and whir — this was the nightmarish finale, the tunnel of fear. After their wild ride in the truck, the birds were dumped onto a broad belt that rolled into the dark mouth of the factory. Inside, most of the room was bathed in black light — it calms the birds down, I was told — and the stench was overwhelming. Assaulted by screaming machinery and Top 40 radio, the birds were jerked from the belt by a row of eight workers, wearing black goggles and industrial tunics, and hung by their feet from a running chain overhead. The chain whipped them into the next room, where they were squeezed through mechanical bottlenecks, stunned by bolts of electricity, and then beheaded by a rotary saw. If a bird happened to lift its head to avoid the saw, a worker reached over and slit its throat. "The live hang job is about the nastiest job in the business," Schaffer admitted. "But a lot of people seem to like it."

These are things we don't want to know, that we zone away beyond city limits, and most meat producers are happy to oblige us. Every year we eat more chicken meat and see less and less of the living birds, and this strikes us as right and normal. Animal-rights activists, of course, condemn poultry factories as well as cockfighting, but most of us aren't that consistent. We're appalled at blood sports, yet when activists picket slaughterhouses or send lurid photos to the media, we resent them, deem them unrealistic. Like cockfighters, they threaten a cherished illusion: that society, in growing up, has lost its taste for blood.

When I was nine years old, and the only blood sports I knew were those my brother had invented, my family rented a house with some chickens in the back yard. It was a crumbling old adobe in a quiet part of Pasadena, where my father would do research in the summer, and the chickens seemed to have been there forever. After a while, I got used to their sudden flights of rage when I fed them, their strange, hysterical secrets. But I never got used to the dawn. In suburbia, more than most places, a cock's crow can sound like the end of the world.

One afternoon, when my mother answered a knock on the door, she found a policeman standing awkwardly on our stoop. "It's about your rooster, ma'am," he said. My mom stared at him blankly for a moment. Then, with a twitch of a smile, she asked: "What's he done?"

Our bird was arrested for disturbing the peace. After the humane society dragged him away — kicking and screaming as only a chicken can — we never saw him again. Looking back, we always laughed at my mom's reply and at the rooster in the paddy wagon. But the funniest part, we thought, was the fact that we had a suburban chicken coop in the first place. Now I think that the joke was on us. We thought of our neighborhood as an ideal of sorts, clean and safe and free of life's old brutality. But we lived in a glass bubble, one so fragile a rooster's call could shatter it.

These days, the stories we tell ourselves about ourselves grow ever more polished and predictable. We play out our primal urges on the Internet, in cineplexes, or in therapy, rather than in the town square at midday. Yet cockfighters still stir in the dark, incubated by secrecy and the heat of resentment, far from the glare of popular culture. Judging from the pits I visited, the twilight suits them best. "You can't stop us," Demoruelle says. "We have more gamecocks being fought this year than we've had in the history of this country." If they jangle a few nerves, so be it: disturbing the peace is a rooster's business.

How I Won the Minnesota Statehouse, by Jimmy (Big Boy) Valente As Told to Garrison Keillor

FROM THE NEW YORK TIMES MAGAZINE

AT INTERNATIONAL WORLD WRESTLING, I, Jimmy (Big Boy) Valente, was the headliner, Mr. Magnificent, the Boss Man.

I brought wrestling into the modern age.

I was the one who introduced rock-and-roll. I was the first to use loops of accordion wire in place of ropes. I was the one who introduced pyrotechnics. A flaming genius! Every night it was a Ring of Fire! I was the first to employ sweat-seeking cruise missiles in the ring. The first to use explosives: we liked to have one wrestler throw another in a Dumpster and blow it up. Our slogan was "Come See Extreme Wrestling — No Children Under 6 — Not for the Squeamish — Don't Wear Your Good Clothes." The blood flowed, the monster truck roared, the ring burst into flames and the fans went away happy. I was sitting on top of the world, earning millions, getting a million hits a day at jimmybigboy.com.

Wrestling gets hard when you pass 40, though. Your back hurts from lifting 300-pound guys and heaving them into the seats.

One night in the Boston Garden, Hump Hooley and I fought a marathon tag-team match against the Messenger of Death and Mr. Disaster, a real shorts-scorcher involving quarts of blood, thousands of vampire bats, a pack of rabid wolves, six suicide bombers from Hamas and 12 Tomahawk missiles, and in the finale I hoisted the Messenger over my head and heaved him into the turnbuckle, only to have him ignite a moat of gasoline around the ring, and I passed out from the fumes and lay unconscious, the flames licking at my feet, death near at hand — and then pain awakened me! I leapt up and called in an air strike on myself! The cruise missiles came straight at me! Smoke and flames! Utter confusion! And when the smoke cleared, there was a heap of ashes in the middle of the burning ring where I had been! The crowd screamed: "No! No! Not Big Boy!" And then I jumped up and brushed the ashes away and Old Glory descended from the rafters and I took hold of a corner and was lifted to safety as the ring exploded and burned.

When the match was done, I lay on the dressing-room floor, too tired to shower. The Messenger of Death brought me a beer and Hump helped me into a chair. I glanced at myself in a mirror and was shocked at the grayness and blankness of me, the fatuous look in the eyes, as if I were on powerful medications. Or else, as if I wasn't and should be. I looked like a snake that had swallowed a dog.

"Loved the flag bit," Hump said. "Write that into the act from now on."

I said, "Boys, I believe I need a vacation."

In the morning, I went to a doctor who diagnosed a nasty case of testosterone poisoning. The pills I took to keep my energy up were causing a metabolic vasodilatation of the nerve endings. I was getting numb above the neck.

One night in Dallas, a man sat waiting for me in the dressing room and stood as I entered and extended his hand and said: "Jimmy, I am Earl Woofner, the chairman of the Ethical Party of Minnesota. And I've come a thousand miles to say that our state needs a man like you."

My skull glittered with sweat, my pink tights were spattered with blood and I was wearing a peacock-feather headdress, cobalt blue shades and a cape with 600 flashing light bulbs. Plus, a python named Virg draped around my neck. Earl did not flinch.

He set down his briefcase and sat on a bench and looked up at

me with utter sincerity and said: "The people of Minnesota are crying out for a champion to break the liberal choke hold and open
up politics to common sense and honesty. And I am looking at
him."

I took off the glasses and set down the snake.

"What about it, Jimmy?" he said. "The troops are ready. When do
we get the order to march?"

By rights I should be a Democrat, because I am for the little guy,
but the Democrats are run by yuppie liberals trying to remake
American society into a day-care center for adults. Making folks
stand outdoors to smoke a cigarette. Making a teacher fill out a 14-
page questionnaire if she says boo to a kid. Labels on beer cans
warning that alcohol is not good for your health and may cause you
to fall down on the floor.

The Democrats started out with the New Deal, a good idea for its
time, and then delusions of grandeur led them to keep adding on
to it, like a guy who sets out to make carbonara sauce and starts
throwing sausage and peppers and onions in, and pretty soon
you've got hearts of palm and peas and anchovies and water chest-
nuts and pineapple swimming around in it and the thyme and
oregano are at toxic levels and nobody is hungry anymore. That's
the Democratic platform. Programs for everything — programs to
combat grumpiness, stupidity, discrimination, covetousness, im-
proper lane changes, low math scores, flat beer, poor taste and too
much air in the Cracker Jack box, and all of the programs require
battalions of social workers and reams of paper.

So I look to the Republicans, and what do I see? The Me First
Party: squeeze the maximum profit out of everything, strip it clean,
gouge what you can, clear-cut the forest, to hell with everybody else
— lay off the 20-year guys and hire cheap replacements, cut costs,
inflate the stock, sell out, make your pile, leave town, head for your
compound in Palm Springs, buy an electronic security system and a
team of Rottweilers, sit around the swimming pool, enjoy your
brains out and feel no more remorse than a fruit fly.

So I thought, What the heck, why not the Ethical Party, a grab
bag of bikers and bird-watchers and disgruntled dishwashers and
surly seniors and people who call in to talk shows to gripe about the
mailman.

It was May 1998. I took a week off from the IWW tour and got
in my Porsche with the "Mess With the Best, Die With the Rest"

bumper sticker and took a run around Minnesota to think about the governorship.

I prefer the gravel roads, where you can make time, roads that would shake your fillings out at 30, but at 140 you fly over the bumps like melted butter. From Moorhead to Worthington, on some of those straight stretches, I held it at 200 for a while. I think better when I'm moving fast.

I cruised the state and I pondered the future.

Out in the country, farmers were in hock and going broke, having bought fancy combines at 20 percent interest, and now the price of corn was bottoming out and the loans were coming due. In the cities, the factories had gone south and the old factory buildings were turned into restaurants serving lamb chops the size of chickadees, plus an artichoke and a small red potato, for $30.

I saw a picture of a candidate for the Democratic nomination for Governor, eating tofu at a fund-raiser and wearing a T-shirt that said "I Really Could Use a Hug Right Now." And a picture of a Republican hopeful dedicating a milk-producing plant where 40,000 genetically engineered Holsteins, heavily sedated and lying on canvas slings and fed with stomach tubes, could produce two million gallons per day.

I called Earl Woofner. "I can't do it," I said. "I am not a politician. I don't have the stomach for it."

"That is your strong suit, your honest independent nature," he said. "Sleep on it. Call me tomorrow. The brochure is at the printer's, ready to go. The 'Jimmy for Governor' beer is bottled, all we have to do is slap on the labels."

That morning, as I often do when I'm on the road and have an extra minute, I dropped by the local hospital to visit children, and as it happened, there was one, a 12-year-old boy named Tommy, who had lost his left hand in a corn picker.

"Big Boy," he said, "how can I grow up to become a wrestler without a left hand?"

I told him: "You can be anybody you want to be. Don't ever give up. And it would be a great gimmick. Tommy (the Talon) Anderson. Jump in the ring with your eagle-feather headdress and clack your prosthetic device and get the audience to chant, 'He fought the claw and the claw won.'"

He was a chipper little guy, and he looked up at me and said, "How did you become what you wanted to be, Big Boy?"

And I was about to say, "By sheer determination and imagination," and then I thought: "Hey, I'm not there yet. I want to be Governor. For once in my life, I want to be taken seriously." And I looked down at his freckled face on the pillow and said, "Tommy, I came here to help you out, and instead you helped me."

I called my wife, Lacy, and told her I had decided to run for Governor.

There was a long breath of a pause, and she said: "Fine, but I don't campaign. I don't do the candidate's wife thing at all. No fund-raisers, so don't even ask." I understood, I said.

"Why are you doing this?" she asked. I said I was tired of people making fun of me for wearing pink-feather boas.

Felix, my promoter, offered to manage my campaign. Felix is a hatchet-faced little guy with a toupee that looks like a raccoon that got crushed by a semi. He favors livid green-plaid sport coats and is very sallow and liverish looking, all splotches and rheum and exploded capillaries, a stub of a cigarette smoldering on his lower lip.

"No, thanks," I said.

I put on my Australian bush hat, my running shoes and my "Gopher It" T-shirt, and for five months I rode around Minnesota in a motor home, green, the interior a soft beige that reminded me of the inner thighs of a woman I met once in Miami, and lived on Cheez Doodles, Ho Hos and root beer, which gave me so much gas I could hardly keep my socks up, and addressed every Kiwanis Club, Elks, Moose, Jaycees, Sons of Norway, Knights of Columbus, VFW and Eastern Star that cared to hear me and roamed the coffee shops and Kmarts, handing out literature, pressing the flesh, chewing the fat.

I told the people: "I am not a joke, I am a decent clean person you could bring home and not be embarrassed by. Yes, I wore a pink boa and gave flying mules and nipple lifts and atomic handshakes, not to mention the deadly and infamous Long Nap, and will employ them against the Special Interests. I am no smarter than anybody else and I don't claim to have all the answers, but it ain't nuclear physics and I will work hard and accept no special privileges, and what I don't know about state government, I'll know a month after I take office."

My platform was exactly as follows:

1. I will not tell a lie.
2. I make no promise except to do my best.
3. Any tax surplus goes straight back to you, the folks.
4. I will scorn Big Business and Special Interests in favor of you, the taxpayer and voter. The trough is closed.
5. There will be action, not just a lot of yik-yakking.
6. No weenies need apply.
7. Let's party.

Career politicians like to act as if government is the Mystery of Mysteries, unknowable except to the Grand Pooh-bahs of the Sacred Elect. Well, I came out of the weeds to face a weaselly Democrat and a wascally Wepublican who each thought he was a great statesman and I was the idiot with the hump, and I ate their lunch.

I destroyed my opponents in the televised debates. I hung them out to dry.

The weaselly Democrat talked about government needing to create jobs. I said: "There used to be a country for people like you, but it doesn't exist anymore. Its capital was Moscow."

He whimpered and looked toward the corner of the studio, where his advisers and pollsters were standing, holding his cue cards. They were helpless to save him.

The Wepublican was a scrawny runt with one wet finger in the wind who used the word "family" in every sentence, as if this might win him an Amana gas range, and said he favored social welfare programs if they "strengthened the family." I leaned forward and said, "You flat-headed, fish-eyed, sap-sucking belly-scratcher, all you do is bark when the big boys yank your chain."

I said, "If a person is smart enough to live in Minnesota, then he is smart enough to take care of his own self and not look around for a handout."

Nobody else dared to say it plain like that.

And in gratitude, the people of Minnesota put me in the Governor's office.

I was sworn in on Monday, January 4, and the national press was fawning all over me. *Newsweek, Time,* you name it. Al Gore phoned that morning and wished me luck. "Thanks, Al," I said. "See you in Iowa." He had a coughing fit. We had a fabulous inaugural ball at the Civic Center, at which I appeared at the end of the arena, in a spotlight, standing on a tiny platform a hundred feet in the air, and lowered myself hand over hand down a length of barbed wire to the stage, where I stripped to the waist and bench-pressed 400 pounds, and then some blues bands played for five hours and we sold 30,000 gallons of "Jimmy Big Boy" beer and 12,000 "Love the Gov" T-shirts.

I'd like to see any governor match me for merchandise sales. I'd like to see Al Gore sell half of the shirts I sold.

Al Gore is obsolete. The fringe is the center now. TV has made a joke of politics, and a joker like me can beat a stuffed owl like Al. He is living in the 19th century, when the President stood at a lectern and read a speech in a big pipe-organ voice and everyone listened and nobody's dog barked. Those days are gone.

And he is disadvantaged by being Bill's Best Friend.

He is a cigar-store Indian, and I look forward to whipping the pants off him in New Hampshire and Iowa. Two independent states full of notoriously cranky voters who delight in depantsing the anointed front-runner and sending his gravy train onto a sidetrack. Al will be the 10-to-1 favorite, and when he falls he will crumble. When he garners 18 percent of the vote in New Hampshire, compared with 52 percent for the 300-pound candidate with the big pink noggin, I am going to enjoy watching him go on TV to explain what happened, like your kid explaining why the car went in the ditch on a bright June day.

Al will wind up running the Ford Foundation and I will be a President you can be proud of and land in Air Force One and inspect honor guards and do my duty, and none of that groping in the West Wing — I will do mine upstairs in the First Bedroom.

The thought of Inauguration Day 2001 keeps me toasty warm on these cold winter nights.

I'll be sitting ramrod-straight in my seat on the flag-draped platform before the U.S. Capitol in Washington, D.C., dressed in my black suit and Led Zeppelin T-shirt, a big wad of Copenhagen in my cheek, and on the back of my big bare head I'll feel, like dancing snowflakes, the cold glares from all the big bonzos in the seats behind me and I'll smile my Big Boy smile to the cameras on the platform, and then, after one of those mealy-mouthed "O Thou Who Didst Once on the Sea of Galilee" prayers read by some pathetic dope in a collar, I'll stand and raise my right hand and place my left hand with the World Tag-Team Champion gold ring on the third finger upon the Holy Bible held by my foxy wife, Lacy, and look Chief Justice Billy (the Robe) Rehnquist straight in his black cobra eyes and shift the wad into the left corner of my mouth and vow to preserve, protect and defend the Constitution of the United States and then turn to give Lacy a smooch and hug my daughter, Tiffany, and my son, Adrian, and shake hands with Bill and Hillary and squeeze Al Gore's hand, maybe bear down a little until his eyes water and he looks queasy, and say, "Tough luck, buddy boy," and hold my arms up so that my supporters out in the cheap seats can see me, and I'll cock my ear to that distant cry of "Jimm-ee, Jimm-ee, Jimm-ee!" and turn to go to the limo and look up and see every senator and congressman and justice and ex-President and ambassador standing, mouth open, in shock and confusion, as if they had just witnessed the explosion of the *Hindenburg,* wondering, "How did this happen?"

It's called democracy, boys.

Bottom of the Ninth

FROM ESQUIRE

PEOPLE WILL COME, Ray.

No, really, they will. They'll come for reasons they can't even fathom. They'll turn up your driveway . . . well, not really *your* driveway. It's Ilitch the Pizza Guy's driveway. Anyway, they'll turn up *somebody's* driveway, not knowing for sure why they're doing it, although some possible reasons — like Genuine Authentic Replica Gear! — will be suggested at top volume by the kids howling in the backseat.

They'll walk through what used to be called a neighborhood before we had new "urban villages" with "shops, restaurants, offices, and other attractions." They'll enter through one of three gates: the one with the eighty-foot bats, the one with the two immense sculpted tigers, or the one that has big bats *and* a big tiger and that faces the new "restaurant/retail" complex at the other end of the avenue. People will come, Ray.

There'll be one cash register for every 125 fans. (Did you know, Ray, the typical ballpark has one cash register for every 200 fans?) They'll wander through the food court. They'll ride the carousel. Later, perhaps exhausted, they'll sit in the large, open-air beer garden. They won't even have to come inside, Ray. They'll sit on the roof decks along Witherell Street, which will be "easily accessible" from the food court and the carousel and all levels of the ballpark.

The one constant through all the years, Ray, has been baseball. America has rolled by like an army of steamrollers, but this field, this game, is a part of our past. It reminds us of all that was good and could be again if we can just line up the bondholders. And now, Ray, look out there. Now it's baseball that's rolling by like an army of steamrollers. Not clumsy metaphorical ones but real ones, the kind that build new and modern things, like urban villages and genuine authentic replica ballparks.

Oh, people will come, Ray. People will most definitely come. They'll arrive at your door, innocent as children, longing for the past.

And, by God, Ray, we'll be there to sell it to them.

(Is this heaven?)

No, Ray. It's Detroit.

The ball has a cushioned cork center and the signature of someone named Gene Budig. It also has a black splotch where it came off the bat, and, tight against one seam, there's a very suspicious-looking scuff mark approximately the width of two fingertips, which may account for the fact that a promising young Detroit Tiger infielder named Frank Catalanotto was able only to loft the ball foul, along the third-base line, through the velvet evening rain and up into the outdoor auxiliary press section at the very top of Tiger Stadium.

I found the ball there, sitting in a small pool of rainwater. I was alone. There's little call for an outdoor auxiliary press section during a game between the Detroit Tigers and the Anaheim Angels on a softly flowing night at the beginning of May, not even at the beginning of the last May in which baseball will be played at Tiger Stadium. There was nobody to fight me for the ball.

I am not sentimental about old stadiums. Which is odd, because I have spent most of my life around Boston, where ballparks and arenas generally find themselves afflicted with talismanic characteristics as though they were concrete Kennedys. The relentless palaver about Fenway Park leaves me cold because, far too often, especially during night games in April, so does the ballpark. (David Halberstam claims to love even Fenway's smells. I don't know. Maybe the smells remind him of the good old days in the Mekong Delta.) In the first game I ever saw at Fenway — and, yes, I saw it with my father — the Red Sox lost by a fat pile of runs on their way to a 62–100 season. There were about ninety-five hundred of us there, and nobody was talking about history, tradition, quaint patriarchy, or lyric little bandboxes.

Because I am not sentimental about old stadiums, I am equally unmoved by the new ones, the plasticine nostalgia palaces that have sprung up in places like Denver and Cleveland and, most famously, Baltimore, a place of the kind of ersatz instant tradition perfect for a time in which television anchormen fancy themselves historians. The new ballparks are comfortable tributes to the modern service economy, and they are not as ugly as old Crock-Pots, and that is all that can be said for them.

Now, on this soft and liquid evening, Tiger Stadium was about as empty as Fenway was the first time I saw it. The two parks are rather married to each other; both opened on April 20, 1912, although neither event received the attention it might have, since the *Titanic* went down that same week. However, whereas Fenway has become an icon, Tiger Stadium is looked at now as an anachronism: old, a bit leaky, and possessed of far too much inherent architectural democracy to meet the oligarchic demands of modern baseball economics — to wit, luxury boxes, club seating, and a babelicious young hostess to bring you refreshments.

Even to those people whose memories of the place are the longest and the fondest, Tiger Stadium is ending its days as something of a public inconvenience.

"It's time," says Ernie Harwell, who broadcast his first game for the Tigers in 1960. "I mean, I'm ready. I'm not one of those Good Old Days guys. History and tradition are great, but it's time for them to go forward in a new ballpark."

I looked down from the outdoor auxiliary press section. The field was bright and wet and impossibly green. Tiger Stadium always has been an odd mix of impressions. From the outside, it dominates the corner of Trumbull Street and Michigan Avenue with a blank and cheerless facade. (Harwell and Al Kaline both had the same initial reaction to the park; they thought it looked like a battleship.) Inside, however, it is a warm, self-contained universe.

Tiger Stadium is the only major league ballpark that is double-decked all the way around, from home plate to the thin wedge of bleachers in dead center field. It is done up in deep blue and bright orange, like a child's happy castle, and running along its top level is a series of wooden enclosures that look for all the world like the running chutes in a stockyard. Unlike Fenway, which forces baseball to adapt to its weird, procrustean angles and corners, Tiger Stadium encompasses the game within itself.

Next season, the Tigers will move into Comerica Park, a $290 million nostalgia factory along lower Woodward Avenue for which the public will pay nearly half the tab. I will miss Tiger Stadium, which is remarkable, because I've been here only six or seven times in my life, and even more remarkable because baseball has very little to do with why I'll miss it.

I rolled my last souvenir of the place around in my hand, and my fingertips once again stuck in the peculiar abrasion along one of its seams. I don't trust immaculate history, one impeccably straight-line, survey-course, and sound-bite ready. Give me history that's suspiciously scuffed, a touch of rough mischief that you can put your fingertips on so that you can make it sail and dive, a kite in gypsy breezes. It can break all the rules, this history. You can make it dance.

Shortly before the turn of the century, Samuel Brooks built his lumberyard on the corner of Cherry Street near Michigan Avenue. It was a time of frenzied wood-cutting, with thousands of newly arrived Swedes and Germans and Lithuanians plunging into raffish settlements deep within the wide forests around the Great Lakes, and Samuel Brooks prospered. In 1896, he saw a baseball field rise on what was once an old hay market at the corner of Michigan and Trumbull. Over the next twenty years, after Samuel handed the business down to his son, Arthur, the Brooks family and their employees watched as what was once Bennett Field became Navin Field.

Then when the great teams were in town — the Athletics with Al Simmons and that burly gobblehog Jimmie Foxx, or the Yankees with Ruth and Gehrig — the men working in the lumberyard would hear the crack of the bat and look up through the spreading twilight for the ball. The men would chase after the ball. You could get a half dozen in one afternoon if you were quick enough.

Arthur Brooks handed the company down to *his* son, Arthur, who is retired now and living in Florida. His first memory of what would become Tiger Stadium is of sprinting from Jefferson Intermediate School in order to make the 3:00 P.M. starting time. In the days before night baseball, the games started at three so the men coming home from work might be able to catch the last few innings. Arthur Brooks would run to Trumbull Avenue and hop a streetcar to the ballpark. He'd pay his fifty cents and sit in the bleachers, and he'd watch the home runs soar into his father's lumberyard.

"They wouldn't always find them all," Brooks says. "Used to be, especially if those Yankees were in town, I could still find half a dozen balls all over the lumberyard."

The home runs stopped coming regularly in 1938, when Walter Briggs finished the job of enclosing the stadium that had been started by Frank Navin, Arthur Brooks's godfather. It was a whole new ballpark, considered to be state-of-the-art. There would be no more rickety temporary bleachers, the fans atop the last row standing and craning their necks until it seemed the whole structure would capsize onto Cherry Street. Baseball was contained within itself. The cheers reached the streets in softened roars. To hit one into the lumberyard now required a luckless conjunction of Homeric power and a truly terrible curveball. "Ted Williams did it a couple of times, though," Brooks recalls. "He put a couple into the yard for us." Reggie Jackson almost did it in the 1971 All-Star Game, but his rising line drive banged off a transformer that sits atop the right-field roof in what is still one of the defining home runs of the age.

The baseballs don't come as frequently these days, but Brooks Lumber is still where it always was. It's baseball itself that's moving now. The home runs will soon go sailing by the Hard Rock Cafe and into a whole neighborhood that is part of the ballpark as surely as the whole ballpark was once part of a neighborhood, baseballs falling into the new urban village like so much captive rain.

One day in 1987, a Tiger scrub named Jim Walewander knocked a ball into the right-field seats to win a game. It was Walewander's first career home run. It was also his last. There was a nice crowd that day, and everybody cheered, especially four sallow youths sitting in the boxes near the Detroit dugout. Their names were Dean Clean, Joe Jack Talcum, Dave Blood, and Rodney Anonymous. They were the Dead Milkmen.

No matter how hidebound its bureaucracy, baseball was the sport of choice among the countercultural Left. Back in the days when only FBI informants had any money, baseball's bleachers were always cheap and, therefore, suffused with the spirit of "participatory democracy," that charmingly impossible philosophical

template so central to, among other things, the Port Huron Statement, composed by Michigan native and Tiger fan Tom Hayden.

This has not always been easy for the game's purists to accept.
George Will, who has replaced the late Bart Giamatti as baseball's preeminent dilettante nuisance, once even blamed the rise of
those awful multipurpose stadiums in places like Cincinnati and
Pittsburgh on the "wretched excesses" of the sixties, on which Will
also blames the popularity of professional football. It should be
noted that those same purists — a coalition of corporate and political elites — are behind most of what have been called, with no apparent irony, the "new vintage ballparks."

Rather, the people most directly involved in that "wretched excess" of the sixties hated football — *too militaristic, man* — and
loved baseball, which is why the center-field bleachers in Tiger Stadium were once regularly bathed in the aroma of certain American
Indian religious compounds. In fact, that same season in which
Walewander brought joy to the Dead Milkmen with his one and
only home run, Tiger Stadium also played host to something called
the Eugene V. Debs Memorial Kazoo Marching Band.

So, as the tie-dye faded and the Grateful Dead turned into a cab-
aret act, it was no real surprise that the young ballplayers of the
eighties developed a jones for ham-fisted drumming and atonal
guitar strangling. And the ham-fisted drummers and atonal guitar
stranglers came to love baseball. Thus did the Paycheck Lounge in
Hamtramck meet Tiger Stadium. Walewander hit his dinger, and
the Dead Milkmen cheered, and everybody got together afterward
in the Tiger clubhouse, where Walewander talked about his homer
and the Milkmen talked about their breakthrough album, *Big Liz-
ard in My Backyard.* After a while, Detroit manager Sparky Anderson
came out of his office and sized up the Milkmen.

"Jeez," Anderson said. "Them boys don't see much sunlight,
do they?"

There are people who come to Tiger Stadium and can still hear
Ty Cobb cursing the pitcher from second base, or they can still
hear one of Hank Greenberg's home runs hitting the second deck
in right field, echoing deep and solid like a ripe melon dropped
into a barrel. Me? I look down at the boxes along the first-base line
and hear my favorite Milkmen single, "Methodist Coloring Book":
"But don't color outside the lines / Or God will send you to Hell."

Alas, the Dead Milkmen broke up in 1994, and Jim Walewander

was out of baseball not long after that. People say he's in California now, working as an investment banker, which isn't bad for a guy who once used Hefty bags for curtains.

On the last weekend I was there, Jon Beavers and his friend Louis Koroyanis had come to Tiger Stadium as part of their annual spring ballpark tour. They found themselves trapped in the no-alcohol family section deep in the left-field seats and were returning from a thirsty eastward pilgrimage through the grandstand as the rain fell, steady and percussive, on the empty seats. Far away, Tiger center fielder Gabe Kapler caught the better part of a fastball. The ball stayed on a line, nearly flat, dipping just slightly as it approached the low fence in left field. Jon Beavers, beer in hand, turned back toward the plate just in time for Kapler's home run to hit him right in the stomach.

Louis Koroyanis, of course, in the tradition of all those who once ran through the Brooks lumberyard, immediately dove past his wounded friend and grabbed the ball.

"Do you believe this shit?" Beavers said, laughing. "I get hit in the gut, *on television,* and he winds up with the ball."

My personal history of Tiger Stadium took its last little mystifying break when Gabe Kapler went long to Jon Beavers's midsection. It sailed with the Eugene V. Debs Memorial Kazoo Marching Band, and it dipped once each for Jim Walewander and Dean Clean and Rodney Anonymous. My history here had some stuff on it. It never moved the way things will move in the new urban village, which will be a safe and convenient place, where the line will run straight and true, from Ty Cobb to Gehringer and Greenberg, to Cochrane and Kaline and Alan Trammell, who played shortstop for twenty years and who played it only in Detroit.

Before the game, Trammell talked about the old ballpark and the new one and about the difference between history and sentiment, a subtle distinction often lost on the people who build new stadiums or write about baseball. In fact, it's a distinction that eludes quite a few historians who look for life to color between the lines because they're afraid we'll all go to hell if it doesn't.

"Look, I'm not saying that I'm not going to miss this place," Trammell said. "This was home, and I'll cherish that. But you don't erase twenty years. I'll have that right here." And he puts his hand over his heart.

"But," Trammell went on, "the history will travel. It will come with us, I hope, and there will be some new history in the new ballpark."

I have a little piece of that history to carry with me, an inauspicious foul ball that fell into a small pool of rainwater during an extraneous game on a rainy night in May. The ball is nowhere near as significant as the one that hit Jon Beavers amidships, or the one Reggie Jackson pounded off the transformer, or the one with which Jim Walewander delighted the Dead Milkmen, or even most of the ones that went rattling through Brooks Lumber. There is a black mark on my ball, and there is a suspicious scuff on it, and that's why it will bring forward for me Tiger Stadium, where history always dove and sailed and fooled you, because it was a place where history always had its very best stuff.

RICK TELANDER

His Love Never Dies

FROM THE CHICAGO SUN-TIMES

AMERICA'S GRANDPA drives slowly down the winding cemetery
road.

If there were anyone here on this chilly December Saturday, they
would see the vintage silver Cadillac with the license plates reading
"DEPAUL" come to rest near a lone spigot that rises from the
ground, not far from a row of flat stone markers with Christmas
wreaths in front.

"I park near the hydrant or whatever you call that," says Ray
Meyer, 85. "I could find my way here in the dark. In the summer, I
get water for the flowers from the faucet."

Fifty-five years at DePaul, 42 years as head basketball coach, 724
victories, Chicago through-and-through, Meyer is the epitome of
the hard-working, modest, family-centered, vanishing American
sports teacher. "Coach" is all you need to call him. "Coach" is all he
wants to be called.

He climbs out of his car and walks slowly but sturdily over the tan
grass and past the barren trees.

A handicapped-parking sticker dangles from his car's rearview
mirror. Coach got it a couple years ago when he had a knee replaced.

"I hurt my knee in college at Notre Dame," he says. "About
1936."

Everything with Meyer is steady and cheerful and decent and
self-deprecating.

Why worry about a bone-on-bone knee joint for a half-century or
so? How insignificant such a thing is when you have your family all
around.

First there were the six kids, and now the 16 grandchildren, seven great-grandchildren and tons of parties, reunions, holiday gatherings, on and on. Many of the festive times still take place at the modest split-level house in Arlington Heights where Coach has lived for 30 years. The kids and everybody pile into the basement with the tiny pool table and the plaques and trophies and the funny sign Ray's wife, Marge, put up behind the bar: "The opinions expressed by the husband in this house are not necessarily those of the Management."

"And there's another grandchild and another great-grandchild on the way," Coach says. "I live alone now, but Marge wanted to move out here to be near our daughter and grandkids. Barb and Pat live near here. Tommy coaches at Niles West. Bobby is a lawyer. Joey's doing TV work."

One of his daughters, Maryanne, died two years ago, and Coach is dealing with that. He's working on the transition that everyone and everything must make, the risk we take when we extend ourselves and have our hearts broken from doing so.

He walks past tombstones that are head-high, past a grave with fresh sod marking its dimensions, then stops at a mid-sized stone with a carving of the Madonna and child at its center. Below the carving is the name "Meyer."

"Here it is," Coach says. "Here's Marge."

The old man's beloved wife died August 9, 1985, from complications of a heart attack.

On the right, the stone reads, *Mother Margaret M.* Below that is chiseled, *1913 — "Marge" — 1985.*

To the left of those markings the stone says, *Father Raymond J.* Under that, *1913 — "Coach."*

Meyer looks down.

"Someday I'll be on this side," he says.

Oh, he gets misty-eyed out here at times. But he comes because he wants to, once a week, every Saturday, without fail. Well, there are the six weeks each summer when he and Joey are working the family basketball camp in northern Wisconsin, times when he can't stop by.

But otherwise, it's simple clockwork.

"I don't know," Coach says, thinking about the number of visits he has made. "Forty-six weeks times 14, what's that?"

It's 644. A number like the victory total. Large. Amazing.

He'll come and talk to Marge. He'll tidy things up, place a wreath or cut flowers in front of the stone, depending on the season. He'll tend the ground cover he planted. ("I don't know why it doesn't grow as well on that side," he says, perplexed.) And he'll reflect.

The life of basketball.

"It's all entwined," Coach says, the wind rising and blowing his white hair. "I met her as a basketball player. She was at St. Agatha's on Douglas and Kedzie. One of the few churches that had a parish gym, so I hung out there. She was a good player. I think she won the *Herald-American* free-throw shooting championship. She could shoot, but she wasn't very fast. That's how I caught her."

Aw, Coach, you rascal.

There was the bad finish with DePaul, the firing of Joey as head coach and the chilliness that has accompanied the end of the Meyer era at the school.

"There was a power struggle," Ray says with a shrug. "They won, we lost."

And that's about it. Coach is OK with just about everything that goes on at the school now. He's not shunning DePaul. But he's not running to it. Those vanity plates, they were given to him by a state senator 10 years ago. If they weren't already on his old car, they probably wouldn't go on.

Coach isn't bitter. It's just that, well, family is so much more than an institution. And you stand by your family. You don't even question it.

"She was Irish," says Coach, the career German. "Delaney. Everything about her was Irish. Oh, she was something. On St. Patrick's Day, she had all green clothes laid out on the bed for me, even down to underwear. She said I was Irish by marriage."

John Wooden, the octogenarian former UCLA coach, is a close friend of Meyer's. And like Ray, John lost his wife, Nell, many years ago.

"God, he was so devastated," Coach says. "He went into a shell."

There are stories that Wooden visits his wife's grave even more than Ray visits Marge's. At some point, one must move ahead. A man shouldn't live in mourning, should he?

"To each his own," Coach says. "John Wooden is a man you would be proud to know. What a wonderful man. He always talked to all the little guys, the young coaches. They loved him. That's the test for a coach after all the years: They still love him."

There are some geese nearby, grazing on the graying stalks of summer's bounty.

Coach Meyer wipes his nose. Probably from the cold.

"We had a great time together," he says. "Forty-six years married. Together six before that. Oh, we had a great life."

He backs up a little. He looks around. It's not like there is routine to such things, such visits. Everything changes. Time moves on. Coach himself will have a birthday in a few days.

"She's fine," he says, like a father tucking in a child. "She's at rest."

On Saturday, Ray Meyer will be 86. And before he and his family celebrate, he'll come visit Marge.

DAVID HALBERSTAM

He Got a Shot in the NBA, and It Went In

FROM THE LOS ANGELES TIMES

IT BEGAN about a year ago as the most casual kind of palship, one formed in a New York gym. We were working out next to each other on stationary bicycles. He came over and said that he understood that I was working on a book on Michael. Michael, of course, is Michael Jordan. He knew Michael a bit, he volunteered, because he was a Carolina guy, and had played ball there a very long time ago. Perhaps he could help with the access. That did not strike me as likely. Somehow he did not look connected to the high-powered modern-day world of basketball. Instead, he looked quite ordinary, just another man in his sixties, a little shorter than me, perhaps 5 feet 9 inches or five-ten. His name, he said, was Tommy Kearns, and for a long time the name meant nothing to me; during most of the ensuing three or four months of our regular conversations I did not think of him by his name, but rather as the pleasant, helpful Carolina alumnus from the gym, a man who was, judging by the sweat on his workout clothes and the slightly chunky outline of his body, working even harder than I to keep his weight down. In the modern age when a player is usually at least six-five, and with a body fat content of under 7 percent, he did not look like a player; that was emphasized by the fact that the New York Liberty players practice at our gym and from time to time as we talked we would look at the sleek, powerful bodies of young female professionals, all of them, it seemed, stronger and taller than we were.

But our palship progressed. We both liked to talk basketball.

He was smart and likable, and he clearly knew the inside of the Carolina program extremely well, who was in and who was out. Dean Smith was Dean to him, yet he clearly was not a name dropper. After a few weeks during the early months of the legwork on my book, he began to guide me through the intricacies of the Carolina hierarchy, and at a time when I was still struggling to gain access to Smith himself, he tried to be helpful.

The Carolina basketball world, it should be noted, is tightly bonded and largely sealed off from the outside world: a cult, Chuck Daly, the former Penn and Detroit coach, once told me, a good cult instead of a bad one, but a cult nonetheless. Outsiders, particularly writers, are likely to remain outsiders forever. Kearns was clearly in the club; he played golf with Smith at Pinehurst each summer with many of the best-known Carolina alumni, a kind of Dean Smith Invitational. That is very much an insider's game; Carolina coaches, Carolina alumni and a few trusted outsiders who had treated Carolina players well, like Jerry West, Rod Thorn, Kevin Loughery and Daly, were the ones asked to play.

Our friendship progressed over the year. We talked about the game, and about Michael, and Kearns tried, unsuccessfully, to get me to try spinning, a hyped-up form of stationary bike riding. Then, late in the season when I was checking out the Carolina basketball brochure, looking up some of James Worthy's statistics, I happened to stumble into some of Kearns's records. Tommy Kearns, it turned out, had been a third-team all-American in the mid-fifties, but even more, he had been the playmaker — that was before they were known as point guards — on the Carolina team that in 1957 had gone undefeated and beaten Kansas and Wilt Chamberlain for the national championship.

Bringing the City to North Carolina

I mentioned this to him with some measure of apology the next time we spoke at the gym: "You really *were* a player, weren't you?" And with that he started telling me a very good basketball story from a very different era. He had been in the vanguard of New York City kids whom Frank McGuire had recruited back in the mid-fifties and put on his reverse underground railroad to North Carolina, as part of a plan to bring winning basketball to a school (and region) which, in basketball terms at least, was largely an underdeveloped area. Basketball was not yet a truly national sport and the game was still more often than not a city game — played best, it was believed, in New York. But it was a bad time for the college sport in New York. The point-fixing scandals of the early fifties had destroyed the sport locally. Once-powerful programs had been closed down. McGuire himself had coached at St. John's before seeking a kind of sanctuary at Chapel Hill.

After landing at Chapel Hill, McGuire had almost immediately started to import his own boys. He was the son of a New York cop and he was good at recruiting city boys; if in Carolina he had something of a strange accent, and if he seemed a little flashy, very much the outlander, then neither of these things was true when he went after kids in the boroughs. He was very good at visiting kids in their homes, usually accompanied by someone very successful from the same neighborhood who vouched for him. He liked to do most of his recruiting in the homes — where he could make a better read on the life style and the ambitions of the parents and therefore tailor his pitch accordingly — rather than in fancy restaurants where the parents might be uncomfortable. He visited the home of Tommy Kearns, who was a big-time schoolboy star in New York, some four or five times. In those days the Catholic high schools held tryouts for scholarships — the players the coaches wanted got them, and Kearns had played for Lou Carnesecca at St. Ann's, a traditional powerhouse; he had been an all-city playmaking guard, quick, scrappy, and smart with the ball, with a good outside shot. Under his direction, St. Ann's in 1954, his senior year, had been national Catholic school champion.

McGuire badly wanted Kearns, and the fact that the senior Kearns was also a cop living in the Bronx did not hurt — it was an easy house in which to make a read. The recruiting sessions were, Kearns remembered, largely devoted to McGuire's attempts to overcome the doubts of Kearns's parents about sending their son to so alien a part of the country. After all, Chapel Hill was in the heart of the Bible Belt South, and Tom Kearns Sr. was wary of what would happen to a good Irish Catholic boy down there. But, Kearns remembered, McGuire was a masterly recruiter, and if you listened to him, the conversion was going to be quite different —

he and his boys were going to convert the Protestants to Catholicism, and do it through the Trojan horse of basketball. And so in time Kearns became one of four New York City kids McGuire recruited for his class of 1958, fittingly enough, all of them Catholic. Already waiting for them down there, a year ahead of them in school, was a young man of consummate talent who was a great pure shooter, Lennie Rosenbluth, also a New York boy, who was Jewish. That would make their team essentially all New York, four Catholics and a Jew: Kearns; Pete Brennan from St. Augustine's in Brooklyn; Bobby (no kin to Billy, who came after him) Cunningham, from All Hallows in the Bronx; Joe Quigg from St. Francis Prep in Brooklyn; and Rosenbluth from James Monroe in the Bronx.

Jumping Center Against the Stilt

Their arrival marked the beginning of big-time basketball at Chapel Hill. They knew the game, they were well ahead of the national curve in basketball savvy, they knew how to shoot and set picks and make cuts and, above all, how to pass. They compensated for a lack of height by deft defensive positioning. Freshmen could not play for the varsity in those days, but the Carolina freshmen were undefeated and often beat the varsity in practice. As sophomores, they played regularly and went 19–7, and then in their junior year everything tumbled right and they went 32–0. The heart of the team, as the *Raleigh News and Observer* later noted, was Kearns. In the National Collegiate Athletic Association semifinal, they beat Michigan State in three overtimes. Then, playing in Kansas City, Missouri, they had to play against a Kansas team led by the seemingly unstoppable Wilt Chamberlain. They were ranked number one in the country because they were unbeaten, and Kansas, which had lost once, was ranked number two, but there was no doubt which team was favored; it was Kansas by about eight points, playing virtually at home and led by the mighty Wilt.

Before the game, McGuire, wanting to fire his players up and wanting to end any possibility of intimidation, had turned to Kearns, the smallest player on his starting team, and said, "Tommy, you're not afraid to jump center against Wilt, are you?" and Kearns had shouted out, "Hell no!" So he had jumped center, and Wilt had got the tip, but having Kearns jump center had set a tone of Tar Heel cockiness. ("My wife still says that jumping center against Wilt in the national championship game is the defining moment in my life, the one sure thing which will be in my obituary," Kearns said the other day.) The message had been given, Carolina was not afraid of Kansas, and it eventually won, again in triple overtime. The game, little underdog Carolina against awesome Kansas, had caught the imagination of the country and the region; from that time on, noted the writer Jonathan Yardley, who was about to enter Carolina, basketball became not merely a sport, but a religion in the area — in that sense, what McGuire had promised the senior Kearns proved to be true.

The Brief Career of a Perfect Pro

Their next year was not so successful. Rosenbluth was gone, and Quigg was injured and they did not do so well. The irony of a great athlete's story — deeds once so important to so many people, thousands cheering, but deeds now largely distant memories for all but those few who actually played, men who had regained anonymity in their lives — struck me forcefully as he finished the story. He had told this story outside the locker room of our gym and as we were about to part, he said, almost casually, "I played in the NBA, you know." He paused and added: "Briefly. I still hold the record for the best field-goal percentage. One for one." And then he was gone. Not sure whether to believe him or not, I went home and took out my trusty National Basketball Association record book, and there it was, a great line: one game, one field goal attempted, one field goal made.

It was a statistical line for the Walter Mitty in all of us — and I thought based on that we ought to have lunch so I could hear the rest of the story, and so we met again. In 1958, when he had graduated from Chapel Hill, there were only eight teams in the fledgling NBA — with 10 players each. The year that Tommy Kearns came out, the league was just beginning to change and there was the early surfacing of black players — Elgin Baylor went first in the draft that year. Even more important, Syracuse, which took Kearns in the fourth round, took a seemingly unknown guard from Marshall named Hal Greer in the third. Kearns, who had played in a number of all-star games, had never even heard of Greer. Basketball drafting and scouting was hardly big time, and Tommy Kearns had never, as far as he knew, been scouted. It was several weeks after the draft when a letter arrived from the Syracuse owner, Danny Biasone, setting Kearns's salary at $7,500 if he made the team. Nothing in those days was guaranteed.

The numbers, he soon realized at preseason camp, were going to be tough given the limited 10-man rosters and the need to keep the payroll down. The veteran guards on the team were Larry Costello, Al Bianchi and Paul Seymour, then 30 years old and a 12-year veteran. The question was whether Seymour would be a coach or a playing coach. If he only coached there was one more spot on the roster. But Biasone was not a wealthy man — his money came from the ownership of bowling alleys, and so all economies were critical. The competition was tough: the coach himself if he chose to play; Costello, who was very, very quick; Greer, clearly an ascending star ("a little bigger, a little quicker and a little bit better shooter than me"), and Bianchi. Some teammates thought it was going to come down to a choice between Greer and Kearns, and that was ominous to Kearns.

Kearns had a good camp, but in one of the last preseason games he came down off balance from a rebound and hurt his ankle and it cost him several weeks. When he was finally ready to play, it was in a game against Cincinnati. Syracuse, as Kearns remembers, was well ahead in the second half when Seymour sent him in: in time, the ball had come to him on the outside ("four or five feet outside the foul circle") and he had taken his shot and it went in. "It would be a three in today's game," he noted proudly. All told, he had played seven minutes. The next day Seymour made his decision. He called Kearns in and said: "Tommy — it's been great. We really like you and your game. But I've decided to stay on and play, and so we have to let you go." That was it. There were no agents to call European teams in those days; he was gone that day. Hal Greer, who came in with him, went on to play for 15 seasons (39,788 regular-season minutes to Kearns's 7), becoming a Hall of Fame player who averaged 19.2 points a game. Kearns played for a time in the Eastern League and then went back and married a girl who had gone to Duke, and worked in Greensboro for 10 years as an investment banker before returning to New York. He was, he told me, a man with no regrets: he had got a great education from a great school, he had helped win a national championship, and in the record book it still shows that he was the best shooter ever in the NBA. You could look it up.

JEANNE MARIE LASKAS

America Is a Bull

FROM ESQUIRE

"BULL RIDING? Okay, bull riding is 90 percent mental. Anybody tells you any different, they're lying. Because when you get on your bull, you have to, just, be on your bull. And that's all that matters. Because bull riding is not a natural human behavior. Bull riding is 99 percent practice. Basically. Because it all comes down to timing. Riding jump for jump. Because these bulls here have been on TV. They've been to the PBR on TV. Yeah, you've got a rank pen of bulls here. And every one of them has a different bucking style. Like Achy Breaky, that red-and-white Braford right there? A pretty little bull. He lunges. Feet out this far, he lunges. And then Skywalker over there? He gets air. Just reaches out forward and stretches out like he's walking on air, like he runs on the air, front feet out. It depends on the bull. You've gotta more or less, just, whatever he's doing this second, that's what you have to be doing. Just trying to say, Hey, bull, I'm here, I'm with you; my hips are square with your shoulders, and my shoulders are square with my hips. Just a straight line. Because bull riding is 75 percent balance. Basically. That's why it's gotta be feel. Because it's, well. It is. Bull riding is 99 percent feel."

He's got his vest on. His hornproof vest. It's brown and matches his chaps. Which are plain. At least comparatively. There are boys here with bright-blue chaps adorned with stars and stripes and their initials in shiny red. There are boys here with fancier chaps than that, chaps you would imagine only Liberace or maybe Elvis wearing — all shimmer and glitter and pink and purple. Chaps that say, GLORY TO GOD in letters as big as a thighbone. Chaps that say, RIDIN' WITH JESUS. But Billy's chaps are plain. Buckskin-brown with a subtle navy-blue design element. He's got his plaid shirt on and a white hat with a turkey feather in it, which, he wants to point out, is just like the one 1987 world champion Lane Frost had in his hat when he got killed by Taking Care of Business in 1989. But Billy has never been, well, killed. Worst that ever happened to Billy was a few broken bones and an hour or two unconscious. Which is a whole nother story.

He's ready to ride. He's draped over the pen, his lower lip holding a good wad of Copenhagen. Watching bulls. Spitting. Watching bulls. Spitting. He could spit and watch bulls all day. Plenty of days he does.

"Did you see Organ Donor? That little white-faced brindle right there? He's wild. He'll get that high and then just roll over one side or the other. And that little black bull, that's CX-101. Oh, I love CX-101. All them CXers are buckers. But 101, I'd say he's the meaning of bucking bulls. No tricks. No snappy turns. No slinging his head. He just bucks. When the gate opens, he just bucks. He may make only five jumps in eight seconds. He's in the air that high off the ground every jump. But you never know. You come to a show, you draw a bull, you say, That's my bull. That's why you never know. Because bull riding is 90 percent luck. You just gotta ride the bull. Jump for jump. Hanging on with your legs. Bull riding is 75 percent legs. Your arm just gives you a balance point. A teeter point. You ride bulls with your knees and your feet, more or less. You get set up in the box. Because bull riding is really made in that box. Getting set. If it's wrong, everything is going to be wrong when they open that gate. But if it's right? Awesome. I mean, it's just, the *power*. I don't know. Something that strong, but smooth at the same time. It's . . . I don't . . . There are not words. I mean, adrenaline. That's all it is. Bull riding is 99 percent adrenaline. I've been shot at, I've jumped out of airplanes, and nothing comes close to nodding your head and callin' for that gate. You won't do it and you won't continue to do it and you won't get to this level if you don't love it. Because it has to be love. More or less, that's it. I mean, if you want to know what bull riding is, bull riding is love."

The show tonight in Elkin, North Carolina, is, thank Jesus in heaven, just a bull ride. Not a full rodeo. He can get so sick of waiting through the saddle-bronc riding, the calf roping, the barrel racing. Because in a full rodeo, they always put bull riding last. Because it's what the crowd waits for. Maybe they'll see a cowboy get stomped. Maybe they'll see a cowboy get hung up, his hand knotted in the bull rope, feet in the air, body whipped round and round like a dead coon in the teeth of a thrashing dog.

The music is starting. "Ladies and gentlemen." A lone bugle works up some patriotism. "Right now, I'm going to introduce you to a group of guys who are, well, they're the last of a dying breed." Billy listens. He listens but he doesn't listen. He hears "role model." "Hero." "Professional bull rider." He hears "Billy Nichols!" He steps into the arena, takes his hat off, lays it across his breast. Soon, all the cowboys are in a line, bowing to the crowd.

He loves the sound of that: "professional bull rider." Because that's what he is. A professional bull rider. He is twenty-two years old, a card-carrying member of the Southern Rodeo Association. A cowboy makes it here, he could go all the way to the National Finals Rodeo in Las Vegas and become a world champion, like Tuff Hedeman and Jim Shoulders and Larry Mahan and the rest of those famous men. He could also become rich like Tuff, the first cowboy to amass $1 million as a bull rider. But he is not one to focus on the numbers, much less the odds. He knows his place. A lot of the guys who win the big money have been riding, what, nine, ten, thirteen years? Last year, he made probably $7,000 riding bulls. And that was only his third year. Of all the bull riders who ever lived, his hero is 1962 world champion Freckles Brown. He loves Freckles Brown mainly because Freckles Brown didn't win the world title until he was forty-two years old.

Time, to a professional bull rider, is a consideration. For Billy, there are basically two units: eight seconds and four or five or six or seven or eight or nine, ten, eleven, twelve, thirteen, fourteen hours. Eight seconds: That's what your bull ride is. You hang on eight seconds, you get a score. Anything less and you're disqualified. And all the rest of your time is spent getting to the next rodeo. You drive and drive, get to the show early so you can look at bulls, spit, look at bulls. Until it is time for your eight seconds. He will tell you that he lives for the eight seconds. He told his father this, back home in Pennsylvania. His father said, "You're living in a dream world right now. One of these days, you're going to have to wake up."

"No," Billy said. "All I gotta do is ride bulls and die."

"No," his father said. "All you gotta do is start making your truck payments, because I'm getting tired of it."

Billy: I am a professional bull rider.

Dad: Well, I'd rather ride girls than bulls.

The crowd is cheering, and the professional bull riders are waving. There are about three hundred people here, moms and dads and kids from nearby towns looking for fun on a Friday night. Soon, a pretty cowgirl in a sparkly shirt comes bounding out on a beautiful white horse. She is carrying the flag of the United States of America while the singer sings about being proud to be an American, where at least he knows he's free. And Billy watches. Believes. Feels. Because there is no cynicism for a cowboy. There is no irony for a cowboy. It's all here, straight ahead: truth, justice, power, guts, glory.

"Our gracious Heavenly Father." Billy bows his head, closes his eyes, listens good. "We ask that you be with us at this bull ridin', and we further pray that you will guide us in the arena of life. We don't ask to draw a good bull or not to draw one that we know is impossible to ride. But Lord help us to live our lives in such a manner that when we make that last inevitable ride to the country up there, where the grass grows lush green and stirrup-high and the water runs cool, clear, and deep, that you, as our final judge, will tell us that our entry fees have been paid in full. Amen."

And with that he puts his hat back on. The music changes. Now it's . . . Axl Rose. "Welcome to the Jungle." The first five bulls are in the chutes, including Conehead, a big muley with a particularly huge blob of fat and muscle sticking out from on top of his neck. This is the bull Billy has drawn. The last time Billy met up with Conehead was two years ago in Asheboro, North Carolina, and Conehead came out, made one jump, turned, whipped his head high just as Billy's head was coming down low, and *bam, slam* . . . nothing. Floating. Sinking. And all those little stars. "Just like in a cartoon," Billy is saying to the boys. "You see little stars going in a circle over your head." He is laughing. The boys are laughing. Because it's the funniest thing. Every injury is a story to tell, worthy of honor and praise and laughter.

"All right, well, get him this time, Billy," says Jeff, Billy's riding partner, who helps Billy into the chute. Cowboys always help cowboys. Because cowboys are united, all cowboys throughout time. United in the poems and the songs and the stories. Billy's got a wad of Copenhagen in his mouth larger than usual. He's spitting everywhere — left, right, over his elbow, careful never to spit on Conehead. He climbs on Conehead's back, a mighty, hairy, rolling barrel of rawhide and steak. Axl is screeching. The cowboys back here are all slapping Billy. "All right, Billy. Come on, Billy boy. Get turned on. Let's go, Billy boy. Let's go, babe. Loosen up, loosen up." He wraps the bull rope around his hand, trying the split-finger wrap that eight-time world champion Donnie Gay himself once taught him. "Take your time, baby. It's you and him, Billy, it's just you and him, baby. Get it on, get it on!" Billy nods, his eyes bugged out in a mixture of fear and happiness and love, his white hat bouncing one time, two times, three times, signaling the guys to open the gate.

Conehead thunders out, two front feet in the air, green bull poop flying out at all the cheering cowboys, who don't even duck. It's hard to tell exactly what is going on. It's just a lot of dust and then all of a sudden Billy emerging high on top of the dust, up in the air, soft and floppy like a stuffed animal. He lands with a thud in the dirt.

"You had him! You had him, Billy!"

Except he didn't. He didn't make his eight seconds. The truth is, he hasn't made his eight seconds in weeks now. In other sports, this might be called a losing streak. One hell of a losing streak. But not for Billy. He is sweating. He is ripping off his glove, pulling off his chaps. He is not upset. He is . . . thrilled. *Conehead, you are so fucking beautiful.* He is telling the story of Conehead to as many as care to listen. "I had a good seat, I was with my bull rope, I was locked, he couldn't rock me, he couldn't shake me, so, a veteran bull, he had to try something, like I said, he's been to the finals, he's a smart bull, he felt my body weight slide to the left, and so he went right while I went left, and he said, 'Now I got you, boy, now you're mine.'"

It will go on like this long into the night, in the truck, in the bar. He will tell Conehead stories. This story. That story. A whole nother story. It will be amazing to none of his listeners that this many stories can actually occur in less than eight seconds of real-world time. Because they will have their stories, too. They will laugh and get bucked off over and over again in their stories, leaving the bar, heading to tomorrow's rodeo, five hours away in Lynchburg, Virginia, where maybe they'll meet up with Warthog or 3-D or Yellow Jacket or Rampage. They will pull over at a rest stop, sleep in Jeff's Blazer, and in the morning look around for a hose. A drink. A shower. A howdy to the new day.

When he was little, he rode pigs. You could say that's how it all started. A pig would get loose in the yard, and Billy, still in a diaper, would grab that pig by the ear and climb on, hang on, screaming for joy.

And then, naturally, he started riding the dog. Samson. Such a great dog. Then he rode the goose. It was Homer's goose. A big old gander, bigger than Billy, who was only three. And this goose was mean — he would bite anything. He'd bite Billy. Three times, to be exact. Billy was so terrified of that goose. So one day, here comes the goose, all spread out and hissing. And Billy's dad told him, he said, "Get the goose." He said, "Just grab him by the neck and shake him." So Billy did it — grabbed that goose by the neck with both hands. And the goose started flopping, and they went all the way down Homer's driveway that way, Billy never letting loose.

He killed the goose. The goose was lying down there at the edge of the hard road, Billy on top of it, still holding on to it, straddling it, crying his heart out, riding that dead goose. Later, they cooked it.

This is the way his dad tells the story. Sometimes it seems to Billy that his dad is waiting for him to stand up to a bull the same way he did to that stupid goose. Then again, his dad is the one to call this season a losing one.

Dad: How'd you do?

Billy: Got bucked off.

Dad: Again?

He is getting sick of this conversation. Because he does not, himself, care about getting bucked off. Bucked off is not losing. Bucked off could have more to do with the bull you draw than anything. You could be drawing the rankest bulls in the pen, over and over again, the rankest bulls. Like Billy is. In that way, this is a winning season. Because in bull riding, only half your score is how well you ride. The other half is the bull's: how well he bucks. So a cowboy making eight seconds on some stupid little hippity-hop bull is nothing to brag about. But a cowboy climbing on the back of Magic Man? CX-101? There is no shame in getting bucked off one of those amazing, beautiful, rankest, buckingest bulls.

But anyway. Despite Billy's well-rounded upbringing riding pigs, dogs, and a goose, he didn't actually begin riding bulls until he was eighteen years old, fresh out of high school, a marine stationed at Camp Lejeune, North Carolina. He met a guy from Oklahoma who talked about bulls. And one weekend they went over to a pen in Jacksonville. And Billy got on one, just a practice bull, a trashy thing that hardly fit the definition of a bucking bull. Even so, Billy was bucked off before the clock started.

And that was the exact moment he fell in love.

He continued to ride at the pen as often as time would allow. Because he was first and foremost a marine. He loved being a marine. Who wouldn't? He could have lived his whole life as a marine, if it weren't for the stupid stuff. Like when he'd return from a mission and be back at Camp Lejeune and there was nothing to do. Nothing. So they gave you stupid stuff, like they'd take you down to the motor pool and have you clean Humvees — grease, oil, just stupid, stupid stuff. He couldn't take that. So every weekend, he'd ride. He bought chaps, a bull rope, Wranglers, and a good set of spurs. He hung around bull riders. He learned the mythology. He learned Tuff and Lane and Cody Lambert and Jim Sharp. He learned Freckles Brown, who, incidentally, when he was 47 years old, came out of chute 2 and rode Tornado, an 1,850-pound Braford that had never been ridden in 220 times out. He learned Taking Care of Business and Conehead and Organ Donor and all them CXers. And, of course, he learned Bodacious, the most famous, buckingest bull of all time. An 1,800-pound Charolais-Brahman crossbreed that practically killed guys. When Tuff drew Bodacious at the 1995 PBR World Championships, Bodacious made two jumps and then, on the third jump, flew into Tuff's face, breaking one of Tuff's cheekbones into five pieces and the other into six, not to mention shattering his nose, jaw, and several teeth. It took surgeons six hours and six titanium plates to get Tuff's face back together again.

Billy and Jeff, whom he met at a rodeo, they would get together to watch Bodacious videos. Aw! Ugh! *Yee-ouch!* They watched cowboy after cowboy get beat up by Bodacious. But Billy would always be the first to defend Bodacious. "He's not a mean bull," Billy would say. "It's just his style of bucking. It's not his fault." Billy loved Bodacious.

Billy and Jeff became riding partners. Billy would drive to Jeff's house every Friday, take off with him for the weekend, and go from rodeo to rodeo. They listened to the poems, and they listened to the songs. Tape after tape in Jeff's cassette player. *Folks don't seem to realize the thrill I get from every ride. / That bronc feels like pure dynamite to me. / Scratched and bruised, my body aches from the day-to-day abuse it takes. / Lord only knows the way it sets me free.* They'd drive, usually Jeff at the wheel, Billy sticking his pointy-cowboy-boot toes out the window, on and on down the Blue Ridge Parkway. And then he'd come back to the base, and there was nothing to do. Nothing. Just stupid stuff, like clean your rifle seven times a week.

"Sir, that's fucked," he found himself saying. He couldn't take it anymore. He couldn't handle somebody telling him what to do, how to do it, when to do it, where to do it. He thought, I'm a cowboy, just like the songs say. I'm too proud, and I want to be free.

He bided his time, got out last spring a corporal, not a sergeant like some guys. He was a cowboy, fully transformed. *He's heard the call of the wild. / The mountain's callin' to him like a mother calls her child. / He's heard the call of the wild.* He and Jeff got to know Brian and Dennis and C. E., everybody sharing in the dream. They got close. Like Lane and Tuff and Cody and Jim — brothers, practically. No, closer than brothers. Winning titles together, like in 1988, when Jim won the world title and Tuff came in third and Lane came in sixth and Cody came in seventh. Could it ever get any sweeter than that? That's how they were, just like Lane and Tuff and Cody and Jim. Except without the titles.

And without the money.

Which bothered Jeff a lot more than it bothered Billy. Jeff was getting . . . moods. What was with Jeff? Jeff couldn't take losing. Plus, there was Amber. Jeff loved Amber. And Amber? Amber loved . . . Billy. Which is a whole nother *nother* story. Amber would go to the rodeos, hang out. But Billy didn't love Amber. Like he'd say to Dennis, to Brian, to anyone who asked: "The only problem with Amber is, Amber is not a bull."

*

Broke, not knowing where else to go, fresh out of the marines, Billy moved back to Fredericktown, Pennsylvania, the small farming community on the West Virginia border where he grew up. Where his dad and brother, Tommy, are, and Patti, his dad's woman, and Levi, his dad's horse. And where Homer still lives next door. His dad has all the work Billy can handle at the excavation company, Nichols & Son's Excavating. Digging ditches. Putting in sewers. Laying roadbeds. Billy likes the work just fine. It's what he does with his week. He calls it "waiting for my life to start."

His life starts Friday at noon, when he bundles all his bull-riding gear in the back of his pickup and wraps a blue tarp around it. He dips into his Copenhagen. He puts in a tape, and then for seven or eight or nine or twelve or fourteen hours, he climbs into his life. *I took a chew just the other night — it made me feel so fine. / I grabbed my honey baby and I pinched her ol' behind.*

And every once in a while, his dad will come with him to the rodeos. Because his dad loves Billy. His dad carries pictures of Billy and shows them to customers, saying, He made eight seconds here, he scored an 82. But the pride thing, maybe it's wearing out. Because his dad is getting scared. His dad doesn't want to see Billy end up like Lane.

Billy and his dad are in Tazewell, Virginia. A huge rodeo. Lots of events. Lots of entertainment in between. Whew. Let's get on with it, already. Billy is back here spitting, watching bulls, spitting. Hoping he makes his eight seconds tonight, tomorrow night, every night until he gets to the NFR in Las Vegas, to the world championship. But, well, what's the rush? Keep in mind that Freckles Brown was forty-two. And it's funny. A lot of cowboys pick Lane Frost to be their hero, what with him dying on the cross like that; well, not exactly *on the cross,* but that's how some guys make it seem. But as Billy sees it, Freckles is to Lane as, well, as God is to Jesus: the Father. Because Freckles was the one who taught Lane to ride. And Lane so loved Freckles. Hell, Lane so loved Freckles, he won the world championship the same year Freckles died, 1987. Lane was only twenty-four. Jeezus, that's only two puny years older than Billy is now. But Freckles won it at forty-two. And that's — what? — that's twenty whole huge years older than Billy is now.

A cowboy comes up. "Did you hear?" he says. "Your dad's in bull bowling."

"Jeezus . . ." His dad is really starting to get on his nerves. His dad is not a cowboy; a cowboy would never do this. A cowboy knows better. Because in bull bowling, the people are the pins. And the bull is the ball. The last person standing in place wins. Billy's dad has no idea how dangerous this is. Billy runs to find him. To stop him. To save the son of a bitch.

But it is too late. His dad and nine other idiots are lined up like bowling pins in the arena. Timberwolf is the bull — a massive brindle with turned-down horns and a nose as wide as a pasta bowl. The gate opens and Timberwolf comes after the men. Because this is what bulls do: They come after men. Nine of the men dart, just run like sane people toward the arena gates and leap for their lives. But not Billy's dad. He stands there, the only one. Oh, here he goes. Billy knows. His dad is doing it again. Giving his son a lesson. *You want to spend your youth toying with death, boy? Well, this is what it looks like.* Billy gets it. Okay, Dad, get out! Get the hell out! But his dad is not done. His dad stands there and braces himself for what is about to come. Timberwolf charges, rams right into him, knocking him on his back, head-butting him, head-butting him, head-butting him.

There is dust, and more dust, and the crowd is on its feet. Are they finally going to see a man get killed by a bull? Two bullfighters in their bright costumes come charging to the rescue, waving their arms, screaming at Timberwolf, trying to convince him that they are more fun to kill than Billy's dad. Which apparently they are. Because Timberwolf makes his choice. And Billy's dad is saved. (And the bullfighters were just kidding.)

"You ain't never coming with me nowhere again," Billy says to his dad later, much later, after his dad gets considerable help from the medics.

Billy: Why would you do that? Professional bullfighters wouldn't stand in that circle. There is just something wrong with that.

Dad: You know what I think there's something wrong with? Doing all these miles every weekend just to get thrown off a bull.

Soon, he's going to rodeos alone. Jeff is nowhere in sight. For one thing, Jeff's Blazer blew up. But Billy doesn't mind: He got himself a dog. A blue heeler he named Freckles Brown. Him and Freckles, they're traveling partners.

Right now, he feels pretty good about his professional bull-riding career. Even though he's probably out the $7,000 he won last year. But still. It's going to happen. That's obvious to anyone. With the way he's been drawing bulls? It's happened again here at Stan Steagall's bull ride in Concord, North Carolina. He's drawn a bull called Five. Well, that's a weird name. Five? But it's good. Oh, this is so good. *Because Five has never been ridden for eight seconds.* Not all summer. Is this amazing or what? This is Freckles drawing Tornado in 1967. This is Lane drawing Red Rock in 1988.

Amber is here. He can see her over by the concession stand, working on some nachos. Because Amber still loves Billy. Amber does not mind the way Billy bucks her off. And she does, well, look good. But that's, well. No. He will not go up to her. Because he has to watch the bulls. He is draped over the pen, watching bulls, spitting, watching bulls. Has any man in the history of the universe ever had such a perfect life? He's got his vest on. His hornproof vest. It's brown and matches his chaps. Which are plain. Buckskin-brown with a subtle navy-blue design element. He's got his plaid shirt on and a white hat with a turkey feather in it.

Then comes the announcer, the blessing, the cowgirl on the pretty white horse carrying the flag of the United States of America. And then Van Halen. AC/DC. And boys are getting bucked off left and right. And before Billy's ride, the announcer says it's time for the Tight Fittin' Jeans Contest. Does he have some volunteers? Some ladies out there who want to come into this arena and shake, rattle, and roll for the panel of cowboy judges?

Why, yes, he does. It's . . . Amber. The crowd cheers. More girls come out. Billy is with Five. Grinding his foot into the bull's back, oblivious to Amber, her jeans.

Amber makes it into the finals of the Tight Fittin' Jeans Contest. It's down to five girls! But now let's get back to some bull ridin', ladies and gentlemen. The cowboys help Billy get the flank strap around Five. And Billy feels something. He feels this is it — the so-called losing streak is over. Not that he himself would call it a losing streak. But people are starting to wonder. And because it has to be this way. *And the spotlight's on the sawdust that shines in his brain. / And his dreams are the bones in his soul. / And it's all comin' true, right in front of his eyes. / Cuz he's the feller who won the big rodeo.* Because it happens this way in the poems and in the songs and in the mythology. Like

the way it was for Lane when he was having that streak of injuries in
1989 and all-around cowboy Roy Cooper walked up to Lane and
told him he could feel it, that the bad streak was finally over. And
then, of course, Lane got on Taking Care of Business and . . .

Well, no, it's not like that. Okay, erase that. Find another story.

Billy is next. He climbs onto Five, hoping to get a good seat. It is
not a good seat. Five is squirming. Suddenly Five starts leaping —
Aw! Ugh! *Yee-ouch!* He's throwing a fit in the chute, trying to climb
out of that chute. Billy gets knocked clear up in the air, back into
the arms of the cowboys.

That bull is crazy, people are saying. There is something wrong
with that bull. Billy thinks, Well, it's not the bull's fault. Let him
calm down. Okay. Billy puts one leg over, lowers himself, gets on
again, wraps his bull rope around using the split-finger wrap that
eight-time world champion Donnie Gay himself once taught him.
And Five, he's snorting. Twitching something fierce. Trying to
communicate something. Something like, "That's it. Off with the
cowboy. I am not a goddamn monster here to perform some circus
trick. I am a bull — a mighty, mighty bull — and whoever the hell
you are on top of me, I will be rid of you." He leaps, curls, stomps,
and Billy gets sucked down into the chute beside the bull, where
there is just a sliver of space into which a man of some 155 pounds
can slide. And all the cowboys united in the code, united throughout time, they're trying to save Billy, reaching for him, but the bull
throws his head high and knocks them onto their backs. But somehow one of them gets up, somehow he reaches in, reaches in and
finds the cowboy drowning in there with that crazy bull, getting
sucked into the drain of madness, and he pulls, he pulls and pulls
with both arms, bringing Billy out of there, back up out of there,
back to him.

There are sighs. All around the arena, sighs. Is the cowboy all
right? What's the cowboy gonna do? Does he dare try to ride that
wild monster? Billy is hurt. Barely able to stand. To see. He's looking for an answer. A hero, a story to follow, a song, a poem. Jeezus,
maybe it is like Lane and Taking Care of Business. Maybe it's Billy's
turn to be Lane. Maybe Billy's dad was right, saying it would take
Billy getting killed to wake him up from this dream. Maybe he
should just take this turkey feather out of his hat.

So what's the cowboy gonna do? The people are waiting. Five is
waiting. The cowboys, they're waiting.

And Billy, he does the thing he's never done before. Not in his entire career as a professional bull rider. He holds his hands up, shakes them, shakes his head, takes his hat off. He turns the bull out. And when that happens, a cowboy doesn't get another ride. Because the cowboy made his choice. The cowboy surrenders. Jeezus. He wonders if there are any songs about surrender. Even one line of poetry? Surrender is not in the cowboy code. *In the rodeo arena I'll take my stand. / I wanna be known as a rodeo man. / I'll come flyin' from the chute with my spurs up high, / Chaps and boots reachin' for the sky.*

"Good decision, Billy, good decision," the cowboys are saying. Oh, please. *Please!* He rips off his gloves, chaps, says goodbye to no one. Because he has to go. Leave. But then here comes . . . Amber. Oh, God. And Amber has won what? First runner-up in the Tight Fittin' what? The *what?* He has no idea what she is talking about. He has to go. Leave. Get out of here. He gets in the truck. *So what am I doing here, / Lord, what am I doing here? / There's got to be something better up there. / So what am I doing here?* He hits the eject button, puts in another tape, another one, cranks the volume so loud you can't even make out the words, the poems, the stories. Because none of them matter. Because there is no answer here.

He dips into his Copenhagen, spits, thinks, scratches Freckles behind the ears. And sooner or later, sometime in the night, he begins singing. *If it's a horse, ride it. If it hurts, hide it. / Dust yourself off and get back on again.* Because sooner or later, sometime in the night, he thinks: Wait a second. What about Tuff? Bodacious? What about in 1995, when Tuff wouldn't ride Bodacious at the National Finals? Tuff didn't think it was worth another busted-up face. And did anyone argue with that? No, nobody argued with that. So why is he arguing with himself about Five? He thinks about this, up I-79, into the dawn. *That's cowboy logic, every cowboy's got it. / It's in the way he lives his life and the songs he sings.* Maybe Tuff surrendered for him, for all cowboys, sort of like Jesus died on the cross. But not exactly. But, well, thank you, Lord. And he really means it. Thank you for the cowboys united throughout time who share with him this life on this beautiful earth where the grass grows lush green and stirrup-high.

MARK LEVINE

The Birdman

FROM THE NEW YORKER

CARLSBAD, CALIFORNIA, which is situated along a hundred-and-twenty-mile strip of sand between San Diego and Los Angeles, is a town where the impulse to stay upright on a fast-moving piece of wood has spawned two closely related but rivalrous tribes — the surfers and the skateboarders. Skateboard lore concedes that the sport was more or less invented in the early sixties by barefoot "street surfers," who took to the pavement on days when the waves were flat. Over the years, however, the surfers and the skaters have grown apart, like cousins who secretly despise each other. The rift was to be expected. In Carlsbad, the surfers, who can be seen, day and night, strolling through town in wetsuits with their boards slung under their arms, are regarded as heroes. The skateboarders are viewed as something of a public menace. Like countless American municipalities, Carlsbad has banned the sport from many of its public byways: grinding a downtown curb with your board puts you in danger of getting slapped with a fifty-dollar ticket.

Still, Carlsbad recognizes that the local appetite for skateboarding can be contained, if not eliminated, and recently the town opened a small public skate park. One evening this spring, I went to check it out with a Carlsbad resident, Tony Hawk — aka the Birdman — who is widely acknowledged to be skateboarding's grand master. Hawk, who at thirty-one is a venerable figure in a sport dominated by teen-agers, stands a gangly six feet three, and has a touch of gray in his sandy-blond hair. He was dressed as usual: in baggy corduroy shorts that came down past his knees, a pair of thick-soled, black skate shoes that looked appropriate for a character in an "Archie" comic, and an oversized sweatshirt bearing the logo of the skate-shoe company Adio. A garish column of pink and purple skin flecked with scabs ran down his right shin. As we pulled into a parking area, he pointed out laconically that the city had seen fit to locate the skate park on the grounds of the Carlsbad Safety Center, between the police station and the firehouse.

Even so, the skate park, which was about the size of a baseball diamond, seemed designed to facilitate injuries. It consisted of three shallow concrete bowls, which were rimmed and linked by steeply sloping ramps and ledges, interrupted at various points by cement obstacles. We watched as one of several dozen skaters, a boy who had a shaved head and wore a black T-shirt that said "Products of Corruption," dipped into one of the bowls, tucked his torso into a crouch, and glided along the sloped perimeter in a birdlike posture. Suddenly, he popped out of the bowl and flipped his board; feet and board parted company, and he kicked the air frantically before coming back to earth, with a quick stutter-step. "Cool," Hawk said.

Hawk put on bulky elbow pads, knee pads, and a black helmet. Then he slapped his skateboard to the pavement, slanted his right foot across the board's front (or "nose"), kicked his back foot in the manner of an agitated mule, and glided into the skate park. Although he is the devoted father of two children and the client of five stockbrokers, the William Morris Agency, and a public-relations firm, he looked as single-minded as a child sprinting toward a carousel.

At first, Hawk seemed scarcely more adept at staying on his board than the others. When he tried to snap the board up a bank with his feet, he fell, and the board darted away from him. He got up, retrieved the board, skated along a ledge, and fell again, his impassive expression never changing. In this way, he blended seamlessly with the swarm of skaters, most of whom were half his age, and all of whom seemed immersed in the private rituals of flight and collapse. Skateboarding, I was beginning to realize, involves an almost masochistic willingness to fall, again and again, in pursuit of a perfect landing. It is also an intensely solitary activity. Despite the whine of urethane wheels on stone, and an occasional explosive curse, there was a prevailing hush in the park.

Finally, Hawk paused on a plateau in the center of the park. He

careered down a ramp, scraped the tail of his board along the edge
of one of the obstacles, bent his knees, went airborne, flicked the
front of his board with a toe, turning the board into a perfect spiral, landed with his feet planted back on the board, and glided
away. Then he signed autographs.

I called Michael Brooke, who is the author of *The Concrete Wave,*
a recently published scrapbook history of skateboarding, and he
gave me an account of the sport's origins which might have come
out of *The Hardy Boys.* Skateboarding's roots, he said, "go back
to the early nineteen-hundreds, when kids banged roller-skate
wheels onto two-by-fours. Sometimes kids attached orange crates
with handles to the two-by-fours, for steering. Sometimes kids
broke the T-bar handles off scooters. This kind of thing continued
through the Depression and the Second World War."
   It wasn't until the early sixties that large-scale commercial production of skateboards began. Made by a firm in Los Angeles
named Roller Derby and priced at a dollar ninety-nine, the boards
were narrow slabs of wood with steel wheels bolted on. Boards
with smoother-riding clay wheels soon followed, as did surfboard-
shaped decks. As more people grew enamored with what Brooke
called "the freedom of gliding," skateboarding became increasingly acrobatic, incorporating wheelies, spins, and headstands. In
the sport's halcyon days, in the mid-sixties, fifty million skateboards
were made. In 1965, *Life* ran a cover featuring a perky blond
woman named Pat McGee doing a handstand on a skateboard;
the headline read, "THE CRAZE AND MENACE OF SKATEBOARDS."
Other warnings appeared, and, in short order, skateboarding was
banned from the sidewalks and streets of twenty cities. Skateboarding's reputation as an antisocial sport was born.
   There are now nine and a half million skateboarders in the
United States. Ninety percent of them are male, and nearly all of
them are too young to hop off their boards to vote. They are not,
however, too young to spend money: this year, skateboarders are
expected to drop eight hundred and thirty-eight million dollars on
boards and related paraphernalia. Municipal skate parks are prolif-
erating, and at last count there were about three hundred of them
in places as far apart as Boca Raton, Florida, and Ketchikan, Alaska.
The sport has also become a media attraction as never before. In

1995, the cable channel ESPN introduced the Extreme Games —
now known as the X Games — which spotlight skateboarders and
other alternative athletes, and the event has been highly successful.
This fall, NBC is planning to air its own Gravity Games.

Still, skateboarders cling to their outlaw past. Most of them are
white and live in suburbs, but they tend to cultivate a taste for the
baggy clothes and backward baseball caps, the music and the vocabulary, of hip-hop culture. Their rallying cry, which is repeated
on T-shirts and bumper stickers, neatly combines a sense of persecution with bravado: "Skateboarding is not a crime." A recent letter to the editor in one of the leading skateboarding magazines,
Thrasher, begins, "Yo, waz up, I'm 14 and been skateboarding for
four years. . . . Georgia has nowhere to fucking skate." In *Thrasher*
and its rival skateboard magazines, like *Big Brother,* which is published by Larry Flynt, the sport's most beloved heroes are the rene-
gades who persist in doing their stuff outside the bureaucratically
sanctioned skate parks. These are the so-called "street skaters," who
infuriate landlords and security guards by riding their boards on
whatever terrain is available — railings, steps, ledges, benches, hy-
drants, and loading docks — regardless of their safety or anyone
else's. Today's leading street skaters, like Jamie Thomas, Chad
Muska, and Eric Koston, are endowed with some of the street ca-
chet of rap stars. On the other hand, as Kevin Imamura, the editor
of *Warp,* a "skate snow style sound" magazine, told me, "The image
of Tony Hawk is not so hard-core. But," he added admiringly, "that
guy, his level of skating is so ridiculous."

In 1977, Alan Gelfand, a thirteen-year-old skateboarder, whose
nickname was Ollie, spent hours in an abandoned, empty swimming pool in Hollywood, Florida, teaching himself how to pop his
board into the air with his back foot, then stabilize it with his front
foot and take himself airborne with the board seemingly stuck to
his feet. This maneuver has been known ever since as the Ollie, and
it has become an essential part of every serious skateboarder's rep-
ertoire — the equivalent of a plié for a ballet dancer. Whenever
you see a skateboarder sail along the pavement, lower himself into
a crouch, then jerk himself and his board suddenly upward, you
are seeing an Ollie. It's the skateboarder's way of expressing his desire to fly.

Currently, the skaters with the greatest public visibility are the masters of the "half-pipe" — a steeply graded, U-shaped chute, into which the skater plunges, only to spring up, an instant later, on the opposite wall. Tony Hawk might be called the Baryshnikov of the half-pipe, a skater who combines speed, aerial elevation, and agility with fearlessness. Indeed, it's easy to forget that he is a skateboarder as he bounds above the rim of the half-pipe, twisting his almost horizontal body into a spiral, as if he were trying to disappear into thin air. Performers like Hawk display their aerial skills in contests devoted to vertical, or "vert," skateboarding. Vert competitions get prime coverage on ESPN, which has made stars of such half-pipe artists as Hawk and two of his neighbors in Southern California, Andy Macdonald and Bob Burnquist.

One afternoon, I went with Hawk to the place where he does most of his professional workouts — a thirty-two-thousand-square-foot skate park at a YMCA in Encinitas, ten miles south of Carlsbad. I followed him up a flight of stairs to the deck of an eighty-foot-wide half-pipe. As a teen-ager, Hawk had pioneered the art of vert skating by learning how to Ollie off the ramp at the end of his upward ride, springing into the air with the board still clinging to his feet. On his runs at the Y, Hawk managed to sail six or eight feet above the top edge of the half-pipe; getting this "air" gave him time to perform stunts before descending to the ramp again. He also sometimes combines his aerials with "lip tricks," precisely timed maneuvers on the narrow edge, or "lip," of the ramp.

Hawk has been credited with inventing dozens of tricks. In recent years, the splashiest one he's come up with is called the Loop. It requires him to skate a loop-the-loop on a ramp that he compares to "a twisted Hot Wheels track." In another trick, the Kickflip McTwist, he flips his board with his feet while spinning his body five hundred and forty degrees. To pull it off, as he put it, "the stars have to align." He added, "I have dreams about skating all the time — anxiety dreams. Dreams in which I'm riding a board with a sawed-off tail, or in which the ramp is made of carpet. And dreams that I can't skate."

For Hawk, this was an unusually revealing statement; generally, he had difficulty talking about skateboarding in anything but the most technical terms. Unlike baseball, skateboarding was not to be analyzed; it was to be experienced. The moment Hawk's feet touched the board, he became a kind of genius of recklessness, propelling himself high into the air, stretching and twisting his frame into Brancusi-like postures.

Hawk was born in San Diego in 1968. When I asked him about his family history, he said that all he knew about his parents' origins was that they were both raised in Montana; he had no idea where his grandparents had come from, or what had brought them West in the first place. Hawk's father, Frank, who had been a Navy pilot during the Second World War, worked as a salesman. He and his wife, Nancy, raised their four children in comfortable suburban surroundings. Tony's older brother, Steve, was a dedicated wave rider who went on to become a longtime editor of the magazine *Surfer.* One day, Steve allowed Tony, who was then nine, to jump on his narrow fiberglass skateboard. I invited Hawk to relive the moment of his first skating experience. He paused. I waited. Finally, he said, "I don't know. It was fun."

Like many other skateboarders I met, Hawk told me that, as a child, he had been something of a misfit. When he was eleven, he committed an act of serious filial disloyalty by quitting his baseball team during his father's tenure as president of the local Little League. Around the same time, he also quit playing basketball. "I just liked being freer, not having to submit to some practice schedule of repetitive passing and shooting, not having to rely on all the other players in order to do well," he told me. "There's a lot of practice and repetition in skateboarding, but it's at your own pace. It's not someone telling you what to do. That was the bottom line. I just didn't want to be ordered around."

Hawk's mother had told me that Tony was "a very intense child, difficult and stubborn and hard to handle," and that his discovery of skateboarding had come at just the right time. "It's a wonderful means of containing all the hormones and rages that a kid goes through," she said. "We were just glad that, after a while, he took out his energy on the skateboard and not on us." Hawk doesn't challenge his mother's memory. "My brother and sisters had moved out by the time I was a kid, so it was like being an only child," he said. "I was impatient and uncooperative. I'm sure it had something to do with my diet — soda, candy, ice cream all the time. I'd drink Cokes until I had a sugar buzz. If I were growing up now, teachers would probably say I had attention deficit disorder."

His passion for skateboarding, Hawk told me, made him an "out-

cast" in high school. "I just didn't relate to anyone," he said. "I
never went to a single school function — sporting events, dances,
prom. I just didn't care. I was going to school because I had to."
Hawk dressed like a skater — in tight shorts when those were the
fashion and, later, in neon-colored Jams. Like other skaters, he listened to the cutting-edge rock music of the time — bands like
Devo and Depeche Mode, and punk groups like X, the Dead Kennedys, Circle Jerks, and Agent Orange. His boyhood hero was Evel
Knievel: "Just seeing someone overcome danger and fear — he
seemed like an immortal."

A 1983 photograph of Hawk in a skateboarding magazine shows
a scrawny kid, looking closer to eleven than to fourteen, with one
hand on hip, helmet on head, and shredded pads around an elbow, as he glares at the camera with a tense, glum expression. "I'd
take the bus to the skate park after school every day, and my dad
would pick me up at night," he recalled. "I'd skate for two or three
hours, stop, hang out at the park, then skate again for another two
or three hours. I was *living* at the skate park."

One afternoon in Encinitas, while I was watching Hawk practice,
the YMCA skate park was overtaken by a large group of teen-agers.
Many of them were shirtless in the midday sun, and many displayed
the scars of nasty skin-shaving falls. It was a school day, and I
learned that they were students from the San Dieguito Academy, a
nearby public high school that Hawk had attended for one unhappy year, in the ninth grade. Now, however, the school offers a
skateboarding-for-credit class — one of the few in the country.

I stood on the deck of the half-pipe with Lani Madrid, a burly in-
structor. "We really had to fight the school board to start this program," he told me. "The authorities would rather have the kids
reading *Macbeth* than skating. They don't understand that this is a
way of life, and that the kids are stoked on it. These kids definitely
have discipline problems at school. A lot of them stay in school only
to attend this program. They're great athletes, but they wouldn't
excel at team sports. And they're tough. Look at how banged up
they are. If they fall down, they don't cry for their mothers."

Several members of the class were girls. One of them, a freckle-
faced, blond-haired eighteen-year-old named Ashleigh Mull, told
me that she dreamed of becoming a professional in a sport in
which the presence of females ("skate chicks") is rare. "Everybody

looks on me as one of the guys," Mull said, and, as if to prove it, she told me that after recovering from surgery on a torn knee ligament she had broken a wrist and then, skating with a cast on, an ankle. "Yeah, it's a scary thing, the half-pipe — it's so big," she said. "But I love the feeling. It's adrenaline, it's a rush. Pulling the trick you've been trying for a month — there's nothing like it."

After the class broke up, Madrid told me, "We were all talking the other day, and the kids were saying, 'We don't want to be captain of the football team, we don't want to go to Yale, we don't want to live in a box house, we don't want to drive a Volvo. Just give us our skateboards.'"

There are about three hundred and fifty professional skateboarders in the United States, most of whom live in California. The vast majority of them make only a modest living — enough, say, to share an apartment with a couple of other skaters and to spend their days looking for appealing places to skate. Perhaps ten of them, like Hawk, earn six-figure incomes from endorsements.

"I never imagined any future for myself outside skateboarding," Hawk said when I visited him in a subdivision of Carlsbad where his Spanish-style house stands amid other, nearly identical stuccoed houses, each with a neatly trimmed lawn. A fifty-thousand-dollar emerald-green Lexus was parked in the driveway next to a Volvo station wagon. He shares the house with his wife, Erin, a former ice-skater, their son, Spencer, who was born this past March, and Hawk's six-year-old son, Riley, from a first marriage. Hawk has a spacious home office, whose walls are adorned with plaques and trophies celebrating his skateboarding triumphs, and with a large photographic portrait of his extended family, all of whom are wearing bluejeans and white T-shirts. An enormous gumball machine stands in a corner.

Hawk turned professional when he was fourteen. He was invited by Powell-Peralta Skateboards, the major manufacturer of boards at the time, to join the company's team of sponsored skaters. In the early eighties, skateboarding was not big business, and his financial success was gradual. He received free equipment and modest endorsement fees, and competed in weekend contests that might offer a hundred dollars as the top prize. Then, in 1982, Powell-Peralta introduced the Tony Hawk signature-model skateboard, which featured the ghoulish graphic of a bird's skull on its under-side. By the late eighties, Hawk was collecting monthly royalty checks of approximately twenty thousand dollars.

A few years later, however, the skateboarding craze was over, partly because of the growing allure of rollerblading — an activity that skateboarders regard as contemptibly risk-free. Hawk found himself pleading with his first wife — a manicurist whom he'd met at a shopping mall in Fresno — for a Taco Bell and Ramen-noodle allowance. Skateboarding competitions were rarely held, and Hawk, who was not yet twenty-five, was skating toward forced retire-ment. Then, in the mid-nineties, a demographic bulge in the eight-to-eleven age group emerged. The doors of skate shops opened once again. At the same time, ESPN began giving prominent cover-age to skateboarding events. Hawk took the top prize at the X Games in 1995 and in 1997.

Hawk, like most top skateboarders, is now a virtual billboard on wheels for his sponsoring firms, and his clothes and skate gear are plastered with logos. A top-selling signature shoe can net a skater a hefty annual income. Hawk's shoe of choice, as his T-shirts will re-mind you, is made by Adio. He is sponsored by 55DSL, a hip line of Diesel clothing, as well as by Swatch wristwatches, Arnette sun-glasses, Fury skate trucks, and Club Med. He is also the co-owner of a skateboard company, Birdhouse, whose 1998 revenues were fif-teen million dollars. He has been featured in a television commer-cial for the Gap, and his electronic likeness will soon be accessible via a video game devised by Activision called "Tony Hawk's Pro Skater." ESPN announcers routinely refer to him as "the Michael Jordan of skateboarding."

If there are some in the skateboard culture who feel that he has sold out, he doesn't care. "There are skaters who don't want any-one to penetrate their world," he told me. "But if my role is to be skateboarding's link to the mainstream, I'm willing to accept it. My business card for Birdhouse gives my title as 'Media Whore.'"

In May, I traveled to Richmond, Virginia, where ESPN was mount-ing the X Trials, a made-for-cable-TV warmup for this summer's full-blown X Games. Hawk was appearing as a goodwill gesture, since the competition was moot for him; he had long ago qualified for inclusion in the games. The site of the trials was a defunct ironworks on the banks of the James River which had once provided the Confederate Army with cannons and ammunition. For the X Trials, the place had been spruced up with enough asphalt to cover half a football field, and over Mother's Day weekend it was bustling with activity. Several hundred young athletes — skateboarders, rollerbladers, and riders of those pesky small-wheeled stunt bicycles that can be seen jumping the curbs of major cities — had come for four days of competition. Live alternative rock music filled the air. Two paramedic vehicles stood at the ready. The X Trials charged no admission fee, and the event had drawn more than eighty thousand curiosity seekers, many of them teen-agers in packs, and families with small children.

"There's a bit of a revolution going on out there in sports," Chris Stiepock, the director of marketing and communications for the X Games, told me over lunch one afternoon in Richmond. "The X Games show a forty-year-old dad why his twelve-year-old son isn't picking up his baseball glove anymore." Stiepock went on to say that the rise of so-called "extreme sports" had everything to do with the growing disaffection from traditional team sports among teenagers. He informed me that this year's X Games would feature such "disciplines" as "street luge," "freestyle motocross," and "big-air snowboarding." (This last event was to be performed on a ramp coated with shaved ice.) He also mentioned an event called "sky surfing," which would involve leaping from an airplane with a board strapped to the participant's feet.

What interested ESPN, Stiepock said, was the youth market's buying power. "The X Games is looking for Generation Y — twelve-to-twenty-four-year-old males," he told me. "They're nebulous and hard to reach, because nobody knows what to call them or what they are or what they're doing. All we know is that they're not doing traditional stuff anymore. But on any given telecast on ESPN of the X Games there are about fifty males ranging from twelve to twenty-four for every hundred households watching. That's higher than for any other sporting event on television. That's a direct hit. That's a household concentration that's very attractive to the Mountain Dews, the Taco Bells, the Marines, Snickers, Pringles, AT&T — right down the line."

One of ESPN's ambassadors of extreme sports is Rick Thorne, a wiry twenty-nine-year-old bicycle stunt rider and the host of the cable channel ESPN 2's "X 2day," a monthly survey of athletic pursuits that you'll rarely find discussed in *Sports Illustrated.* I sat with Thorne on a knoll at the edge of the X Trials site, as he delivered a high-volume monologue. "I never consider myself an athlete, dude," he said. "I think of myself as an *artist.* Bike riding is like painting or sculpture or writing a song. There's a lot of freedom. There are no standards. I'm a rock star, and the instrument I play is the bike."

Thorne was wearing a black T-shirt with the word "Split" stencilled across the chest. His teeth glittered with gold caps, and a good proportion of his visible skin surface was covered with colorful tattoos. I asked him whether he felt that the pure bliss of extreme sports was in danger of being diluted by all the commercial attention that these sports were suddenly receiving.

"It trips me out that we're so accepted now," he said. "I liked it when we weren't accepted — when we were the bad boys. I liked when we'd go grind a curb and people would be like 'Get the fuck out of here.' Now they're like 'Are you on ESPN?' And it's weird, because I'm like 'Dude, chase me, call me a name, let me throw a bottle at you.' Those were the days, and they're never gonna come back. Damn!"

The vert-skating competition was the big draw at the X Trials, and Hawk was going up against a field that included some of the world's top skateboarders — among them Andy Macdonald, who was the champion of last year's X Games, and Bucky Lasek, another Carlsbad-based skater. Each skater was allowed three forty-five-second runs in the final round, and he would be scored by judges on the difficulty of his tricks as well as on more subjective considerations such as fluidity and style. The highest score on a single run would determine the winner.

I sat behind the judges, who were all skaters themselves, and thought about how anomalous contests are in the world of skateboarding. The notion of being timed is at odds with the practices of real-world skaters, who will attempt a difficult move dozens of times, crashing on the ramp again and again, for the elation of nailing a trick once. Falling — or, as skaters say, "bailing" — is the skate-park norm, but contests tend to encourage fairly conservative skating because a time-wasting fall will cost a skater dearly. As a result, a skater's rank on the competitive circuit is far less important to him than his reputation in the skateboard culture — which is determined through word of mouth, magazine coverage, and videos. The skaters held in highest regard are those who are said to "take it to the next level." ESPN's extravaganza, I was beginning to suspect, was really a kind of dog show for the skateboard illiterates at large.

The first skater to make a run was Lasek, a rather perplexed-looking young man who had grown up in a blue-collar neighborhood in Baltimore. He sailed above the lip of the ramp, spun himself one and a half times in midair while clutching his board, and then rejoined it on the ramp, with perfect, ringing precision, like an opera singer hitting a high C. "Sick," one of the judges scrawled approvingly on his score pad.

Next up was Macdonald, who is called Andy Mac by fans. He is a skater's skater — an extraordinary technician, whose self-containment belies the speed and the ferocity of his effort. He strung together a dazzling series of tricks, twisting himself in compact midair spirals, switching his forward and backward feet from one descent to the next — an accomplishment similar to a baseball pitcher's delivering a fastball with his fielding hand. The rap on Andy Mac, though, is that he is a bloodless wonder in a sport that's all about passion; he is much admired but not much loved. One judge jotted down "robotic" while assigning Macdonald a high score.

Hawk's great appeal, I had noticed, was his vulnerability. Like Wayne Gretzky, he is not exactly one's image of a perfect physical specimen, and because his feet, which are size 13, seem barely to fit on his board, he always appears on the verge of losing his balance. ("The guys whose styles are appreciated are the ones who look like they're almost out of control," he told me. "They look like they're on the edge the whole time, and then they bring it together.") When Hawk skates, his mouth hangs open in an awestruck expression, and his fingers are spread stiffly, like claws. Now he dropped onto the ramp, zoomed up the opposite wall, and got great air. He did a tuck-knee invert — a one-handed handstand from the lip of the ramp, his back bowed in an elegant crescent, his knees bent, his feet nearly touching his head, and his free arm thrusting the board toward the crowd — in which the dizzy speed of the skating was suddenly captured in a moment of emblematic stillness. And then, when he had seven seconds remaining in his run, his board slipped under him, and he slid to his knees. "Pretty sick," a judge noted in praise. "Still doin' it."

Lasek had a superb second run, but after that he seemed to have peaked, and on his final run he bailed. Andy Mac continued to nail his tricks, and his last run was a stunning assortment of aerials. From my vantage point, I could see that the scoring was very close.

Hawk took a modest bow before beginning his last run. Then he unleashed himself on the half-pipe. He hit a pair of 540s — airborne twirls of a turn and a half — and during one of them he rotated his board while his body was spinning, so that he looked like an organism with many moving parts. He followed with a 720 McHawk — a double-revolution spin that he was the first skater to land and that only a few other skaters have ever successfully performed. It happens so quickly that one is uncertain of what one has seen: the body is launched; the body floats to the crest of its arc; the body does its dervish; the body realigns with its wheeled instrument and skates back into real time. His execution was flawless.

Much of the crowd had dispersed by the time the winners were announced. Indeed, the skaters themselves seemed unconcerned about the outcome. Hawk accepted first prize — forty-five hundred dollars — as if it seemed OK. Lasek stuffed his check, for third place, into one of the floppy pockets of his floppy shorts. Andy Mac left the contest as the runner-up, which happens to a lot of great skaters when they compete against the Birdman.

One summer day two years ago, at Point Loma High School, near the San Diego airport, one of the superstars of street skating, Jamie Thomas, performed what has become the most notorious stunt in the annals of skateboarding. First, he glided along an outdoor landing to the top of a double flight of concrete stairs — twenty-seven steps in all. Then he Ollied over the steel handrail, momentarily grabbed his board with one hand behind his legs, released his grip, extended his arms, and flew. In photographs of Thomas clearing the rail, he looks as if he were inhaling his own face. His body, compressed in the beginning of the jump, seems to open up as he approaches the concrete below. The board stays on his feet. When he lands, the board cracks in half, and he crumples and rolls over on the pavement. The stunt is known as the Leap of Faith.

Thomas grew up in small-town Alabama. "It was just a redneck haven, and skateboarding was not acceptable," he recalled. At seventeen, he dropped out of high school and made his way to San Francisco, where he supported himself by panhandling in the Embarcadero, waiting for his skateboarding prowess to attract the attention of sponsors. Now, at twenty-four, he owns a house on a quiet suburban street in Encinitas. I was invited to drop by one evening, after midnight. When I arrived, he was just finishing an interview with a reporter from *Thrasher.* He and I talked until dawn.

"I got off lucky," Thomas told me, discussing the Leap of Faith. "I just charley-horsed my ass, that was it." (The Leap of Faith gained greater renown last year, when an unknown skater from Texas attempted to duplicate the feat and fractured a shin with such force that the bone tore through his jeans.) "Everything I do is about fear and danger," he continued. "I scare myself every day."

Thomas has a shaved head, plenty of tattoos, and the sulky looks — part thug, part tortured soul — of the late Kurt Cobain. As I listened to him, I began to worry about his life. I had seen him on the video "Misled Youth," released this spring by his skateboard company, Zero. "Misled Youth" is a masterpiece of the genre, a film with handmade production values which moves through thirty-five minutes of aggressive skating at warp speed, yet seems to luxuriate in the ugliness of concrete and steel. To see these guys streaking down handrails and over stairwells — and, in one instance, across the hood of a car — is to see skaters in search of something that is beyond their capacity to understand. If the young Jean-Luc Godard had made a skate video, "Misled Youth" would have been it.

Thomas stands on the other side of the skate-culture divide from Tony Hawk. He is darkness to Hawk's daylight. Hawk is a skateboarding classicist. His venue of choice — the half-pipe — is an artificial realm designed specifically for skating. Hawk puts himself to the test in a setting that can seem like a metaphor for the world at large, with its symmetries and asymmetries, its inclines and declines, its hollows and flats, and its precipices. Hawk's world, like that of an abstract sculptor, is one of struggle with ideal forms.

As a street skater, on the other hand, Thomas is the creature of a haphazard, denatured environment. He is one of the legion of skaters who still prowl the urban and suburban landscape for skateable terrain, motivated by the longtime skateboarding cry "Skate and destroy!" When I asked him where he liked to skate, he said, "I'm constantly on the lookout for a place where I can fight my battles. As soon as I get off the plane in a new city, I'm excited. I start noticing things. I even notice things as I'm landing, like barriers around the airplane. Mostly, I skate at colleges and apartment complexes, and I'm looking for anything aesthetically pleasing that I want to try something on." Aesthetically pleasing? "You know, like there's a big handrail and there's a palm tree there. Rails are kind of my thing."

The fact that the street skater's chosen stage places him constantly in confrontation with various authorities — Thomas has been arrested once, at a power plant in Phoenix, and can talk at length on the subject of security guards — only adds to the breed's mystique. So does the street skater's refusal to wear protective gear, like helmets. "Street skating is about image, and feeling a certain way when you do it," Thomas said. "You don't want to feel nerdy when you're doing it. And, anyway, what's going to protect me?"

Thomas has had his share of broken bones, like any serious skater, and in each of the last four years he estimates that he has also suffered two or three concussions. One of them, which is captured on the "Misled Youth" video, is particularly chilling: Thomas grinds a handrail, misses his landing, and smacks his head on the pavement; one arm rises stiffly in the air, then falls; he looks dead. "You can get in a zone when you skate," Thomas told me. "You feel physically perfect; you have no dizziness in your head; you're completely focused. When you feel like you can't be stopped by anything, you're in the zone."

The X Games were held in San Francisco at the end of June and the beginning of July, and Hawk was again going up against Bucky Lasek, Andy Mac, and a corps of other top skaters. I tuned into the skateboarding competition on television, and I found the experience somewhat disheartening. Watching televised skateboarding is a little like looking at a postcard of a great painting. The sense of scale disappears, and the textures and tones of the experience are flattened out. When I stood on the deck of the ramp of the half-pipe in Encinitas, or sat in the scorching bleachers in Richmond, my sense of Hawk's fallibility — his precarious foothold on his slab of wood — had been very immediate, and that was what made him seem so human and so heroic to me. On television, he and his peers looked like mere technicians, succeeding or failing at their assigned tasks. It felt like sports, not like skateboarding. Hawk skated proficiently, but this time he was bested on the judges' scorecards by Lasek, who took gold, and Andy Mac, who placed second.

Nonetheless, before the X Games were over, Hawk managed to upstage not only the other skaters but his own previous achievements. During a segment of the games devoted to "Best Trick," Hawk decided to chase after what is often referred to as the Holy Grail of skateboarding: a two-and-a-half-revolution midair spin, called the 900. He made one attempt after another, and with each try he seemed to move a bit closer to landing the trick. On his eleventh try, he sailed above the top of the half-pipe twice to gain speed. Then, during his third time in the air, he spun his body two and a half turns counterclockwise, while grabbing the board with his right hand and bending his left arm above his head. His body was nearly parallel to the ground, and it was a beautiful sight — deliriously ephemeral. When he hit the ramp, he looked as though he might tumble again, but he kept his footing, regained his balance, and stood upright. His mouth hung open, astonished. He drifted on his board across the half-pipe in a diagonal line, looking lost. Skaters mobbed the ramp. Andy Mac, Lasek, Bob Burnquist, and other competitors slid down the half-pipe from the deck and hoisted Hawk on their shoulders. Hawk staggered off to find his wife and baby. ESPN announcers quickly declared Hawk's feat to be a historic moment in alternative sports. "This is the best day of my life," Hawk said, after returning to earth.

On my last day in Carlsbad, Hawk presented me with my first skateboard. It was a longboard — about a foot longer than a standard skateboard, and with larger, softer wheels, which are intended to give a smoother ride. It's hard to do tricks on a longboard, Hawk told me, adding that it takes a few months of daily practice to accomplish even "a teeny, tiny Ollie on it." Nonetheless, he said, it's "great for cruising."

My board is a very sleek model of Russian birch, covered with glittering grip tape on the top, and adorned with a tasteful black-and-red "G," which stands for Gravity, the name of the manufacturer. On the back end, it has a small kick tail. It tapers toward the rear, flares out subtly in the center, and has a front end carved into what looks like a mushroom cap. It's a beautiful piece.

That night, after dark, I went out into the parking lot of my Carlsbad motel. I placed my front foot on the board, kicked with my back foot, and got myself going. I bent my knees and spread my arms for balance. I went down a slight incline and knew that I couldn't stop. I jumped off, fell, and banged a knee. One knuckle was bleeding a little. I got back on the board. A shallow ditch that ran through the lot was surfaced with smoother cement. For the next thirty minutes, I skated back and forth in the ditch, undisturbed. The nearby San Diego Freeway hummed, muffling the Pacific surf beyond. The cement vibrated pleasantly. It was a new discovery of the paved world below.

JEFF MACGREGOR

Less Than Murder

FROM SPORTS ILLUSTRATED

SOMETHING TERRIBLE is about to happen. There, in the upper-left-hand corner of the screen. Behind the goal and a step to the left. The videotape is probably a copy of a copy of a copy, as grainy as a Navajo sand painting. A hockey game. The camera pans too fast, too slow, chasing knots of players back and forth across the ice. Medium wide-angle coverage, very likely shot from the press box, panning blue line to blue line, blue line to crease, blue line to blue line. It looks like team tape, overbright and jittery, something coaches use to show players how a penalty kill broke down or to mock their clay-footedness on a breakaway. The date — apr.17.1998 — appears across the bottom of the screen.

You've been told about the incident, so you know what to look for, and where. You think you know how bad it's going to be. The camera pans left and then rests, showing an area from the blue line to the goal. A clumsy rush forms and dissolves, and a blocked shot shakes the puck loose. It squibs into the corner, left of the goal. Two men skate in on it. They look small, but they aren't. The white jersey gets to the boards first; black jersey vectors in a second later, delivering a cross-check to the back, left elbow high. The puck slides past them and is cleared up the ice. White jersey turns, gives black jersey a shove, and they both glide toward the net. They are three feet from each other, no more, the black jersey a step nearer the goal. They pause for a second or two, the time it takes to read from here to *here*. But the moment seems to stretch on and on, elongated and made dense by the number of possibilities it contains.

Then it happens. White jersey lifts his stick and swings it hard at the head of the player in the black jersey. The long, flat arc of the swing drives the heel of the stick into his face, and he goes down. Goes down like an empty suit of clothes dropped to the floor. Goes down and stays down. The player in white stands over him as the camera pans away to the right. The tape abruptly cuts to a shot of the scoreboard.

Several seconds later you remember to breathe again.

This is a sports story in which no one wins. Everyone involved has already lost, and all that's left is the reckoning.

Who Ya Gonna Believe?

From hockey officials, on the record: "I didn't see it."
From officials, off the record: "The worst thing I've ever seen."

The Synopsis

On Friday, April 17, 1998, during an Ontario Hockey League play-off game at the Compuware Sports Arena in Plymouth, Michigan, 19-year-old Jesse Boulerice (pronounced BOWL-er-iss) swung his stick into the face of 19-year-old Andrew Long. That fact is not in dispute. It is, after all, on videotape. Jesse was in white jersey number 18; Andrew wore black jersey number 19. It was early in the first period of the fourth game of a seven-game series. Jesse's team, the Plymouth Whalers, was down three games to none. Andrew's team, the Guelph Storm (pronounced GWELF), was on the verge of advancing through the divisional eliminations toward Canada's lesser grail, Major Junior hockey's Memorial Cup.

When Jesse swung his stick, he produced immediate consequences for Andrew: a broken nose, multiple facial fractures, a Grade III concussion accompanied by seizure, a contusion of the brain, two black eyes and a gash in his upper lip the size of a handlebar mustache. Had the stick landed a hand's width higher or lower, Andrew might have been killed.

The consequences for Jesse, arriving more slowly but with a grinding weight and gravity of their own, have been these: a one-year suspension from the OHL and a suspension from the American Hockey League, his next step up the professional hockey ladder, that ended last November 15. He has also been charged by the Wayne County (Michigan) Prosecutors Office with a felony: assault with intent to do great bodily harm less than murder. A conviction could carry a $5,000 fine and 10 years in prison.

For every action there is an equal and opposite reaction. These are the applied physics of violence. Arc and acceleration, cause and effect. Swing a hockey stick hard enough, and you can bring the world down on yourself.

A Question of Fact

On April 30, at the Toronto Marriott Hotel, the OHL held a hearing on what it called the Jesse Boulerice/Andrew Long Matter. The video was reviewed. Reports were taken from game officials, coaches, the players and their agents. Jesse and Andrew were interviewed separately and did not talk to each other.

The OHL's confidential 35-page report is largely what you'd expect: witnesses explaining what they saw, agents and coaches speaking about the character of their players and the viciousness or the unintentional nature of the hit. A few intriguing points emerge. The first is Jesse had broken his right hand several games before the Guelph series, and he was wearing a playing cast on the night he swung that stick. The OHL report says Jesse was on painkillers that night, but no conclusions are drawn as to how that might have affected his behavior. Also interesting are these questions to Jesse regarding what he said as he was led off the ice that night.

Question: Do you recall the statement allegedly made by yourself to Referee [Pat] Smola, "You didn't even see what happened"?
Answer: I knew what I did was wrong — I was upset — I was not sure what else I should be saying.
Question: Do you recall the statement to linesman [Steve] Miller, "But Smola did not see what I did"?
Answer: I knew what I did was wrong and I was not sure what I should be saying or doing.

It could be argued that Jesse had checked to see where the referee was looking before he hit Andrew. Prosecutors expect to seize on this when the case goes to trial.

Other Things Jesse Said on April 30

"When I went into the boards, my hand got crushed."
  "I have been picturing the incident ever since."
  "I never meant to hurt him like that."

Some Things Andrew Said on April 30

"All I want to know is why."
  "I don't understand why [he] would do that."
  "I don't understand why."

What It All Means, Part I

So far the story unspools the way these stories always do: good guy–
bad guy, right-wrong, black-white. You don't have to read past the
headline to know what happened and form an opinion. It is another tidy front-page morality play that teaches the kiddies a valuable lesson in sportsmanship before working its way backward
through the newspaper until it evaporates completely. Seen out of
the corner of your eye among the NBA box scores and the strip-
joint ads and the PGA Tour money list, the story is just another
messy collision between sports and the law, a not very memorable
footnote to an age in which athletes seem to spend as much time in
court as on it.
  But to understand any part of this story, you have to understand
all of it.

Oh, Canada

There is no analogue in the U.S. for the almost chromosomal role
hockey plays in Canada's national life. It is omnipresent — everywhere and in everyone — at such a molecular level that even Canadians who hate the game (and there are a few) understand its nu-
ances. In a nation with so much winter and so much ice, hockey is
an inevitability; it is as inexorable as the weather. In Canada hockey

is the manufacturer of good character. It is myth and science. It is a kind of national dream state. Baseball, the only fitting point of comparison in America, has always been optional, no matter what George Will says. Hockey is to Canada what capitalism is to America: a functioning ideology.

Hence Major Junior hockey.

Major Junior. Jumbo Shrimp

There are as many divisions in organized Canadian hockey as there are diminutives in the language.

Before a Canadian is old enough to lace up his own skates, he has a league to play in. (Yes, the sport is still mostly about boys, although girls' and women's hockey is growing.) By the time a boy is 10 or 11, it's time for him to start taking the game seriously. His family should, too, because that's when it gets ruthless. And expensive: Equipment. Gas. Registration fees. Food and a room for those weekend tournaments. If you've got more than one child playing the game, better buy a minivan because the average hockey bag is now the size of a Lake Louise summer cabin. And bring a book, because your kids are going to be playing more than 70 games a year by the time they're 12. And don't forget to set aside some cash for power-skating camp next summer. Little Pierre and Gump Jr. and Sue had better attend; by the time they're 13, if they're any good, they're already being scouted.

At the top of this food chain is Major Junior, last stop before the pros. It is made up of 53 teams in three leagues: the Western Hockey League, the Quebec Major Junior Hockey League and the Ontario Hockey League. Together, they make up the Canadian Hockey League, which advertises itself as the largest hockey league in the world. If it is not, it is at least the most complicated.

CHL teams are spread over eight Canadian provinces and four U.S. states (Michigan, Washington, Pennsylvania and Oregon). A few teams are in big markets such as Toronto, Ottawa, Seattle and Calgary. (The Plymouth Whalers, for whom Jesse played, are a suburban Detroit franchise.) The heart of the CHL beats loudest, though, in small towns, places like Kamloops and Kitchener and Kelowna; Lethbridge and Medicine Hat; Moose Jaw, Swift Current and Victoriaville; Brampton, Belleville and Guelph.

Players between the ages of 16 and 20 are eligible, but the bulk of the CHL is made up of kids 17, 18 and 19. These are most of the best young players in North America. They are drafted (yes, drafted) out of the regional or divisional minors at 15 or 16. In western Canada they can be drafted at 14. That's why scouts start tracking these kids in utero. According to CHL figures, 70 percent of the NHL's coaches and 65 percent of its players graduated from the Major Junior system, including Gretzky, Lindros and Lemieux.

Young as they are, these kids may move thousands of miles to join their new teams. Billeted with local families, they carry a full high school schedule while playing more than 60 games a year (not counting playoffs) in front of crowds that often exceed the population of a team's home town. They practice almost every day. For this they receive room and board and a stipend of about 45 bucks a week. If they choose to continue their schooling after the CHL, the teams provide for that, too. CHL folks are very proud of the league's record in educating players, and they resist no opportunity to define Major Junior hockey as a largely educational enterprise.

Upside, players are being scouted by almost every team in the NHL almost every night they play. Downside, it's tough to finish that book report on *Ivanhoe* during a seven-hour overnight bus ride.

Upside, every team has an educational counselor. Downside, it's likely to have a boxing coach, too.

Upside, players become local celebrities. Downside, they might miss the prom because they've been traded.

Upside, players wear the best equipment money can buy. Downside, they need it.

Upside, this is their best chance to make it to the NHL. Downside, only one in hundreds ever does.

The CHL boasts season attendance of more than 6 million and pumps nearly $200 million into the Canadian economy every year. The league has more than 1,800 employees. It supervises more than 1,900 games annually. It has a comprehensive new four-year television package to broadcast games regionally and nationally. Again, this is amateur hockey, not to be confused with professional hockey. In pro hockey the pay's better. And there's no homework.

Uh-oh, Canada

Any character-building system this elaborate and profitable involving young people — children — is going to have critics. Major Junior hockey has plenty. Every decade or so Canada undertakes to reform its national game. Generally this involves a series of scathing editorials in newspapers and some self-loathing rhetoric in magazines. Canadians bemoan the state of the grand old game for a few months, rending their garments and tearing at their hair. Then the two-line pass rule is modified, and everyone heaves a grateful sigh and shuts up.

Whereas in the past it was the quality of the game and the players that engendered those cyclical reexaminations, now it is the nature of the system in which the game is learned and played that is coming under scrutiny. The Graham James sexual abuse scandal in 1996 arrived just in time for one of hockey's 10-year checkups, and the stakes went way up. For those who don't remember, Graham James was a Major Junior coach convicted of serial sexual assaults on Sheldon Kennedy, who later made it to the NHL. (In the space of one week last October, James was released to a halfway house on parole and Kennedy entered rehab for substance abuse.)

The most immediate fallout from the James case was a hurried investigation of the CHL *by* the CHL that was later criticized as a whitewash. But the investigation — and the events that precipitated it — stirred Canada to take a long look at every aspect of the business of Major Junior hockey. Toronto's *Globe and Mail* published a four-part series scalding the CHL for its win-at-any-price philosophy. It referred to the players as "slaves to a junior hockey monopoly that is run by a gang of buccaneers who would do Blackbeard proud." The systematized violence of junior hockey and the intractable code of silence surrounding it were also roundly denounced. Its editorial pages recommended scrapping the junior draft and remaking the entire development system. In addition to being morally unsound and Dickensian, it was, worse yet, not turning out very good hockey players. (The number of Canadian players in the NHL has been going down steadily, so Canada is losing gold medals *and* jobs to players from Europe whose names read like bad Scrabble racks.) The *Globe and Mail* also asserted that verbal, emotional and physical abuse of players occurred because "the Canadian Hockey League structure demanded that you keep your mouth shut and do as you were told. Anyone who did otherwise — and to this day, anyone who does otherwise — in Tier I junior hockey in Canada risks never playing again. Period."

Laura Robinson's 1998 book, *Crossing the Line: Violence and Sexual Assault in Canada's National Sport,* has also been brewing up rancor with its delineation of drinking, brawling, hazing and sexual assault throughout junior hockey. "Violence is the vocabulary" of the game, Robinson says. In November, *Maclean's,* Canada's leading newsweekly, ran a piece slugged "Thugs on Ice" that looked hard at the manly traditions of goonism and the quick fist.

Off the record you'll hear plenty of horror stories about a *Lord of the Flies* hierarchy that prevails on and off the ice. The entire system seems pressurized by a get-tough-or-get-out Darwinism. And it is druidically secretive. "These kids are terrified," says one leading agent who knows Canadian junior hockey, "but they learn never to say anything to anyone about it." Jesse Boulerice may be from upstate New York, but he is entirely a product of this Canadian system.

Major Junior hockey still thrives because it is part of the golden mythology of Canada. For generations it has been a way to rise above a lifetime of bucking bales at the grain elevator in Wakopa or Assiniboia or Cut Knife. It is the rural equivalent of boxing or ghetto basketball, a ticket out. And it inspires as much false hope. But even mythology changes when it has to. Major Junior hockey is under a cloud right now, under the microscope, under the gun. Any business with that many metaphors ganging up on it is in trouble.

What Those Last 2,732 Words Add Up To

Andrew and Jesse still want more than anything else to play in the NHL.

Why Fighting Is Still Allowed in Hockey

It is by definition a violent sport. Apologists for the game say that fighting acts as a safety valve, preventing other, more serious expressions of frustration with sticks or skates. "They're always saying that," says Kevin Young, a sports sociologist at the University of Calgary, "but I'd like to see the study that proves it. There isn't one."

When asked in a recent Internet poll by the OHL if fighting should be banned from hockey, more than 85 percent of respondents said no. Unscientific, but perhaps indicative.

Fighting is a leading cause of injury in the NHL. It is also a great tradition.

Clichés Make the Man . . .

Andrew is referred to as a "skills" player, a "finesse" player. Jesse is regarded as a "physical" player, a player with "some skills," a player "who sticks up for his teammates" (no pun intended).

. . . and Numbers Don't Lie

In four seasons at Guelph, Andrew played in 189 regular-season games. He scored 48 goals and had 92 assists. He accumulated 96 penalty minutes. In three seasons at Plymouth, Jesse played 150 games. He scored 32 goals and had 42 assists. He had 529 penalty minutes.

Things You Might Not Expect

Jesse turned down a chance to attend Brown to play in the OHL. He played on two U.S. World Junior teams. He is a regular church-goer. His favorite television show is *Jeopardy!*

Things You'd Never Expect

Jesse and Andrew seem like nice young men with a lot in common. Both are right-handed forwards. Both are polite in conversation. No brag or swagger in them — like sitting next to the deacon's son at a box social. Both are tall and move with the space-creating assurance that characterizes professional athletes. The two have similar features and share a smudged sort of handsomeness. Despite his injuries, Andrew's face is still the more smoothly engineered. Jesse's face is all broad angles and worried planes. Pale in the sick-room way that only fictional Victorian heroines and real-life hockey players are pale, each young man has wavy hair; Andrew's is black, Jesse's brown. Andrew has hazel eyes and a big, terrific smile. Jesse hasn't smiled much lately. His eyes are blue. Jesse and Andrew were born on the same day: August 10, 1978.

Each has a steady girlfriend. Both enjoy video games. Jesse is crazy about golf and plays whenever he can. Andrew enjoys golf too and is starting to play more often. (They are much longer off the tee than you are.) Each has one sibling and two parents at home. Both young men were selected in the fifth round of the 1996 NHL draft. Andrew went 129th, to the Florida Panthers; Jesse went four choices later, to the Philadelphia Flyers.

People speak highly of them, both as players and as young men. They seem never to have been properly introduced.

They also have in common the fact that each, directly or indi-rectly, may have shortened or destroyed the other's career. Both suffer troubling thoughts about the future. And there must be times, maybe before the morning skate, or after dinner, or late at night, balanced on the dark edge of sleep, when they hate each other with a purity and purpose you couldn't begin to understand.

Plymouth and Guelph

Plymouth, where Jesse played, is about 25 miles west of Detroit. Downtown Plymouth is as small and neat as a hatbox, with gift shops and bookstores and a restored Art Deco movie theater. The Compuware Sports Arena is on the western edge of town. It is nearly new, and the money that went into it shows. There is a land-scaped pond out front, and you can reach one of the arena's en-trances by a bridge that swans across the water. Inside there are two rinks and a nice restaurant. The 4,300-seat rink where the Whalers play is bright and open and has four suites. There are a couple of brightly painted concession stands that look like the kind you'd stop at for a four-dollar hot dog on the Universal Studios tour.

The team draws a youngish crowd, enthusiastic, with plenty of puck bunnies: high-school-age girls wearing cocktail-party makeup. During breaks, the PA system plays the same deafening rock-and-roll snippets you hear at big league games. The whole thing is like a one-quarter-scale rendering of an NHL arena.

The Guelph Memorial Gardens in Ontario, where Andrew played, is a half-century-old barn of a place, like a zeppelin hangar with a rink in it. It is downtown, across from the Black Stallion Saloon and Acker's Furniture. The training area is in the oldest part of the building; one wall is whitewashed stone. (Players must feel as if they're lifting weights in a root cellar.) Up in the rafters, in the dark, is a banner from the 1951–52 Biltmore Mad Hatters of the old Ontario Hockey Association. This rink is the one where, some say, the phrase *hat trick* was born. The banner may make the trip across the street to a proposed new 5,500-seat arena.

The crowd in Guelph is older than the one in Plymouth: lots of former players, guys thick through the hams and hunkers, with graying crew cuts that look as if they were done with a belt sander. One codger spends the night roaring like Lear whenever a fight breaks out. He's as deaf as a post, but he knows what he likes. Amid the cowbells and the great farting horns, the PA plays the same denatured rock, but you can't hear it; the sound system isn't very good, so the canned excitement dissipates into the rafters like smoke.

Newmarket and Mooers

Newmarket, Ontario, is a northern suburb of Toronto. The Longs have lived there for 10 years, in a two-story brick house with blue trim dropped onto rolling farmland. David and Brenda Long share the house with Ryan, Andrew's older brother, and Rudy, a schnauzer. Andrew's bedroom, at the top of the stairs to the right, is pretty much as it was when he left home to play Major Junior hockey. There is a bunk bed along one wall, and next to it are shelves that hold many of the plaques and trophies he has accumulated. He was on skates for the first time when he was four.

David and Brenda are in their early fifties. Brenda works part-time in publishing, and David is the president of several professional associations. David is a good-looking man, gone a bit gray at the temples. Brenda is a blonde, pretty woman who gets animated when she talks about what happened to Andrew. David grew up in the same neighborhood as Ken Dryden, a Hall of Fame goalie for the Montreal Canadiens and now the president and general manager of the Maple Leafs. They used to play a little hockey together and are still friendly.

Sitting in their kitchen, you begin to understand what all of this has done to them. "Andrew was nearly killed," says Brenda, "and Boulerice gets to go right on skating? It's not fair." The kitchen table is covered with newspaper clips and Internet downloads about the incident. David and Brenda both look tired. There have been a lot of interviews and phone calls and conversations since the assault last April. It's late. "I've never seen anything like this," David says. "He took two hands and swung his stick into Andrew's face."

Do they want to see Jesse go to jail? Brenda answers. "No," she says, as though measuring the word, "but somebody should take his hockey away from him for at least a year."

On the big-screen TV in the den, David plays the video of that night. He has seen it many times. He talks until the moment Andrew gets hit; then he is silent. A few seconds later he says, "I'll never get used to that." Brenda is still in the kitchen. Brenda still hasn't seen the tape. She can't bring herself to watch it.

It's late when you leave, when you've heard all their stories about the distant tournaments and the driving and the many successes and the rare failures. About how happy and jokey a kid Andrew is, and about the grind of trying to get organized hockey to pay attention to what was done to him.

Mooers is in the northernmost corner of New York State, only 40 miles south of Montreal. It is farther north than Toronto and Guelph and Plymouth. Like lots of rural towns, Mooers is just a few tattered businesses laid out at a crossroads — the A&L Cafe and Monette's Furniture and Dragoon Farm Equipment. The Boulerices have lived outside Mooers for 19 years, in a trim white farmhouse. It's pretty country, dotted with dairy farms. You can see the Adirondacks rolling away to the southwest.

Mike and Lisette Boulerice share the house with Marie, Jesse's younger sister. Jesse's bedroom, at the top of the stairs to the right, is much as it was when he moved to Plymouth to play Major Junior hockey. There's a low bed along one wall and a dresser and a few jerseys hanging in the corner. Leaning on their stocks next to the dresser are two shotguns that Mike and Jesse use when they go bird hunting. There are no trophies or medals; those are across the hall in a little attic space. There is also a letter in there from some local schoolkids saying that Jesse is their favorite hockey player.

Mike and Lisette are in their forties. They celebrated their 23rd anniversary on Valentine's Day. Lisette works for a commodities company that handles grain. Mike works for the highway department, doing roadwork and plowing snow. He takes extra work doing construction and welding when he has time. The Boulerices used to run the 148-acre farm as a dairy operation, with 60 cows, but they had to sell out a few years ago. "You can't go 15 years just breaking even every year," Mike explains. They kept the land.

Lisette is a pretty blonde who still has Quebec French in her voice. Mike has curly brown hair. He is meaty through the chest and shoulders, like most farmers. He gets agitated when he talks about their son's impending trial but doesn't always have the words to express his feelings.

Sitting in their kitchen, you begin to understand what all this has done to them. "We think it was a terrible thing," says Mike, "but this kid has had no trouble with the law *whatever*." Mike and Lisette both look tired. There has been a lot of bad press about all this and a lot of talk around town. "You really find out who your friends are," Mike says. Lisette says she has tried to talk to Jesse about that night, "but he doesn't say much, just keeps it all inside."

What would they say to the Longs if they had the chance? Mike knits up his face and says, "We're sorry, I guess — we're just so. . . . I wish we could just get in a room and talk to them. . . ." Tears well.

"How sorry we are," adds Lisette.

It is nearly midnight. You've heard all the stories: Jesse driving a tractor when he was eight, putting in a full workday like a hired man. How he started hockey late, at 10, and practiced out front shooting into a goal Mike welded up himself; about what a good kid he was and is, and how nobody here can make sense of this. How hard he worked to overcome his late start. How tough he had to make himself.

You walk out into a night so dark you can't see the keys in your hand to unlock the car, and you remember what Mike said about driving back from the arraignment in Plymouth: "You cry all the way home. Nine hours. Then you get home, and you cry some more."

The Time Line, Part I

Jesse's stick was most likely traveling between 50 and 75 mph when the heel of it slammed into Andrew's face. It probably crashed into that little groove that runs from your nose to your upper lip. Doctors and dictionaries call it the philtrum. The blade of the stick bowed Andrew's face shield back into his nose, cutting him, but the shield didn't shatter. Remarkably, neither did Andrew's teeth, although he wasn't wearing a mouthpiece. The blow fractured his nose and his right cheek and a small bone tucked away inside his sinuses. It opened three cuts under his nose, the longest of which ran laterally and was the length of a tall man's little finger. The force of the blow may have slammed Andrew's brain into the front of his skull, because the contusion that the doctors found on the brain was just behind the forehead. Or the bruise may have occurred when Andrew fell and the back of his head hit the ice, his brain sloshing forward in his skull on the rebound. He was knocked unconscious.

Shane Mabey, the Guelph Storm trainer, got to Andrew first. "I knew he was in serious trouble," Mabey says. "When I got back there behind the net, he was curled up in the fetal position and in seizure." After kneeling to assess Andrew's condition, Mabey jumped up and beckoned team doctors onto the ice. The paramedics in attendance were taken under the arms by players, lifted and literally skated out from the bench.

Getting knocked cold slows bleeding, so until Andrew regained consciousness, it was mostly a matter of making sure that he was breathing and that there was no spinal injury. When he came to, though, the bleeding from the broken nose and the facial lacerations started in earnest. "I had to have my equipment guy wipe my face off three times, because every time Andrew breathed out he was blowing a lot of blood," says Mabey. "I had blood all over me. He was sort of blowing it out like a whale. Two feet in the air."

Head trauma is often characterized by disorientation and agitation. Andrew experienced plenty of both for the next 20 minutes. "He didn't really know what we were trying to do for him," says Mabey. "We had to hold him down to work on him." Six men couldn't keep Andrew still enough to get an oxygen mask on him or start an IV. He was screaming and swearing in the sold-out, now silent arena. "He was yelling 'f — a lot," says Mabey.

By this time the refs had skated Jesse off the ice with a match penalty for attempting to injure another player. He went to the locker room.

A fan who witnessed the incident and wrote a letter offering to testify in any case that might proceed from it said, "Parents were grabbing the many young children to remove them from the sight." Several Guelph players admit to having cried on the bench that night, no small thing in what is often described as the toughest league in hockey. "We knew it was bad when the coach went out on the ice," one player said. "Coach never goes out on the ice."

Andrew remembers only shards of this.

Andrew's parents were at home in Newmarket. In their bedroom they listened to all this being described on the radio.

The Time Line, Part II

It took several minutes to get Andrew stabilized and restrained on a backboard, to put a cervical collar around his neck and wheel him off the ice. By the time Mabey saw him put in the ambulance, play had resumed. The trainer went into the Plymouth dressing room to clean up. "I looked around and saw that Jesse was sitting beside me," Mabey says. "He was in his underwear. He was crying. My clothes were all covered in blood. I remember him saying he didn't mean to hurt him."

With lights and siren it was a 12-minute ride down to St. Joseph Mercy Hospital in Ypsilanti. Andrew arrived there Friday night around 8:30. Mabey got there around 11:30 and spent the night. When Mabey arrived, Andrew's parents had been called and told what to expect, and Andrew had been stitched and scanned and tested and was out of immediate danger.

Jesse left the arena, perhaps on the advice of the Whalers' staff, and went back to his billet. He changed clothes and met up with his teammates a few hours later for what had become a somber season-ending party. (Plymouth had lost the game and was done for the year.) Jesse was still upset. According to Robert Esche, a Whalers goalie and Jesse's best friend, "He felt really bad about it. It's not like he planned it or anything."

Andrew's parents arrived the next morning, and Jesse was still asking his coach if he could go to the hospital to apologize to Andrew. He was told not to, that the Longs were too upset. He called Andrew instead. That didn't go well. Neither of them remembers exactly what was said, but it wasn't enough.

By Sunday the 19th, Andrew was ready to be released. His performance on the neurological observation flow sheets and Glasgow Coma Scale tests was nearly normal, and CAT scans revealed that the bruising to his brain had stabilized. He was told not to play any contact sports for three months and to have his own doctors monitor his condition. His parents took him home to Canada, where he spent a lot of time on the couch watching TV and eating pasta one strand at a time. The long-term prognosis was good.

Andrew visited his teammates a few times as they made their postseason run at the championship. He cracked some jokes in the locker room, led stretching exercises and saw how his mates all touched his jersey, which hung by the door, for inspiration on their way out to the ice. While watching them play, however, Andrew got very worried. "The game was so fast, so confusing, I couldn't really follow it," he says. "It didn't seem like I'd ever played it."

There is a newspaper photo from an appearance Andrew made in Guelph about a week after he was hit. The crowd has just given him a standing ovation. He is smiling as best he can, but the face in the picture looks like a pillowcase full of doorknobs.

On May 6, 1998, the OHL, saying that Jesse Boulerice had "used his stick in a most alarming and unacceptable fashion," suspended him for one year. It meant that he could not return to the league, which he was unlikely to do in any case, since he would move up to the American Hockey League at the start of the following season. It was the most the OHL could do under the circumstances. The OHL has refused further comment on the decision.

On May 17 the Guelph Storm lost in the 80th Annual Memorial Cup Tournament to the Portland Winter Hawks, 4–3 in overtime. According to former Storm coach George Burnett, Andrew, one of the team's leading scorers and playmakers, might have made the difference.

That same week AHL president, CEO and treasurer David Andrews ruled that Jesse would be suspended for the first month of the AHL season. Though the AHL and OHL are not affiliated, Andrews has been severely criticized for not honoring the junior league's one-year penalty. The assault "didn't happen in our league," Andrews has said, adding that there was a potential civil liability if his league interfered with Jesse's right to earn a living. "Under the circumstances, I'm comfortable with the decision." The AHL is the primary minor league for the NHL. The NHL has never formally commented on the Boulerice-Long matter.

During the last week of May, David Long called the Plymouth Township police department for instructions on how to file a criminal complaint. On June 4 Andrew Long filed a formal assault complaint against Jesse Boulerice. On July 6 a warrant for Jesse's arrest was issued by the Wayne County Prosecutors Office. On July 14 Jesse, accompanied by his parents, surrendered himself to Plymouth Township police. He was fingerprinted, and his mug shot was taken. Later that afternoon he was arraigned in 35th District Court and released on a $10,000 personal bond.

Over the summer Jesse was allowed to attend the Flyers' training camp. In the fall he joined their AHL affiliate, the Philadelphia Phantoms. He practiced with the team but was ineligible for game play until November 15.

Andrew's rehabilitation continued over the summer. He was able to cycle and work out, but he began skating again only in July. He played some shinny games, practiced with friends in Guelph and felt well enough to go to the Panthers' training camp in late summer. He joined their AHL affiliate, the Beast of New Haven, in the fall.

On August 17, five months to the day after he was hit in the face with that stick, Andrew took the stand in a preliminary hearing in Detroit to determine if the case would be brought to trial. Jesse and several of his Plymouth teammates were there, too, but they were not called to testify. Andrew identified Jesse as the man who hit him and testified that Jesse had called him the day after to apologize. The court's decision at the end of the hearing: "It is a question of fact that the crime was committed and probable cause exists to believe this Defendant committed the crime. He will be bound over."

A defense motion to dismiss the charges has been denied, and a trial could begin as early as this summer. Jesse has options that would avert a jury trial: alternative programs that allow for a lengthy probation but no jail time. But they would require a guilty plea, which is unacceptable to Jesse on principle and would increase his exposure in a civil lawsuit, even though the Longs express no interest in filing one. "This isn't about money" has been their assertion throughout.

Precedents in the criminal matter are hard to come by. Eleven years ago Minnesota North Stars winger Dino Ciccarelli spent a day in jail as part of a plea bargain for whacking Toronto Maple Leafs defenseman Luke Richardson in the neck with his stick. In 1969 Wayne Maki and Ted Green of the St. Louis Blues and the Boston Bruins, respectively, were both charged with assault when they went at each other with their sticks. Both were acquitted.

Sports and the law coexist uncomfortably in situations like this, the rules of one having little to do with the rules of the other. All that's required for a hung jury is one juror who watches the tape and thinks, It's just part of the game.

Jesse and Andrew

Trying to talk to Jesse about all this is frustrating. He is a quiet young man by nature, and his attorneys are present to make sure he stays that way. Questions about the incident are off-limits.

The programs list him at 6'2", 200 pounds, and he's every bit of that. He has huge hands — not much scarring on the knuckles yet — that he folds and unfolds while he talks. He freely admits to having made himself tough to get ahead in the game, but he is surprised how far all this has gone: "I never thought I'd be in trouble with the law for playing hockey." He sounds genuinely sorry that he hurt Andrew but seems determined to view it as an isolated incident, an aberration. Has the experience changed him or changed the way he plays the game? "No," he says, honest enough to give his real answer.

When Jesse skates hard, he is all ass and elbows, effort and angles. Off the puck, sizing up the play, he is as expressionless as a guy waiting for a bus. He is tough to get out of the crease, goes into corners as if he's got a lifetime gift certificate for chiropractic therapy and skates much bigger than he is. Splitting time between the Phantoms and the New Orleans Brass of the East Coast Hockey League, Jesse has amassed 120 penalty minutes in 36 games. The Flyers consider him to be one of their top prospects.

Andrew hasn't played much for the Beast of New Haven. Because it's affiliated with both the Panthers and the Carolina Hurricanes, the Beast roster is large for an AHL team, and ice time is scarce for first-year players. He has been loaned out twice to the Miami Matadors of the ECHL to get more ice time.

Andrew remains a very upright, fluid skater. At 6′3″ and 190 pounds, he is nearly willowy compared with some of the bruisers he skates against. He seems to be aware of everything in the offensive zone and sends passes where they need to be before you even see the opening for them. Good wrist shot, good slap shot, good nose for the goal. He is a playmaker and has, as they say, all the tools.

The game he's had to play against himself has been the toughest part. "I almost talk to myself about it, just kind of convince myself that stuff like that can't happen again," he says of the Boulerice incident. "And I'm not worried about it happening again — it's just that . . . sometimes I ask myself, What if I take a big hit tonight? I try to say to myself, You gotta do it, because I want to play in the NHL. If I'm scared out there, I'm not going to make it."

Andrew's only ongoing medical concern is his concussion, so he wears a helmet with a little extra padding. It was his third concussion, and he's only 20 years old. When New York Rangers forward Pat LaFontaine retired last season because doctors said he couldn't risk another major concussion, he'd had five. He was 33 years old. The Panthers have been patient with Andrew and foresee no special problems in his development as an NHL player.

Does Andrew want to see Jesse go to jail? "I don't care to see him go to jail," he says. "What I really, really want — and I talked to the prosecutor about this — is for there to be a precedent, some sort of serious probation, and for him never to be able to lift his stick, or do something even *remotely* close to that on the ice. Anything even close to that, like an 'attempt to injure' penalty, and he's gone. Never play again. Playing in this game and not being able to bring his stick up when guys are coming at him would be punishment enough."

What It All Means, Part II

This is a sports story in which nobody wins. The final reckoning won't fit in a box on the sports page or add up clean in the mathematics of a nightly highlight show.

Stories like this drag too many questions behind them. What was turning in the heart and mind of Jesse Boulerice on the night of April 17? Was there criminal intent? Or was it simply iron-man hockey? Does the tape show Jesse sliding his hands up the stick? Did he shift his weight to get a lumberjack's leverage on the swing? And how do you differentiate this act, other than by its terrifying result, from 1,000 other unseen moments in that same game, the many small, subtle acts of enthusiastic violence that hockey prizes? What is most surprising about the Jesse Boulerice–Andrew Long matter is not that it happened, but that it doesn't happen more often.

And when it does happen, who bears responsibility? What about the hockey factories that tirelessly promote themselves as "quality organizations" and "builders of character"? If what they manufacture short circuits, should they not be held accountable? They're always eager to talk in the euphemisms of risk, of "role players" skating close to "the edge." But when they lose a kid, when the edge crumbles and he falls, you won't hear a word. The code of silence won't allow it, and locker-room signage is sparse on the topic of regret. Players spend years in junior hockey practicing to do things right. How much time is spent learning to do the right thing? Is Jesse Boulerice, then, a criminal or simply the product of his elite education?

And what about us, you and me, fat and happy as a couple of whorehouse bedbugs up in the seats in our souvenir jerseys, spilling our beer and screaming for brain matter whenever two guys drop the gloves? How much responsibility do we bear?

Hall of Famer Ken Dryden knows better than most: "We love to turn up the temperature, in part because it means that we go off into territory we've never been as players, and it's exciting to be where you've never been. The problem is, where you've never been may be where you shouldn't be.

"Whether it's the motivation of the coach, the chanting of the crowd, the taunting of the crowd, the rhythm of the music inside the arena — all of those things are intended to pitch the emotions higher and higher and higher . . . and then, when something really dumb happens, we sort of step back and say, 'You fool, how could you allow that to happen?' Then we shake our heads and walk away."

And something terrible has happened.

ALLISON GLOCK

Touch of Knievel

FROM GQ

EVEN THOUGH Sault Sainte Marie, Michigan, borders majestic Lake Superior, the Kewadin Casino and Hotel slumps pitiably just off Shunk Road on an arid lot boxed by an RV park, a rehab center, a Head Start facility and a convenience store. Inside the hotel, the lobby flooring has been scuffed by the wheels of portable oxygen tanks, which are being pulled behind every other patron like luggage. The rooms are sparsely furnished, and there is no cable. There is only the casino, heavy on slots, the buffet restaurant and the bar, where Kaptain Robbie Knievel is slouched, drinking a Jack and Diet Coke.

He will knock back several before it's all done. He's pissed, see, because although he is in Michigan in July to attempt to set a world record by soaring his motorcycle more than 235 feet in the air over a bevy of semis, the tribal council that runs the Kewadin Casino isn't paying him his jump fee. It has advertised the event. The life-size cardboard cutout of Robbie in his red-white-and-blue leather jumpsuit is propped in the lobby, in front of the platform show-casing his extra red-white-and-blue motorcycles, but the council won't come off the coin. And Robbie doesn't suit up without the money in his pocket.

"Jumping is my meaning in life," he says, lighting a cigarette. "It's natural. It's what I love to do most. But," he pauses, exhales, "I won't do it without the cash."

He signals the waitress for another round. "You get older and the jumps become more about the mental than the physical. I'm 36. I've been jumping motorcycles for 29 years, so mentally I can overcome what I need to," he snorts, laughs. "But this sucks. Nobody knows what it's like to do what I do, to be in my shoes."

He used to perform at tractor pulls when he started, triple-billed behind jacked-up monster trucks roaring in slop and rednecks butting bumpers in the demolition derby. He would be hopped-up or hungover — these were the crazy times, before he cleaned up his act and narrowed in on one path of potential self-destruction. Now Robbie gets his thrills from wheels alone. He's not a lunatic anymore. He wants to settle down with a nice girl, follow God's word and maybe sail over the Snake River Canyon just once. As daredevils go, he's very mature.

"I'm not afraid of death. I want to live forever. And I believe I will. Really, my only competitor is death," he growls playfully, "and I'm gonna nail his ass!"

To understand the son, you must first know the father. It has always been thus, and is especially so when the father is Evel Knievel, the P. T. Barnum of daredevilry, a man who single-handedly created an industry by charging folks to come watch him play Russian roulette. Evel earned millions hurling himself over trucks and canyons and livestock, sniggering and waving his ass at the bulging eyes of death.

"My father was real good at being an American hero," says Robbie. And for a time Evel was the biggest, becoming more recognizable than the president, his dolls outselling GI Joe, his squinchy face adorning everything from toothbrushes to pinball machines. George Hamilton played him in a 1971 feature film, while in real life he made himself an idol via outrageous behavior, either as a human shuttlecock or as the nation's no-horseshit bad boy. He once served six months for clubbing a former publicist with a baseball bat. Three years earlier, he had made the cover of *Rolling Stone*.

Evel hit his apex in 1974, when he tried to ride his Skycycle X-2 over the Snake River Canyon in Idaho, a flight that was ingloriously aborted when his parachute opened prematurely. It was one of the highest-rated shows ever on *ABC's Wide World of Sports*. By 1975 there wasn't a child jumping curbs in any cul-de-sac in the U.S.A. who didn't pretend he was Evel Knievel.

"When I was growing up in Butte, Montana, I never knew how famous he was," says Robbie. "I didn't realize until I was 11, and then all of a sudden the trailer house turned into three yachts, Lear jets, a vacation home in Florida on the water. We were partying with movie stars and athletes. We were on the road every month."

When Robbie was born, Evel was in jail in Twin Falls, Idaho, for speeding. When Robbie started jumping, Evel imploded. "My dad said I was a better rider than him when I was 15, but he never wanted to move over. He still doesn't want to move over. I left home because he wouldn't let me jump more than ten vans."

So at 16 Robbie rented a $60-a-month hole and spent his days working on motorcycles and his jumps. He already had his own doll — Robbie Knievel: Teen-age Stuntman — but that was a gift of heritage, and when Robbie left the umbrella of Evel, he had to start over, to build his own fame train. The athletes and the movie-star friends disappeared, along with the boats and the jets, till all that remained was the jumps.

"My dad trained me. It's easy when you make a kid drink Wild Turkey and beat him with a cane." Robbie laughs. "The first time he ever taught me to ride a motorcycle, he tied a rope around me and put me in a ditch on a minibike. He used the rope because if you get paranoid, you grab a handful of the throttle. So with the rope he could yank me off." Robbie runs his palm over his hair. "See, my dad loved us — me, my older brother, Kelly, my younger sister Tracey and the youngest, Alicia. He was proud of his sons. Then I started jumping, and he got a little pissed off."

Robbie looks like his father. He has the same improbably petite nose, the same attenuated upper lip. But he is softer, handsomer. His skin is flushed, pink, babylike. His gray-brown hair curls above his T-shirt collar in the back and is vigorously brushed off his forehead in the front. His chest balloons. His jeans strain. Chicks peck after him, like they did his father. Some swoon.

Now 60, Evel is broken up and craggy, his bones melded stiffer and sharper than plywood. His last jump was with Robbie in 1980 in Hollywood, Florida. Now Evel lives with his 27-year-old girlfriend in Clearwater, Florida, where he's recovering from a recent liver transplant.

"I love my dad," Robbie says wearily. "I spent so many years hating him because he was jealous of me in a way. But he loved us. He's my dad."

But know this, too. Know this most of all. Though Robbie is, like his father before him, a one-man sideshow, earning his wage jumping trucks for bucks, Kaptain Robert Edward Knievel is named after his grandfather. "I'm a second," he stresses. "Which is good, because I never wanted to be a junior anyway."

The thing about daredevils is they are never alone. They have groupies — men and women who find their way to every jump, men and women who want to get a taste of a man who is not sleepwalking through life, hands extended into the black to break his fall. Daredevils also bring their team, the crew that constructs the ramps, lubes the bikes and relives the past with vigor. They eat together, drink together, carouse; it's a never-ending stag party where the men adore the groom with a ferocious intensity usually reserved for lovers.

For Kaptain Knievel, the posse includes Joe Little, the ramp builder, a man who looks like a Native American Sonny Bono and who wears an unflagging grin and 79-cent sunglasses. There's J. D., the pyro guy, and his corps of fire starters, who routinely blow up enough heat to shake a stadium. And Fred Bezark, the Knievels' attorney, who, with his shock of white hair and thick build, projects the solemn vibe of a man who eats shit storms for breakfast. Also in regular attendance are the Fox TV crew and producers, who discovered last Fourth of July that "the name Knievel still kills in the demos" and who are therefore on hand to record every jump — and perhaps its bloody aftermath.

And then there is Bill Rundle, the linchpin of Team Knievel since 1975. "I met Robbie when he was a kid. He used to come out to the racetrack in Butte and watch," explains Bill, who was himself a jumper. "We've been together ever since."

Though short, Bill cuts an imposing silhouette. His arms hang six inches from his sides at all times, as if he's waiting to draw a pistol and speed a level adios to whatever irritant is buzzing in his atmosphere. On his left hand, he wears a gold-and-diamond ring the size of a palmetto bug. It's a motorcycle studded with stones, a gift from Evel. On his right hand, he sports a smaller ring, gold too, a gift from Robbie. They weigh heavily on his fingers.

"I put them on for jumps," he explains. Bill was Evel's chief mechanic. Now he's Robbie's. He tunes the bike by listening to it, straining to detect disaster in the cackle of the engine.

"I hear every little thing. I hear all kinds of stuff other people don't. I'm always listening to it. You always have two thoughts," he explains: *"I hope I didn't leave anything out* and *Imagine if the bike seized.* I don't want to see him miss the landing. So I go over the ramp. Jump up and down on it, check for nails. This is for real. This guy's pulling the trigger. He's risking his life. People don't understand that this may be the last thing he ever does."

Bill understands all too well. He's seen jumps come unhinged and riders end up in wheelchairs for life, watched as friends have been thrown to tomorrow, heads severed, limbs collapsed like telescopes. He's watched Robbie skitter like a Frisbee over yards of pavement, seen him bleed plenty, seen the angel of death nodding toward the exit sign and waved him off.

"I come to make things go smooth," he says modestly. "Robbie and me, we're like brothers. I know him better than anybody. He relies on that. The older we get, the harder it is to do this. Take a look at the ramps. Four feet wide. Ten feet high. Imagine hitting it at 95 mph. It scares the hell out of you."

The waiter at Abner's Restaurant won't be coming to the Kewadin Kaptain Knievel jump: "With Evel, he'd jump and crash, like that time at the Grand Canyon or whatever it was. He broke every bone in his body. With Robbie you get to see him break another record. Who cares? It'd be more exciting if he crashed. That's what people want to see."

Once, years ago, after a smashup, Evel and a young Robbie were in the ambulance together, Evel with IVs jammed in his veins, clothes cut open, skin bubbling up, blood underneath.

"Look at me, son," he said. "Look at me good. Never do this. Never do this."

Robbie said nothing.

"I was deaf as a child."

Here's how it works. The members of Team Knievel descend on a jump site about ten days before takeoff. They suss out the landscape, erect the needed ramps, park their trucks, wire the pyro, frequent the bars. They spend their days in the parking lots and on the fairgrounds where the jumps usually happen. They spend their evenings living hard, like it's the last chance they'll have to be together, which it could be. There is a constant awareness of the end. To hell with the rapture, they say, we got ourselves a doomsday every month.

"You know, nobody really knows what doing this is like," Robbie says. "And the drinking, the smoking — it kind of goes along with the package. The eighties were kind of wild. I don't do drugs anymore. But I indulged. I tried things." Now Robbie has replaced the candy with Christ. He has, as friends attest, given himself over to the Lord.

"Now I'm a believer," he chortles, coughs. "Do I have a choice?"

Robbie leaps sober, shaking at the extremities, a man of Jesus adhering to the word. And when you watch him launch into the blue, chin tucked, wheels spinning, in the hush of your held breath, in the intermission of your heartbeat, you pray, too. And you feel as keenly as you ever have that God is in the details.

When he can, Robbie gives interviews, does radio and local news, chats about positive risk taking and how he's only "doing what he does best. Isn't that what everybody wants?" How "no harm can ever come from telling the truth." How on the takeoff site he says, "Hey, God, watch this!"

Eventually, the fans show up. Families, couples, teens with hardons for speed. He has regulars: the Beauchamp brothers, who travel to every jump, tape it with their camcorders and later send the videocassettes to Robbie, even though he's told them, nicely, "I never want to see myself jump again. I can still picture every one of them in my head — know what I mean?" Then there are Terry and Karen, thirty-somethings from Ohio who drive to as many events as they can: Green Bay, Wisconsin; Vegas; the Iowa state fairgrounds. When they arrive at the jump site, they hang around waiting to help. Sometimes Joe lets them paint and sand the ramp.

Robbie embraces them all. Even those he doesn't know too well. Even those who don't volunteer to paint the ramp. What other celebrities consider stalking, Robbie labels loyalty. And when the same faces bob enough outside his trailer window, he doesn't escort them away; he hands them VIP passes.

Today the bobber is wearing cutoffs, strappy sandals and a crop top. She checks her hair in one of the motorcycle mirrors. She strokes the fuel tank with a French-manicured finger.

"You like it?" Robbie asks. He jumps from his trailer wearing his trademark jean shorts, white Reeboks and T-shirt.

"Like it?" she gasps. "I *looovvve* it." She stands back, hands on her hips, belly sucked in. Her long earrings rattle in the breeze like wind chimes.

"Maybe later I'll take you for a ride," Robbie says as he towels down the bike.

"*Greaaaattt,*" she answers, flipping her long auburn hair. She turns to go, then spots a slew of other female fans waiting outside the security fence, many with ball caps in hand to be signed, many with crunchy blonde hair and similarly strappy sandals. She decides to wait, encamping near the Team Knievel truck. Bill rolls his eyes.

Not that you can blame her. How many people get to say they rode with a Knievel? Got to press their pelvises hard against his back while he slammed the throttle until time bent at the corners? Because when you ride at 100 miles per hour uncovered, air smacking your cheeks like a wet belt, sound amplifies. You feel your connective tissue vibrate. You think about nothing. You forget to swallow. Then it stops. And the world never seems more still.

"Once Robbie took this reporter for a ride and she peed her pants," says Bill. "She had to do the whole interview with her legs pressed shut."

Robbie is back in the Kewadin Casino bar, hunched over his ashtray, draining cocktails as if they were Kool-Aid. There is only one day to go, and Kewadin management is still hemming over the delivery of the cash. There's some snafu. Some fiscal misunderstanding. Promises are made almost hourly, then broken. Robbie is growing perturbed.

"I can't believe it," he mutters, all hangdog confusion. "How am I supposed to psych myself up?" He shakes his head, smiles. "I'm gonna go call my lawyer. I'm gonna go do something." And he exits, tramping out the door.

How does a daredevil walk? Like he doesn't give a damn. Like his balls are unhappy being stuffed into a tight denim pouch. Like if he doesn't get where he's going, it doesn't much matter, because he's been there a thousand times before — when he's airborne, you know, taking wing and the petty ticker tape of his life is unwinding fast and he knows this could be it, game over, and then he hits the landing ramp and his whole body compresses like a wrung sponge, including his vertebrae, including his intestines, including his brain — and so who really gives a rat's about how he travels on foot, least of all him, because, Holy Mother of God, when he wants to, he can fly.

Robbie eats and drinks the same way he walks. He even smokes without affectation. The only time his vocation becomes evident is when he drives, which he does as if he's wearing a bridle, speeding in spits, gunning the engine to 95 miles per hour, then releasing the pedal. Heel to the floor, then nothing. It is not relaxing.

His verbal cadence mirrors the driving style. He will shout a Journey lyric, hoot and holler, then he will mumble under his breath, out of the side of his mouth. It's because of the song he hears in his head. His own never-ending sound track. The effervescent grumble of motorcycles, the squeals of children, the screams of fans, the explosions, the screech of melted tires, the simultaneous gasp of 20,000 people, the galvanizing symphony of life at the edge of the world.

He can't turn it off. No matter how many voices he surrounds himself with, it's always there, the hum of possibility, the law of averages, the improbability of surviving a career as a human missile, of retiring as a walking, talking member of society, as a man without a wheelchair. It whirs just beneath his skin, waiting to puncture through and speed him, surge, purge straight to the gates. It is not relaxing.

"I once spent 45 days at a juvenile detention center for robbing a music store," says Robbie, under his breath. "They did Rorschach tests, all kinds of therapy. They found me to be completely normal." He laughs — the very idea. And then, articulating only the backfire of a truncated rant he doesn't share, he says, "Extreme sports, my ass."

Freighters Restaurant looks out over the St. Mary's River. Robbie likes to go there when he's in town for jumps. "It's nice," he explains, "for Sault Sainte Marie." The menu features prime rib, and although Robbie swears he's on a diet of Jack and Slim Fast, prime rib is what he orders, with a gravy boat of horseradish.

Like his father, Robbie is a clown. He tries hard. Like when the waitress comes and he asks her to sip his cocktail to make sure it's diet. She doesn't understand, so he tries again, with three more corny gags, one about O. J., but nothing.

"No one gets me," he says. "Doesn't matter where I am."

"Maybe you're just not funny," quips Bill.

"Like you'd know, fuckin' used-car salesman on Rogaine."

Bill laughs.

"One day back in Butte, I painted 'Evel Junior' on Robbie's old '66 Chevy," he says. "He got so mad, he painted it black. Then he tried to run it off a cliff."

Robbie changes the subject. "I had a girlfriend for seven years, but it recently ended. I'm accumulating friends now, and they're nice girls, but I'm picky. Relationships aren't like they used to be. It's not the *Leave It to Beaver* days anymore. The Devil's taken his stand with the world." He sips his drink. "When it comes to girls, I don't want nothing to do with you, I don't care how cute you are, I don't want to go to bed with you unless I want to wake up with you."

He pauses, mugs.

"Unless I'm real drunk."

He and Bill laugh. Bill's disintegrating into an improbable giggle.

"Seriously, I've always wanted a nice girl because I had a wonderful mother. She prays for me a lot. I help her with that. I say, 'Mom, there's meaning for me. When I die, I'm gonna go to Heaven. I'm gonna have a new body. I'm gonna live forever. So why do you get so upset? God's got a plan for all of us. You know the word.' You know, she's never been with another guy her whole life besides my dad."

Robbie stops, lights a cigarette.

"The whole family was hurt when my dad left ten years ago. It took me eight years just to forgive. But now I feel sorry for my dad. I feel sorry for him because he's dying."

After dinner, as he is leaving the restaurant, Robbie starts singing. It's a silly song, but he sings it straight, riding the notes high and low.

> You hear his name in every town.
> Is he for real or just a clown?
> Does he have wings, how does he fly?
> Is he a man like you and I?
> Everybody calls him Evel, Evel, Evel Knievel.

He starts laughing. "That's an old song came out in the seventies. I used to sing it in my bedroom as a kid." Bill nods.

"I'd never want my dad's life," Robbie says as he steps outside. "I know, because I lived it with him already."

The Kewadin prejump trailer is sparse. No cheese tray, no fridge full of bottled water. Robbie's leather suit is hanging off a cabinet knob. On the counter sits his opening speech, a scrawl on a torn square of cardboard. Robbie sits stiffly on a folding chair, smoking. J. D. is there, listening sympathetically as Robbie spits out a loose monologue about the folly of trust in the daredevil business.

"This sucks. It's got me all ticked off, but I'm trying to stay mellow. They still haven't paid me. They think I'm gonna go anyway, just because there are a few thousand people out there. But they're wrong. I did some practice runs. I didn't disappoint the kids."

"Yeah, that's true," says J. D.

"I can't wait to get this over with. They've screwed me for a year. I'm doing these guys a favor, that's what I'm doing."

"Yeah, that's true," says J. D.

"My dad taught me, and I learned. You get your money up front. These guys will screw you. They're morons. God love 'em."

"Yeah," says J. D.

"I want to feel good tomorrow. I want to feel good every damn day. I want to wake up without a hangover."

"I hear that."

There's a knock at the door. In comes a posse of Native American businessmen, led by the moron promoter. In his hand is a manila envelope stuffed thick. He nods at Robbie, tilts his head.

"We need to do this alone." The trailer empties.

Outside Bill is tuning the bike, tightening and retightening, smelling the exhaust, patting the pipes, checking the heat. "Todd Seeley died Saturday. He was jumping a four-wheeler 150 feet. He'd jumped the same in San Antonio without a hitch. About five years ago, Randy Hill was decapitated performing a midair car crash. That's how fast everything can change."

Five minutes pass. Then Robbie emerges, grinning, and lets out a whoop. The show will go on. He will fly.

Later J. D. shares a story about Vegas. Seems the day before Robbie's history-making Caesars Palace fountain leap in 1989, he did seven practice jumps over thirty limos. Evel was there, watching from his wheelchair. Each time Robbie jumped, Evel would flinch.

"Evel wanted him to stop. He kept yelling, 'Stop! Stop!' but Robbie wouldn't. Then Evel got up from his chair, took his walker and confronted Robbie, told him, 'Enough.' But Robbie begged, 'One more time,' and Evel said OK."

That last time, Robbie sailed over no-handed. He made it to the safety ramp, but only by a foot.

"Look, Dad, no hands."

That night Robbie cleared the 150-foot jump over the Caesars Palace fountains that had left his father in a coma for 29 days.

Bill's face is stiff. With thirty minutes to go, his fingers twitch and his eyes dart from the ramp to the safety fencing to the gas tank to the flags flapping in the breeze.

"Wind isn't good," he mutters, squinting to read the weather. "Sometimes Robbie comes up before a jump and says, 'I don't want to fly this thing,' meaning he doesn't want to go too high. He knocked the wind out of himself one time in Butte. By the time we got to him, someone had already stolen his RK belt buckle off him."

In the corner, Fox gets the prejump interview.

"What's the biggest obstacle here? How do you do it? What are you thinking when you take off? What makes you do this?"

Robbie answers patiently, but his eyes struggle to keep from rolling, as if to say, "There are no answers. Clearly, I'm insane."

"When do you know if something has gone wrong?"

"I know I'm going to crash when I leave the takeoff ramp. And when you know you're going down at 95 miles per hour, you don't relax. You turn into a brick. I visualize flying through the air before I take off. The landing ramp looks like a Popsicle stick. You go down, you hit the semis, you're done."

By now the crowd is five deep. One look and it is clear the Knievels are still products, action figures packaged in red-white-and-blue cellophane. They transcend class much like they defy gravity. The hip embrace them as kitsch, the intelligentsia as an example of the id unbound; the rest see them as heroes, or at least fine entertainment, especially if they crash. All are here today, most decked out in Knievel-theme apparel.

"I never eat before a jump," Robbie tells Fox, "in case they have to cut me open."

And now it is time. Robbie ducks into his trailer to yank on his leathers. He coats his body with baby powder and tugs — one leg at a time, then the arms. He needs help zipping the front. His hands are flapping like wings.

Once he's dressed, the ritual is the same. Sirens squeal. The emcee thanks the sponsors. The national anthem is sung. Kaptain Knievel is introduced, and Robbie breaks from his trailer and walks to the landing ramp to make a speech, what may be his last words. He keeps it short.

"I wasn't planning on jumping tonight," he says, helmet tucked under his armpit. "But I'm going for it."

Then he warms up by making speed passes at the ramp and popping 90-degree wheelies. Then, when his belly says so, he sucks a last breath and vaults into the clouds like a shot put.

He sticks the landing. The crowd erupts, a frenzy of release. Robbie flew, but he blew the record, missed it by more than 20 feet. Nobody seems to notice, least of all the fans, who swarm around him like gnats, fingertips aching for one touch.

The jump later that July at the Oneida Bingo and Casino in Green Bay is different. It has been heavily promoted. Safety bales have been stacked. Trees have been padded. Television crews have been alerted. Robbie has been paid up front. (Pals estimate he will clear a million this year, but when you're paid in cash, details are sketchy.) He has had time to prepare, to think about the implications of his commitment.

Camp Knievel has been set up for days, and Robbie, hoping to break his own no-handed record, is wired. He whizzes around on his scooter. His hatred of the waiting time, the lull between life and life at 100 miles per hour, jets off him like heat. The song in his head is loud today. It is screaming. So he takes fans for rides. Poses for snapshots. Paces. Monkeys around with his fetching blonde daughters, Karmen, 19, by an early girlfriend, and Krysten, 12, by his ex-wife. They've been coming to a few jumps this year, donning red-white-and-blue sequined vests to watch their father cheat death.

"Karmen looks like Kim Basinger," says Robbie proudly. "I just met her for the first time last year. It was one of those things where I needed to step out of the picture so her mom could do what she needed to do." Though she's known her dad for only a short time,

Karmen is now using his last name. She has ideas. Like maybe one day she'll be the one in the white jumpsuit.

"My dad says no way," she says, grinning. "But he can't stop me forever."

At the site, a fan has trucked out a replica of an old bike of Evel's. Robbie takes it out, pops some wheelies, listens to the rumble of history as he zooms around the parking lot.

As Robbie thunders by on one pass, Bill looks up from the tuning area. His forehead wrinkles reflexively, but it is too late. Robbie has already decided. He is headed up the ski ramp on the bike.

The ski ramp is the imperfect answer to a shortage of pavement. Because there is not enough distance in the Oneida parking lot to pick up the travel speed required to sail over 17 semis, the ramp men have erected a gravity-enhancing starter platform about three stories high, with a narrow plank of wood unrolling from the top like a tongue. The ski start rests on scaffolding and is accessible only via speeding motorcycle or cherry picker. The plank has been painted Knievel blue.

The bike doesn't freeze until a couple of feet from the top. The engine is hung too low, and when it meets the sharp angle of the plank, it flat-out quits, leaving Robbie balancing at the ramp's peak, with no means of gracefully sliding off.

It takes less than a minute for his posse to scale the scaffolding. Bill gets there first. He always does. He was there first in Hawaii, where the rain kept everything slick as liver and Robbie hit the ramp wrong, sailed too high, too soon and plummeted through the safety deck like a falling piano, breaking the swing arm off the bike and grating his leathers to his flesh. Bill was there the next day, when a hobbled but intact Robbie jumped again and set a world record — 150 feet no-handed.

When Bill and the gang get to Robbie, he is hanging on by one hand from a support pole. Inches up or down and he would not have been able to reach the pole. Inches in either direction and Robbie and the bike would have been pitched to the ground like an anvil.

"Well, the show was almost canceled," says Robbie, laughing, as Bill helps him eke his bike down the ramp. Bill shakes his head, spits.

*

It is twenty minutes before jump time.

"Want to know the definition of *far?*" asks Fred Bezark, the Knievels' attorney. "The distance between the takeoff ramp and the landing ramp, and it doesn't matter how much space is in between." He shudders.

"I suffer every time they jump. You can't watch this without having your heart in your mouth. You're watching someone become a living bullet."

Fred was introduced to Robbie back in Butte, in the seventies, while he was busy keeping Evel out of jail. The afternoon they met, Robbie was popping wheelies.

"Here was this little kid who says, 'Hey, Fred, you want a motorcycle ride?' and I say, 'I guess so,' and I jump on the back of the motorcycle and he drives me straight up the mountain. And at that time people wore those shoes with the high platforms and the heels, and I burned off one heel completely from the heat of the friction."

Fred has other memories, too, darker ones about a father and son who collided like rams, bashing heads until one or the other was quivering unconscious.

"Time was, my hardest job was to get them onto the same page. I talk to Evel and Robbie probably thirty times a week. Evel has a much tougher personality. Robbie loves his father dearly. He's always professed his love for his father. And eventually Evel came to understand Robbie loved him."

With three minutes till takeoff, the emcee won't shut up. He is wearing a ballooning gray Chess King suit, circa 1984, and his thick fingers grip the microphone like it's a life preserver as he rambles on in a contrived baritone about the legend of Evel Knievel.

"It all started with the world's greatest daredevil, Evel Knievel," he bellows like Ted Knight as he paces atop the landing ramp. "And now the tradition continues with his son, Kaptain Robbie Knievel, here at the Green Bay, Wisconsin, Oneida Bingo and Casino, attempting to break the world-record no-handed jump over — now, listen — over 17 semis. He will attempt to go more than 185 feet before your very eyes."

As he blathers, Robbie paces in his trailer a short walk from the jump site. Outside, his crew members cradle their walkie-talkies, awaiting direction. The emcee is dragging on — Knievel this, Knievel that — and Robbie, already anxious, already primed to the jolting point, crackles over the speaker: "Tell that guy to get the hell off my ramp."

The crew laughs, and without another word the emcee is unplugged. Van Halen starts blaring from the loudspeakers, fireworks explode, and Kaptain Robbie Knievel emerges from behind the smoke like a leather-clad hallucination, walking tall, one arm raised to God.

"Hey, Robbie," a reporter shouts from the crowd. "Do you prepare differently for a no-hands jump?"

"Nah," Robbie replies above the squealing din of 30,000 fans. "I put the one bullet in the gun as usual."

Onstage Robbie preps the audience.

"Ever since I was eight, I've been looking down these ramps. I've set over a dozen records, conquered the fountains at Caesars. I had the best teacher in the world, a man who created his own sport. My father, a huge legend, Mr. Evel Knievel!"

The crowd detonates. So do the fireworks.

"I've been in major meetings with the city of Twin Falls, and hopefully someday I'll stuff my ass into that contraption called a Skycycle and blast my ass zero to 450 miles per hour over the Snake River Canyon to keep the name Knievel the most famous on two wheels. I hope to see you after the jump."

And with that he mounts his motorcycle and begins his speed runs. As he thunders by — once, twice, three times — popping wheelies, standing on his seat, zooming like lightning between the ramp and the fence, the fans tighten up. They cheer, but in hushed tones. They squeeze one another's hands. They think about life. They hear, for a moment, the song Robbie hears every day of his full-throttle life.

And then he does it. He hits the ramp at rocket speed and lets go. He soars like an angel. He points skyward. And the world is silent. He lands. He folds over the bike like a monkey. His bones crush together like cymbals. And the unbridled joy of collective relief explodes like confetti above the crowd. He is alive. And for a little while, so is everyone who watched him.

He has broken the record. Shattered it by 34 feet in front of God and everybody. He is celebrating in the nearby Radisson hotel bar, pounding back booze to calm his heart. His posse is there, plus a few extras — fans, groupies, witnesses who want to share air with the man they watched fly a motorcycle, hands to Heaven, steering by will alone.

There's a lot of hugging and "ah, man"-ing and meaningful nodding. The mood is thick with victory. There is love in the Radisson bar. And it is this love that propels Robbie to the microphone around 1:30 A.M., moving with his phantom gait to the stage, where no one notices him until he signals for the music to cease.

He clears his throat, then smiles.

> You hear his name in every town.
> Is he for real or just a clown?
> Does he have wings, how does he fly?
> Is he a man like you and I?
> Everybody calls him Evel, Evel, Evel Knievel.

Bill's jaw drops. "I can't believe he's doing this," he says, laughing.

> They call him Evel, Evel, Evel Knievel.

ROBERT HUBER

Joe DiMaggio Would Appreciate It Very Much If You'd Leave Him the Hell Alone

FROM ESQUIRE

JOEY HAS THE BLINDS down in his trailer on Mike's big side lot, where Broadway dead-ends at Grizzly Bay. It's quiet here, next to Mike's rancher; nobody bothers him. Just the muted yakking of gulls. It's the edge of spring now — the northern-California light is still sweet, the afternoons merely warm. In the other direction, a few miles south beyond the lazy stucco squalor of Bay Point, the Diablo foothills are as soft as thumb-pressed clay, and now they're sporting a pretty green fuzz that'll brown out in summer's heat — not that Joey bothers to look. Midafternoon on a March Saturday, he's holed up, sucking down an Old Gold Lite.

An Amtrak train rumbles by on the tracks between Mike's billboard-sized plywood fence and the bay, heading west, bound for Oakland, then the city. Joey cracks another Old Gold, still has half a twelve-pack at his feet. Him and Arden put a new power-window motor in the '87 Coupe DeVille they bought to sell; it's nice, nicer than they thought it'd be, a blue almost black, interior a lighter blue. Fucking cold this morning over at Brentwood — Mike's junkyard — down in the forties. Joey lies down, pulls a blanket up. He hates the cold, sips his beer. Half in love with that Caddy — maybe he should keep it. Cruise around in a fine old Coupe DeVille. Joey nods off still holding his beer.

A knock. Joey, groggy, waits. Mike always knocks and then comes on in. Another knock. Joey doesn't move. A third. Then — nothing, just the gulls. Joey relaxes. But suddenly a presence, a shift in light — fucker's got his face pressed to the window. Then he's gone. But this is trouble. Joey downs his warm Old Gold. The sun out there is getting stronger. He gets under the blanket and goes back to sleep.

Later, daylight fading, Mike helping him kill off the Old Golds, Joey says, "Why now? Why are they dicking with me after fifteen years?"

"I don't know, Joe-Joe."

But he knows, and so does Joey, who's tense, breathing heavy. The old man is dying. They want the shit. They want to know why he lives in a trailer, why he doesn't work except at Mike's junkyard — fucking field day there! — why he's been living this way for better than a decade, why he's not in Florida with the old man.

Joey needs to go to the hospital so he can load his inhaler; stress kicks up his asthma. When he and Mike walk out to Mike's pickup, the guy's waiting there in the shadows. But Joey is ready: "I know who you are." He bounces slightly on the balls of his feet — it pisses him off, this guy waiting for him. "I live this way because I want to!"

They go to the hospital, Joey gets his medication. Then he wants to get a pizza. Mike takes him to Pizza Hut. Joey wants to get it to go — he doesn't like being around strangers. They escape ten miles down the freeway to Martinez. It's where his grandfather Giuseppe came after leaving Sicily in 1898, a fisherman testing the waters of America. It's where his father was born in 1914. It's where Joey ended up when his life fell apart.

Joey hooked up with Mike, who owns two junkyards, a few months ago. Mike's grandmother was a DiMaggio, and Joey has worked for him off and on over the years. He's latched on to something good, crashing in the RV on Mike's side lot next to a trash truck and old mattresses and rusting, fucked-up farm plows — Mike's idea of lawn ornaments — hitting Mike up for fifteen or twenty bucks whenever.

He asked Mike the other day why he was gutting the little bungalow out back. "I'm redoing it for you, Joe-Joe," Mike said. "You'll live there."

"No," Joey said. "It's too big for me."

Mike just shook his head — it's the size of a two-car garage. He'll keep trying.

They eat their combo at the marina in Martinez, watch four-by-fours pull boats out of the water. A thirty-footer with a proud glassed-in control room like a widow's walk rises tall like . . . like money. They eat silently. The day's last light makes trace bruises out of low clouds.

Joey seems edgy, pissed. Mike looks past him, to a twenty-two-foot Chris Craft motorboat with peeling paint, up on stilts. It's the *Joltin' Joe,* and it was given to Joe DiMaggio at Yankee Stadium in 1949, along with a Cadillac, a Dodge for his mother, two TVs, jewelry, money, other stuff. The boat was restored by the city of Martinez and mounted in '94; Joe D. couldn't make the unveiling.

Joey doesn't give it so much as a glance. That day at Yankee Stadium in '49, when his father was feted like a king, Joey was seven years old, and all he got from seventy thousand staring people was a set of electric trains.

Now they want something from him — they're pressing in. They've got to know why Joe Jr., fifty-seven years old, the dying Joltin' Joe's only kid, is a bum.

Joey's mother, a showgirl who wanted to be an actress, fought a losing battle. When Joey was ten, Dorothy Arnold marched into court with him to get more child support out of his father, whom she had divorced eight years earlier because all he did was play baseball and hang out at Toots Shor's nightclub. Now Marilyn was in the picture. They were taking Joey on some of their dates. So she wanted more money.

The judge dismissed Dorothy, informing her that she'd made a mistake divorcing Joe DiMaggio in the first place.

She moved from New York to L.A., put Joey into Black Fox Military Institute, a fancy dumping ground for the kids of Hollywood's too-busy famous like Dorothy Lamour and Jerry Lewis. Joey's mother, who lived six miles away, pursued her career, eventually appearing in about a dozen movies for Universal that nobody remembers. She was loud and sweet and seductive, and her agent's son, Georgie Milman, would hang around the house afternoons, while Joey played football or baseball, just to be with her, because, well, he was fourteen, fifteen — three years older than Joey. Sometimes, together, they'd pick up Joey, who'd be steamed at himself. "If you're a great athlete and have a bad game," says Milman, now a lawyer in L.A., "that's one thing. But Joey's was more an abiding disappointment that he wasn't more of a football player or more of a weight lifter or taller or bigger. He was just generally pissed off."

Joey and his mother started playing golf with a Black Fox teacher, a scratch golfer. Dorothy — so beautiful, and such a good athlete, with a swing so beautiful she could have been a pro. Joey? He got pretty good. Not as good as his mother, though.

But she couldn't compete against Joey's father, living up in San Francisco with Marilyn. It's hard for anybody under sixty to get why DiMaggio was such a huge deal; post-baseball, he was an image-polishing coffeemaker salesman, a snotty guy in forever-pressed slacks who'd once gotten on a fifty-six-game roll and then somehow, horse-face and all, got the blonde. But DiMaggio was once supreme cool. There's a telling stat in that two-month run of 223 at bats in '41: He struck out only seven times. Seven! That's why old-timers still go on about DiMag — when he pulled the trigger, he connected; when he floated over that vast outfield in Yankee Stadium, he caught it. And he had the class to keep his mouth shut.

When Joe and Marilyn would go down to L.A. in the early fifties, he was done playing baseball, and she was riding the wave of *Gentlemen Prefer Blondes* and *How to Marry a Millionaire*. But Joe was still the bigger sensation.

Small wonder, then, that Joey would get a little nervous when his father was coming to town. Every few months, Georgie and Joey would pick up Joe and Marilyn at the L.A. airport in a limo and take them to the Beverly Hills Hotel. "Joe DiMaggio was a god — this great shining light," Milman says. "And any time Joey was around him, he was invisible."

Georgie and Joey and Dorothy and a female friend would sometimes drive down to Baja for the night, rent a couple rooms. Dorothy knew people there. She'd go out with her friend, have a few drinks, return a little loud, a little drunk.

Joey's mother was embarrassing. She couldn't touch his father, who he was. But neither could Joey.

Joey prepped at Lawrenceville back east in Jersey. He was a kicker on the football team; his father, who still came to New York in the late fifties to hang out, never bothered to take a train down to a game. Then Joey got into Yale. He could cut it there — "A very bright guy, very quick," remembers one of his roommates, now a lawyer in Washington. "He was one of us." But he hated the winter in New Haven and, after his first year, hotfooted it back to L.A. Joey roomed for a while with Georgie and Georgie's buddy, Tom Law, who got him a night-shift job in his uncle's rug factory down in Santa Monica. They liked Joey; he was a nice kid, like a younger brother, trying to figure himself out.

"But he was a needy guy," Law says. "He was inward, kind of a shut-down soul. Something was missing."

Good-sport Joey had another side he kept hidden from them. When he joined Dorothy at her sister's summer place near Duluth the next summer, he was a demanding little shit who tried to run everything, told his aunt when it was time to eat, set the agenda for the water sports. It was an attitude that had been stoked by his mother's friends, who doted on the great DiMag's son, wanted to give him a little fathering. Joey's cousins hated him. But they were just his mother's people.

Back in L.A., Joey tried to get Tom, the guy with wheels, to go see Marilyn with him. She'd been divorced from his father for half a dozen years, but she and Joey were still buddies. Marilyn was living in a bungalow in Brentwood.

But Tom, who had grown up in L.A. and had worked as an extra in movies since he'd been a little kid, took a pass on bugging her. Now Law kicks himself; not because he missed a chance to hang with Marilyn, but — who knows? — going there just might have done her some good. Her connection to Joey was strong — not on a motherly level but as a friend, somebody with a screwed-up childhood who could understand him. A relationship with her separate from his father's, no bullshit.

Joey talked to Marilyn by phone the night she died, just chatting, even laughing; she seemed fine. His take on her death was the conventional one: a lethal combination of booze and sleeping pills. "It was a real punch in the gut to Joey," Law says.

He went to her funeral in his marine uniform. He'd enlisted the year before; the military was like boarding school — structured, a place to be kick-ass good. And he'd married a seventeen-year-old San Diego girl while he was stationed there. It lasted a year; at the divorce proceeding, Joey testified that she "badgered" him about working too much. Afterward, he knocked down a newspaper photographer trying to take his picture. This was a new side of Joey: Nobody fucks with me.

But Joey wasn't a hard guy. He was charming, smart, a good talker, and he was strong from weight lifting and the marines. A very attractive guy, in fact. It's just that he had no idea what to do. As his father padded his grief over Marilyn with booze and girls up in San Francisco, Joey drifted back east, showed up at Uncle Dom's office one day in the mid-sixties. Dom, the ex–Red Sox center fielder, owned a polyurethane-foam company near Boston — big rolls of foam cut to order.

"He was just kind of roaming around at the time," remembers Dom, who's eighty-two now and splits his year between Florida and the Northeast. "And he just kind of floated into town." Dom found out Joey had been missing marine reserve meetings, took him to the local office, got it straightened out. It was also obvious that Joey needed a job, so Dom put him to work. Joey helped run a plant division, then was put in charge of another polyurethane plant Dom owned in Baltimore.

Joey met a woman there who had two little girls but had lost her husband, a helicopter pilot, in Vietnam. Sue fell madly in love with Joey. She was a golden opportunity to prove something.

"He told my mother one time," Sue says, "'Maxine, your daughter was brought up really well, and that's one of the main reasons I married her.' It made me feel yucky. I filled the part his father wanted him to have." Sue never met Joey's mother. He had, by now, rubbed her out of his life.

They'd been married two years when Joe called Dom, in 1970, from California. He wanted Joey to become partners with him and two other guys in a polyurethane business out there; Joey would run it. He didn't hesitate: Joey moved Sue and Kathie and Paula west.

He had figured right on one thing: The granddaughters were a big hit with Joe, who was fifty-six now. With his little girls he was soft, sweet, was coming over to Joey's apartment in the East Bay to see Kathie and Paula almost every day. It was Sue's job to cook, to kowtow to Joe's idiosyncratic diet: No salt! Watch the starch! Barely a nod from Senior at how Joey was working his butt off running the business. But Joe D. would do anything for his little girls.

And why shouldn't he — Joey — do well? Joe had sent him to the best schools, given him every opportunity; he was a smart kid. The old-school silent-treatment crap now ruled even Joey's living room.

But for a little while, there on Second Street in Lafayette, Joey and Sue got in with a fun crowd, would cross the bay and do up early-seventies San Francisco, sometimes fly down to L.A. for dinner, fly back the same night. And Joey, with his father and wife and two girls in his house — this is what he never had, what his father's incredible fame couldn't begin to provide. Joey could.

But it was a straight line Joey couldn't walk for long. Getting no credit from Joe was infuriating; he felt bottled up. Sometimes he'd head for North Beach in the city, come home at three or four. Sometimes he wouldn't bother coming home at all. Sue would let him have it; Joey would respond by beating her up.

There had always been women who wanted him simply because his name was Joe DiMaggio — he was close enough to the real thing. Sue remembers that one night, when they were still back east, she and Joey were having dinner with the couple who lived downstairs. Sue looked across the table. The neighbor, a tiny blonde, was staring at Joey, running her tongue around her lips. Sue pitched a scene. Later, alone with her upstairs, Joey broke two of Sue's ribs and made a mess of her face.

But Joey would be contrite as hell, and he could be sweet and charming, and he was very smart, knew so much that she didn't, and Sue was crazy in love with him still.

Then the business fell apart. One of the polyurethane partners, Steve Alexakos, an ex-NFL guard with the Giants, pushed the DiMaggios out of the company. Joe blamed Joey, who was supposed to be running things.

"More than anything in the world," Sue says, "Joey wanted to do something right, to impress his father. Every time he failed, it crushed him."

Joey managed to land on his feet, running a trucking company in Oakland, but now he dug in hard against Joe, took it out on Sue. Not only women — Sue realized Joey was getting into drugs, especially speed. He posed as a cowboy, with the hat and boots, roared around on a big Norton, rubbed noses with the Hell's Angels. He was barely speaking to his father. And his anger was getting more and more out of control.

One day Sue found a note left on their fence in Lafayette, the fence of the place they were thinking about buying. It had two pussycat drawings and read, "When are you coming back? I miss you so much." She confronted Joey. He sent her screaming across the street to a neighbor. Then he left her for a twenty-year-old.

And then he crashed.

It was 1976. Joey and Sue had been split up for two years, but he was still in and out of her life, had borrowed her little Ford wagon and totaled it. A piece of his brain had to be removed to get rid of a blood clot. The doctors warned that his personality might change.

"It did," Sue says. "Joey had even less control of his anger." He blamed Sue. She fucked up his life by signing for the operations that left him this way — pissed, self-destructive. Sue doesn't buy it. The anger had been building for a long time, a frightening, unpredictable, hair-trigger response. Not just over women. Once, back east, he and Sue were driving in the snow when somebody cut them off. At a stop sign, Joey got out, went up to the other car, opened the driver's door, punched the guy, came back, got in, and drove around him.

Sue, despite everything, still cares about Joey, and she takes the long view. The problem was how he'd been treated from the beginning: "When he was a little boy living with his mother in New York in the Waldorf, his only entertainment was riding up and down in the elevator. Then it was camps and military school and boarding school. They threw the man away!"

As he recovered from the accident, Joey dug in even harder, decided that whatever life he was supposed to lead, he wouldn't — not that he ever knew what that was. He started driving a truck. Joe bought him a $75,000 Peterbilt cab. He showed up one day in 1983 at Dorothy Arnold's Charcoal Charley's restaurant near L.A.; she was married again, ran the place with her husband. Dorothy and Joey hadn't seen each other for about fifteen years. He seemed at loose ends; Dorothy hooked him up with a guy she knew, a trucking-company owner who needed a union rep. They arranged a meeting in Las Vegas. Joey never showed. He did make use of the credit card Dorothy gave him, though. A year later, she was dead.

He started sleeping in his Peterbilt. Then he wrecked it. By the late eighties, people saw Joey as just another full-time bum and beer drinker.

Still, no matter what, he was a DiMaggio. It's Peter, Dom's son, who really nails what that's like: It's like when the elephant's in the room. You can't turn or go anywhere; the elephant's still there. Always. But Peter has no idea, really — his father was a nice little center fielder who wore glasses. Try being the son of the Yankee Clipper. Try whipping out the goddamn name every time you write a check in the drugstore.

Sue, who gradually weaned herself away from Joey, remarried. Kathie and Paula went on to high school and college and marriages without him, presented Joe with great-grandchildren that Joey has never gotten to know. And in the last decade, Joey saw his father less and less.

The few friends Joe had knew better than to ask him about Marilyn — not if they wanted the continued privilege of the great man's company — and they didn't ask about Joey, either. It was as if Joey were dead, too.

Sam Spear, a San Francisco racetrack publicist, met Joe in 1977 when he came out to bet on the horses, and for fifteen years, until Joe got old and stayed in Florida, they'd often spend Tuesdays, the nonracing day, together. Maybe start with a steam — Joe loved his steam — then take a drive, go up into wine country. Sam would bring tapes — Joe enjoyed strings, stuff with violins, nothing too jazzy. They'd go to a winery, eat figs, have a glass of wine, sit in the sun, and Joe would spin old baseball stories.

Sometimes on the way north, they'd stop off in Martinez. He wouldn't tell Sam what they were up to, just direct — Sam always drove them in his green Buick. Sometimes Joey would be waiting for them after a relative who was putting him up had passed the word he needed help. Joe would give Joey some cash, try to rouse him with a history lesson about how his grandparents got themselves all the way to New York from Sicily at the turn of the century, then all the way across the country, and made something of themselves. What he had to do was stick with a job, work hard! Joey just stared.

And sometimes, Sam and Joe would simply troll the streets of

Martinez, looking for Joey; Joe wasn't always sure where he was living. Often they wouldn't find him. But occasionally they'd spot
Joey, walking his beat-up Schwinn downtown, maybe heading to
the marina, in his uniform of the eighties: the same cutoffs and
Raiders jersey day after day.

Once, there he was walking along on the other side of Berrellesa.
Sam stopped. Joe got out.

"Joey! Joey!" he called.

Joey kept walking.

Joe called again, louder. Joey heard him — certainly he heard
him. But he ignored Joe, kept walking. Joe got back in the car. Sam
drove them silently up to Napa.

They didn't discuss Joey. Even with his brother Dom, Joe didn't
discuss Joey. But it was obvious what a heartache it was. Joe didn't
discuss heartaches. This was all he could do for Joey: give him some
money, have family in Martinez keep an eye on him. That and take
care of his daughters.

So Sam and Joe drove on into wine country. Sam had a friend
who ran a winery and had once played trumpet for Glenn Miller.
They had lunch, and Sam sat back listening to stories of the grand
old days of New York nightlife.

Coming home, Sam's tape of old standards landed on "I've Got a
Crush on You."

"That," Joe DiMaggio said, "was Marilyn's favorite song."

The last five years or so, when Joe almost never left Florida and Joey
rarely saw him, things got worse. Mostly, Joey holed up in the Ice
House at the end of Arthur Road in dumpy Vine Hill, outside Martinez. The Ice House was the back of a refrigerator truck plopped
in a field, a long metal box with no heat or insulation, no water, no
windows — just a big sliding door. One afternoon four years ago,
he wrecked his bike into a van, had to have hip surgery, and got arrested for drunk driving to boot. When he recovered, he'd ride his
Schwinn, or walk it, up Pacheco Boulevard to his cousin Bobby
Marazzoni's on Grangers Wharf, burned from the sun, filthy, his
long hair matted; he wouldn't even bother putting in the false
teeth Joe had paid for. Bobby's place — once a boardinghouse for
fishermen and later a family home where Joe would sometimes stay
— was now just a place for Joey to hang with Bobby, drink.

He was on the edge now. One afternoon a guy from Mike's Brentwood junkyard saw him limping along the freeway toward Pittsburg. It was midsummer, the heat intense. He stopped and asked, "You want a ride, Joey?"

"No." Joey seemed pissed.

"You want something to drink?"

"Yeah. What you got?"

"Coke. Or bottled water."

Joey looked at Mike's guy for a moment, shook his head, limped on.

Joey had now taken on a trait of Joe's: He had only a few friends, guys who didn't ask questions, wouldn't probe. Except Joey had no interest in regaling them with stories from the old days; he hung with guys who would drink with him or ride bikes or do nothing. No girlfriends. Guys who didn't give a shit that he was a DiMaggio.

At Rick's place there in Vine Hill, Joey and Rick would barbecue steaks and drink beer. Rick's a pipe fitter, three quarters Apache, living with his mother and his kids, Richie and Nicole, in a tiny bungalow. Rick's take is that Joey used to be close to his father, but something happened; he thinks it was wrecking the truck. They built bikes together, Rick and Joey, took long rides. Joey got to know Rick's kids real well, played Nintendo with them, helped Richie with his homework. Rick had no idea, until somebody recently told him, that Joey once had a family.

And Rick helped Joey outfit the Ice House; they ran water from a warehouse nearby, electric from a pole, cut out windows, patched them with Plexiglas. Joey got an electric heater, then a radio, TV, stereo. Quite the pad. But he seemed antsy, unhappy, said he might move: to the city, maybe Vegas. Sometimes they'd down a lot of beers. Sometimes Joey slept all day. Rick thought Joey missed his dad.

Little did he know. Rick, though, would never bug him, never pry for more of the story. But then Joey outed himself a few months ago; a TV tabloid kept after him, sweetened the offer to fifteen grand — why not? He'd tell them things were cool as they were, that he just wanted to be left alone. But they didn't buy it — who the hell lives like he does because he wants to? Joey, cornered on camera, came back with: "What's Joe DiMaggio's son *supposed* to do?"

Then Joey started talking about his father. He said that things were fine between them. Whatever his father had given him, it was always the best, never second-rate. That if his father asked, he'd go right down to Florida to be with him. Anything else? "Nothing other than I'm glad he's better" — lately Joe's health seemed to have turned a corner. But now Joey's voice got thin, close to breaking: "And I love him, and all the things that are felt but never said, I guess, between people." He hadn't seen his father for two years.

Georgie Milman, down in L.A., was watching. He hadn't spoken to Joey for thirty-five years, not since Joey left his mother's world behind, but it was heartbreaking to see him like this — toothless, old at fifty-seven, in so much pain. It took Georgie all the way back, to the way it always was: Just look at a photograph of Joe DiMaggio in the Yankee clubhouse, late forties, there in his uniform, after a game, laughing with a teammate. Joe seems oblivious to the seven-year-old boy with his arms wrapped around his neck. Joey.

Sometimes they'd go somewhere, Rick and Joey, like on a long bike ride, meet somebody who wouldn't believe who Joey was. Not that Joey would throw it out to strangers, but it came up once or twice that he was Joe D.'s son, and now people wouldn't believe it. *This* guy? Joey wouldn't get mad. He'd merely shrug. It was funny, in a way. The name still fucking him, just in a new way.

Sunday morning. Joey feels shitty, his asthma is still bothering him. Last night at the marina, he and Mike decided that today, whenever Joey got it together, they'd get propane for the trailer. He sleeps all morning. But Joey's doing better at Mike's. Mike, almost twenty years younger than Joey, has money, watches out for him. When Joey finally comes out, Mike is talking to some guy out back who wants to sell him a truck. Mike's always got something going on. He drives Joey out Broadway in the RV, along Willow Bay where the bums wander.

In a few hours, this Sunday night in March, Joey's father down in Florida will be dead. It's a death befitting his dignity; his granddaughters and their husbands, his lawyer, his brother Dom have taken turns helping out the last few weeks. Joe has had hospice care at home, and it makes his passing as gentle and caring as it could be. He even ate a little these last couple of days. Joe dies with his granddaughter Kathie holding his hand.

Joey ignored Dom's phone call to Martinez a couple months ago trying to track him down, fill him in on Joe's condition. Joey will get a call tonight — or rather, Mike will, since Joey doesn't have a phone.

Now, in the RV, he's sitting sideways, half facing Mike. Suddenly Mike veers to the shoulder; Joey almost falls off his wheel-well perch.

"What the fuck — ?"

There's a guy on the shoulder on a bike, with filthy white hair that circles his whole head like a baboon's, coming their way. His slit eyes ball in fear, then, when Mike swerves back onto the road, the guy gives them a thin smile, nods. Mike laughs. Joey shakes his head. Fucking Mike, just dicking with the guy. He's got his finger in everything, wants to help everybody — it's a guy he feeds sometimes. Mike gets off on feeding the homeless.

STEVE FRIEDMAN

Up from the Gutter

FROM ESQUIRE

It was after midnight. I knew that sometimes in matches like this, you
either lose a lot of money or, if you win, you're lucky to get out of
there. We look around the parking lot. I'm thinking, We're gonna get
mugged. I'm thinking, This is ugly.
— Professional bowler David Ozio, remembering bowling an action
game against Rudy Kasimakis

MOST MEN don't leave bowling alleys at sunrise, but he has left
many then. He has staggered out of bowling alleys into cold dawns.
He has opened bowling-alley doors and blinked at fragrant mornings and hot, sticky mornings and cool, autumnal mornings, exhausted but fulfilled, his pockets bulging with so much cash he
would rather not discuss it. He has walked out with nothing: "No
gas in your car, no toll to get home, sometimes you're not eating
for three days." This has been his job. He has driven five hours to
bowl six hours. He has drilled holes in hundreds of bowling balls,
until he made himself expert in the ways they were balanced and
weighted. He has carted bowling balls to a hospital, where a medical technician allowed him to watch as the balls were X-rayed. (In
self-consciously ironic moments, he refers to himself as "a recovering ballaholic.") He has bought advertisements in small bowling newspapers and challenged top professional bowlers — "professional" in a legitimate, corporate-endorsement type of way, from
the clean, well-lighted world he once tried and failed to enter — to
meet him after midnight in smoky, loud places filled with hard, unsmiling men, and many of the professionals have come. Hours
later, oftentimes, he has swaggered into the sunrise with gas money

to burn. He has taken money from many less-famous bowlers, too. He has made a good living at that — a much better living, it is safe to say, than many of the bowlers who labor in the clean, well-lighted world he once tried and failed to enter.

He has bet on frames, high odd scores, and high even scores. He has bet on a single ball and on "concourse games," in which bowlers fling their balls from behind the scorer's table. (He has not bet on "towel games," in which bowlers fling their balls from towels, though he has beaten players who have played that way.) He has bowled when the lowest score won (but only if the bowler hits at least one pin per ball). He has bowled "telephone-book matches," in which two bowlers meet in a town and open a phone book, one player closes his eyes and stabs at the page listing the bowling centers, and, wherever his finger lands, that's where they bowl. He has bowled badly on purpose, but only to persuade other bowlers to play and to bet against him. "To keep the fish interested," he says. "I was always cleaning the bottom of the tank. It was dirty, and I had to clean it." He has bowled "four-game freeze-out," which means the first bowler to win four games wins everything. In the world of action bowling, which is where Rudy Kasimakis has ruled for the past fifteen years or so, "everything" can represent an impressive sum of money, oftentimes bet by hard, unsmiling men. Think of a good year's salary. That sum, large but intentionally vague at Rudy's request, might be what's at stake in a single action game.

But action bowling's most successful practitioner is pulling himself from the game now. He is once again trying to leave the four-game freeze-outs and bleary sunrises behind so that he can enter the clean, well-lighted world with the television lights and corporate endorsements. This spring, he is attempting success on the Professional Bowlers Association tour — at thirty-four years old, going legit. But like Michael Corleone and Joseph Kennedy and Don King and Mark Wahlberg and other skilled men who have tried to leave one disreputable world in order to enter a different, better-lighted, and more complicated one, his trip is fraught with difficulties. And in the case of action bowling's greatest action bowler, a question: Why?

Most bowling fans know him as Rudy Revs, because, when he cocks his bowling ball back, his right hand points straight up and he torques his wrist and then releases the ball with more power than almost any other bowler alive. Among bowlers, Rudy is said to possess a "high revolution" ball. Thus Revs. He weighs 240 pounds and stands 5 feet 7 inches, and he has forearms like thighs and a neck like a waist and dark eyes that glower and burn in a head like a boulder. He is loud and swaggering in victory and moody in defeat. He is obsessed with winning. His survival depends on winning. Professional and top amateur bowlers speak of "throwing" a bowling ball. In Rudy's case, the expression is accurate. When Rudy strikes, pins jump and scatter with cartoonish alacrity. When he doesn't strike, he leaves more pins than a professional bowler should or can afford to. He is known as an all-or-nothing bowler. He has a heavy New York accent and a reputation for betting big money on games whose outcomes have, for whatever reason, never been in doubt to Rudy. He looks and sometimes acts like low-rent muscle, and he is making a life change for the loftiest kind of ideal.

> He gets right in your face and says, "I'm the best, you can't beat me. I'm the best, there's no way you can beat me." He'd just demoralize a guy; the guy would just be shaking.
>   I bowled him twice, beat him twice. The last time, I beat him two straight games, and he was in my face at the end of the second game, still screaming, "You can't beat me, you can't beat me!"
>   — Former professional bowler Brian Berg

There are two commandments that action bowlers live by. The first, especially for an action bowler who wants to keep his belly and his gas tank full, is that you play the percentages. "You don't play a straight guy in a straight guy's house if you're a hook bowler," says David Ozio, the thirteenth-winningest professional bowler in history, a man who has bowled his share of action games, and who still does.

The second imperative is, you play anywhere. "The code of any good action player," says PBA commissioner Mark Gerberich, a man who has a strange and twisted relationship with action bowling and action bowlers like Rudy, "is 'Anytime, anywhere, any amount of money.' That's what action bowling is — you and me, you get done working, I get done working, we're gonna lock the doors, and we're gonna bowl."

To thrive as an action bowler — and Rudy has thrived better

than any other — means devising a way of synthesizing those two absolute but ostensibly conflicting imperatives. In some ways, it's like being a pious murderer.

So action bowlers try to make sure the lanes they are bowling on are oiled to their liking and not to their opponents'. Oil patterns influence how a ball hooks, where it hooks, and even *if* it hooks. Some action bowlers arrive at a lane early and tinker with the pin-setting machine so that the resulting pin configuration favors balls thrown from certain angles, angles that happen to be the ones those bowlers who tinker are best at. One action bowler, a man who throws the ball even harder than Rudy — "His ball could basically knock down tree trunks," Rudy says — used to travel to action games with four cases of 3–8 Brunswick Red Crown bowling pins in the trunk of his car. "That's three pounds eight ounces." At the time, the Red Crowns were heavier — and more difficult to knock down — than normal pins.

In the world of action bowling, where Rudy has long been the chief aquarium cleaner, strange and exotic creatures scurry and skitter in the murky light. There are "gutter players," men with sweeping hooks who spend their entire careers bowling on the board right next to the gutter, because they've made sure the rest of the lane is heavily oiled. A gutter player's ball avoids the oil before hooking into the headpin at the last minute. A gutter player's opponent usually bowls down the middle of the lane, only to watch helplessly as his ball slides and slips out of control. There are "dump artists," excellent bowlers who make most of their money placing secret bets against themselves and on other, lesser bowlers, then losing on purpose.

One dump artist became so notorious that one night, with one ball left to bowl, a ball that would decide the outcome of the game, many of the hard, unsmiling men who had — perhaps foolishly — bet on the dump artist thought he might throw the game, so they threatened him with grievous bodily harm if he didn't make his spare. But other hard, unsmiling men, who were counting on him dumping the game, threatened him with grievous bodily harm if he *did* make his spare. So the dump artist faked a heart attack. "Clutched his chest, yelled, fell over, the whole bit," says Rudy with a laugh that is at least a little admiring. "Made an ambulance come to get him outta there."

Dump artists and gutter players are unpopular creatures, shunned by other denizens of the action aquarium. But, among bowlers, their cunning and skill are recognized. Sometimes they are even honored. Such is the case with the pro bowler who discovered in the early seventies that if he soaked his bowling ball overnight in a chemical resin that he had found in a hardware store, the ball would become soft and grip the wood of a bowling lane with amazing traction and hook powerfully into the headpin. The year he made his discovery, the bowler, a career journeyman, made more money than any of his colleagues and was named PBA player of the year. He is described at the International Bowling Museum and Hall of Fame in St. Louis as "an innovator in the game."

Rudy is not above gimmicks and trickery. When he bowls at his favorite action spot, Deer Park Bowl in Deer Park, Long Island, he tries to make sure the match takes place on lanes 11 and 12. "Lane 11 is the easiest lane in America to throw a strike on," he says. "Lane 12 hooks early and stops in the back. You have to circle the lane, make sure you get the ball to come around the corner and kick the ten." It takes a while for Rudy's opponents to figure that out.

Bowlers who have opposed Rudy at Deer Park Bowl refer to the venue as the Cage, in part because it always seems to be crowded with Rudy's hard, unsmiling friends. "A lot of hassles, fights broke out," David Ozio says, "and you could tell Rudy was the general there." Rudy yells at other bowlers there and slaps his hands in front of them after he has bowled a strike. He'll say, "Now, that's a *real* strike." He belittles his opponent, insults his game, and then watches him. Rudy knows that when a man is bowling with his own money, he is often scared, and Rudy senses others' fear and feeds off of it.

"I'm kind of like a dog that way," he says. "When I can sense him shaking, it's kind of like a high."

"He was an animal," says Norm Duke, the eleventh-winningest man in the history of bowling. "The hardest thing about beating Rudy was not being intimidated. He takes a sixteen-pound ball and makes it look like a piece of popcorn."

"I bowled him at the Cage," says Ozio. "That was suicidal on my part. Everyone feared Rudy in the Cage."

*

He tried the pro tour twelve years ago, but he didn't make it. There are no fish on the pro tour, and there's more oil than on regular lanes, and the oil patterns are equally tough on everyone. And while Rudy's all-or-nothing ball scares opponents in dark, dim alleys, it didn't scare anyone on the PBA tour. Too many times, the all-or-nothing ball was nothing. The most successful PBA bowlers aren't the men who make the pins jump or whose balls can knock over tree trunks. The men who make the money on the PBA tour are consistent, mostly quiet men with consistent, mostly quiet bowling styles. They could even be considered boring. The man Rudy says is the greatest clutch bowler in the game — the man "I'd bet my last dollar on to throw one single ball" — is Norm Duke, who is 5 feet 5 inches, 123 pounds, and unfailingly polite to bowling fans, and who says thank you and dips his head when people applaud. The Duke, as he is known, is not flashy, but he's consistent. The richest bowler in history is a man named Walter Ray "Deadeye" Williams Jr. Williams doesn't throw a particularly powerful strike ball, and if his style is notable for anything, it's a certain clumsiness. But he's accurate, and he's consistent.

To succeed on the tour this time, Rudy knows he'll have to adjust more and go for broke less. He also knows that even with his two sponsors — Hammer bowling balls and Turbo 2-N-1 Grips — giving him monthly checks, plus incentives if and when he wins, competing on the PBA tour means spending about $1,300 a week on travel and expenses. When you do the math, Rudy stands to make much less money as a pro than he has made as an amateur. In fact, every Saturday you see him on TV, he stands to lose money, a concept that is anathema to an action bowler.

"Everybody's ego exists to the next level," says David Ozio, by way of explaining Rudy's otherwise inexplicable return to the PBA. "If you don't do it, you'll always wonder how you would have stacked up against the best of the best."

Rudy is having lunch with Mark Gerberich at an Applebee's restaurant in a mall on the outskirts of Scranton, which is like the most notorious and trash-talking street-basketball hustler you never heard of sitting down to break bread with David Stern, though they probably wouldn't end up at Applebee's or in a mall outside Scranton. Gerberich is at the table because he knows what an action bowler with Rudy's dark charisma and big hook and boulder head with glowing eyes can do to draw fans to the sport; because he knows what Rudy's penchant for mano a mano, in-your-face confrontation can do for television drama; and because he also knows that some people already think badly of bowlers — think they're less skilled than other professional athletes, somehow ruder, louder, meaner, *seedier* — and he worries that too much of Rudy's dark charisma and boulder head and mano a mano confrontation might reinforce that notion. So Gerberich, who has bowled action himself and loves the color and drama of action, who loves the *action* of action, wants people to know about Rudy. But the commissioner also knows about the bad image some people have of bowling, and he doesn't want them to know *too* much about Rudy. Rudy — who honestly seems interested only in the next week's tournament — is here because Gerberich asked him to be here.

"There are some pro players who couldn't win an action game if their life depended on it," Rudy says.

"What Rudy means," Gerberich says, "is that while pro bowlers are the best in the world, when it comes down to a single match, with everything on the line —"

"Bowling action," Rudy says, "means you're putting up your own money on one game, everything riding on it, and it means you're facing some serious consequences depending on how you bowl."

"What Rudy means —"

"What I mean is, to bowl action, you gotta have ice water in your veins and a set of big keisters. I remember one match — it was in West Hempstead — I got beat up so bad, I left that place in a body bag and —"

"He doesn't mean he literally left in a body bag," Gerberich says.

"Yeah," Rudy says. "Not literally. But he beat me up bad. I was talking to myself that night."

Gerberich thinks Rudy could be just what the PBA needs. He hopes he'll bring some of the drama and flair of the action game to the PBA. But Gerberich worries that too much drama and flair might scare some people, might jeopardize the already-fragile alliance the PBA has built with its corporate sponsors. Gerberich would like to make professional bowling more colorful without alarming the middle-class audience it is trying to broaden.

"You wanna do that?" Rudy asks. "Here's how you do that. When Walter Ray wins the next TV tournament, I walk up to him after, while the cameras are still rolling, and I say, 'Hey, Walter Ray, you might have won the tournament, but I don't think you're so hot.' Then I say, 'How about me and you just go to an alley down the street and we just rough it up, just me and you?' Then we do it, and the cameras follow us. Now, that would be something."

Gerberich tells Rudy to hold off on that idea for a while.

JONATHAN MILES

Ay Caramba! The Fish Drink Tequila Like Goatsuckers!

FROM SPORTS AFIELD

LATELY, IN THE NORTHWEST Mexican state of Sinaloa, there'd been rumors. Livestock and pets had been turning up dead, and local farmers were pinning the blame on a creature they called the *chupacabra,* or goatsucker, a five-foot-tall ogre variously described as resembling a giant rat, mad kangaroo, hirsute alien or punk rocker à la mid-seventies London. Chupacabra sightings first emerged in Puerto Rico, in the town of Loíza in late 1994; a few years later, they had moved west onto the mainland, to Sinaloa — one of Mexico's poorest provinces, a narcopolitical state where marijuana farmers cruise the dirt roads with bottles of Tecate and pistols between their legs and where the air quivers with the distant buzz of helicopters manned by pot-seeking *federales.* Pressed by public outcry, the state government assigned a team of 15 scientists — flanked by 50 police guards — to investigate. The task force could neither prove nor disprove the chupacabra's existence, though one official, quoted not so long ago in the Mexican press, curiously ventured, by dint of explanation, that "pollution is now so bad that it's driving ordinary animals mad, giving them the behavioral trappings of crazed alien creatures."

I'd be lying if I denied this was on our minds as we drove, my pal Bruce Browning ("like the shotgun," he is wont to say) and I, in a car rattling with fishing gear, our eyes peeled, straight into the maw of chupacabra country. I'm a sucker for the gothic, willing to half-believe anything that expands our world into a more fitful and mysterious place. But then, more to the point, we were seeking crazed alien creatures of another stripe: the large-mouth bass of Lake Huites (pronounced WHEE-tez), a 33,000-acre reservoir on the roughshod outskirts of the Sierra Madre Occidentals, where the fish, we were told, were brawny and prolific enough to warrant rumors of their own.

At least this was the shadowy claim of a friend of a friend of a bartender who had just returned from Huites, a lake that has yet to show up on most maps. An American fishing maven, he said, had stocked the nascent reservoir, created via a dam on the Rio Fuerte that was finished in 1993, with upward of 80,000 Florida bass fingerlings; they'd grown, those bass, blessed with a year-round growing season and a glut of bluegill, tilapia and shad to feed upon. It was said to be remote, its only access a 30-mile burro trail just barely wide enough for a four-wheel-drive truck, and because it was Mexico's first-ever catch-and-release water, it wasn't headed for the sort of glum bust that so many other Mexican bass lakes had suffered when local tilapia netters quickly and efficiently decimated their fish populations. Bruce and I had been cradling our Thursday afternoon martinis when the bartender leaned in, like a wartime *confidante,* and told us what this friend of a friend had said: This new lake in Mexico, this Lake Huites, may be the best bass lake in the world. Of course this is not the sort of thing you whisper to men whose obvious lack of regular employment leads them to drink martinis at four o'clock on a Thursday. That goatsuckers were afoot was not a bother. The preternatural be damned: There was fishing to be had.

There is something just shy of full-blown loony, however, in driving some 2,000 miles to catch a galoot of a fish readily located in almost every pond and puddle near home — or so I concluded, somewhat foul-headedly, driving southbound in the northbound lane of Highway 15 in Sonora, between the towns of Navajoa and Guaymas, en route to Sinaloa. You travel thousands of miles to catch trophy marlin or salmon or even trout, if you live in a place such as I do, where trout are an exotic species that most folks have heard plenty about but only a few have ever seen, like Catholics. But it takes a firm leap beyond logic to point yourself toward the ugly fat bass of a foreign nation.

"This is akin to flying to Paris for a Snickers," I told Bruce, who, several years ago, retired from playing conga drums with a reggae band to intermittently teach canoe classes, less intermittently fly-fish, and quite regularly drink martinis with me. Bruce is a big, bearded, white-haired fellow — for a few years, he did a one-man show in Florida playing Ernest Hemingway — and ageless in that way of big, bearded, white-haired fellows.

"Wasn't this a four-lane road before we stopped?" he asked.

"What time is it?"

"I don't know — maybe sevenish, but in a dark, eightish sort of way," he said. Semis whirred by, and beyond the highway lay the spartan Sonoran landscape that one can see north to Phoenix — a crisply famished bed of nameless scrub, organ-pipe cacti and miser-able-looking mesquite trees. That I grew up in such a landscape seemed to matter little; the desert never welcomes you home. It suffers lovelessly, without memory. It doesn't even want its dead, leaving them for the sun to devour rather than pulling them earth-ward for absorption.

"Did I finish the port?" asked Bruce. His voice was drowsy. "I think I did. That was a good bottle. Australian, to boot."

"We were supposed to meet Rene Salazar an hour ago," I mut-tered. "And I thought port came from Portugal."

"This is all too mysterious for me," said Bruce. "'Go to the town of El Fuerte. There you will meet a man named Rene Salazar. He will lead you to the bass. The bass, oh, they will be bigger than Chevrolets.' I swear this was four-lane 10 minutes ago. Ah, here's the port. All gone, yep, and it was Australian. A shame."

"Australia's not so bad. I once caught a trevally there that —"

"I meant that it's a shame it's empty, not that it's Australian. That truck just flashed its lights at us."

"My lights are on," I said. "I think in Mexico that means hello. Like the one-finger hidy wave in Mississippi. Anyway, I was fishing with two Japanese tourists and an English soccer hooligan, this heartbroken, cross-eyed guy I'd been drinking with for a few days, but he kept trying to goad the mate into a fight by —"

"We're going the wrong way."

"— eating the baitfish, like that old college goldfish shtick —"

"Oh, God."

I spun the car into the median as the thick front of a semi skidded past the corner of our bumper. There was a burst of gravel, a whirl of lights and then, with a *thunk,* we leapt into the southbound lane, as if we'd always belonged there, which of course we had. The tinny roar of offended honks faded behind us. Inside the car was a long, pronounced silence, until finally, in the dark, I said meekly: "He called it the best bass lake in the world." My pal Bruce had no comment, but then he's always been a bit of a trout snob.

Permit, if you will, a brief, if slightly digressive, note of caution: If you intend to catch bass in Mexico, then you must be careful where you drive. It's not simply a matter of driving in the correct lane on the highway, though naturally that's got its relative merits. But it is all too easy to turn right here, and then maybe left there, and suddenly you find that the road ends in the cobblestone maze of a *pueblo* with a 17th-century stone church at its plaza, where even now a festival is in full swing and girls more winsomely pretty than any you have seen at home are slipping lightly past the *tacquerias* and *tortillerias,* and a young man with a guitar is playing on the corner, and at the *palacio,* it appears that all the townsfolk have turned out to see the baritone Artura Barrera and the mezzo-soprano Adriana Diaz de Leon sing from the works of Rossini and Mascagni and the great Mexican composer Alfonso Esparza Oteo. A man on the street will tell you: *Si,* you can make it to El Fuerte, but it is best not to drive the old road in the dark, for the marijuana farmers are making their runs at this hour and wouldn't it be better just to stay for the festival and eat some bass seviche and drink tequila from the strange round gold bottle kept on the shelf with the radishes and cilantro and tomatoes while the local Mayo Indians perform their deer dance and a hundred thousand bats flutter above the trees of the plaza and I tell you grand stories of the chupacabra? The answer, of course, is yes.

Like all desert reservoirs, Lake Huites looks *wrong.* Because the lake itself, in a purely metaphorical sense, is a sort of crazed alien creature. With its weird, half-cruel juxtaposition of starchy desert and bountiful blue water, it evokes less a scene from nature than it does a bad abstract painting. Those poor blackish skeletons of dead organ-pipe cacti up there on the mountainside: They spent their entire existences moaning for water only to find themselves, on that clear fine day when the Rio Fuerte began flowing backward, neck deep in it. It's a queer thing to cast a Zara Spook toward the drowned arm of a cactus. Even more queer to cast one toward the chipped stone crucifix of a church steeple poking out from the water.

But then, queer as it may be, this is the routine for catching fish by the hundreds on Lake Huites. We set out at dawn, in the flinty-cold gray light, a 55-horsepower Evinrude hustling us through submerged canyons flanked by 400-foot red walls while an unseemly gyre of vultures circled above the water — a funnel of death birds. Our young guide's name was Manuel, and he's the brother of the mysterious Rene Salazar, a giant of Mexican bass fishing, who, like Manuel, grew up fishing with his father on the much-older and much-netted Dominguez Lake near El Fuerte. Guides here tend to make, on average, about $12 a day, not including tips, which, compared to the $4 per day average of the local farm laborer, isn't quite so dreary as it sounds. This is one reason that local officials are working to keep netters off the lake — patrolling the lake, shooting holes in the bottoms of netters' boats, and working with the new crop of lodges to provide tourism-based incentives for the locals — and greeting the stream of gringo fishermen with wide and welcoming grins.

The magistrate in the nearest town of Choix, in fact, was so determined to make us fishermen feel secure that he posted 24-hour guards at our lodge. A kindly act, but it was nonetheless slightly disconcerting to stumble across two scowling men with bandannas over their lower faces and submachine guns at their sides as we hauled our tackle out to the trucks in the predawn darkness. "In case of goatsuckers," Bruce said. I nodded dimly.

There is a very precise difficulty involved in describing fishing of this variety. I could, for instance, do it this way: I cast into the brush; I caught a three-pound bass. I cast into the brush; I caught a four-pound bass. I cast into the brush; I caught a six-pound bass. But this would go on and on, ad nauseam, like a never-ending Buddhist mantra that wouldn't be much of a joy to write, truth to tell, and less so to read. Or, more concisely, I could simply tell you how many fish we hauled in; but then I've always been one who believes that the counting of beers drunk, fish caught or women bedded is a noxious vulgarity that should under no circumstance be tolerated.

So I find myself with almost-empty hands, forced to dip into anal-ogy, however banal: Perhaps you remember, as a child, after you'd spent a good half-hour and a pocketful of quarters, finally being able to hit every target at the carnival shooting gallery so that, all at once, the monkey was clapping, the cuckoo was cuckooing, the bottle was spinning, and the piano player's bowler hat was leaping off his head like he'd just caught a peek of the neighbor lady's nitchy. If so, then you will certainly understand: Bass fishing at Lake Huites is rather like that. By the afternoon of our first day on the lake, I was able to predict my catches. "Right there, in front of that little pocket of rocks," I would tell Bruce, and then lob a 10-inch red shad-colored worm right there, in front of that little pocket of rocks, let it sink for a two-second count, twitch it slightly, then feel the worm swallowed, hard, and feel the line go taut as copper wire while Manuel just shrugged as if he'd seen it all before, which, I suppose, he certainly had.

Getting your lure to the fish was the sole objective; these were lazy bass, accustomed to jutting out their necks for their lunch but never putting too much effort into it, which meant that topwater lures were about as useful on the lake as a cello, golf clubs or a thick Victorian novel. But as to that whammo of a question, whether or not Lake Huites is the best bass lake in the world: It's a silly qualifier in the first place, hinging so preposterously on the inter-twined vagaries of season, weather, water level, skill and blessedly dumb luck. Let's just leave it at this: Even the trout snob was eu-phoric, giggling in the sun.

Meanwhile, back at the lodge. The atmosphere among the return-ing anglers was heady, like that of a room choked with big-shot ca-sino winners. Caught this, caught that, went the song, and oh, gee-whiz, the one that got away. That the greater bulk of the chitchat of half-drunk bass fishermen is wholly insipid bears no mention, but I was startled by one guy who said he'd landed a bass bigger than a tit. That night I dreamt of a bass with large bosoms, a dream I'm still not able to classify as erotic, aquatic or simply deranged.

Bruce and I took our perch in the *palapa* at the center of the lodge. Because we had driven the wrong way on the Mexican in-terstate — and narrowly survived — we were accorded a certain prestige among our peers, who, being more pragmatic sorts, were nonetheless puzzled as to why we had opted to drive at all. We drank heartily. Included in the fishing package were all the margaritas we could devour, which is never a good thing for someone like me, who spent most of his early 20s scouring sofa bottoms for enough change to buy a cocktail. I have two dogs who spent their puppyhoods on the periphery of starvation and even now, half a decade later, can't control themselves around a full bowl of chow; there is a corollary there, I'm afraid, but it's one I'm trying to better manage.

Sometime around sunset I thought of how, as a youngster, I'd stood fishing on the banks of Lake Pleasant, a reservoir in the beige-colored badlands near Phoenix, and felt an abrupt pop on the line, watched the water churn and a silver-green tailfin slap the lake's surface and then vanish and, not knowing quite what to do, began reeling in the line, excitedly, with a pink-cheeked, breathless sense of mystery one can liken only to that which accompanies first love. I remember that bass still, and the thundersome beating of my small heart. One might expect, lo these many years later, that such histrionic glee would soften, that the heart, after so many fish, would develop a crust demanding bigger and better fish to penetrate. One would be mistaken. I sat there in the palapa, reveling in the happy twitching of my chest, until the sun had slipped behind the *cordilleras* and the guards had begun lightly dozing with their M-16s dangling off their kneecaps, and somewhere in the mountains the chupacabra was coming alive, stretching his limbs, like me, in the reddish Mexican half-light.

DANIEL COYLE

Peerless

FROM OUTSIDE

THREE-THIRTY ON A Monday afternoon in Whistler, British Columbia. The snow is falling, the lifts are shutting down for the day,
and within the lacquered-oak confines of the Keg at the Mountain,
the boys are starting to gather. There's Tommy Charron, Richie
Schley, Peter the Swede, and adventure-filmmaker Christian Bégin
— a fair cross section of Whistler's top backcountry skiers and
snowboarders. And sitting in the corner, rolling a cigarette, there's
Eric Pehota.

Tommy says, "Spanky's was going off. Flat as slate, perfect pow."

Richie says, "Falsies. Falsies was total cream."

The Swede says, "The snowpack's snapping into shape. It's good
up top, but a few death cookies down low."

The rest of the boys hoist their pints of Kokanee — yes, death
cookies. As if on cue, four fetching snowboard betties — two bru-
nettes, a redhead, and a blonde — materialize at the next table
and start issuing signal plumes of Marlboro smoke. From a back-
pack they extract a freshly developed sleeve of photographs, including some snapshots taken last night after they got home from
the bars and slipped on their pajamas and got a little crazy and . . .
well, they make such a commotion over these photos that they just
have to pass them over. The boys, however, barely take notice. Even
as they leaf through images of fleshly temptation, even as the de-
lectable betties perch expectantly a few feet away, the boys end up
ignoring them because the boys are doing something more important.

The boys are telling stories, stories of their day on the mountain,

they might do. They speak in the
ng of ripping fresh pow (powder),
acks), scoring schwag (gear) and
ucking big air. They tell stories in
ot that they'd ever admit there *is* a
g there's a hierarchy is the hierar-
here it is nonetheless, the primal
round a table seeing who's stron-
at one local writer has dubbed the
nd Christian are punching each
s how he got fired from his waiter
week's forecast looks totally sick,
and Christian says how he's psyched his new ski film is doing so
well, and the Swede says he's thinking about a big expedition to the
Tantalus, and everybody agrees that would be righteous. Then
Tommy gets up to use the facilities and asks the betties if it would
be all right if he borrowed the photos for, oh, about ten minutes,
and everybody's laughing, basking in the glow of the day and the
beer and the flow of words, the hucking and chucking, the freshies
and the pow, the stories that pile up like snowflakes.

And Eric Pehota? He sits in the corner, observing the proceedings and doing absolutely nothing. To be more precise, he's working on his Kokanee and rolling another cigarette, and he's sitting
the way he usually sits: perfectly still, his head slightly down, his
eyes quick and watchful. When someone in the group courts his
opinion, Pehota makes his signature move, an artful maneuver that
he repeats to perfection a dozen times in an hour, a hundred times
a day. He gives an easy smile and a matter-of-fact shrug — "You
probably already know this," the gesture says — and utters a few
words in his tobacco-y Canuck voice, something concise and agree-
able, like, "The snowpack's shaping up just like it did three years
ago," or "Yeah, that was one hell of a day," or something else designed to steer the conversation back on track. Which is to say away
from him.

Not that Pehota (pronounced pay-O-ta) lacks for stories. He
could talk about the 40 major first ski descents (or maybe it's 50, or
60 — he doesn't bother to keep exact count) or the half-dozen
close calls with avalanches, including two last winter that left him
digging out corpses. Or the time when, after helping his partners

make a nasty 20-foot rappel into the you-fall-you-die steeps of Mount Currie's Pencil Couloir, Pehota yelled at them to look out, planted his poles, and just *leapt.* Or the time he went hand over hand along a chairlift cable to rescue that little girl who had slipped off and was hanging by her brother's leg. Or the stories about the things he hasn't done — like ski that unnamed 55-degree couloir south of Pemberton, the one he's obsessed with, the one he's hiked to each of the last six winters only to turn around when the conditions proved dicier than he liked. Or any of the stories that have accumulated in such stealthy magnificence that the boys, who dun one another with nicknames like Puddles and Sweet Cheeks and Ragu, refer to Pehota only half-kiddingly as The Legend. But the thing about Pehota, the thing that sets him apart, is that he doesn't tell stories. Not to the boys at the bar, not to the ski media, not to anyone. When I spoke to his brother, Dave, who's a farmer in Grand Forks, British Columbia, I asked what he thought of Eric's adventures. Dave paused. "I don't know," he said. "He's never told me about them."

The other thing about Pehota that you learn right away is where he's from: namely Mackenzie, B.C., a logging town of 6,000 and wellspring of that bacon-eating, plaid-shirted, hardass avatar of Canadian manhood known as the Mackenzie redneck — a term employed to define Pehota by everyone I spoke with, including Pehota himself. Amid the neon-swathed glitterati of Whistler, the Mackenzie redneck tends to stand out — particularly one with a hatchmarked Eastwood squint and a penchant for showing up spattered in cement, sawdust, engine grease, or, as happened last fall, the blood of a sheep he'd just finished butchering. When he walks into the bar, eyes follow him. People may not know who he is, but they sense his authenticity; they know he's somebody. And they're right. He's the cinematic figure in western mythology, the lean-muscled, laconic hero from the backcountry who comes strolling down Main Street while the townsfolk point and whisper. Pehota's even got a long white scar on his left check, the result of a childhood encounter with — what else? — a horse's hoof.

"A lot of people are intimidated by Eric," says his friend David Hughes. "It comes from the look in his eyes, this real cold, hard look. Not that he's mean — it's just that he's intense, very intense, and most people can't tell the difference."

It's a fine line. During our first evening together, after some beers and encouragement, he was telling about the time he fought a logger from Revelstoke and had just reached the part about pitching the man out the barroom door when he hesitated, as if suddenly realizing where he was.

"Truth is, I'm not much of a fighter," he said, slowly unwrapping his fingers from my neck. He shrugged harmlessly. "Don't fight much at all, really."

When I ask Pehota to describe his profession, he has a hard time finding the words. He tests various possibilities, dismissing "extreme skier" as inaccurately dangerous-sounding. He tries "all-mountain skier," then the current industry alternative of "free-skier," and finally throws up his hands and reaches, as he often does, for a cliché — this one a quote from his friend Steve Smaridge. "It's the ultimate paradox," he says. "The closer you get to death, the more alive you feel."

Paradox abounds, because the fact is, his closest compatriots are mostly dead, not only Stevie but so many of the *ski d'extreme* pioneers of the eighties — Patrick Vallençant and Jean-Marc Boivin and Bernard Gouvy and most recently Pehota's best friend and longtime skiing partner, Trevor Petersen, all neatly erased by rock climbing, parapenting, and skiing accidents. Or they've lost their soul, like the sport's acknowledged founder, Sylvain Saudan, who called for his lawyers after Whistler-Blackcomb had the gall to name two runs in his honor without providing proper remuneration. The remainder of Pehota's peers have steered themselves into the stability of heli-ski guiding, lodge-owning, or ski-industry promotion, as in the case of famously mohawked Glen Plake, who attends conventions dressed as the Energizer bunny. They've been followed by a wave of canny, peroxided kids who want the same thing, only faster — kids who've already bought into the packaged rebellion of the International Free Skiing Association and its various extreme contests, kids who view skiing as a career path. At 34, Pehota is one of the last of a breed, an extreme skier still true to the movement's founding creed: to climb mountains and ski steep faces for the love of doing it. He does not enter contests or attend trade shows; he has no agent, little money, and no plans for a life after skiing. He possesses a redneck's deep-seated distrust of whiz-bang modernity. Pehota cooperates with the corporate machine as much as he has to, getting photographed enough to keep his small handful of sponsors sending him equipment, teaching the occasional backcountry ski clinic. But the rest of the time, he's living a life he's carefully designed and guarded, a life that, because it depends on no one outside of his family, allows him to do what he wants to do. As ski filmmaker James Angrove says, "Everybody pretends to be a mountain man, but Pehota actually is one."

Pehota twists the points on another cigarette and looks up to see 29-year-old Richie Schley. Schley is wearing a gray knit cap pulled low over his brow and nursing a stein of cranberry juice with an orange slice. Schley is one of the hottest skiers in the game, sponsored by Salomon and Smith and Valid and PowerBar, and spends more than half his time away from Whistler on photo shoots. Pehota notices the drink, and Richie follows his eyes.

A flicker crosses Richie's impenetrable slacker gaze. "Yeah," he says, all nonchalance. "I gotta go lift after."

Pehota's brow creases. Lift? The lifts are closed.

"No," Richie says, flexing his arm. "You know. Lift weights."

Pehota looks bemused. To him, the notion of a skier engaging in formal exercise verges on the unfathomable. A few years ago when Pehota broke a couple of ribs on a 50-foot leap into a mogul field, he came up with a line he used when people asked if it hurt.

"Only thing is," Pehota would deadpan, "I can't do my sit-ups."

Now Richie, emblem of the next generation, is pumping iron? The moment cries out for a comment, a little tease, at least an acknowledgment of the gap between veteran and whippersnapper. But Pehota doesn't do that. Instead, he leans back, pulls a long draw of smoke into his lungs, and wrinkles his face into a smile — a surprisingly gentle smile, one that embodies the core reason Pehota is king of the mountain: He's got nothing to prove.

First there are chickens. Thirteen of them, nice plump Rhode Island Reds, along with one exceedingly satisfied rooster, in a neat little coop on Pehota's two-acre property in the quiet rural town of Pemberton, 22 miles north of Whistler. They're good layers, too — every Friday Eric's wife, Parveen, takes a few dozen eggs to Whistler and sells them to friends. Beyond the coop lies a garden of beans, peas, potatoes, garlic, onions, tomatoes, carrots, and sweet corn that grows tall enough for Logan, four, and Dalton, two, to get lost in. To the east lies the Lillooet River, to the south the newly built barn, and to the north the Lumbermate Mark III sawmill where Pehota transforms the trees he fells into massive posts and beams. He makes his own timber-pegs, of course, and with the pegs and the timbers he's built the barn, a shed for the sawmill, and the basement beneath the trailer where the Pehota family lives.

Ah, yes, the trailer: that mustard-colored, 12-by-60-foot 1972 corrugated-steel job he bought for a song and has remade into a sort of backwoods castle. "I'm pretty good with my hands" is how Pehota explains the fact that he did the cement work himself. As well as the framing. And the finish carpentry. And a fair bit of the wiring and plumbing. For heat, he hand-splits cottonwood and fir, running five cords a winter into their living room stove. The Pehota estate is rounded out by a diesel truck, a 1951 Cessna airplane, a snow machine, two kayaks, two mountain bikes, and a shiny green-and-yellow riding lawn mower. When I point out the irony of the world's best all-around skier trundling along at two miles per hour on a John Deere, Pehota doesn't laugh. He doesn't get the joke, because the lawn mower — along with the trailer, the garden, the woodstove, and the chickens — are part of his system, as much a part of his life's essentials as his skis or poles.

"My goal is to be totally self-supporting," Pehota says. "Why should anybody depend on someone else for something they can do themselves?"

These days, not everybody understands that goal, particularly some of the suburban-raised, cyberliterate, Church of the Moment boys who come out to visit. Though they stand in awe of Pehota's seemingly depthless redneck savvy, though they're dazzled to experience the cultural antithesis of their own frat-house, laundry-bomb milieu, they can't help but assume that the whole thing was a big score, some kind of megaschwag. And that kind of talk — well, it ticks Pehota off.

"If there's one thing I'm tired of," he says, "it's people coming out here and saying, 'Oh, you got such a great life, such a great job, a plane, a nice piece of land.'" He slams a fist into his hand. "Hey buddy, I earned this. I worked for every bit of it — every fucking bit of it, OK?"

Pehota has two basic expressions: amiable and dead serious. When he's dead serious, his facial muscles tighten, his eyes narrow, and words come with difficulty. When he's amiable, his face relaxes and his eyes open up, enabling quick bursts of conversation. As we walk around, I ask Pehota about his life: his motivations, his attitude toward risk. I ask about his wife, a Vancouver-born snowboarder of Punjabi descent, and his kids, and his own childhood. And he answers — shrugging and giving his matter-of-fact smile, disposing of the questions as cleanly as if he were hammering pegs. Childhood was good. Parents strict, and he needed it. Ski-raced locally for a while, didn't like it, headed backcountry. Not real big on risks — try to be careful. Parveen? Worked with her at the bar, liked her a lot, and, well, you know how it goes.

Looking for insights, I try his friends.

"Eric doesn't let anyone in his head," says Mike Jensen. "He's not what you would call a communicator."

"What motivates him? He likes drinking beer and rolling cigarettes, and he's damn good at both," says Hughes.

"Here's the deal with Eric," says Peter the Swede. "He works hard; he's got a good wife, a good job, a good life doing what he likes to do. It's simple, no?"

Perhaps it is. Pehota and I make our way back toward the trailer. The garden hose hangs coiled on its hook, the firewood is immaculately stacked and tarped, the skis rest in their rack of two-by-fours, the kids' boots stand in soldierly pairs. He shows me his workbench and his woodworking tools — drawknives, wood chisels, cold chisels, block planes, all arranged neatly in drawers and on pegboard, a place for everything and everything in its place. It reminds me of my grandfather's basement, so I tell him, attempting to turn the conversation toward family, toward memories, toward the deeper questions of why we are the way we are. But Pehota doesn't take the bait. As we stand down there, looking through tools in comfortable silence, it occurs to me that Pehota's not going to answer these questions for the same reason that my grandfather wouldn't be able to answer them: because life is busy enough without such foolishness.

"That's right, everything's raised up," Pehota says when I ask about his shelving. "When the river rises, I'm ready."

Pehota's grandfather was a logger, his father was a logger, and Eric would have been a logger except that Mackenzie had this hill called Little Mac, maybe 400 vertical feet, that he could walk up and ski down. By the time he was eight years old, Eric could do front and back flips. Dyslexia made high school difficult and college unthinkable, so on graduation day he loaded his car and drove to Apex Ski Resort, got a job as a liftie, and met a ponytailed, beret-wearing firebrand named Trevor Petersen. While Pehota had never traveled as far as Vancouver until he was in his late teens, Petersen was interested in emulating the extreme skiers of Europe. Petersen, who spent several months in Chamonix in the eighties, educated Pehota in the ways of French-style ski-mountaineering, which stood in stark contrast to the big-air, big-attitude approach of Glen Plake, Scot Schmidt, Mike Hattrup, and other members of the burgeoning American extreme-skiing scene. In 1984 Pehota and Petersen relocated to Whistler and started to make a name for themselves. Pehota skied the northwest summit of Mount Waddington in 1987 and notched the second winter ascent and first ski descent of the north face of Dalton Dome in 1988; he made the second ascent and first descent of the north face of Mount Fitzsimmons with Petersen in 1989. In 1991, Pehota won the first extreme-skiing contest, defeating favorites Dean Cummings and Doug Coombs. Pehota hadn't planned on entering — and hasn't entered a contest since — but he was broke and needed the prize money to go on an expedition to Mount Rainier's Liberty Ridge. On the last run he worked his way out on a narrow rib no one had dared ski, flew 40 feet over a rock pile, and collected his check. Word started to get out.

"Petersen and Pehota were a perfect partnership," says ski photographer Paul Morrison. "Trevor was the charismatic one, while Eric was the quiet buddy. They didn't do show-off, lift-oriented stuff — it was the real deal."

A small taste of these days is captured in videos, RAP Films' little-seen *The White Room, Cosmic Winter,* and *Tales from the Snow Zone.* Filtering out the throbbing sound track and the relentlessly cute narration that is the nemesis of the ski-movie genre, you're left with a series of stunning images. Pehota and Petersen perform any number of superhuman feats — hucking huge air into thick groves of trees, snaking through granite mazes, blasting down couloirs as the snow avalanches around them like sea foam — but in every case the eye is drawn to Pehota, to the way his body becomes a rhythmic extension of the terrain. "I try to flow," is how he puts it, and it's accurate enough. Skiing the steeps or working his way through the stem-christying weekend crowd at Whistler, Pehota moves downslope like water.

"Virtually every skier has some weakness," says Morrison. "You can't see it with the naked eye, but it shows when you look frame by frame through a camera. Pehota is different because he doesn't have a weakness. He looks good at every point during a turn."

"Eric's like a cat," says former World Cup downhiller Rob Boyd. "He's ungodly smooth, he picks wise lines, and he's got this way of staying on his feet no matter what's happening around him."

"Skiing steeps like Pehota it isn't about a thrill ride," says Johnny Chilton, a top extreme skier and Pehota's sometime expedition partner. "It's about control, staying connected to the snow by using your skis like you'd use an ice ax. Eric stays connected to the snow better than anybody on the planet."

Pehota and Petersen never broke into the big time, not like the Americans did. This didn't always sit well with Petersen, but it was fine with Pehota. Besides, by the midnineties, things were settling into a new and mellower phase. Petersen and Pehota each got married. Pehota was thinking of buying his land; Petersen had his young son, Kye, skiing like a dervish. The plan was in place — they'd keep adventuring together, start bringing the kids along; it would be simple. Then, in February 1996, Petersen died in an avalanche.

"Everything went crazy," remembers Chilton. "All of us were crying, freaking out, getting drunk together. But Eric kind of withdrew. The rest of us had to let our feelings out, but whatever he was thinking, he kept it inside."

In the Church of the Moment, there was no greater saint than Petersen. His happiness, his energy, his ability to communicate the wonder of the mountains, all were held up as proof of his worthiness. His equipment was given away as keepsakes; his ashes were scattered in his favorite spots; his ice ax was mounted on Blackcomb Peak. The circumstances of his death were mined for poetry. Petersen had been skiing alone in a remote couloir above his beloved Chamonix. He had not suffocated, but had died by the quick mercy of a broken neck. To raise money for Petersen's widow and kids, a relative printed a bumper sticker that remains ubiquitous on Whistler vehicles: TREVOR WOULD DO IT. It's a sentiment that proves unsettling to some locals, including Doug Sack, a local sports columnist. "Trevor would do it? Well, Trevor did it, and Trevor's dead, and he left two kids who are going to grow up without a dad," he says. "Pehota would impress me a hell of a lot more if he dialed back the John Wayne act and lived long enough to bullshit his grandchildren."

After Petersen's death, Pehota drifted from the group, eased off skiing for a year to spend time with his family, including his newborn son, whom he named Dalton Trevor. Eventually he returned, though his friends sensed that something had changed. As Jensen puts it, "When Trevor died, he lost something. He'd never talk about it, but you can see it in his face."

One afternoon, when we were talking about Petersen, I asked Pehota what he thought of Sack's sentiment.

"Hey, it's a numbers game," Pehota said quickly. "You never know when yours is going to come up."

But, I asked him, isn't it the point to control those numbers? Wasn't that the goal of all his organization, his discipline, his carefully built system of life?

Pehota thought awhile, his eyes narrowing while he looked for the words. Then he again reached for the quote from Steve Smaridge.

"The closer you get to death," he said quietly, "the more alive you feel."

Then he said it again, repeating the mantra as if he were trying to convince himself of something he couldn't entirely believe.

Do you have the bumper sticker on your truck? I asked.

"No," Pehota said. "I used to. But now I don't."

There's a river just south of Whistler called the Cheakamus. It's a 20-foot-wide band of fast green water banked by cathedral stands of hemlock and fir. On the afternoon Pehota takes me there, it's snowing. We leave Tommy and the Swede and the rest of the boys at the Keg and drive out of Whistler, first swinging into a liquor store.

"Gonna have a drink with Trev and Stevie," Pehota explains.

We climb down to the river's edge and are enveloped in the sound of the water. Pehota shows me the plaques cemented on the rock. There are three — in memory of Steve Smaridge, Trevor Petersen, and a woman named Kim Wetaski, along with a larger plaque urging us to live our dreams. Pehota looks at the words, walks out onto a boulder that protrudes over the river, stands on the edge, and drinks his beer.

In my few days in Whistler, I've heard a lot about Stevie, crazy, lanky Stevie who was always up for anything, Stevie who never wanted to rope-up on climbs because he knew he wouldn't fall and thought the others might, Stevie who drowned in 1993 on the Upper Elaho River. I've heard about Kim, too — beautiful Kim, a wonderful athlete and former figure-skating champion who missed an eddy on the Lower Green just above an unrunnable waterfall. But now, Pehota isn't thinking about Stevie or about Kim or even about Trevor. He's thinking about something else — staring into the water, hunting for words. And then, in a sudden rush, the words come.

"You know, you get out into it," Pehota says, turning toward me. "You get out into it and it's shitty weather, you're freezing and you're out of fuel and food, and the fucking mountain's going to avalanche." He pauses a moment, as if startled by the sound of his own voice, and then resumes. "And it's getting dark so you huddle up, press against each other to stay warm, and make it through the night, because either things are going to get worse and you're going to die, or they're going to get better. The next day, you get up and you start moving, you start walking and you keep going, and all of a sudden . . ." His eyes widen. "You're back. You're in the car drinking beers and you're joking around and you're *back.*"

Around us, the rocks and trees are slowly being painted white. Every once in a while, a branch receives one snowflake too many and bends to release its burden. After a long silence, I ask what happened that day in Chamonix, the day Trevor didn't come back.

"Trev had skied that couloir before, eight years ago," Pehota says. "The slide wasn't even two feet deep, but it had a lot of rock and ice. It must've knocked him off his skis. It's just one of those things."

I ask if Pehota would have gone skiing that day, alone, in a couloir he hadn't run in years.

"Hard to know," he says finally. "I chalk it up as something that's out of anybody's control."

After Petersen died, amid his friends' sadness and shock there existed a small but significant element of anger — anger that Petersen had taken such risks by himself in a place he hadn't skied in so long. Pehota would never go so far as to voice such an opinion, but the question hangs in the air nevertheless. His two best friends — two happy people, two guys who lived their dreams — are dead, and he's still here. There are two possibilities: Perhaps Pehota's lucky, and he unquestionably is. Or perhaps there's something in the way he approaches life, something in the redneck virtues of being organized and humble and hardworking, something to that cold gaze and that matter-of-fact smile. Perhaps he is simply in touch with truths that the rest of us can so easily forget: that we live our lives in an indifferent, dangerous place, a place in which a river can flood your basement, a corporation can steal your soul, an insensate chunk of snow can take your best friend. You want to survive? Enthusiasm isn't enough. Happiness isn't enough. You've got to be vigilant, obsessed, even a little dangerous yourself.

Pehota drinks the rest of his beer and shakes the last drops into the river. We talk awhile longer, about his childhood in Mackenzie, and something occurs to him, something important. He leans in close and locks eyes with me, and his face tenses into its dead-serious expression.

"When I was a kid, my mom used to tell me something," he says.

The river's loud, so he leans closer — he doesn't want me to miss a word. "The world doesn't owe you anything," he says.

Green water rushes toward the ocean, snow piles silently on the fir trees, and Eric Pehota has finally found a story worth telling, so he shouts it.

"That's what she would tell me, all the time. She'd say, 'Eric, the world doesn't owe you anything — not a single thing!' And she was *right*."

MICHAEL FINKEL

Running Like Hell

FROM WOMEN'S SPORTS AND FITNESS

I KISSED Janet Runyan because I fell in love with the way she ran. I fell in love with her stride — the way her legs appeared to arc instead of scissor, the way her feet seemed to brush the pavement rather than pound. The swing of her arms. The slight, steady bob of her chin. These are not the only reasons. I kissed her because she is beautiful. I kissed her because her life had become a jumble of sleep deprivation and physical pain and a training schedule that was the equivalent of running nearly five marathons a week, and I wanted her to know that I, an outsider, did not condemn her for her choices, however unorthodox they were, nor did I pity her or want to change her. I kissed her because there seemed no way to explain all this. It was five o'clock in the morning, and everyone around us was paired off and kissing. Kissing seemed to be on the agenda. So that is what we did.

I met Janet early last summer, in Boulder, Colorado, in the midst of a long and extraordinary run. I had come to Boulder for two reasons. First, to conduct research for a book I am writing on the motivations and lifestyles of people who seem addicted to excessive exercise. Second, I wanted to aid my own pursuit of exhaustion. Over the past year I had been methodically preparing to run an "ultra" — that is, a race longer than the standard marathon distance of 26.2 miles. The race I had my sights on was the 100-mile-long Western States Endurance Run. But in June, less than a month before the event, I found myself daunted by the enormity of running 100 miles and overwhelmed with doubts. My training began to stagnate. I came to Boulder seeking inspiration. I came to find a group of people known as Divine Madness.

Nearly everything I knew about Divine Madness I'd gleaned from a pair of articles published in the *New York Times* and *Newsweek* during the summer of 1997. The articles had a strong effect on me; I cut them out and pinned them to my office wall. According to the stories, Divine Madness was a strange and insular group consisting of a guru and approximately 40 followers, men and women whose ages ranged from mid-twenties to late fifties. Their way of life included communal living, all-night meditation sessions, and no shortage of unconventional sexual behavior. There was also a lawsuit, filed by three ex-members (two of them women), accusing the guru of systematically destroying their lives.

What fascinated me most was the running. Spurred on by their guru, about 25 of the Divine Madness members had taken to ultra-running. They logged incredible distances — sometimes 50 miles in a day — hours upon hours of running; an entire lifestyle, it seemed, built around running. All this training had resulted in some remarkable performances. A Divine Madness member named Steve Peterson had triumphed in each of the past four years at the Leadville 100, a race that is the equivalent of running nearly four successive marathons combined with an elevation gain in excess of 15,000 feet, more than the rise from the base to the summit of Mount Everest. His winning times were usually between 18 and 19 hours. In 1996 Janet Runyan won the U.S. 100-kilometer national championships, covering the 62 miles in less than nine hours. *This guru is on to something,* I thought. His runners had evidently tapped into an energy source I had not discovered, one I hoped they'd be willing to share.

Establishing contact with the group was surprisingly easy. I phoned a Boulder running-shoe store (where, it turned out, Divine Madness members receive a discount) and asked how I could get in touch with a member. I was promptly given the phone number for Art Ives, one of Divine Madness' strongest runners. I called and left a message.

Art rang back a few hours later. We had a friendly chat, though strictly about running. I told him that in the Northern Rockies, where I live, the mountain trails were still clogged with snow and that I planned to be in Boulder the following week, in order to train for my ultra. I told him about some of my recent training difficulties. Neither of us mentioned the name Divine Madness.

"We do a pretty good run on Wednesdays," Art said. He paused. "I suppose you could join in."

I told him I'd be honored. "Where should I meet you?"

"Well," said Art slowly and, it seemed, a bit evasively, as if he were weighing his invitation. "I won't know that until Tuesday night."

I gave him my cell phone number. The next Tuesday I flew to Boulder and met friends for dinner. Around eight o'clock, I began to get antsy. Perhaps Art had discussed his invitation with the other members and felt that the presence of a stranger was not a good idea. Perhaps they were concerned I wasn't a strong enough runner. I didn't even know if I was strong enough. At nine o'clock, I called Art. No answer. At ten, I called again. Still no answer. Then my phone rang. It was him. "We're on," he said. He gave me the name of a trailhead on the outskirts of town and told me to be there at 8 A.M.

"Be ready for 30 miles," he said. "Maybe more."

Ultra-running is a strange and all-consuming sport. There are very few ultra-runners in North America (a rough estimate is 8,000), and for good reason: It is the point, I believe, at which running crosses the line from sport into obsession. Ultra-running is hard on the body: hard on the joints, the muscles, the hips, the spine. It may be punishing right down to the molecular level; doctors are beginning to question whether excessive running can corrupt healthy cells, resulting in maladies such as chronic fatigue syndrome and even cancer.

Ultra-runners are on a first-name basis with misery. I know this because I have been an ultra-runner. For many of us, the longer we run, the more sleep-deprived we are, the closer we come to absolute exhaustion, the more satisfied we feel. I have experienced the throes of such an obsession, and it's not difficult to imagine how soothing it would be to find someone who could guarantee my body endless challenges, who was willing to manage and schedule and plan my pain.

Divine Madness, in fact, is not the only guru-led ultra-running community in the U.S. The 2,000 or so followers of Sri Chinmoy, based in New York City, include a large contingent of ultra-runners, several of whom have completed the group's annual 51-day, 3,100-mile-long race. A few weeks before meeting with Divine Madness, I had spent time in New York, watching and occasionally running with several Sri Chinmoy disciples as they plodded around a one-mile loop for 10 consecutive days, stopping only for catnaps. There was a contingent of ultra-runners in the EST movement who called themselves the World Runners, and a group known as Nichiren Shoshu of America, or NSA, occasionally embarked on long sessions of group marching.

In describing Divine Madness, the *New York Times* bandied about the word "cult." Divine Madness, of course, hates that label, preferring to call itself an Ultra Club. But Divine Madness is "definitely cultic," says Carol Giambalvo, director of the recovery program at the American Family Foundation, a group that keeps tabs on cultic groups nationwide. "All the ex-members I've spoken with consider themselves former members of a cult." The lawsuit against Divine Madness supports Giambalvo's belief that the group meets most of the criteria that indicate an organization is operating as a cult. According to the suit, which was settled out of court last year, Divine Madness isolated its members from the outside world; attempted to control members' physical needs and finances; and inculcated fears or phobias.

Divine Madness is centered on one man: Marc Tizer, whom his adherents call Yo. Tizer spends most of his time at the group's retreat in central New Mexico. He is small and gaunt, with wild eyes and an unruly Brillo pad of a beard and mustache — an appearance that can, without too much imaginativeness, start a person thinking about leprechauns. Tizer, who is now 51 years old, came to Boulder from Philadelphia (via Berkeley, California) in the seventies and began teaching a healing system of his own creation called harmonizing. It is a grab-bag of religion, mysticism, and self-help programs, including meditation, group therapy, holistic healing, and frequent consultation of the I Ching. The goal of harmonizing is to achieve a state Tizer calls transformation. Yo, his followers believe, has reached this state. He is a transformed being. This gives him superhuman powers: He can, he claims, influence people's thoughts, inflict someone with cancer, and control the win-loss record of the Denver Broncos.

Evidently, harmonizing was profoundly appealing to certain people, and within a few years Tizer had enough adherents to establish his group, which called itself the Community. Members rented a series of houses in and around Boulder and began living in groups of five or six, men and women together, with the housemates selected by Tizer and rearranged annually. The lawsuit alleges that contact beyond the boundaries of the Community is limited: "Tizer forbade reading of outside literature; forbade travel outside of Boulder; forbade watching television and required daily reading and study of the notes of his lectures." Most members are self-employed, working in town as caterers, music teachers, or house cleaners, and reportedly donate portions of their incomes to the group. The 160-acre New Mexico retreat is said to have been paid for in cash by a member; another said she turned over a $100,000 inheritance to the group.

Tizer introduced running to his followers about 10 years ago, after witnessing an ultra-race at the University of Colorado. Tizer, himself an avid runner, seems to have made the sport a metaphor for the state of one's mental health. Aches and injuries and other troubles encountered on a long run have their direct counterparts in deficiencies in one's pursuit of transformation. Extreme distance running seems to fit perfectly into Tizer's ideas of self-fulfillment through deprivation and exhaustion. His rambling, stream-of-consciousness lectures frequently last all night, and group meetings can go until dawn.

The emphasis on ultra-running and sleeplessness, explains Giambalvo, are variations on a classic cult theme. "A cult leader often seeks to have his followers in a weakened state," she says. "People who are sleep deprived or physically exhausted are more malleable, more suggestible, and far less likely to disagree with the leader's demands."

According to the lawsuit, one of Tizer's demands is sex. Marriage and monogamous couplings are discouraged; Yo believes such relationships sap too much of the spiritual energy needed to accomplish transformation. "I am tired of feeling the sexual pressure," wrote one ex-member in a letter included in the lawsuit. "I am tired of having to field that energy and feeling guilty when I don't want to make love. . . . It reminds me of a battering relationship where the woman is not allowed to communicate with the outside for fear of other influences." The lawsuit states that Tizer has had open sexual relationships with many women in the Community and that he "told female members of the Community that their emotional health required that he control their sexual activity." His regular partners are part of an inner group known as "the Yo ladies."

Tizer denied all charges of wrongdoing in the *New York Times* article. "There is such an illusion that I control people," he was quoted as saying. "A cult is where everyone shaves their head and you have to give all your money over. This is something else, where people who are sincerely trying to improve themselves have a teacher who is more or less evolved and is trying to help them lead a more balanced, harmonious life."

Of the 40 members of Divine Madness, there are about a dozen men and a dozen women capable of completing ultras. It is no coincidence that Tizer's top students seem to be those who can run the farthest. "The community revolves around the best runners," one former member told me. "Those who don't run have to work as support crews for those who do; they have to kiss the runners' butts. When I was in Divine Madness, I was sure it was the coolest running club in the world. It took me years to realize that the cost of admission was my mind and my spirit and my independence."

On Wednesday morning, the day I was scheduled to run, I arrived at the trailhead a minute late. Art was already there, looking perturbed. Divine Madness members are exceedingly punctual; I soon discovered why. Art took off up the trail, which headed across a cow pasture and into the craggy foothills of the Rocky Mountains. It was a gorgeous day: 70 degrees, with puffball clouds meandering across the sky, the peaks still pleated with snow.

Art had a quiet, loping stride and the physique of a spider. He told me he was in his early forties and had run several hundred-mile races, including a twelfth-place finish at Leadville in 1997. It was just the two of us on the trail. Two or three miles into the run, though, Art began to check his watch. We sped up a bit, came to an intersection with another trail, and there, as if by design — it *was* by design — was another runner.

He was introduced to me as Kevin, and the three of us continued together. A mile later came Rebecca. Kevin and Art soon surged ahead, and Rebecca and I locked into a slower pace. She had long blond hair and a muscular figure and a forceful, perpetual-motion machine of a stride. She wore a pained expression, not uncommon for ultra-runners, that suggested to me she was doing this solely because it would feel so good once she stopped.

Rebecca, it turned out, hadn't run at all until she joined Divine Madness four years ago. Now she was completing runs that lasted upwards of seven hours. In a few months she was scheduled to compete in a 100-kilometer race. She had just turned 30. I had reached the same milestone a few months earlier, and there was something about this minor coincidence, I think, that made her open up to me. "The last half of my twenties were the worst years of my life," she said, though she didn't elaborate further. Had things been better since she'd turned 30? "Sort of," she said, in a tone that implied not.

I had the impression that she wanted to say more, that the opportunity to speak candidly with an outsider was a rare one, but it was only a matter of minutes before Kevin and Art slowed down and we were all together. Over the next dozen miles other runners started appearing at various intersections. This was the way Divine Madness operated: an intricate interlinking of workouts, everyone on their own schedule, and yet, as the run reached a crescendo, everyone running together. We cruised along the Table Mesa trail and down the Big Bluestem trail and then, more than 20 miles into the run, we jumped onto the paved roads and a woman came toward us from the opposite direction, running with an extraordinary fluidity, moving as if the road were transporting her.

"This is Janet," said Art.

The woman came upon us, slowed to a stop, and pivoted. Then she fired up her stride and continued with us. We'd run nearly a marathon by this point. We ran in a tight, churning group, a sort of runners' peleton. The pace picked up. Seven minutes a mile. We all clicked subconsciously into the same cadence. Our footfalls became synchronous. There was an energy encircling the group, almost a centripetal force, that made me feel as though I'd shed my individual burden and was part of a single multi-legged entity. I was swept along by the rhythm, swept past pain and fatigue and concern. I felt *less* tired as the miles passed.

I ran behind Janet. Her hair was twined into a dusty-blond braid that fell halfway down her back. She had golden skin. I watched her calf muscles flex and relax, pump and deflate, like something on a steam engine. The source of her stride, though, appeared to come not from her legs but from someplace in her center. Her braid scarcely swung. There was an intensity about her, about the way she ran, that I couldn't quite grasp, like a sound so high-pitched it

can only be heard by dogs. Occasionally she would say something
aloud, a scrap of imprecise coach-speak to keep the group moving
in tune: "Shorten the stride. Round the hips. Lean forward."

We shortened and rounded and leaned. I tried to emulate
Janet's pace. She seemed to be running in slow motion, and yet we
were moving faster. Six forty-five. Six forty. We were closing in on
30 miles. I sidestepped to my right, opened my stride, and pulled
beside her. We started to talk. We talked the way runners talk when
they are running — in staccato phrasings, to the tempo of our
breathing.

She told me of her running credentials: winning the 100-kilome-
ter championships and then, the next year, finishing second in the
50-mile championships — back-to-back marathons, nearly, in just
over seven hours. Later this summer, she said, she'd be shooting
again for the 100-kilometer title. She'd come from Texas, she told
me, shy and timid and seeking fulfillment. She came to Boulder
and found Tizer. She hadn't started running until she was 24, and
not seriously until she was 32. She'd just turned 40. We charged
up a short, steep hill. Janet burst into song, "Chattanooga Choo
Choo," sung to the cadence of our pace. "I live to train," she said
when we had reached the crest. It was apparent: She was radiating
the pure spent joy of exhaustion. She told me she ran 120 miles a
week.

Janet hadn't started running until she'd joined Divine Madness
and now she was one of the finest ultra-runners in America. What
had happened? There was her piercing intensity — the type of single-minded drive endemic to almost all top athletes — but through
the slits in that intensity I could sense something slightly off. She
had a purity of focus that seemed too pure. "I'll never marry," she
told me, matter-of-factly. "All I really do is run and eat and sleep." I
couldn't help feeling that she was afflicted with an odd sort of low-
grade fear, a deep-seated nervousness, as if she thought something
terrible might happen to her if she stopped running. It was impossible to know if this were true, of course. All I could do was run beside her.

We came to the trailhead where the cars were parked, and the
run was over. Four hours solid, more than 30 miles. One of the best
runs of my life, maybe the very best. I mentioned this to everyone,
along with my thanks. Rebecca hopped into a car and was off. Janet

smiled and glanced at her watch and said she hadn't finished her workout, and she took off down the road.

Art chose this moment to ask me if I knew about the group and its leader. I said I'd read the articles about Divine Madness but had come with an open mind. Art told me he'd been upset by the charges against the group. "If Divine Madness is a cult," he said, "Christianity was a cult."

The more I thought about the run, the more unsettled I became. I wondered what these runners had subjected themselves to and why. The next day, seeking explanation, I went to see an ex-member I'll call D. She had joined Divine Madness when she was 24 years old; she left the group in 1997, when she was 42.

D.'s home sits on a bluff overlooking Boulder, where she runs a New Age cooking school that she calls a nourishment center. We sat in her backyard in plastic lawn chairs, catching wonderful tomatoey whiffs of the Tuscany bean soup stewing on her stove. When she spoke she continuously patted my forearm, as if to add punctuation.

I began by asking about the guru. At first, D. claimed that much of her time with Tizer was rewarding. "Yo can be an incredible teacher," she said. "At times his ideas seemed magical. He held my essence. He slowed down my aging process. He was the one who told me that my destiny was with food." When I mentioned some of the eccentricities I'd read about — the isolation, the sleep deprivation — her tone shifted abruptly and her eyes narrowed. "You kind of surrender yourself to Yo," she said. "You live in a cocoon with him. Sometimes we'd listen to Yo talk all night about running. What a waste. I never had a full night's sleep. Yo said it wasn't necessary. He said the organs in the body have their own time to sleep and that as long as you got your liver sleep, between 3 and 5 A.M., you were okay." D. also said that Tizer did not allow his runners to eat their first meal of the day until after their workout, even if the run was five or six hours long. "And if you don't finish the run," she said, "you don't eat after, either."

Tizer, she went on, had frequent sex with women in the Community, often while drunk. She confirmed the existence of the Yo ladies, though she wasn't one of them. "Oh yeah, I had sexual relations with Yo," she said. "He needed to make love every night. One time, in the morning, I said I didn't feel like having sex and he said, 'Oh, you'll get over it.' And we did it, just so he could get his rocks off."

Toward the end of our visit, I asked D. if she still ran. "No way," she said. "And I don't miss it. I don't miss it at all."

On the drive back down to town, my cell phone rang. It was Art, calling to invite me to a party. "You seem like the type of person who wouldn't mind staying up late," he said. There was a gathering that evening, and he gave me an address. "Come around midnight," he said. As I hung up, I was reminded of something D. had told me. I had asked her how she was first enticed to join Divine Madness. "I was invited to a party," she said.

The gathering was held in the loft of a renovated barn behind one of the group's communal homes. The loft was windowless and steam-room hot and filled with at least 30 people, two-thirds of them women. Vinyl records were being played — classic rock, a good amount of Beatles. Many of the men were shirtless and dancing wildly, legs and arms aflap, hips pumping, hair spraying sweat. Women mirrored their moves. A bottle of Maker's Mark was pressed into my hand. I took a long swig and passed it on. Soon another bottle was in my palm. I drank again.

It took me several minutes to realize what was going on. For 30 seconds into each song there was regular rock 'n' roll dancing, but this would soon devolve into dirty dancing and then body-smearing and then, quite abruptly, passionate kissing. Some of the couples ended up rolling about on the carpeted floor; others sat and fondled each other. No one, save me, seemed the least bit self-conscious. I took another drink.

Janet and Rebecca were both there, and I sat on the floor near the turntable and watched them dance. When a new song started, I saw Janet dance with someone else and, soon enough, kiss him. After a dozen songs I had watched her kiss four men. This stirred in me a surprising jealousy. I'm not quite sure when it happened, but one moment I was watching Janet dance and the next she had flopped down beside me. My pulse jumped; I began to sweat. We got to talking — about running, about the mechanics of her exquisite stride, about the endless pursuit of faster times — and somewhere during this talk she wound herself about me, so that when she started telling me of her injuries, she'd glide my hand to the site of the wound. I had the feeling I was slipping headlong into trouble, but I did nothing to stop her. She told me about ripping her calf muscle during a 100K race and running through the agony. Down went my hand to her calf. She guided my hand to just above her left knee, where I felt a button-sized scar, and then near her hip, where I could feel a second scar. She told me she'd broken her femur while running and had to have a metal rod inserted to hold the bone together. She had even competed with the rod in place.

It got to be late, very late, and suddenly people were pairing off and leaving. I felt that strange dizzy energy on the far side of exhaustion, so I said to Janet, "Let's go outside and look at the stars," and we unhooked ourselves and walked downstairs, holding hands. But there were no stars outside, because the sky was already turning blue. We laughed — we'd both lost track of time — and Janet said, "Do you want to go running at nine?" I wanted to go, but I needed more than three hours' sleep, so I said, "I can't, Janet, I really can't," and I leaned forward, and we were very close. The moment seemed to beg for closure, like a first date, so I kissed her — or maybe, in truth, she kissed me — but it was an innocent kiss, dry-lipped and brief. We were too tired for passion and I think we both knew it, but we tried again, and again it was the same, and so I said, "Good night," and she said, "Good morning," and we laughed again and I walked to my car and drove away, watching the alpenglow work its way down the mountains.

Two days later Art invited me to join the Sunday run, the most intense workout of the week. I ran for six hours, covering more than 40 miles, and again I found the experience profoundly strength-giving. I spent much of the run with either Janet or Rebecca.

Rebecca and I ran together for the first part of the day, just the two of us, and she continued the conversation where she'd left off on our previous run. She expressed doubts about her desire to continue running, and fears about her spiritual growth. It was impossible for me to remain neutral. And so, as we ran through the foothills, I told Rebecca of the joys of travel, of the pleasures of riding a bike and swimming in the ocean and sleeping late and goofing off and generally being in charge of one's own life. I could tell she was listening, thinking about the path she had chosen, weighing her choices.

For a long time she was silent. Then, suddenly, her foot caught a tree root and she went down hard, skidding on all fours over the rocky path. She jumped up, but already blood was gathering at both knees and tears were pooling in her eyes. She kept going.

"I know why that happened," she said after a few minutes.

"Why?"

Again there was no sound save the slap of footfalls and the rasp of her breathing. "I lost my concentration," she eventually said, "because I was wondering if it would be okay to call you sometime."

Her confession unnerved me. In an instant, she had seemingly transferred to me all of her pain and chaos and confusion. I told her my e-mail address, and she memorized it, but after one exchange of pleasantries a week later, the messages stopped.

I ran my final miles with Janet. When my six hours were up, and I had been pushed yet again beyond what I'd thought were my physical limitations, I gave her a brief hug and watched her run on alone. Janet, I realized, had become habituated to Divine Madness. She had reached the point, I believed, where she would be miserable if she left the group, even though I felt she was surely damaging herself by staying. She had become an athletic machine, constantly running, constantly exhausted, never quite finished, never quite transformed.

It was clear to me that there are secrets the Divine Madness runners possess that I'll never gain access to — secrets that require a sacrifice to unlock I'm unwilling to make. At its very edges, among a certain type of people, ultra-running may become a choice between running and freedom. Janet has chosen running. I selected freedom. I left Boulder, but not before tucking the memories of my runs into a spot where I could access them when necessary, deep into a difficult workout.

Three weeks later I completed my 100-mile race. I finished in 23 hours and 48 minutes, and I'm convinced my runs with Divine Madness helped me break the magical 24-hour mark. My race strategy was uncomplicated: I simply envisioned Janet's stride every step of the way.

JAMES HIBBERD

Poker Face

FROM THE PHOENIX NEW TIMES

THE OTHER HIGH ROLLERS call him Sam. He's the bearish, wealthy owner of two clothing stores, and a regular here at the Bicycle Club card room in Los Angeles. Normally a dominating rock of a card player, Sam is anxious and fidgety. He has about $2,000 in chips lying in the middle of the poker table. And he hates to lose.

The game is Omaha Eight-or-Better, a poker variation where the best hand and the lowest hand (below an eight-high) split the pot.

The other players have folded, and Sam is going heads up against his remaining opponent.

Chewing his toothpick, Sam bets $800 from his waning chip stack.

When his opponent raises, Sam doesn't look up. He knows this particular player is impossible to read.

The dealer peels off the final card, and Sam watches intently as it falls onto the green felt: a three of diamonds.

Normally, a three is an ideal low card. But there are already a couple of threes on the board, and Sam has unavoidably paired up, detonating his low hand. His opponent, who reveals an impressive flush to the ace, has him beat for the high end. There's no consolation prize for getting stuck in the middle.

While the other players marvel at his unfortunate turn, Sam stares at the improbable trio of threes.

"How the fuck did they do that?" Sam asks, his voice cold.

Nobody responds, and Sam's hands begin to shake.

"How the *fuck* did they do that?" he demands, and a jacketed casino supervisor silently appears behind Sam's chair, ready.

Red-faced, Sam reaches into the middle of the table and snatches the offending three of diamonds. He folds it in half, furiously creasing the card, and throws it at the dealer's face.

The dealer doesn't flinch and the supervisor quickly replaces the deck. This is done unobtrusively and without comment. There is significant revenue generated at this table.

The dealer, who has seen such tantrums many times, pushes the whole pot into the waiting hands of Sam's opponent, Johnny Chan.

Chan is the world's greatest poker player, and he says something as he arranges his new chips into tidy stacks.

He says it low, so other players won't hear.

He says, "Just another day at the office."

Johnny Chan lies on a floor mattress in Tawa's Shiatsu Spa, a landmark Japanese massage parlor in Little Tokyo. He often comes here to prepare for a high-stakes poker session, stretching out in the steam rooms, saunas and Jacuzzi baths. The deep-tissue therapy in the communal massage room is his favorite part, and these female Japanese masseuses perform particularly aggressive shiatsu.

The room is silent, save an occasional sigh and the popping of joints.

Chan, 42, has twice won the World Series of Poker, played annually at Binion's Horseshoe Casino in Las Vegas. His second victory, in 1988, is legendary: He lost the biggest pot in the history of the tournament, then came back to take the title.

Two months ago, he signed an exclusive contract with Fort McDowell Casino off the Beeline Highway to develop card games and play heads up against tournament winners. Spectators say he cleaned out his first challenger in less than 10 minutes.

Interviewing Chan is nearly as difficult as trying to read his play. Every detail of his past needs to be dug out with repetitive questions and long pauses. He'll shape his image as it suits him — saying he graduated from college, for instance, when he actually dropped out. Or saying he won $30,000 in his first casino poker game, but telling another reporter in 1988 that it was $20,000.

The more formidable a player's reputation, the more cautious and nervous his opponents. So if Chan doesn't always give the most honest answer, he can always be trusted to give the response that will serve him best in future competition.

On the massage mat, Chan breathes heavily, drifting in and out of sleep. He played poker until 8 this morning and is exhausted. As the masseuse digs her toe into the sides of his spine, another customer recognizes him from his role in *Rounders:*

"Weren't you in that movie?"

"Yes."

"You looked scarier in the movie."

"They filmed me wearing dark clothing."

"You lost to Matt Damon in that scene, right?"

A pause.

"No, I didn't lose to him," Chan says. "I *allowed* him to bluff me out."

Chan doesn't mention that his catch phrase was excised from that scene. When Matt Damon takes the pot, Chan's line was: "What's yours is yours."

It's not a phrase of any particular significance, just something Chan likes to say when he loses a large amount of money to another card player.

He doesn't say it often.

An hour later, Chan dresses in the locker room: black sandals, cream pants, black-and-white shirt, gold bracelet, gold necklace, black-and-gold Versace sunglasses and black Rossignol baseball cap.

He tips the masseuse $10 and gets on his cell phone.

"What's the best action you've got?" he asks, not needing to identify himself.

Chan is told there's a high-stakes game in progress at the Bicycle Club.

He closes the phone. "Let's go."

Chan navigates his red Mercedes convertible through the L.A. freeway maze, a bright blur against the thick afternoon smog. He drives fast, not wanting to miss the action at the casino. His license plate spells out a full-house hand that once paid off for him — threes over jacks.

Following Chan is difficult. He drives aggressively, changes lanes often and rarely signals. You cannot anticipate his next move.

Millions in laundered drug money helped build the Bicycle Club. Extortion has been committed within its walls, and armed robbers have followed its winners home. The casino was eventually confiscated by the federal government and was recently sold back into private ownership.

Card rooms are legal in California because players don't compete against the casino. The house rakes a portion of the betting, but the majority of the pot is for the players to fight over.

A common misconception is that poker is a game of chance, that it's the cards that determine who wins the pot. Among professionals, luck is a joke that only amateurs find funny. Put two professional poker players and two average players at the same table, and sooner or later the pros have all the chips.

Sitting behind a professional poker player in a card room is considered an honor. You're watching his play, glimpsing behind the wizard's curtain. Sitting behind Johnny Chan is nearly unheard of, and it takes some wrangling and discussion before he concedes.

"Sit very close to me," Chan says. "Don't talk to the other players. If you have any questions, ask me later. Players don't like somebody talking when they're losing money."

The table with the best action is in a far corner, and several staff members hover nearby. On a wall there's a sign posted to prevent cheating: "English only to be spoken at all times — Mgmt." The players, all of whom have played with Chan before, don't look very happy to see him. They'll smile at his jokes and engage in some conversation, but there's no love at this table. Just money.

The game is $400/$800 Mix, which means the ante is $100, the minimum bet is $400 and the maximum raise is $800. "Mix" indicates that the game rotates — from, say, Texas Hold 'Em to Seven-Card Stud to Razz — every 10 hands. It takes a very experienced player to keep pace with all the changes of strategy at a Mix game.

Chan takes a seat, and his $10,000 buy-in is placed at his side. He orders a fruit plate of oranges, cantaloupe and watermelon. At the World Series of Poker, Chan kept an orange wrapped with a rubber band throughout the tournament. The second year he won, other players brought bananas, grapefruit and apples in joking reference to his orange fixation. Although Chan admits to being superstitious ("all gamblers are"), he swears he liked the orange for the fresh smell that he says kept him alert amid the Camel and Marlboro smoke. The rubber band is left unexplained.

"Hello, captain," Chan says to a passing floor supervisor.

"*You're* the captain, sir," the supervisor replies.

Chan is wealthy, but he won't say how wealthy. He owns a home in Cerritos and one in Las Vegas, as well as a fast-food franchise in Vegas' Stratosphere Hotel. He plays the stock market and consults for casinos and game manufacturers. His annual income has been estimated at around $1 million, but with all his side games with the likes of L.A. Lakers owner Jerry Buss, Vegas entrepreneur Bob Stupak and publisher Larry Flynt, his actual income is anybody's guess.

The opponents today include Sam, the clothing-store owner; Frank, an anxious thirtysomething; an advertising executive named Rick; and a shaved-headed pro named Freddie, who recently beat out 581 players in a Hold 'Em tournament to win $430,000.

The cards came out and $100 antes are tossed into the pot. Chan's cards aren't dealt quite close enough, and the dealer quickly scoots them forward another two inches.

The dealer is well-trained. Chan harshly chastises card dealers for minor infractions. One novice Bicycle Club dealer apologizes when rebuked, while two others just give him the Dealer Stare, a withering look used by card dealers in lieu of a retort that could get them fired.

Fort McDowell card room manager Mike Byrne, who suffered Chan's scrutiny when he was a dealer in Vegas, defends the bullying as part of Chan's game strategy.

"It's part of his intimidation," Byrne says. "A player can own the table and get everybody on the run."

Within an hour, everybody *is* on the run. Chan's initial $10,000 stake increases to $12,000, to $14,000, to $16,000. The other players check when Chan checks, fold when Chan raises. The players are being played.

Watching Chan, it's clear he isn't some sort of magician with the cards. He checks or folds when he doesn't have it, and raises when he does. He plays simple, aggressive poker.

What gives Chan such extraordinary edge is his even-keel demeanor and ability to read other players. When the cards come out, most players are eager to see what they've been dealt. Chan doesn't even look at his hand until he watches every other player react to their cards. He'll toss in a $100 ante before he's seen his cards if other players' expressions excite him.

Game after game, Chan maintains his famous bored appearance. He'll crack a joke, or make an occasional Texan brag ("All I
need to see is one of your up-cards, just one card, that's all I
need"), but any emotional response to his hand is kept somewhere
deep inside him.

"It doesn't matter to me if I'm dealt two aces or a three and a
five," he says later. "In fact, I don't need any cards. I just play the
person."

By contrast, his opponents' emotions rise and fall with the height
of their chip stacks. Elated and buoyant. Then sad and angry. They
glare at their cards suspiciously, trying to decide if they're holding
next month's rent. Chan is purely reactive, the responses to given
players and given hands seemingly hard-wired into his nervous
system.

During a game of Lowball, where the lowest hand takes the pot,
Rick suddenly throws his pair of jacks at the young Asian dealer.

"Same fuckin' cards," Rick says.

The dealer looks up and gives him the Stare.

"Same fuckin' cards," Rick says. "You dealt me the same fuckin'
cards as the last game."

The tension is broken by the chirping of Rick's cell phone — all
the high rollers keep one nearby — and he takes the call at the table. A few seats down, Frank stands up to stretch, ready to call it a
day. As he leans back, his pants zipper is wide open. Nobody tells
him.

The game changes to Seven-Card Stud.

Chan is dealt a five and a three up, with a pair of sevens con-
cealed in his hand.

"I have to raise," Chan says aloud, teasing. "After all, I have a
pair."

The other players look at his up-cards. The usual assumption is
that his three or five is paired, but would Chan play such a lousy
hand? And if his hidden cards are paired, might they be aces or
kings? That is, assuming he's telling the truth in the first place.

Chan's next up-card is a seven, and the other players relax a bit,
not knowing Chan now has three of a kind. He raises aggressively
and ends up taking a pot worth nearly $3,000.

"Fuck this! Fuck this!" one player says, throwing his cards toward
Chan.

A king lands on the edge of the table and Chan flicks it away with a finger.

In two hours, Chan made $11,000. He cashes out while he's ahead.

Chan is so accustomed to angering other players that their frustration doesn't even register.

"Poker brings out the real you," he says, shrugging. "You play with somebody long enough and the real person comes out. I used to have more heart — and I still do, but not when playing. 'Don't leave sugar on the table' is what I always say."

It's a conditioned response. The action, the awards and consequences of high-stakes poker shaped him. And during his formative years, Chan was transplanted into the heart of poker country.

Poker is a hybrid of betting games from Persia, France, England and Germany. The American version was born in the late 1700s in New Orleans, using a 20-card deck. During the next century, riverboat gamblers spread the game throughout the Western territories. Poker was not only easy to learn and portable, but it required no fixed dealer and no equipment other than a deck of cards. The ideal game for a growing nation.

In the 1970s, poker experienced a second boom — in Texas. There was so much fresh money, so many oil barons looking for high-risk excitement. Two of the best-known poker players — "Amarillo Slim" Preston and Doyle Brunson — were celebrities from the Lone Star State. And Texas Hold 'Em, the official game of the World Series of Poker, rose out of dance-hall back rooms to dominate the attention of serious players.

Chan's family moved from Hong Kong to Phoenix in 1968. Five years later, they relocated in Houston, where both Chan's cousin and his father owned restaurants. It was expected that Chan, who worked in his father's restaurant for $200 per week, would continue in the family business when he finished school.

At 16, Chan was an avid bowler. He bowled for money and says he did well. Playing card games was an afterthought. Poker was something Chan played at his cousin's restaurant after the bowling alley closed. His weekly game was nickel/dime/quarter dealer's choice — the garden-variety poker night held in thousands of houses, dorms and storerooms every week. Chan and his friends played games with tough names, like Mexican Sweat, Anaconda and Three-Card Gut. Games that were easy to learn and whose outcome depended a great deal on the luck of the draw.

Poker was also a hobby he had to conceal from his father, who would ask him where he spent his nights.

"Bowling, playing poker," Chan would say.

And his father would get angry. Chan was going to attend the University of Houston, he was going to major in hotel and restaurant management, he was going to continue the family business. Not gamble, not play games. His father wouldn't change his mind about Chan's gambling until his son won $875,000 at the 1987 World Series of Poker.

Chan was playing for fun and low-stakes cash. Then, one night at his weekly game, a repairman fixing the restaurant's air conditioning invited him to a different poker night.

"How much will it take?" Chan asked.

"Oh, not much," the repairman said. "About $300 to $500 to play."

Back then, $500 was high stakes for Chan. More than he had ever risked at poker. He accepted the challenge.

"I beat them," Chan says. "I beat them every week."

Playing at K.C. Air Conditioning against electricians and construction workers who were 30 years his elder, Chan says he made about $1,000 per week. He was also introduced to Texas Hold 'Em, a game that would change his life.

Just when it seemed Chan had discovered a new source of weekly income, his newfound poker buddies said they were calling it quits — no more poker night.

The next week, Chan drove to the air conditioning store anyway.

All the familiar cars were parked outside.

Honoring his father's wish, Chan attended the University of Houston, majoring in hotel and restaurant management. He dropped out at 21. He was a gambler and he knew it.

"I just couldn't work 9 to 5," he says. "The action always gets me. The action makes me who I am."

Chan married his Taiwan-born girlfriend, Judy, and in 1978 drove to Las Vegas in his beige Camaro and rented a studio apartment.

It wasn't his first time in Vegas. He had flown there and gambled many times since his late teens. His first casino poker game was at the Golden Nugget at age 18, where he sat down with $500.

When he stood up, hours later, he had $20,000.

For a young gambler, winning thousands of dollars during the first visit to a casino card room is like a heady injection of a powerful drug. His gambling addiction, already a dominant force in his life, now bound him irrevocably to the poker table.

Chan lost his winnings the next day.

During those early Vegas years, Chan's bankroll was on a roller coaster.

He says he worked menial casino and restaurant jobs, then lost his paycheck to blackjack, craps, sports betting and poker. He bet recklessly and compulsively — the lights, the cards, *the action.* He smoked four packs of cigarettes a day, and ate and slept on casino comps while gambling 14 to 16 hours at a stretch. He awoke in hotel rooms that smelled like smoke, then descended into the casino to start it all over again.

When he slept, he would dream of poker. He would dream he was at a Hold 'Em table, a pair of kings in his hand. He knew his opponent had only a pair of queens. But then comes the river — the final community card — and it's a queen. He loses and the chips go away.

Even when he won, he needed to win with caution. The casinos were mob-controlled, and smart gamblers were wary of offending the wrong player.

"The casino was the law," Chan says. "Back then, you just kept your mouth shut. You didn't want to step on anybody's toes. You never know who somebody is connected with."

Even cheaters, the scourge of the 1970s poker table, were sometimes untouchable. Chan says he would spot crooked dealers and players marking or holding cards. But he never knew if the cheater in the seat beside him secretly was working for the casino or had mob connections. The wise move was to stand up, take the loss, and walk away.

In the early 1980s, a convergence of changes in Chan's life caused Chan to start playing strictly for the money. His first son, Jason, was born. Chan quit smoking, started eating more healthfully and exercising. He stopped playing poker for the social rewards — no more sugar on the table. Poker became his profession.

Mike Byrne remembers Chan coming into his own.

"All the pros have an intimidation factor, but he got this huge intimidation factor," Byrne says. "He plays real fast, and when he's looking at you, it's like he's looking right through you. He's like a mercenary at the card table."

During one game, Byrne recalls Chan aggressively raising and reraising. At the showdown, Chan's opponent sheepishly turned over his cards, revealing a terrible hand.

"Okay, you got me," the player said. "I was bluffing."

Then Chan turned over his cards, revealing an even worse hand, much to his opponent's delight.

Later, Byrne asked why Chan had bet — raised, even — with such an awful hand.

"And Chan said to me, 'Well, it didn't matter what I had, I *knew* what he had,'" Byrne says. "Chan knew the other guy was playing out of line. At that moment, it really struck home that, as much as it's the cards, it's really the player. That was the first time I positively discerned the difference between a pro and an amateur."

Mike Caro, poker author and self-proclaimed "Mad Genius of Poker," calls Chan "one of the most intensely competitive players in poker. There are some who've achieved publicity based largely on short-term luck, but Johnny Chan's achievements are solidly based on long-term ability."

In 1983, Chan won $130,000 in Bob Stupak's America's Cup Tournament, launching a streak of high-profile tournament wins. During the match, he blew through 13 of the 16 players in minutes. Stupak called him "The Oriental Express," and the nickname stuck.

Earlier this month, 112 poker players entered the Hold 'Em tournament at Fort McDowell Casino.

After two and a half hours of play, the last remaining player was declared the winner.

That man, local retiree Ron Holden ("Like 'Hold 'Em,'" he says, "only with an *n*"), won the right to play heads up against Johnny Chan for an additional $1,000 prize.

Chan's presence at the tournament is another in a string of Arizona gambling precedents set by the Fort McDowell Casino.

The casino was the lone holdout during the 1992 Indian casino raid, where FBI agents attempted to confiscate slot machines. The much-publicized stand-off lasted three weeks before Governor Fife Symington agreed to negotiate a gaming agreement.

Fort McDowell was also the first Arizona casino to offer poker. Previously, poker had been played in poker parlors that profited from liquor sales.

Byrne remembers ordering those initial 12 tables in April of 1992, and then having to order 33 more a few months later. Each table generates about $60 in revenue every hour. Although Byrne sees more and more professionals in Arizona card rooms here to take advantage of the relatively novice players ("A good player can easily make $500 a day at Arizona poker tables," Chan says), no side game or tournament has been big enough to regularly attract Chan.

But Byrne, who's known Chan since their Vegas days, convinced him to sign an exclusive deal with Fort McDowell. Now, he's scheduled to play tournament winners (his next showdown is in August) and help develop new games such as Action Jack, a variation on blackjack where players play against each other rather than the house. The Action Jack at Fort McDowell has had spotty attendance so far.

At the tournament table, winner Ron Holden waits for Chan. A crowd of players has gathered to watch the match, and the game will be carried on closed-circuit monitors throughout the casino.

Chan is on the other side of the card room, having shown no interest in the poker tournament. He's intent on the U.S. vs. China soccer game on the game-room television.

"I'd rather be lucky than good," Holden says. "If he's as good as they say, I'd rather have the luck."

When a commercial interrupts the soccer match, Chan comes over to meet his opponent. The two poker players smile and shake hands: a retiree in tight white socks and bifocal glasses, and an Asian celebrity sporting a pricey watch and a new haircut.

Byrne grabs a microphone to call the game, and play begins.

For a while, Holden keeps pace with Chan. There are no dramatic showdowns, and the chips swing back and forth. Those who have studied Chan's style of play, however, know that Chan is putting his opponent to the test — deciding what makes Holden fold, check, call or raise. Silently collecting this information for an upcoming showdown.

"The last time he was here," whispers a spectator, "Johnny tricked the guy into going all-in when he was holding a pair of pocket [face down] aces. It was all over in a second."

Chan draws a pair of pocket aces this time, too, and raises viciously.

Holden, sensing a trap, folds before the showdown, but not before losing a large pot.

The balance of chips, and the probability of victory, shifts to Chan. As a new hand is dealt, an employee of the casino approaches the table to give Chan the soccer score.

"I saw it," he says, loud enough for his audience to hear.

There's a television set broadcasting the soccer game on a far wall. Chan, so confident in his eventual victory, is practically ignoring his opponent and the cards dealt to him. His arrogance surely must have an effect on Holden's play as well.

More cards come out, and Holden's chip stack erodes further. It seems Holden wins only the small pots, and Chan takes the large ones.

The next hand is pivotal:

Both players raise and re-raise until a large mound of chips sits impressively in the center of the table. If Chan wins, his victory today is almost assured. If Holden takes it, he's back in the game.

The players go into a showdown, and Holden turns over his hand — a king-high.

Witnesses are positive Chan has him beat. And he does — practically any decent hand could take the pot. But when Chan turns over just an ace-high, the crowd gasps.

"Now, if you can figure out how Chan knew that he had a king, and only a king," says an onlooker, "then you'll have a story to write."

Holden's remaining chips are quickly drained away. Chan wins — again. It took about 25 minutes.

The players shake hands once more, a flash from a camera, and Chan steps aside. As he walks away, a fan asks Chan if his opponent had any tells. Chan, knowing neither modesty nor restraint, and never leaving sugar anywhere near the table, nods his head.

"He had tells," Chan says. "He had tells from here to Las Vegas."

STEPHEN RODRICK

Blown Away

FROM GQ

FREAKS. I'm surrounded by 6,000 freaks. Freaks to the left. Freaks to the right. There's even a Freak family. On the firing line at the Knob Creek Machine Gun Shoot, a camouflaged hobbit blazes away with a Browning .30-caliber machine gun. *Baaddaah ba baaddaah ba.* Bilbo's cap reads, LITTLE FAT GUY. Next to him is a redhead. She maniacally rips rounds from something called a grease gun. *Blaam.* Her cap reads, LITTLE FAT GUY'S WIFE. Next to her is a ninth grader. Harry unstraps a Glock 9mm and holds down the trigger. *Bip bip.* The boy's cap reads, LITTLE FAT GUY'S SON. There's even Little Fat Guy's Daughter. Sadly, Baby Sniper is only 5 months old. She won't start firing a submachine gun until the age of 4. Four. I told you. Freaks.

I know, because I'm standing about 30 feet away. Caressing a rifle. Jim Gilmore, a Michigan dealer in military gear, hands me a succession of automatic weapons. We start with an AK47 clone. *Ping ping.* Boring. Then a British Sten gun. Cost $11 to make during World War II, now goes for as much as $1,800. *Baabam, baabam.* Better. I flip a round of .308-caliber bullets over my shoulder, and Gilmore passes me the M60, a.k.a. Rambo's gun. *Waawaawaawaa.* Excellent. My fingers are loose, fluttering wildly, jonesing for a trigger. Next is the Browning .50-caliber. At $1.50 a round, ecstasy is brief. I lovingly embrace the mounted God of War and pull. *Whiiiiiiipppppp.* In 2.5 seconds, imaginary invaders turn to shredded wheat.

I've shot my load. Post–machine gun stress syndrome begins. Ulcerated eardrums throb out a hard-core beat. Hands quiver. Jim

Gilmore laughs. "Now you know why they call them boner machines." Within my compressed auditory system, I hear the muffled
sound of a man cackling. It is me. I haven't felt this euphoric since
this morning, when I set a Pontiac ablaze with a flamethrower.
I am a freak.

HE IS ALIVE!

WELCOME MACHINE GUNNERS

On Kentucky Highway 44, Baptist churches and discount liquor
stores hail the return of Christ and John Moses Browning, respectively. It's the Thursday after Easter. With J.C.'s moment past, aptly
named Bullitt County preps for the main event: the Knob Creek
Machine Gun Shoot and Military Gun Show.

And what is Knob Creek? Militiaville, sniper fantasy camp and
fun for the whole family. Every April and October, the shoot at-
tracts gun geeks to Kenny Sumner's range, about twenty-five miles
southwest of Louisville. Why? To spend three days firing I-can't-be-
lieve-this-is-legal killing machines. Perhaps you're smitten with the
MP40 submachine gun that just splintered a Gremlin. Make an offer in the barn next door. Unless you're Sirhan Sirhan or loony —
and "loony" has a pretty loose definition in these parts — it's yours
in ninety days.

I arrive in Kentucky with a few facts about Knob Creek rattling
around in my head, none of them cheery. I stumbled upon the
place while reporting on adolescent neo-Nazi bank robbers from
Philadelphia. These junior Himmlers purportedly stopped here
between heists. And they weren't the first hatemongers to pass
through. Turns out Knob Creek is the Six Flags for the revolu-
tionary right. Timothy McVeigh made an appearance in his pre-
terrorist days. Everybody says he was real polite. Now ATF and FBI
agents secretly prowl the grounds. There has also been tragedy.
Three years ago, an 11-year-old died when a machine gun fell on
her while she was shooting it.

Not that I have an aversion to the military-industrial complex.
Grandpa on Mom's side left Alabama squalor to become a highly
decorated United States Marine, in a career spanning from Gua-
dalcanal to Vietnam. Dad rose from the Brockton, Massachusetts,
working class to become an Annapolis grad and an A-6 squadron
leader. He died at 36, flying. Even Big Sis got into the act. She's a

former army captain, and I have videos of her riding through Kuwait City with an M16 on her shoulder. And though I am no fan of Charlton Heston, except in the original *Planet of the Apes,* I have never viewed guns or guys in fatigues as a problem.

Still, Knob Creek sounded too much like Heaven's Gate meets *F Troop.* Neo-Fascists aside, grown men toying with machine guns seemed a tacky disservice to the fallen, not to mention a slight perversion of the Second Amendment. Even before my arrival, I could hear Gramps, the late Master Gunnery Sergeant Melvin Gunter, USMC, hiss, "I fought in three wars, got two Purple Hearts and ate shrapnel so a bunch of crackers could blow up refrigerators with Kraut machine guns?"

Only these crackers are friendlier than my New York neighbors. Here I am talking to a guy from Stamping Ground, Kentucky, about the decline of the American Empire. We're drinking beer and banqueting on his deer tenderloin around a campfire. To my surprise, Knob Creek is populated with reasonably sane men, a few women and children, all communing in peace amid tracer fire and conspiracy theories of epic proportions. Give or take a lone gunman or two, you have mainly *Touched by an Angel* fans here.

This harmonic convergence of the not-so-silent minority reeks of inner peace. These serene people understand why the U.S. of A. is headed down the outhouse. And yet there is little Rome-is-burning bitterness. More like, hey, if 64 percent of America thinks a pot-smoking, intern-screwing president and his Commie wife are good for this country, what can you do? So what if the vox populi refuse to believe that the alphabet soup of NAFTA, the UN and the IMF is systematically dismantling this once great land? Knob Creek Nation can't save the heathen if the heathen don't want to be saved.

See, they're concentrating on the fundamentals: God, country and the right to own your own arsenal. For three blissful days, it is morning in America again. The morning of June 6, 1944. Just ask Gilmore's buddy Shane Duty. A Knob Creek regular clad in a cap proclaiming him the WORLD'S GREATEST BEER DRINKER, he serves as de facto goodwill ambassador.

"This place is better than any fucking psychiatrist," says Duty, sucking down a widemouthed Natural Light with some pals. Our carefully tended fire blazes as the Kentucky sunset turns the sky bloody. In the distance, a Confederate flag flutters. "It cleans you of all the crap going on in the outside world. It's like Oz." Duty crumples his can and throws it onto the aluminum-and-wood pyre. He grins. "Of course, you wouldn't want to live in Oz."

During my own walk down the fully automatic yellow brick road, I learned an awful lot. I now know why schoolkids keep gunning down their classmates. (Ritalin.) I now know why you shouldn't sing along to Leonard Cohen while sitting in a girlie white Pontiac Grand Am in Kentucky. (You will be called a "faggot" by four NRA members from Ohio.) I now know why you shouldn't shoot a flamethrower into the wind. (First you feel flushed, then you feel hot, then you feel fire.) I also know why you shouldn't enter a militia meeting without an invitation. (Fuzzy-chinned Kentuckians brandishing loaded AK47 knockoffs will stop you.)

Most of all, in Knob Creek I learned that happiness is a warm gun.

You hear the Knob Creek Machine Gun Shoot miles before reaching it. The dull *ack ack* kicks in about three miles down a winding two-lane road. At night, when tracer bullets ricochet through the sky like hopped-up fireflies, Knob Creek makes its presence known from an even greater distance. Actual arrival disappoints. You pull into a grass parking lot that rain will turn into a quagmire of Russian-front proportions. You then walk past a series of tents housing Southern-fried interest groups, such as the Sons of Confederate Veterans. When I pop in, two goateed men in gray battle regalia cheerfully teach me that the Civil War had as much to do with slavery as the Revolution did with tea. A pock-marked asphalt road leads to the sixty-five-slot range and adjoining bunker. It's the day before the shoot, and all is relatively quiet. Inside, manager Kenny Sumner sits at his desk. Yes, his office has the requisite IMPEACH CLINTON sticker, but that doesn't mean Kenny isn't a sensitive guy. There's a Natalie Merchant CD near a boom box, a mini New Testament within arm's reach and a Girl Scout plaque on the wall. The sandy-haired Sumner has made the range his life's work. A swarm of potbellied men in Harley-Davidson and KILL THEM ALL, LET GOD SORT THEM OUT T-shirts enter the cinder-block room. They pay for their display tables with fifties peeled from fat wads of bills. Despite the option of using MasterCard or Visa, nobody does. Better not to leave a paper trail.

"My dad started it about twenty-five years ago," says Sumner. "It used to be just shooters and friends. Now we get about 6,000. A lot of people make a family adventure out of it."

And a lot of people make money out of it.

While the masses ejaculate bullets on the range, the savvy shopper heads next door for the ultimate automatic-weapon swap meet. Serious buyers cruise about looking for early-bird specials. There are as many as 200 vendors, featuring all kinds of guns and paraphernalia, from Nazi flags to a Gatling gun–style rubber-band shooter for the kids.

I check out the always popular $2 bumper stickers. New favorite: WHAT MICHAEL JACKSON IS DOING TO LITTLE BOYS, CLINTON IS DOING TO THE COUNTRY. Old standby: BOYCOTT JANE FONDA AMERICAN BITCH TRAITOR. Then there's the one with the silhouette of three KKK members: ORIGINAL BOYZ IN THE HOOD.

Traipsing through aisles of merchandise, I meet Jim Gilmore, military entrepreneur extraordinaire. One of this Inkster, Michigan, native's claims to fame is renting .30-caliber machine guns to Ted Nugent. Gonzo likes to open his Detroit New Year's Eve show by blazing away with screams of "This one's for Sarah Brady!" The bullets, of course, are blanks, but it's still quite a spectacular show.

Then there are the re-creations. A few years ago, a Detroit man paid Gilmore $4,500 to turn his estate into a battleground. As unsuspecting guests sipped martinis, explosions began ripping the Michigan countryside and a full-scale firefight, complete with tanks, broke out between a squad of Americans and 12 Nazis. Everyone clapped when the Germans paraded by, hands on head. Today the 46-year-old Gilmore, wearing thick glasses, a droopy auburn mustache and a parka with what looks suspiciously like a bullet hole in the back, sits inside his booth and analyzes the clientele.

"A lot are Vietnam vets who used to have this amazing power," says Gilmore. "They could get on the radio and bomb any place they wanted. Now they're working at Ford, and their boss is on their case. They're nobody. A lot of people miss that power and come here. Then you've got the militia. They talk big, but come back to me when you have armor and airpower. Then you've got the doctors and lawyers who want to buy whatever Schwarzenegger used in his last movie. Like, before *Predator* came out, nobody had ever heard of the German minigun, and then everybody wanted it.

Which was totally b.s., because nobody can stand and shoot the gun like Arnold did. It'll knock you on your ass."

Gilmore is a gun lifer. Shooting with Dad is his fondest childhood memory. Jimmy with his .22 and Papa with the .30 sniper rifle he brought back from Korea. And Mother didn't stay home and bake cookies. She participated in NRA competitions. Even as a longhaired soundman for Chaka Khan and Uriah Heep, Jim maintained his love for shooting. After a while, it was the only thing he and his old man could talk about.

The events of the past decade have transformed him into Job in army-surplus clothing. For three years, he's been on strike from *The Detroit News* and *Detroit Free Press,* where he worked as a pressman. But that's the least of his troubles. In 1991 his dad was murdered. Four years later, his best friend, a Detroit limo driver, was gunned down by a customer. Last March Gilmore's girlfriend of twenty years had her eye socket fractured by the butt of a pistol during a purse snatching. When she came home, Gilmore jumped in his car and took off in pursuit of her attacker. He left his guns at home.

"No way I'd bring my guns," says Gilmore. "That's murder. I was going to run him over with my car. That's only vehicular homicide."

He didn't find the guy.

Talk turns to last March's Jonesboro, Arkansas, shooting, in which two kids killed five people with family rifles. It's a hot topic in Knob Creek. I ask Gilmore if he doesn't think stricter gun laws would have prevented the murders.

"Let's look at Arkansas," says Gilmore, launching into his stump speech. "Let's outlaw murder. Oh, already did that. OK, let's outlaw kids shooting guns unsupervised. Oh, already did that. OK, the kids stole a van to get to school. Let's outlaw car theft. Oh, already did it. Should we outlaw golf clubs because some guy killed his wife with one?"

Arguing even mild gun control with Gilmore is fruitless. This is the disconnect point between Knob Creek and the rest of America. Before the weekend is out, I will hear the golf-club argument repeatedly, with gunners substituting Ford Pintos, baseball bats and croquet mallets as their metaphors of choice. Over and over, I will hear the old chestnut "Guns don't kill people; people kill people" repeated in a cultlike monotone.

Gilmore informs me, as will another half-dozen gunners, that since the enactment of the 1934 law regulating the sale and ownership of machine guns, only one person has been killed by a properly registered machine gun. And guess what? That was done by a cop.

True story.

The articulation of his philosophical underpinnings dispensed with, Gilmore takes me on a tour of the machinery. There are rows of Uzis, Brownings, M16s, AK47s and all their brothers. Up front, a Maremont M2HB .50-caliber machine gun, retail value $13,500, is being raffled off to raise money for pro-gun causes.

Sadly, the little guy is being priced out of the market.

"A lot of people who made a killing in the stock market are looking to diversify their assets," says Gilmore. "That and the assault-weapon ban are driving prices through the ceiling."

For example, your basic Uzi, Israeli made, nothing fancy, has recently more than doubled in price, from $1,200 three years ago to $2,500 today. The German-made MP5 submachine gun has gone from $2,000 to $5,500 in the same period.

"Things have really begun to change," says Gilmore. "You're getting a different crowd now. It's more doctors, lawyers and accountants."

Gilmore is right. I meet Fortune 500 execs and a big-shot Arkansas defense lawyer. Among the gun elite is David, a Minnesota health-care lawyer who doesn't want his last name used. With his Eddie Bauer–esque casual wear and owlish eyes, he doesn't resemble Woody Allen so much as the kid a young Woody could beat the crap out of. We talk a bit. David tells me about his father, an Auschwitz survivor who didn't like guns but who instilled a message in his son.

"He told me that the only place worth living was a place where the ordinary people had access to guns," says David. "I've always kept that with me. I started in 1986 and bought a Smith & Wesson submachine gun. Now I'm hooked. They're really no different than cars. Machine guns are just one-cylinder engines that run on ammo. Half the fun is finding them and making them work."

I ask David if he would buy a German machine gun that might have been used to kill Jews.

"Yes," he says. "It's not machines that murdered the Jews. It was an authoritarian, evil government."

But what about the bookstall ten feet away selling books that claim Jews were responsible for the African slave trade?

"Hey, this is America," laughs David, chewing his cigar furiously. "It's when I can't buy a German machine gun or he can't sell that book, that's when trouble begins."

Of course, the freak family has a name. George and Laurie Christy run G&L Arms in Williamsburg, Virginia. G&L, they tell me, also stands for Guns and Laughter. Son Harry is only 16, but his name already appears on the business cards. About five-five, with a hint of facial fuzz, Harry packs a Glock 9mm.

"It's not legal out in public," admits Harry, the spitting image of Huckleberry Hound. "It's kind of like moving your car without a license. On private property, it's OK. On the road, it's a felony."

In a way, the Christys represent everything that is Ozzie and Harriet about Knob Creek. Clad in tinted sunglasses and urban gray camouflage, George talks about the family atmosphere at Knob Creek. When his father-in-law passed away, he says, it was the gun community that sent cards and helped the family rally. Pop's line that "the family that shoots together, stays together" isn't really a joke. Unlike most teens, Harry has an affectionate and mutually respectful relationship with his parents. They laugh and joke like peers. It's almost hippieish. As the son presents the Christy cache, father and son wisecrack freely without generational acrimony. The arsenal includes an AK47, a Spanish bolt-action rifle, a basic M16, an MP5 popular with Navy SEALs, a BAR .30-caliber machine gun and a vintage Browning 1919 machine gun.

"Hey, Dad, is this one from the late World War I period?" asks Harry with the inquisitiveness of the scion of a family of Picasso collectors.

Sadly, the kid is a little jaded. He doesn't hold his local law enforcement in very high esteem. "They don't know jack," snorts Harry dismissively. "When I was 12, the SWAT team had to bring in their MP5s because they didn't know how to clean them. That's pathetic." He then points out a spot about fifty yards downrange. "They used to put an old car out there, rig the steering wheel and throw a brick on the accelerator," remembers the teen, his pubescent voice thick with nostalgia. "It would drive around in circles, and you could try and blow it up. They stopped doing it because parts were landing too close to the crowd."

"Ready on the left? Ready on the right?"

The PA system announces it's time to shoot. Harry excuses himself. The Christys lock and load. One family and fifty other people commence firing.

How to describe the clamor. Perhaps fifty Metallicas simultaneously performing in your rec room. The body trembles, and the eyes have difficulty focusing downrange, where the remains of a Pontiac and a washing machine are reduced to metal kindling. I think of how it would take just one misfit about three seconds to turn around and spray the densely packed crowd twenty feet away.

As the Christys fire at will, my previous thoughts about the familial qualities of machine gunning wither away. Watching their faces, all contorted and wild-eyed, I can see that this bonding experience differs somewhat from more traditional recreational activities. Shooting an AK47 as Mom's submachine gun recoils and Dad's .45 chews up rocks is not synonymous with tossing lawn darts and munching s'mores around the bug zapper. Despite the Christys' congeniality and Harry's apparent levelheadedness, I can't be convinced that interminable gunfire makes for a well-adjusted 16-year-old.

Later in the afternoon, I shoot. I'm shocked at the ease of the whole thing. An M16 gives no more kick than Glen Hardin's Daisy. The Uzi is even simpler. No wonder 12-year-olds are popping one another.

Sessions last a half hour. When the all-clear signal sounds, many of the gunners reach for a smoke. Their twitching claws are unable to unite match and cigarette. Some desperately push smokes and lips toward comrades for assistance.

Looking for something a bit more peaceful, I sign up for the flamethrower. Flamethrower operator Stephen Proffitt straps on the tanks and marches me out toward some abandoned cars. The beauty of the flamethrower is that you don't need a permit to own one. Go down to any gun or military show and soon you, like Proffitt, can entertain the neighbors by shooting your flamethrower in the backyard. My fellow flamer is Chad Sumner, Kenny's teenage son. Proffitt instructs us to fire quick bursts and urges me not to set him or myself aflame.

Whooosh. I give the gun a little juice and the sky is alive with fire. It's hotter than a Red Lobster deep fryer. A bit more and the subcompact is ablaze. When I turn to the applauding crowd, I nearly deep-fry Proffitt. That's the problem. It's such a snap to use these tools of mayhem that I forget I could kill somebody with the casual tug of a trigger.

Feeling my tank go empty, I try to flame-paint my initials in the sky. My face feels the burn, maybe a little too much. Soon I'm flameless.

The next day, the strangest thing happens. My forehead breaks out in a rash. I see Chad around camp, and one of his eyes is a ghastly red. Later that day, he's wearing a patch. Proffitt insists he doesn't use napalm, just plain diesel. But I wonder. I begin constructing my own conspiracy theory.

This place is growing on me.

Feeling a bit more weapon literate, I venture into the Knob Creek campground. Despite my recent display of testosterone, *Deliverance* fears still plague me.

With good reason. At the top of a muddy hill, an ersatz guerrilla base appears. As far as the eye can see, there's a sprawl of POW-MIA flags, Harley T-shirts and cherry red Ford pickups. As kids wearing TOMMY HILLBILLY T-shirts kick up mud with their ATVs, parents read aloud from the Constitution. Jokes about Janet Reno's being Hitler in drag pass from campfire to campfire like ancient oral history.

Toward the back of the compound, southern state flags flap in rhythm, resembling the United Nations pavilion. That's where I meet the Kentucky State Militia. An affable lot in fatigues, they invite me into their tent and offer chicken noodle soup. Unfortunately, they forgot bowls. A beat-up pot passes by, and I decline.

Head Kentucky colonel is Charlie Puckett, an impossibly frontiersy-looking man with a flinty grin and cowboy eyes. His boy, Charlie Jr., sits nearby along with two aides. I'd noticed Dad around the range, and frankly, he scared the tar out of me. Up close he's a cuddly bear with an informal army of 8,000. In fact, the Kentucky militia is diversity-friendly. Puckett, mechanic by day, claims 275 black members, plus a couple of Puerto Ricans. They even help local law enforcement. Mind you, that doesn't mean Puckett's a fan of big government.

"We could sit here 365 days, 24 hours, seven days a week, and you wouldn't know the truth," says Puckett, his teeth bared in a smile. "There's 10 planks to the *Communist Manifesto*. The U.S. has adopted seven. You think we have private property? Well, you try not paying your property taxes and see how long your property remains private."

Soon conversation turns to Clinton. While disgusted with the president, Puckett sees him as a wily adversary.

"Clinton's got out of these scandals slicker than snot on a door handle," drawls Puckett with grudging admiration. "I would have given anything if Lewinsky had AIDS and had given it to that cocksucker. Um, I mean cocksuckee."

For an hour, we meander through all the favorite subjects of the militia movement. First up is how the UN is beginning an inexorable annexation of America through national parks' being declared international biospheres. Then we switch to the gun topic.

"The Constitution gave us the right to bear arms to protect us from tyranny, not to shoot at Bambi or hunt," says Puckett. His acolytes nod. By "bear arms," he continues, the Founding Fathers meant "a real gun, not a hunting rifle. And don't give me crap about Jonesboro. When they take your children into the public school and feed them Ritalin, this is going to happen."

It's getting dark, so I make my excuses. Puckett invites me to the national-militia meeting the next day. I ask him what's on the agenda.

"We got to get the extremists out," says Puckett. "You got one scumbag who wants to start taking prisoners. Where you going to keep them? In your hall closet? Another a-hole on April 19 wants to start blowing up federal buildings. That's the anniversary of Waco and Oklahoma City. It should be interesting."

That night, April 17, I think about what one militia expert told me. He sees the movement as more armed fraternity than military threat. Like-minded people gather and share common interests: gun and hatred of government. In terms of real power, they have none and never will, with their fun-house political views. As with the Moose Lodge or the Toastmasters, he told me, everyone wants to be in charge. Whenever a new militia starts up, the army-surplus store always runs out of general bars first. In short, they're just harmless good old boys playing dress up.

The next day, I pull into the Shepherdsville VFW parking lot, about 12 miles from Knob Creek, for the meeting. It's not purely a pickup-truck crowd. There's a Honda SUV and a nifty black Jaguar XJ8. Running late, I hustle up to the door. There I'm met by Charlie Jr. and two locked-and-loaded compatriots. As I open the door, a rifle butt is not-so-gently shoved into my chest. At this point, I view the militia a little more warily than I do the Elks.

"They're taking a vote on you," says Charlie Jr.

It seems my attendance isn't welcomed by all. Every few minutes, a different militiaman pops his head out and asks me a question. One examines my Massachusetts driver's license.

"Taxachussetts. *Mmm.* They put your Social Security number on them. Very clever."

Pathetically, I trot out my family's military history.

"What about *you,* boy?"

I have no answer. For the first time all weekend, I feel like punching someone. My inquisitor's pistol persuades me to just smile wanly.

I lose the vote. Junior tells me it wasn't close. As I head to my car, the VFW doors fly open and two dozen militiamen burst into the parking lot. Everyone's shouting obscenities. And everyone's packing an automatic weapon. For a moment, I'm truly afraid. Eventually, order is restored, and everyone heads inside for more debate.

But I've had enough. I'm heading back to safety. I'm heading back to the machine guns.

That night drizzle serves as another special effect during the annual pyrotechnic show. After a day of deafening shooting and my militia experience, I must cajole my body out of the hotel for another hellish session of sound and fury. I get halfway there, stop at a gas station, look at my shaking hands and vacillate. Eventually, I get there, parking in ankle-deep mud. In the watery twilight, everyone looks like the hollow grunts depicted on the cover of Norman Mailer's *The Naked and the Dead.*

Trying to lift spirits, Steve Proffitt has brought out his entire flame brigade. The orange fire reflecting off the mud puddles transforms his quartet of pyros into the Four Flamethrowers of the Apocalypse. But even that gets monotonous. A backhoe shovels soil over the flames, and the process begins again. Combined with the detonation of dynamite-laced junkers, this is a sensory overload that overwhelms all but the hardiest fans. By 10 P.M. even the Christys have gone home.

It's now 11 A.M. on Sunday. The barn is quiet. Confederate flags are draped over chained-down guns as if over coffins. I find Jim Gilmore holding court and flash him a grin. To me Gilmore is the quintessential Knob Creeker. On the subject of gun use, I know him to reside in a paranoid universe where dissent is not tolerated and the American government is the Great Satan. That aside, I could see myself downing some Stroh's with him in Tiger Stadium's center-field bleachers. Ironically, what Gilmore and the Christys don't realize is that the so-called decadent permissiveness of modern America, brought on by Knob Creek curse words like "the '60s," "liberals" and "government intervention," is precisely what allows them to exist. Supremely weird behavior, such as owning your own armory, is permitted as long as you pay your taxes and don't shoot your unarmed neighbors. If Knob Creekers think they could have held machine-gun jamborees back during the good old days of Ike and Joe McCarthy, well, they're living in their own personal *Twilight Zone* episode.

I tell Jim of my militia adventure. "That's going to be the lead of your article, isn't it?" says Gilmore. "Hey, I noticed you took your earring out. Did you think somebody might shoot you if you wore it?"

Actually, yes. But enough small talk. Before I leave I have to ask Gilmore one last difficult question. How can he enjoy guns after they murdered his best friend and his dad?

"You're jumping to conclusions," says Gilmore with a bitter smile. "My father was beaten with a hammer and strangled. If he had had his gun, he'd still be alive. Shooting these weapons has nothing to do with killing. It's all about the thrill and the camaraderie. Guns are just machines.

"Look, I also love cameras and model trains. I see the same people at all three types of conventions."

Perhaps, but who, aside from Princess Di, was ever murdered by a rapid-fire Leica? And when was the last time a child got cut down in front of his mother by a Lionel train? Yes, the militia geeks scare the crap out of me, but it's a snap picking them out at forty paces: They're the ones in camouflage grease paint, *Lords of Discipline* berets and shiny jackboots.

It's the flipped-out Knob Creek hobbyist who will bring us all sorrow. Picture this. What if Little Fat Guy's Daughter grows up to be homecoming queen? She meets a clean-cut youth named Buck. Buck seems sweet. LFG lets him borrow the SUV, the snowblower and the semiautomatics. No problem. After graduation Buck and his belle tie the knot. There are a few hearty jokes about a shotgun wedding.

Then Buck stops taking his Zoloft. He begins thinking he's Marlon Brando's super-Nazi in *The Young Lions*. On a sky blue Knob Creek Saturday, Buck mistakes Jim Gilmore for Montgomery Clift, Charlie Puckett for Dean Martin. He blows them away. A firefight ensues. The Creek runs red. Buck meets a crispy, flamethrower end. Hundreds are dead, including quite a few dues-paying NRA members. With his dying gurgle, Gilmore recants his comparison of AKs with lens caps and choochoos. A pert blonde goes live at five with one twangy question: "Why?"

It could happen.

CHARLES SPRAWSON

Swimming with Sharks

FROM THE NEW YORKER

SOME SAY the bravest of swims was Ted Erikson's in 1967, when he survived the thirty miles from the Farallon Islands to the Golden Gate Bridge, San Francisco, a trek that took him through waters in which there are more shark attacks than anywhere else in the world. But Lynne Cox's attempt on the Bering Strait was without doubt the most remarkable.

At 9:30 A.M. on August 7, 1987, Cox, a thirty-year-old marathon swimmer, jumped feet first from a rock on the shore of Little Diomede island into the frigid Arctic Ocean and set out for Big Diomede, nearly two and a half miles away. The Diomedes, tiny volcanic islands, situated between Alaska and Siberia, that rise abruptly from the ocean floor, are the peaks of a submarine ridge that once connected the two continents. The international date line bisects the channel between them and forms the boundary line between the United States and Russia. These territorial waters, which are strictly guarded, had not been open to boats since 1948, and had never been swum.

Cox's father had come up with the idea of swimming between the Diomedes back in 1976, when American-Soviet relations were at a low ebb, to show just how close the superpowers were. It had taken Lynne Cox eleven years of negotiation, at the highest government levels, before the Bering Strait swim was authorized, and final permission from the Soviets had been granted only the day before. During those years, Cox had been training and, with the help of medical tests, preparing her body for water temperatures that would kill most human beings within thirty minutes.

Cox had been advised by the Naval Arctic Research Laboratory to expect a strong northerly flow of water through the channel, causing eddies and currents of up to three miles per hour, along with winds that could vary abruptly from periods of calm to gale force. Although the islands were only 2.4 miles apart, Cox would be forced by the currents to swim at least twice as far. The water temperature in the Strait, which freezes over during the long winter months, would vary from thirty-four degrees Fahrenheit to forty-four. She was warned about the presence of walruses and sharks, particularly the fifteen-foot Great Pacific shark, though it wasn't known if Great Pacifics in the Strait would attack humans. Yet Cox refused artificial aid: she would not use a shark cage, or wear a wet-suit, or even coat her body in lanolin grease. Her only form of protection was her swimsuit.

She had arranged to be accompanied by two umiaks — walrus-skin canoes — belonging to the Inuits who lived on Little Diomede in a settlement of shacks clinging to a cliff face. The local mayor, a cynic who wore a baseball cap that said "Patrick was a saint but I ain't," had insisted on five thousand dollars as a fee for the boats, believing that this was a chance to make money for the desolate community, whose livelihood came from seal-hunting and selling scrimshaw on the mainland. Cox, who had borrowed money from her parents to get to Little Diomede and was living on bagels and peanut butter for breakfast, lunch, and dinner, eventually bargained him down to five hundred dollars. Two Soviet naval vessels were due to meet her at the boundary.

When Cox entered the Arctic Ocean, the water temperature was, at forty-four degrees, comparable to a glass of iced water; if she had dived in head first, the sudden impact could have stopped her heart beating. Once she was in the sea, she said later, she concentrated on making her body move, to avoid focusing on the pain she felt. A dense fog had descended, which calmed the surface of the water but also made it impossible for her to see her destination. The umiaks started leaking immediately and had to be bailed out with empty Coca-Cola cans. One boat contained five journalists and the other three doctors, including Bill Keatinge, an erudite Englishman from London University, whose particular field of research was the effect of cold on the human body.

At the beginning of the year, Cox had got in touch with Keatinge and asked if there was a medical system that could register her temperature during the swim: it was essential that her inner body temperature never drop below ninety-three degrees. Keatinge recommended a thermo-sensitive capsule containing a tiny transmitter which had been devised for astronauts. She swallowed the capsule before the swim, and every twenty minutes while she was in the ocean she rolled on to her back and one of the doctors pointed a radio receiver at her stomach in order to register a digital reading. As a further precaution, a rectal thermometer on a lead was inserted into her body and the wire coiled into her swimsuit. If the capsule did not work, a reading could be taken from the thermometer.

The doctors were in a continuous state of apprehension, but Cox remained calmer than the seals in the Arctic Ocean; several rose to the surface to gaze quizzically at this intruder. Every so often, the boats got lost in the fog as Cox sprinted ahead, and she was forced to shout back through the mist to make sure that she was swimming in the right direction. She crossed the boundary after an hour and a half; then one of the journalists thought he could hear an engine, and suddenly the bow of a ship emerged through the fog. The Russians invited the two umiaks to follow them. As they crossed the date line, a journalist called out "It's tomorrow!" and everyone cheered.

Fifty yards from shore, the fog cleared, and the cliffs of Big Diomede loomed above Cox. The closest point of land was a rock directly ahead of her, but a welcoming committee was waiting to receive her half a mile away on a snowbank. Cox knew that a deep trough developed where the island sloped down to the ocean floor, through which a sudden current, with thirty-eight-degree water, raced north into the Chukchi Sea. The ocean here was like a washing machine, with cold water churned up from below and driven out into the Arctic waste. To go that extra half mile would mean swimming against the current. "You should land now," the doctors said, but she refused. The object of her swim was, in her words, "to reach out to the Soviets." She explained later, "Touching a rock rather than someone's hand would have meant so much less. I had to keep on reaching, going." She swam close to the rock to avoid the strongest part of the current, then turned south. Finally, after two hours and six minutes in the water, she struggled up the ice on the beach and felt the warmth of two Russian hands hoisting her. She was engulfed in blankets and presented with a bouquet of flowers and a pair of sealskin slippers. Surprisingly, her inner temperature had remained constant for much of the swim, but after she'd had a brief interview with Soviet television and walked seventy-five yards to a recovery tent, her temperature dropped to ninety-four — borderline hypothermia. She was slurring her words and having difficulty walking. When she slumped to the ground in the recovery tent, a Soviet woman wrapped herself around Cox in order to keep her warm. The Russians and the Americans then celebrated Cox's achievement with a tea party, prepared by a chef in a white uniform. Tables had been set out on the beach and covered with white cloths, and samovars were placed on top.

At the end of that year, Mikhail Gorbachev flew to Washington to sign the INF treaty, which would reduce the number of nuclear missiles. At an official dinner given by President Reagan in his honor, Gorbachev cited Cox's swim as a symbol of the thawing relations between the two countries. "It took one brave American by the name of Lynne Cox just two hours to swim from one of our countries to the other. We saw on television how sincerely amiable was the meeting between our people and Americans when she stepped on to the Soviet shore. She proved by her courage how closely to each other our peoples live." Reagan was mystified by this tribute. The national-security adviser had to call the State Department to find out whom Gorbachev was referring to.

Today, at the age of forty-two, Lynne Cox lives with her parents in Los Alamitos, a few miles from the great beaches that line the California coast below Los Angeles. Los Alamitos is a quiet suburb distinguished by a good fish restaurant and avenues of palm and cottonwood trees. When Cox is not preparing for her swims, she writes articles and short stories, gives lectures to business executives, and coaches swimmers. (One current student is an opera singer who, like Frank Sinatra, feels that swimming might improve her singing.)

A large harbor scene painted by Cox's mother hangs in her room. On top of a bookcase are the sealskin slippers; its shelves are crammed with copies of *National Geographic*. There are no trophies to impress the visitor — they were discarded or donated to a local museum years ago. The Coxes' home is an unremarkable, well-ordered place, but from the confines of that domesticity Cox plans her forays to some of the most desolate and far-flung places in the world, often venturing into seas and lakes where no one has swum before.

Lord Byron was one of the first to swim through dark waters and over great depths, and he did so at a time when the submarine world was still relatively unknown. He crossed the Hellespont, from what is now European Turkey to what is now Asian Turkey, on May 3, 1810, in emulation of Leander's legendary swims to his lover, Hero. The distance is little more than a mile, but the current made it so arduous that Byron doubted "whether Leander's conjugal powers must not have been exhausted in his passage to Paradise." He later wrote of his crossing, "I plume myself on this achievement more than I could possibly do any kind of glory, political, poetical, or rhetorical."

The greatest swim in the history of marathon swimming, however, was Captain Matthew Webb's conquest of the English Channel, in 1875, and the most sensational was the American Gertrude Ederle's triumph there in 1926, when she became the first woman to swim across — using the crawl all the way — and beat the existing record by two hours. On her return to New York, she was greeted by sirens, flowers showering down from planes, and a ticker-tape parade; the enthusiasm for her welcome equaled that for Charles Lindbergh the following year. Captain Webb drowned in 1883 while attempting to swim the rapids below Niagara Falls, in a suicidal bid for "money and imperishable fame." A crowd of ten thousand watched Webb disappear beneath the waves after he cracked open his head on a series of submerged rocks that surrounded a whirlpool where the river bends.

Webb's death was unfortunate, but his financial enterprise and his flair for self-promotion would have appealed to William Wrigley, Jr., the chewing-gum millionaire. In 1927, Wrigley instituted the first professional swimming race in the world: competitors would swim from Catalina Island, twenty miles off the coast of Southern California, to the mainland for a first prize of twenty-five thousand dollars. He had just bought the island as a commercial proposition, and, impressed by Ederle's reception in New York the previous year, concocted the pageant to solve the problem of a lack of tourists in California during the winter months. Some fifteen thousand spectators watched the winner swim home at three in the morning, illuminated by the searchlights of yachts. Wrigley's venture was so successful that he inaugurated an annual twenty-one-mile race on Lake Ontario for a prize of thirty thousand dollars. Other businessmen followed his example, in bays and lakes all over America, and further afield — in Yugoslavia, South America, Australia, Mexico, Italy, England, and Egypt. Like modern golfers or tennis players on tour, the same group of swimmers would assemble in various parts of the world to compete for large amounts of money.

Marathon swimmers are a different breed from short-distance swimmers. Compared with the long, lithe, and adolescent figures you see in the Olympics, marathon swimmers appear in photographs to be built like bisons rather than like cheetahs, with gnarled faces and stubborn expressions, their pendulous breasts and stomachs drooping down to stubby legs. (Only the Dane Greta Andersen has excelled in both forms of competition. After winning the gold medal in the hundred-meter freestyle in the Olympic Games in 1948, she won the English Channel race twice and became one of the greatest open-water swimmers in the world.)

These swimmers need a tenacity and a stocky build to withstand the impact of waves and tides, the sudden nausea inflicted by oil slicks and bilge, the prolonged effects of salt water, which causes the lips and tongue to swell and reduces the face to something resembling fungus. So intense and concentrated are the conditions that marathon swimmers become prey to delusions and neuroses that are often beyond the experiences of other athletes. The huge distances that the swimmers cover, sometimes up to sixty miles, can bring on hallucinations. In 1961, in the first back-to-back swim of the English Channel, the Argentine Tony Abertondo imagined posts and dogs obstructing his path over the last two miles. During the same swim four years later, Ted Erikson saw his pilot boat suddenly fade into a black smear and then turn into a rosebush, at which point he found that there were roses growing all around him. In May 1975, Ben Haggard, a New York policeman, attempted to swim from Florida to Nassau, across the so-called Bermuda Triangle, using a shark cage. As night fell, floodlights from the boats accompanying him revealed sharks circling his cage. Haggard recalled feeling the presence of a hostile force. "I had this feeling that something wanted me to come out through the door," he said afterward. "I knew what would happen, with the sharks outside, but the urge was irresistible. I swam over and grabbed the trapdoor. I was shaking, but I held on to it. I kept saying to myself: I am not going to let it take me out of the cage, whatever it is."

Swimming, particularly long-distance swimming, appeals to the solitary and the eccentric. An informal survey of fourteen champion long-distance swimmers concluded that only two of them were swimming under no particular stress, while the others were all reacting to severe emotional tension. No one knows, for example, why Britt Sullivan, a hard-drinking former Wave from Nebraska, decided to swim the Atlantic Ocean in 1964. She lost touch with her escort boat off Fire Island, twenty miles from her starting point, and was never seen again.

Lynne Cox appears to be devoid of neuroses and delusions, yet no doubt the long hours she has spent submerged in water have made her in some ways remote. Her endeavors seem to defy the limits of human possibility: she was the first swimmer to cross the Straits of Magellan, among the most treacherous stretches of water in the world; she has swum through Lake Baikal, one of the deepest, longest, and coldest lakes in the world. She follows a solitary course: the impulse behind her swims has been hers, as are the organization and negotiation. She is no longer registered with the United States Swimming Association, because races don't interest her, nor does prize money. The purpose of her swims is not to promote rivalry but to create harmony.

For Cox, swimming is an "emotional and spiritual necessity," a phrase used by George Mallory, the mountaineer, to describe his own compulsion to dive into any lake or river that he came upon. Cox is drawn to the challenge of a confrontation with nature — a struggle perhaps familiar to mountain climbers. "It involves a lot of planning, training, and physical obstacles," she says of marathon swimming. "In a pool, you know there's a finish, because there are two walls. In a marathon swim or a mountain climb, you are never sure. There is a much higher risk involved. Basically, you can die." If there is one image, now that all sports are so commercial and technologically sophisticated, that grips the imagination as much as Mallory, dressed like a gamekeeper and glimpsed through a brief break in the clouds, "going strong for the top," it is that of

Lynne Cox, virtually naked, forcing her way through the waves of the Bering Strait.

I first met Lynne Cox by the Pacific, earlier this summer, among the palms of the Hotel Laguna. The hotel, built in 1888, was once dedicated to glamour, but now it is the haunt of earnest couples who seem intent on closing deals and analyzing "relationships." Cox, with her generous smile, lilting voice, and long black hair, appeared to be everything they were not. Like the two plain syllables of her name, Cox was simple and direct. I had been drawn originally to American swimmers by their names, redolent of romance and dash — Donna deVarona, Casey Converse, Chet Jastremski, Zac Zorn — but Cox was in a different category.

We changed and went to swim. The outline of Catalina showed through the haze in the distance. There had been a storm the night before; waves hammered the shore and threw me onto a rock. Cox laughed and shouted that at the start of her swim around the Cape of Good Hope, in 1978, she had had to dive through waves four times as high. At five feet six inches and a hundred and eighty pounds, she is not particularly tall or lean; in fact, her body is between thirty and thirty-five percent fat. (Most women's bodies are between eighteen and twenty-five percent.) What makes her body remarkable, according to doctors who have tested her, is an "even" covering of fat that acts like a wetsuit; the porpoise bulk of her build forms a protective surface that keeps the temperature of her inner body normal in extreme conditions. Most of her power seems to derive from her mermaid hips. She doesn't have the orangutan arms and shoulders of a shorter-distance swimmer, but as we swam I noticed that she kept up a rhythmic, consistent stroke, zigzagging her hand viciously underwater, where it counts. She seemed to melt into the water. (To achieve a similar effect, East German swimmers were rumored to inject gas into their colons.) Her skin looked so smooth that I asked her if she went through the ritual of shaving before a swim, like Olympic swimmers, but she told me that long-distance swimmers preserve body hair for greater insulation.

A harmless jellyfish floated by, which reminded her of the worst jellyfish she had encountered, in warm waters off Sweden. They were "red, yellow, and transparent — the size of a garbage-can lid — with long tentacles that slammed into my face and burned my body," she said. "Every stroke was tentative and I could never relax — I would swim onto the back of one before realizing I was in the middle of it."

As we swam, Cox spoke of her childhood in New Hampshire, and summer holidays her family spent in Maine, on a lake called Snow Pond, where she swam all day and often at night, too, when she was "sticky with sweat." She described her sense of relief on entering the black water, recalling "the smell of pine accentuated at night, the moonlight that turned the edge of the shore to silver." Frogs and snakes and sandfish snatched at her body. Swimming among white and yellow water lilies, she would dive down through the clear water to follow the long stems that attached the flowers to the sandy bottom. A mile out, in the middle of the lake, there was an island that she always wanted to swim to. Years later, she went back to the lake. "I swam around to the original smooth, sloping stone from which I entered the lake as a child," she told me. "I slid off it again and swam out to the island, across a surface disfigured by jet skis and motorboats." At the end of each summer, she hated returning to the local public pool. She loathed the routine and the regimentation, the innumerable laps spent staring at a black line on the bottom of the pool.

In 1969, when she was twelve, her father, a radiologist, moved the family from the East Coast to California. His experience in the Medical Corps on Iwo Jima during the war had turned him into an idealist, and he determined to bring up his four children in a healthy climate and make them all into good swimmers, believing that swimming extended the body more safely than any other sport. In California, Cox started training with a swimming coach, Don Gambril, who was also the coach of the Olympic team. He noticed that she picked up the pace only after a mile, and so had no prospects as an Olympic swimmer, and he encouraged her instead to join a group of young swimmers who were training for the open sea. "Suddenly I felt released from a cage. I was actually going somewhere, not merely back and forth," Cox recalls. "I felt exhilarated by the challenge of swimming against the current and into the waves." When the group swam from Catalina Island to the mainland, Cox was so far ahead of the other swimmers that she had to tread water while they caught up. She was then fourteen.

She returned to Catalina in 1974 to break the record. She started at night, when conditions are usually most favorable. "The whole atmosphere seems somehow refined," she says, "and you feel you are really swimming on the upper inches of the ocean." But on this occasion fog descended five miles offshore. Cox became separated from her escort boat. "I felt the sea welling up around me and huge shapes brush up against my body," she recalls. "Within half an hour, I became hysterical." The boat found her shortly afterward, and she gave up the attempt.

When we finished our swim, we lay on the sand and watched the body of a dead seal drifting about in the shallows; its head had been snapped off by a shark. Although Cox swims often in shark-infested seas, she refuses to use a cage, believing that it divorces a swimmer from the elements and creates currents and conditions of its own, sometimes causing a drag that can help a swimmer along. She says that this is "unfair — like climbing Everest on an escalator." On two attempts made by marathon swimmers to cross from Cuba to Florida which I followed, cages were used. One swimmer was able to relax motionless for hours while being towed along; the other took a ten-minute break every two miles to stand on the bars while he prayed and consulted his psychiatrist.

The first time Cox swam from Catalina Island, she was warned that fear reduces energy. In order to avoid thinking of sharks, she concentrated on her hands moving through the water and the phosphorescent bubbles trailing off her fingertips. She has always managed to divert her mind from what may lurk below the surface. She was forced to confront reality once, however, when a frogman who was protecting her as she swam around the Cape of Good Hope shot a shark that had emerged from the kelp, its jaws wide open, and was making straight for her. She was almost home, but had to sprint the final four hundred yards — a cloud of blood was attracting other sharks.

Sometimes, Cox admitted to me, reflections of clouds could assume sinister shapes in the water and affect her imagination. I asked her how she felt when she studied navigational charts and discovered, as the light blue on the map gradually turned to dark, the depths over which she would be swimming. I wanted to know what went through her mind as she peered down through goggles into two or three miles of water. Anything can rise out of that shadowy line ten or fifteen feet below a swimmer, where the shafts of sunlight fade into blackness. At this point, her insouciance momentarily faltered and she seemed almost to shudder; then she quickly told me to stop my questions.

The English Channel is the ultimate goal of any long-distance swimmer. Cox first became aware of it at the age of nine, even though she had no idea where it was. She was swimming in an outdoor pool in New Hampshire when "there was a sudden hailstorm and strong winds sent waves racing across the surface of the pool," she recalls. "Everyone was ordered to get out and practice calisthenics indoors. Only I remained, and I exulted in the conditions." When she finally did emerge, a woman at the pool predicted that one day Cox would swim the Channel.

In 1972, when she was fifteen, she felt ready for an attempt. Her coach, however, thought her too inexperienced. At this critical moment, she met a Coptic Egyptian living in California called Fahmy Attallah, who describes himself as a "clinical humanist psychologist." He had attempted the Channel on five occasions, between 1939 and 1950, and had failed every time. In 1950, he missed by a mere three hundred feet: he had raised his arms to shield his eyes from the sun as he gazed in disbelief at the nearby shore. The pilot presumed he had given up and bent down to pull him out of the sea. Fahmy was disqualified. (His various attempts made headline news in Cairo, and influenced a great period of Egyptian swimming which followed the Second World War and culminated with Abo-Heif, a suave and brave Old Etonian, and one of the world's strongest swimmers.)

Fahmy inspired Cox to achieve what he hadn't. He described Dover and Folkestone, and told her where to train and how to find a pilot. Her training was much more intense than his had ever been — to increase her speed, she adopted methods used by Olympic swimmers — but he emphasized the discipline required to swim in cold water.

In the summer, Cox traveled to England with her mother. Throughout her swim, she felt that she had the record within her grasp, but two miles off Cape Gris-Nez she was forced sidewise, and a gap of five miles opened up between her and the shore. The currents a mile or so off the peninsula are terribly strong, and she had heard numerous stories of swimmers who got within a mile of the French coast and just couldn't get ashore. They got pulled back into the middle of the Channel, or were swept up toward Calais, or simply gave up.

She spotted a rocky promontory and decided to sprint for that, even though her pilot said that the rocks looked too dangerous and advised her to go for the beach. Her decision was crucial: she made it to the rocks, and her time of nine hours and fifty-seven minutes broke the men's record by thirty minutes and the women's by almost four hours. Telegrams of congratulations followed from all over the world, a few including offers of marriage. Some months later, her record was broken. Cox went back the following year to break the new record: she wanted to prove that her first swim hadn't been a fluke. Stronger currents forced her to swim three miles farther, through rougher seas, and still she broke the record by ten minutes.

On her return to America, Fahmy encouraged her to look for further challenges. She was invited to Cairo to compete in an annual twenty-mile race through the Nile. Fahmy assured her that it would be clean, but years away from Egypt had blunted his memory of local conditions. Cox struggled through fifteen miles of sewage, rats, and dead dogs before she was forced to retire. Fahmy also persuaded her to reattempt the Catalina record after she lost her nerve.

Now aged ninety, the diminutive, dignified Fahmy lives across the road from the Pacific in a Long Beach apartment whose sliding doors open on to a pool. He still swims daily. The author of the recent *Beauty of Being: Psychological Tips for Holistic Wellness*, he has continued to act as a mentor to Cox over the years. "More than anything," she told me, "he taught me to experience the spirituality of water: how we feel embraced and freed and connected to something much larger than ourselves when we are swimming through it."

Whenever I met Cox after our first swim, I noticed that she always veered toward a table by a fountain or a pool. When it rains, she told me, she opens her windows wide, and when it rains hard she drives down to the ocean to swim. To the amazement of her neighbors, she washes her car in her swimsuit in the rain. One night while we were talking, she looked up at the stars and exclaimed how excited she was by the thought of the frozen lakes of Europa.

*

In 1975, Cox flew to New Zealand for an attempt on the sixteen-mile Cook Strait, between the country's North and South Island. This would prove to be one of her most arduous swims. Caught on a massive swell caused by conflicting currents, she found herself farther from the finish after five hours than when she started, but the sight of dolphins spinning and leaping renewed her spirits. The whole of New Zealand seemed to be following the swim. "The escort turned up the radio so that I could hear messages of public support," she recalls. "A cross-channel ferry diverted its course and spectators lined the sides to cheer. Airlines altered their flight paths to fly low over the Strait. When I was halfway across, the Prime Minister called to say that the New Zealand people were behind me." After she touched the rocks at South Island, church bells were rung throughout the country to celebrate.

That swim was the turning point of her career. She felt that she had affected and somehow even inspired a whole nation. For the first time, she became aware of the transcendent power of the solo swimmer. Breaking records no longer interested her: from now on, her swims would be used as vehicles for a more personal goal. She believed that the lone swimmer among the waves, pitting her courage against great odds, could become a symbolic figure. "My goal is not just to be a great swimmer," she told me. "I think people identify with the athletic struggle, and I am trying to use sports to help bring people together." The ancient Greeks felt the same way — wars between city-states were put off during the Olympic games, as if people believed that, through the spirit and example of athletic contest, individual differences might somehow be sublimated and reconciled.

"Lynne was always interested in impossible things done in history by individual people," her history teacher at Los Alamitos High School recalls. And there is something of Joan of Arc about Cox — the enthusiasm and the innocence, the nerve, the vulnerability, the self-belief, the courage to go to people at the highest official levels and make them sympathetic to her cause.

Preparations for a swim are often more torturous than the swim itself, but it is in the course of these negotiations, she believes, that differences between countries are somehow made to look trivial. A year after she swam the Bering Strait, she traveled to Lake Baikal. She arrived in Russia to find herself a celebrity. Thousands of people lined the shore, throwing long-stemmed roses as she passed, crying out, in English, "Welcome, Lynne Cox, welcome, U.S.A.!" A cape on the lake was named after her, next to Cape Tolstoy.

Cox continued to search out political challenges. In June 1990, she swam down the River Spree between East and West Berlin, escorted by East German guards in boats, who could negotiate the various mines and razors they had placed below the surface. Later that year, aware of border disputes between Argentina and Chile, she flew down to the Beagle Channel. Her aim was to somehow break the deadlock by involving the two navies in her swim, across seven miles of fierce currents. At first, the Argentinians and the Chileans refused to cooperate with each other, but ultimately Cox prevailed, and both countries provided escort boats. Afterward, she was told by the American Ambassador to Chile that her swim had set a precedent. A year later, representatives of Argentina and Chile met on an oil rig in the Straits of Magellan to settle the disputes. And in 1994, while Jordan was mediating the peace process between Palestinians and Israelis, Cox swam across the Gulf of Aqaba, a narrow slip of water at the Red Sea's northern tip, which is bordered by Israel, Egypt, and Jordan. The talks, which were taking place at a nearby hotel, stopped while the politicians walked to the edge of the sea to witness the end of the swim.

It is difficult to know if her "political" swims have affected the course of history, but as she described them I was often reminded of the hero of John Cheever's short story "The Swimmer," who swims home one summer day across the pools of his neighbors. I began to visualize his swims as a microcosm of hers. He moves from pool to pool, just as she travels from sea to sea, and his influence is that of some mythical figure at first awakening in those around him a sense of something missing in their lives, a certain generosity and vitality of spirit. He imagines his swims as a romantic voyage into unknown waters, a form of knightly quest. He believes himself "a pilgrim, an explorer, a man with a destiny." As he erupts onto his neighbors' lawns and plunges unbidden into their pools, their reaction is one of puzzled amazement.

Cox's life has been a form of knightly quest, and her spirit has remained essentially romantic — she has swum in the classical Mediterranean, between the pillars of Hercules, across the three-mile Strait of Messina, guarded in legend by Scylla and Charybdis. She has swum in the Orient, through the ancient bridges of Kunming

Lake, below the old summer palace of the Emperor of China. She is drawn, she says, to dangerous places that intimidate ships, and to straits like Cook and Magellan, because they are named after sea captains who opened up a new world.

We had a final swim off Malibu, the day before I left California. Once again, we were the only people in the water. Cox warned me to avoid possible stingrays on the sand in the shallows, and never to wear a yellow bathing suit, because it is the color most attractive to sharks — "Yummy yellow they call it." She had just returned from Fiji and talked about the forty-to-fifty-foot sharks that locals had claimed to spot off the reefs there. She knew which species of shark twisted over to bite, and which didn't. I continued to wonder how, with all her acute awareness of the threat of the submarine world, she felt free to swim far out beyond the horizon. Then I thought of a passage in the autobiography of Annette Kellerman, the great Australian swimmer at the beginning of the century, that might well refer to Lynne Cox: "I learn much from people in the way they meet the unknown of life, and water is a great test. If they've come to it bravely they've gone far along the best way. I am sure no adventurer nor discoverer ever lived who could not swim. Swimming cultivates imagination; the man with the most is he who can swim his solitary course night or day and forget a black earth full of people that push. This love of the unknown is the greatest of all the joys which swimming has for me."

CRAIG VETTER

Terminal Velocity

FROM OUTSIDE

IT WAS TWILIGHT in Yosemite after a day of light rain. Headlights flickered in the dark of the valley floor below as Dan Osman took out his cell phone and called his friends Jim Fritsch and Frank Gambalie. "It's all set," he said. "Why aren't you here? You guys have to do this." Big storm, they told him. The roads out of Squaw Valley had been closed because of the snow. They wanted to be there, had planned to make the five-hour drive south to watch their friend take the longest, most dangerous plunge he'd ever attempted. Both of them were experienced jumpers. Gambalie was also a high-diving parachutist who'd made hundreds of leaps from bridges, buildings, cliffs, antennae — any lofty place with a landing zone; Fritsch, meanwhile, owned a bungee-jumping operation. But the fall Osman was about to make was beyond BASE or bungee. Dano, as they called him, was about to pitch himself off a rock pillar called Leaning Tower and plunge 1,100 feet tethered only to a climbing rope rigged to stop his fall just 150 feet above the boulder field at the base of the cliff.

Gambalie and Fritsch had taken these prejump calls before, had listened to Osman's countdown and then to the whistle of the wind as they marked the interval, had imagined the rush of the ground coming up as both of them had experienced many times themselves jumping on Osman's rigs. Osman himself had used his unique system of ropes, pulleys, and anchors more than a thousand times, and had developed a careful series of safety checks to assure that he and his equipment were ready. This time, however, in the chill of a late-November evening, he seemed hurried. He interrupted the countdown twice. Then, from an angle on the pillar he hadn't tried before, he leapt. The heavy whisper of the wind through the phone lasted 10, 11, 12 seconds, past what Fritsch and Gambalie knew to be the limit of the rope. The phone went dead.

No problem, thought Gambalie. He imagined the phone cutting out from the impact of the rope coming taut as Dano ran out of slack, bounced, and swung in a wide, jubilant arc at the bottom of the fall. Gambalie called back and was put into Osman's voice mail. "That was totally rad," he said. "We're on our way. Give me a call and let me know how it went."

At 35 years old, Dan Osman had long since become a famous name in the world of extreme — many would say senseless — risk sports. For close to a decade his bizarre specialty was jumps like the one at Leaning Tower: single-rope plunges from bridges or cliffs that Osman would make for videos and commercials and, more often, just for the sheer hell of it. Though I'd never met him, I'd read about him, seen some magazine pictures — the long dark hair, the gymnast's body hurtling through the sky like a rag doll. Having taken more than a few unwitting falls on climbing ropes myself, I thought Osman's deliberate leaps into the void were reckless, nuts, a no-net circus act ultimately bound for catastrophe. My opinion was seconded by this magazine, which in January 1996 published a short but highly critical piece about Osman titled "Really Quite Stupid."

Osman began his career, not surprisingly, as a climber. His home turf was Cave Rock, the vaulted outside face of a tunnel near Lake Tahoe's south shore, where he spent years attempting difficult routes that spat him off the wall again and again. After high school he took off for a couple of years in Yosemite and fell comfortably into the lost-boy culture of drifters who live on the rocks during the day, sleep in the dirt at night, scrounge for food and showers, work only enough to earn whatever money it takes to keep them at their sport, and spend long periods away from telephones and mailboxes, outside the catch of ordinary responsibilities. In the mid-eighties he returned to Tahoe and continued his Peter Pan drift: He climbed and worked construction intermittently; he and his girlfriend had a child and then separated. His friends joked about "Dano Time" when he arrived a few hours or a few days late for appointments. His mother's childhood nickname for him, "Danny I Forgot," hung on in the form of unpaid speeding tickets, unregistered vehicles, broken steps to his small cluttered apartment that went unrepaired though he was an accomplished carpenter.

"It disappointed me that he didn't take care of those things," says his father, Les Osman, a Japanese-American man who was once a SWAT team cop. "And I finally told him I wouldn't bail him out when his unpaid tickets landed him in jail. But he never had a lot of money; he was grossly underpaid for the risks he took. He usually earned just enough to take care of his daughter, Emma, and to pay his bills, including his hospital bills. Things like traffic tickets just came last."

Bailing Osman out of his jams often fell to his friends, many of them rock rats like himself, others more attuned to the day-to-day realities of adult life but nonetheless charmed by Osman's perpetual good nature.

"Whatever rough edges there were got smoothed out by a genuine fondness for the guy," said Roger Rogalski, a climber and orthopedic surgeon who became Osman's doctor, as we sat in his south Tahoe office. "He had his demons, sure, but I can't say a single bad thing about him."

By the late eighties Osman had made a name for himself as an accomplished rock and ice climber and as a no-ropes free soloist. Rogalski, who treated him mostly for small injuries — broken ribs and ankles — often suspended his payment, and Osman responded by gifting him with jackets and shoes that he had begun to receive from a handful of climbing sponsors. But Osman's interest in the sport was flagging. In 1989, working with a top rope to put up a 5.13 climb at Cave Rock that he called Phantom Lord, he fell 50 times trying to place a single bolt above a particularly torturous move. In the process he discovered that he was more exhilarated by the falling than the climbing.

"I'm not sure why," Rogalski said. "Maybe when a couple of the hot French guys came along and did Slayer on sight — a 5.14 route that took Dan a year to put up. Sometime after that he sort of drifted away from serious climbing and got very into the jumping. Most of us thought it was crazy, putting your life in the trust of a rope, but he was a passionate guy, and when his passion for climbing cooled he had to replace it with something. And it wasn't going to be backgammon."

*

Osman took small jumps at first, the length of ordinary climbing falls that could be caught by traditional belays and anchors. Then, as the falls got longer and longer, as he grew confident of the equipment, he began designing complex systems to anchor the lines in a way that would spread the load at impact and allow him to plunge from heights that no one had ever dared to try on climbing ropes. In Yosemite and elsewhere, he gathered groups of climbers to take turns at his new "sport," sometimes called "body hurling" or, as one oxymoron had it, "controlled free-falling."

"When I finally did it, my brain just balked," says Gambalie, 28. "This wasn't like skydiving, where the ground is never really in perspective, or even like bungee, where you start decelerating long before you get to the bottom. On Dano's system you got so close to the ground before the rope caught, it really scared me. The rush was just phenomenal, because there was no comfort margin like there is in BASE jumping, no margin for error."

If anyone needed proof of the zero tolerance for mistakes in Osman-style rope jumps, it came in 1994 at a Utah bridge. Bobby Tarver, a 25-year-old climber, rigged a new set of ropes for a 250-foot jump. Climbing ropes are designed to stretch when fallen on, and Osman always prestretched new ones with a series of short falls to determine their maximum lengths, something that Tarver failed to do, though it was part of the detailed written instructions that Osman had given him. Tarver's jump stretched the unused rope far enough to slam him into the canyon wall, killing him instantly. His death was chalked up to pilot error, and Osman continued to encourage his friends to try jumping.

"He wanted me to do it, but I wouldn't," said climber Ron Kauk. "I was intimidated by it — it's super scary. It's against my nature to let go of the rock."

On a bright winter day near Yosemite's Camp Four, Kauk was scrambling like a spider up the side of a big boulder. We were just out of sight across the valley from the overhanging granite wall of Leaning Tower, which rose 1,300 feet behind the thundering rush of Bridalveil Falls.

Kauk, 41, is a longtime valley local and one of its best climbers, and he and I had known each other since my years as a beginning climber on rocks not far from the trees we were under. I'd never gone much past novice climbs, but when I talked about the special fear I always felt when I was rappelling or otherwise depending entirely on a piece of equipment rather than on my hands and feet, Kauk nodded.

"Dano knew what he was doing, knew more about ropes and rigging than anybody," he said, "but I didn't like the idea that others who didn't know as much might try it. It's how I felt when John Bachar started free soloing back in the mid-eighties. I thought it was taking climbing in a direction I didn't want to see it go."

Dean Potter, a 26-year-old climber and Camp Four search-and-rescue team member, was working on a nearby boulder. Potter had helped put up the Leaning Tower rig and had jumped with Osman from a valley landmark called The Rostrum. "I did that one jump and I didn't like it," he said. "My climbing has always been about control, so throwing myself off the rocks like that — thinking maybe I live, maybe I die — pretty much freaked me out. But Dano was a master at this stuff. He had these elaborate drawings, and while we were working on Leaning Tower, he'd get up all excited in the morning, saying he hadn't slept all night thinking about the rig."

Yosemite authorities, not surprisingly, cast a jaundiced eye on Osman's activities. They had outlawed BASE jumping in the park years earlier, and though what Osman was doing was not illegal, the rangers clearly worried about adding him to their already long list of potential search-and-rescue victims. They were particularly irked by the fact that many of Osman's jumps were filmed for commercials and adventure videos and photographed for print ads. To them, Osman's work for the cameras was an open invitation to every adrenaline-addled kid with a climbing rope.

Soon I would get my first look at one of the videos that had made Osman's jumps famous. It was called *Masters of Stone 4,* and I couldn't help but be amused by the warning that opened the film. "If you want a long and happy life," it read, "don't attempt the radical activities depicted in this program."

That's exactly the kind of caveat that makes dangerous games irresistible to some people, including me. I've taken long falls out of airplanes and on bungee cords, I've ice-climbed, ski-jumped, and even gone hand-over-hand onto the wing of a biplane, as if for me, neither a long nor a short life could ever be happy without taking a few gratuitous chances. But most of the risky things I've done, I've done only once, and though they've all scared the hell out of me, none of them has put me or the equipment near the breaking point. But watching Dan Osman cartwheeling off high sandstone cliffs and then riding a bicycle and then a skateboard over the brink, I couldn't shake the feeling that he was trapped in a reach for limits he was most likely to find only in a death fall. It doesn't matter how well designed and executed a system is, things can go wrong, things that might or might not have anything to do with your abilities. Osman, to my eyes, was flying without a parachute in a plane that had "experimental" stenciled on the tail.

Sadly enough, watching someone in danger has an undeniable magnetism to it, and if the many TV shows and commercials built around such thrill scenes are any evidence, our appetite for seeing other people do things that might kill or cripple them is insatiable. And though it's often called sick, I've always considered it just a vivid way of thinking about death, a no-risk look down the dark hole that all of us eventually fall into. But to keep us tuned in, the athletes who star in these video moments have to push further toward the deadly edge every time out. Osman, at age 35, was caught in the hard choice between the nerve it takes to keep going higher, faster, closer to the invisible line between life and death and the very different kind of courage it takes to step back from the game, from the adulation, and figure out what you're going to do with the rest of your life.

Osman arrived in Yosemite late last October determined to make a record-breaking jump. With the help of several friends, he rigged anchors and lines to the Leaning Tower rocks. The rig consisted of a 1,200-foot Tyrolean traverse, a thick line strung like a tightrope, between the tower and a smaller outcrop called Fifi Buttress. The jump line was fastened near the tower side of the traverse so that he would fall away from the rocks. Osman made his first leap on 600 feet of rope, and over the course of a week the jumps got longer — 750, 800, 850, 900 feet.

On October 26, just as Osman was preparing for another jump, he got a cell phone call from his 12-year-old daughter Emma, who lives in Gardnerville with her mother. She was crying, worried about him, she said, and he responded without hesitation. He told his friends he had to leave, got in his truck, and headed off to be

with her. Osman was by all accounts dedicated to Emma and concerned that his high jinks put her in a precarious spot that she had
not chosen. He talked about his anxieties in Andrew Todhunter's
book about him, the breathlessly titled *Fall of the Phantom Lord,*
published in 1998 before the Leaning Tower jump. "By dying,"
Osman said, "I would be letting everybody down — my family, my
friends. . . . My daughter will manage, she'll be okay . . . but I'd be
robbing her."

Two days later, as he arrived back in the Valley, he was confronted and taken into custody by park rangers. The arrest had
nothing to do with his jumps; rather, he was charged with a loose-
end collection of Danny-I-Forgot offenses that had multiplied and
festered as the result of his chronic inattention to the nagging details of everyday life, including driving with a suspended license (a
federal misdemeanor because he was in a national park), a state
felony for having failed to register for probation, and a state misdemeanor for unpaid traffic tickets. He was held in the Yosemite
jail for 14 days — its only prisoner for most of that time — while
friends and family raised money and pledged collateral to post the
$1,500 federal and $21,000 state bonds.

He was released to his sister and brother-in-law, who took him
back to Reno, where he spent time with Emma and filmmaker-
friend Eric Perlman, who had offered his house against bail and
who now suggested to Osman that it was time for him to get his life
in order.

"I told him, 'You've gone far enough, pushed it probably farther
than it should be pushed. Nobody's going to touch this one for a
long time. Take the rig down, show the judge you're serious, that
you're playing by the rules here,'" says Perlman, who filmed *Masters
of Stone 4,* among other Osman videos. "And he agreed absolutely.
He said, 'You know, you're right. It's what I should do. And my
guardian angels need a break anyway. They've been working overtime for me.'"

Despite Osman's acquiescence, Perlman sensed a dour restless-
ness in his friend. "He was depressed as hell after all that time alone
in jail," he says. "And when he got back to Yosemite and saw all the
hard work and creativity it had taken to put up the rig . . ." Perlman's voice trails off.

Osman called his friend Miles Daisher on Wednesday, November

18, and said he needed a ride to Yosemite so he could take the rig down; the rangers had threatened to confiscate it. The two of them left late on the 20th, arrived the next day, and climbed to the tower that night. But the following afternoon, instead of removing the rig, Osman made a 925-foot jump on ropes that had been hanging in intermittent rain and snow for more than a month.

"I asked him about that," says Daisher, "because I'd heard that rope loses strength when it gets wet. He said it did lose a little but that these ropes were the kind they use on Everest, that they were designed to hold up in wet, freezing conditions, that they'd be fine. So he jumped, and it was a good one, no problem. Then I jumped, and it was great. We were having a blast."

That night the two of them shopped for food at the village store and chatted with friends about the record jump Osman intended for the next day. There was no talk about dismantling the rig.

At 4:15 on the afternoon of the 23d, Daisher made a jump and lowered himself to the ground with rope carried in a waist pack. When he got back to the tower at about 5:30, he found Osman hurrying to reset the rig, trying to beat the encroaching darkness to make his grand jump.

"I had a bad feeling about it," says Daisher. "He was jumping from a different angle than we usually did, which meant he had to jump over the retrieval line, which he wasn't even going to be able to see, as dark as it was by then. And he'd added 75 feet to the rope, which was about three times more than he usually added from one jump to the next. So he was jumping on 1,000 feet of line, which meant he was going to be only about 150 feet off the ground when he stopped. I was really skeptical. I kept saying, 'I don't think so, Dano, I don't like this.'"

Osman assured him that all was set and then took out his phone and called Fritsch and Gambalie, snowed in at Squaw Valley. "This is it," he told them, "I'm going big." He put the phone in a case on his chest and began his countdown. Then he stopped. "You got the spot?" he asked Daisher, who was crouched on the rock, ready to throw a coiled length of the jump line once Osman went over the cliff. "Got it," said Daisher. Osman began another countdown but stopped again and asked into the phone, "Did you guys say something?" No, they told him, go for it, and this time he finished the count and flew from the rock.

"I watched his headlamp disappearing into the dark," says
Daisher, "going and going, and in about ten seconds I saw the rope
straighten, heard it start to whip — what Dano called flossing the
sky — but it didn't make the full whipping sound. Then I heard
him yell — 'Ahhhhhh' — and a crash like a tree had broken in
half, and I thought, 'Holy shit, he's swung into one of them.' I pic-
tured him down there hanging from a limb, injured and bloody. I
yelled to him, got on the radio. Nothing. Quiet. Then I started
freaking."

Daisher rappelled to the base as fast as he could and followed the
beam of his headlamp through the rocks and trees until he finally
saw the ragged rope end dangling from branches above him. Then
he spotted Osman, lying peacefully on his side. He checked for a
pulse and, when he found none, sprinted off through the boulder
field to a parking lot pay phone where he made a panicked call to
Fritsch. "Dano's dead," he said, crying. "He's on the ground, I just
saw him, he's dead."

Fritsch and Gambalie told him they'd be there as fast as they
could, and Daisher called 911 to report the accident. A coroner arrived with rangers who started toward the scene but turned back
because of the slippery going over rain-soaked boulders. A while
later they phoned Dean Potter at search and rescue and asked him
to find the body and camp next to it overnight to ward off bears
and coyotes.

Three weeks later, the rig was still hanging between the tower and
Fifi Buttress, as was a long section of the broken jump line. Park authorities were involved in an investigation that was taking longer
than Osman's friends thought it should, and in December a group
of them retrieved the upper sections of the jump line and sent it to
Black Diamond Equipment for analysis. The results, which they
have since submitted to the Park Service, postulate a theory that
seems to indicate not system failure but human error: In short,
Osman had failed to realize that changing his jump angle would
ultimately place an unbearable load on one of the knots that connected the ropes of his jump line. The rangers, who are still working on their report, have not yet confirmed the cause of the accident.

A memorial service was held on November 28 at Cave Rock.

Osman's ashes were scattered over Lake Tahoe while more than 200 of his friends stood in the cold, snowy wind to speak loving words, place flowers, and organize a benefit and a memorial fund for Emma. And to absorb the shock of a death that shouldn't have shocked them at all.

PAT TOOMAY

Clotheslined

FROM SPORTSJONES

THE CONGRATULATORY MESSAGES started flowing in last summer. Via e-mail, the postal service, the telephone, from friends and acquaintances across the country.

"How wonderful for you!" "You must be thrilled!" "We're so proud of you!"

Even today, I get them. Less frequently, of course, but expressing similar sentiments. Now they're a mere annoyance. In the beginning, they were a shock.

The first call came from Ari Susman, a Dallas businessman. "Well, schmuck-o, you could have told me," he said that warm July afternoon. "How does it feel, anyway? To finally hit the big time?"

"What are you talking about?" I wanted to know.

"It's in *Parade* magazine," he said. "An article about the new Oliver Stone movie, *Any Given Sunday*. Why didn't you tell me Oliver Stone was making a movie out of your book?"

"What? You mean Oliver Stone's making a movie called *Any Given Sunday?*"

"Putz," said Ari. "How much did you get for the literary rights? We're talkin' megabucks, right? I mean, this is, after all, Oliver Stone."

I sagged in my chair. I was shocked. I didn't know what to say. I'd written and published a novel called *On Any Given Sunday,* but I'd never heard from Stone, and there had been no sale of literary rights.

Ari and I had known each other for a long time, having met in Dallas, in the early seventies, at Dr. Kenneth Cooper's Aerobics

Center, where Ari was a member and where Dallas Cowboy football players were welcome guests.

I had been drafted by the Cowboys in 1970, a sixth round "project" out of Vanderbilt — a defensive end if I could gain some weight. Access to the Aerobics Center was one of the perks of being a Cowboy in those days. Head Coach Tom Landry and Dr. Cooper were friends. The clients of the club enjoyed hobnobbing with the players.

Ari and I hit it off immediately — I was drawn by his wry sense of humor. We started jogging together, attending local sporting events, and over the years we became good friends. He followed the ups and downs of my ten-year NFL career. He was not a big Tom Landry fan, so he was one of the few people who did not question my decision to leave the Cowboys in 1974, which I did, playing out my option to sign with the Buffalo Bills.

My first book, *The Crunch,* a biting look at life in the NFL, was published that fall. When the Bills put me, after a single season as defensive MVP, on the expansion list, it was Ari who pointed out that the book may have contributed to my becoming expendable there, despite the quality of my performance.

It was less clear to him why the Tampa Bay Buccaneers, the following year, after I played every down of an 0–14 season and again won a booster club defensive MVP award, would want to waive me. But he was as delighted as I was when I turned up in Oakland and there, for one glorious season at least, nearly led the league in quarterback sacks.

I retired in 1980, but even in retirement, Ari remained supportive, especially of my writing. Although he was uncomfortable with the premise of my novel *On Any Given Sunday,* which explored the influence of gambling on the sport, he did agree that the real events that inspired the novel were bizarre and compelling, worthy of the effort to translate them into fiction.

On Any Given Sunday was published by Donald I. Fine in 1984. A paperback edition appeared in 1987. When Ari called last summer, I hadn't thought much about the book in years. When I explained to him that I knew nothing about Stone's movie, Ari said, "Well, it can't be a coincidence. You both have the same twisted point of view. I'd look into it."

I did, but my research yielded only disappointment. Titles, it turned out, could not be protected. If I wanted to write a novel called *For Whom the Bell Tolls,* I could. Similarly, ideas could not be protected, only the expression of ideas. I needed to find out the substance of Stone's script, for only then would I discover if there were grounds for us to talk.

It was not an easy thing to do. It's all very hush-hush, I was told by a Hollywood friend, but finally I got in touch with somebody who had talked to somebody who'd read Stone's script. The story he outlined bore little resemblance to my own. It all made me a little sick, since I was generally sympathetic with Stone's point of view, as I understood it through his films. To have him now turn his attention to a subject I knew well and felt passionately about, to have him appropriate my title without involving me — it was painful.

I wanted to do something about it. Finally, I wrote him a short note. Its purpose was to let him know about my book, to inform him of my sympathies with his take on things, and to offer my help, if he needed it. Some sort of consulting position was what I had in mind. Although I knew it was a long shot, just asking to be involved made me feel better.

I didn't expect to hear from him, but I did a month or so later. A letter from Oliver Stone! I ripped it open.

September 17, 1998

Dear Mr. Toomay,

Thank you for your note and your interest in our movie, *Any Given Sunday.* I was frankly surprised that you had written a book of a similar title, which we then read with great interest. I congratulate you on a very well done piece of work.

The theme of your book is not, however, what our main pursuit is in making this picture. I don't know what it is that we can do together in that we already have several technical advisors on football, and we're already underway in our pre-production. But if we do feel we can call on you for any help, I or my associates will certainly do so.

I thank you again for your generous offer.

Sincerely Yours,
Oliver Stone

Well, that's that, I thought. It was worth a try, anyway. Wondering who on his staff had actually written the letter, I filed it away.

Four months later, they called. "Oliver gave me a copy of your letter," said Clayton Townsend, the film's producer, on the horn from Miami. "We'd like to talk to you about working on our film." Clayton told me that what they had in mind for me was to actually be in the film.

"What? You're kidding me," I said.

"No," he said. He explained that a number of older players had agreed to participate in the film — Dick Butkus and Johnny Unitas among them. They wanted me to play the right-hand assistant to the head coach of an opposing team, a role that would be played by Y. A. Tittle.

Y. A. Tittle! "Yat," as my dad called his hero. Y. A. was my hero, too, growing up. All those division titles for the New York Giants in the early sixties. Countless "Alley-oop" touchdown tosses to 49er teammate R. C. Owens in the late fifties. Yelberton Abraham Tittle, Jr., Canton '71. A legend. He of the bald head. The blood photo. They want me to hang out with Y. A. Tittle!

But then I sensed the dissonance. Dick Butkus. Johnny Unitas. Y. A. Tittle. They were legendary performers, Hall of Famers, every one. Certainly, I'd had a career and achieved some notoriety. But I was a journeyman ballplayer. Nothing more. Still, I was flattered to be included with such an illustrious group. Just meeting any of these guys would be a thrill.

"Sound interesting?"

"More than interesting."

"So what's your schedule like next week?"

"I can clear the time."

"Could you come down Monday and stay the week?"

"I'm there," I said.

Monday, February 1, was the day after Super Bowl XXXIII, and Miami had been the host city. The production company had arranged for transportation, and my driver, when I met him in the Miami airport, looked like he'd been through hell.

"Rough weekend?" I asked, as we drove to the Mayfair Hotel in Coconut Grove.

"I worked 52 hours straight," he said. "I only showered once and never changed my clothes. But my client took care of me pretty well." He looked back and smiled. "I love the Super Bowl."

"Did you see the game?" I asked.

"Game? What game?"

We shared a good laugh.

At the Mayfair I checked in at the front desk, then went up to my room. It was spacious and nice, and I quickly unpacked. I had brought along a copy of my novel, in the event I might find an opportunity to give it to Oliver Stone — somewhere I had the notion that he might want to talk about it. Maybe there were elements of it he could use.

Putting the book on the nightstand, I sat down on the bed. As instructed, I phoned the production office. Simona, one of the girls who worked there, told me I'd be picked up in front of the hotel at 7:30 the next morning. "Look for a white van," she said. "We're thrilled you're here."

When the van pulled up in front of the hotel, four other people were waiting for it. They were movie people from make-up and special effects, part of Stone's team. They talked about other productions they'd worked on for him as we rode to the Orange Bowl.

Security was tight when we arrived. Guards waved us through a big gate topped with barbed wire into a parking lot crammed with trailers and cars. I was amazed at the number of vehicles assembled there. One of the special effects people told me over 500 were employed by the production.

Stepping out of the van, I was directed to a production assistant, who ushered me to a tent where food was being served. There she introduced me to Clayton Townsend. Casually dressed, fortyish, the producer smiled, shook my hand. "Get some breakfast," he said. "It's great you could come."

After wolfing down pancakes, I was led to a trailer positioned along the fence at the back of the parking lot. The trailer had four narrow doors in it, each one sporting a star. Scrawled on a piece of adhesive stuck to one door was the name "Y. A. Tittle." On the door next to Y. A.'s was my name, grotesquely misspelled. Unrecognizable. Laughing, I pointed out the mistake to the production assistant. "Oh, I'm so sorry," she gushed. Then she asked me for the correct spelling, but when she got back with the new tape, my name was still mangled, only in a different way. I let it go.

A few minutes later Wendy from wardrobe showed up. After taking my shoe, shirt and hat sizes, and the measurements of my waist and inseam, she retrieved from the wardrobe trailer a hanger full of clothes: khaki slacks, a green sports shirt, black cross-trainers, a green baseball cap. This was the designated coach's uniform of the Chicago Rhinos. We were to be the opposition in a key midseason game of the featured Miami Sharks.

In the narrow slit of my trailer, I changed into the clothes. For some reason it bothered me that everything was new. Working over the cap, I pulled it on. Dressed now, I stepped out of the trailer.

"Smart," Wendy said, looking me over. "Does everything fit?"

"I think so," I said. "What now?"

"Wait," she said. And smiled.

I settled down on the stairs of my trailer. The day was beginning to heat up. A big Cadillac was pulling in through the security gate. I watched as the Caddy wheeled in my direction, then pulled up in front of me. An old guy got out. Stout but vigorous, six feet tall, he wore thick bifocals and the clothes of a vacationing businessman. He hitched his trousers, looked around. His bald head gleamed in the morning sun. This had to be Y. A. Tittle.

"Y. A.?" I stepped off the stairs, extended my hand. "Pat Toomay," I said. "I believe we're going to be working together."

"Pat? How are you?" Y. A. pumped my hand, took my arm. "Now, you were a ballplayer, too, is that right?"

I nodded. "Dallas and Oakland, with stops in Buffalo and Tampa. But I was a generation removed from you. I played through the seventies. Ten years. I was a defensive end."

"Tom Landry," Y. A. said.

"Yup."

"He was something, wasn't he? I knew him, too. He ran the defense when I was with the Giants."

"I was aware of that," I said. "Tom talked about New York all the time."

"I guess you could say he invented the 4–3 defense, more or less. A keying type 4–3, anyway. He designed this scientific defense that would stop anything if you'd just follow the rules. That's what our guys believed. I didn't. I don't know if Tom did or not. Anyway, there was some conflict between the two units."

"In New York?"

Y. A. nodded. "The defense was a bunch of do-gooders, mostly. Who thought Landry was God. They hated the offense because we liked to have a good time."

I laughed. But the comment had resonance for me. In Dallas the freewheeling quarterbacks, Don Meredith and Craig Morton, drove Tom nuts. He was much more comfortable with the strait-laced Roger Staubach, who became the starter after Meredith re-tired and Morton was traded. "Tom Jr." was one of Roger's nick-names.

"Is that a Super Bowl ring?" Y. A. asked. He pointed to the ring I was wearing, the prize for beating the Dolphins in Super Bowl VII. I didn't usually wear it. It was too big and unwieldy. It put on too much of a show.

"Obnoxious, isn't it?" I held out the ring for Y. A. to see. "I dug it up to wear as a prop. Most of the coaches I knew who had them wore them. So I thought I should wear mine for the part."

"My one big regret," Y. A. said. "It's the one thing I never did. I never won a World's Championship." A sadness came over him, as he stood shaking his head.

"Y. A., if you hadn't told me, I'd never have known!"

He smiled, laughed.

Now Wendy came over and put Y. A. through the same process she put me through. When he emerged from his trailer, he was wearing exactly the same clothes I was wearing. We looked like twins. Mutt and Jeff.

"You know, I'm not too comfortable with this whole thing," Y. A. confessed, as Wendy headed back to wardrobe. "I mean, Oliver Stone. He's got such a reputation. The truth is, I doubt if I'da come if my grandchildren hadn't told me I'd be a fool if I refused the in-vitation."

"Well, he is controversial, there's no question about it. But he gets at stuff other people bury. All the debate is healthy, I think."

Since Y. A. still seemed anxious about putting himself in Stone's hands, I explained how other players of stature had agreed to be in the film, and at that moment, as if to demonstrate the point, around the corner came legendary Cleveland fullback Jim Brown.

"See? There's Jim Brown," I said.

"Nooo," said Y. A., turning, staring. And then: "Look at him. He walks just like he ran."

By that Y. A. meant that Jim, as a runner, seemed to glide along, his feet never leaving the ground, and sure enough, though bent, Jim still moved in that same trademark fashion, as if gliding on skates.

"The sonofagun," Y. A. said. "You know, they'd tackle him, but then he'd never use his hands to get to his feet. He'd push up with his elbows, mostly, because he wouldn't want his hands messed up in case he had to catch a pass. And then he'd just walk back to the huddle, as easy as you please. You'd think he was getting tired, you know. But he was just saving energy. The next play he'd blow by everybody, like they were stuck in cement."

Since Y. A. didn't seem to know Jim, I felt I should do something to facilitate a meeting, so I called out "Jim!" and waved him over. Although I had met Jim once, 27 years before, when my ex-wife sat beside him during Super Bowl VII, I was sure he wouldn't remember me, so I covered it by saying, as he approached, looking puzzled, "Jim, meet Y. A. Tittle."

They fell all over themselves. "Hey, Y! How you doin', man?" "Great, Jim. How are you?"

Amidst the backslapping and hand pumping, I explained to Jim who I was, then listened as they chatted for a while, both men beaming, both men pleased and surprised to have encountered the other, before Jim excused himself, saying he had to get dressed. He was, he told us, the ninth featured actor in the film. He was playing the part of Montezuma Monroe, the Sharks' defensive coordinator.

A production assistant appeared, and took us out to the field. Nothing much was going on there. A camera and lights were set up on the near sideline. Players were milling around. I couldn't tell if Stone was present or not.

We were shown to a row of chairs set up in the shade along the stadium wall and told to await instructions. Flopping down there, we continued to talk. Y. A. told me about his successful insurance business in Palo Alto, California. And how much he enjoyed traveling. Every spring he and his wife took extended trips.

After a while, Jim came out, dressed in black, and passed us, nodding. I wondered if there would be other opportunities to talk to him. Certainly, he was a complicated figure. But there was something intriguing about him, besides charisma. I couldn't put my finger on it.

It surprised both of us when, a moment later, Jim pulled up a chair. It struck me as an act of generosity. After all, he knew the ropes of this business. He seemed to be offering the comfort of his expertise, if we were interested. And of course we were.

For a while, anyway, the talk centered on show business. We discussed what was happening on the field, how movies were made. Jim mentioned the importance, for a performer, of being patient, of completely trusting the director's vision. "That must be tough sometimes," I said. "But you've got to do it," Jim replied. Y. A. brought up Jim Brown's classic, *The Dirty Dozen*. And I thought of *100 Rifles*, in which he played opposite Raquel Welch, and of that old news report that had him throwing a girlfriend off an apartment balcony.

Of course, from such images, it is tempting to make judgments, and many people do: Jim's public image has ranged from Force of Nature fullback, to B-movie actor, to batterer, to militant black — and here was the heart of it. For most people Jim Brown was a radical. Someone who hated whites and wore funny hats. Fiercely proud, but dangerous. My own feelings tilted in favor of Jim's athleticism, but as we sat talking, something started to happen that told me I'd better jettison whatever I thought I might know about him.

Many of the players hired for the film were young and black, refugees from the Arena League or from college ball, looking for a way out and up. As we sat talking, many of these young men approached Jim to say hello and to shake his hand, as if paying respect, not to a mere celebrity, but to somebody else. Someone of depth and compassion. They approached him with the reverent humility usually reserved for a holy man, or sage. It was remarkable to see.

Jim, for his part, greeted each of them with respect and an almost paternal kindness, offering a personal word of encouragement, inquiring how they were doing, patiently answering their questions, whatever they might be, although he did not seem to know any of them by name.

Often these exchanges were deeply personal. One young player, in his pads and helmet, confessed that he was thinking about becoming a Rastafarian. "Let me ask you something, brother," Jim said. "Do you know anything about the history of Rastafarianism?"

"Well, no."

"Don't you think it would be wise, if you're going to become a Rastafarian, to first find out something about it?"

The young man stared at Jim as he proceeded to lay out the history of the movement, in astonishing detail, without ideological bias, almost in the manner of an historian of religion. "I guess you're right," said the young man when Jim was finished. "I guess I should look into it more." "It'd be worth the effort," Jim said. "Whatever you might find."

After witnessing a number of these exchanges, I remembered I had seen Jim on TV during the Simpson trial. He was talking about his decade of work with the kids in South Central L.A., how vital he felt it was that successful members of the black community turn their attention there, and give something back, a gesture Simpson, and others, he felt, had failed to make.

"The killing in the ghettos has got to stop," Jim said. And his ideas about how to stop it were compelling. It was through education, he felt, meeting these kids where they lived, transmuting their rage into a sense of personal responsibility and ultimately into personal fulfillment.

Wondering if this work had created the dynamic I was witnessing, I asked Jim if he was still involved with the kids in South Central.

"Oh, sure. Absolutely," he said. "But I don't usually talk about it around here."

"Really?"

He nodded. "You know," he said.

"What work is that?" Y. A. asked.

Jim gave a brief explanation of what he was up to.

"You mean working with drug dealers, people like that? They belong in prison," Y. A. said. "They should be locked up. There's nothing redeemable about a drug dealer."

Jim sighed. As Y. A. got up to grab a cup of water, Jim leaned over to me. "It's tough," he said. "I mean, it's understandable, why he feels that way. But I don't like to argue about it. That's why I keep it to myself."

Just then one of the production assistants appeared and told us Stone wanted us on the set. We followed her up to the sidelines, where the cameras were positioned, focused on the Shark bench. Behind the camera was a curtained booth with a monitor inside. Stone was smiling as he stepped out to greet us.

He was smaller than I thought. Maybe 5'9", with thick legs. He was wearing rumpled khakis and a sweat-soaked shirt, but he was enthusiastic as he shook Y. A.'s hand.

After introducing us to Al Pacino, who was playing the Sharks'
head coach, he stepped back to look us over. By this time Wendy
from wardrobe had come over, and to her Stone said, "I don't
know. I think Y. A. needs a more distinguished look." They talked
about it for a few minutes, then Stone asked me if I wanted to indi-
vidualize what I was wearing. "No, I think it's okay," I told him.
Wendy took Y. A. back to wardrobe. While they were gone, I
looked around for Jim. I thought this might be a good time to re-
kindle our conversation, but when I saw him slumped in a chair,
deep in thought, I decided not to bother him.

A few minutes later Y. A. returned, now in jacket and tie, and
sporting a snap-brim fedora like the ones Tom Landry used to
wear.

"It's Landry!" said Jim.

"The spitting image!"

Stone was enthusiastic, too. "Now you look good," he told him.
"Now you've got dignity, a little class. Before, you looked like a tour
guide at Disney World."

I glanced at Y. A. A little chuckle had slipped out of him, but it
was strained, a laughter of nerves, not of mirth. He seemed tight
now. Wary. As if somebody had popped him one on the back of his
helmet.

"I don't know about the glasses, though," said Stone.

Y. A. sighed, took off his glasses, rubbed his eyes. Thick bifocals
with rectangular frames, the glasses, like their wearer, were from
another era. The inescapable feeling was that Y. A. would like nothing better than to be ensconced with his wife at their east Texas vacation home, fishing for bass on Caddo Lake.

"I think they're okay," put in Wendy from wardrobe.

"They're, you know, my glasses," said Y. A. "They're the ones I'm
comfortable with."

Wendy was nodding.

"Then we'll go with the glasses," said Stone.

As Y. A. settled down in a director's chair, Stone returned to the
scene he was directing before summoning us to the field. Curious, I
followed him over to watch.

The scene was a sideline shot of the black-clad Miami Sharks. Al
Pacino, their head coach, was sending in a young black quarterback, the replacement for the club's injured white veteran, Dennis

Quaid. Hovering nearby was Jim Brown, the Sharks defensive coordinator. Matthew Modine was the young physician tending players
on the bench behind them. James Woods, another physician, was
watching Modine. Absent were Ann-Margret, the widow of the former club owner, and Cameron Diaz, her daughter, who now ran
the team.

"BACKGROUND!" somebody yelled, and suddenly, the stadium
erupted with a deafening roar. My pulse quickened, the sound was
so loud and real. But it was only a recording. There were no fans
here, only cardboard cutouts of fans scattered strategically about
the stadium, to be digitally multiplied later. Still, it got me. I was
pumped, the juices were back. But somehow I was ashamed of my
reaction.

On the sidelines the camera rolled as Pacino took the arm of
Jamie Foxx, his young black quarterback. The Sharks had recov-
ered a fumble. Quaid's white replacement had been ineffective.
Now it was the black kid's turn.

"You're going in," Pacino said.

"I figured," Foxx replied.

"Feel like throwin' up?"

"Hell no!" Foxx said.

"Hey, last time you puked you had a hell of a game. Make a ritual
out of it and people'll respect it . . ."

Foxx looked at him as Pacino pulled him close. "What I want
from you is concentration. Focus. Downfield. Every inch," he said.
"See it before you do it. You see it, you do it."

"I got it. I feel it," Foxx said.

Then Stone stepped out from the curtained booth where he'd
been watching the actors on a big monitor. Evidently something
had displeased him, for all at once everyone scrambled to reset the
scene. I marveled at the crisp, almost military, efficiency of the
scurrying crew.

But then I remembered and my memories drowned out everything around me. I heard the sound of Fred Biletnikoff's pregame
retching. Every week he'd do it. It was awful to hear, the sounds
amplified by the hard surfaces, echoing off the tiled floors and
walls of the locker room bathroom. Was it fear that roiled in his
guts? Or was it just the black beauties he'd eaten, kicking in,
clenching him up? I wondered if they weren't both part of the

same thing. Maybe the speed gobbled the fear. The fear could make you piss your game pants. Whatever it was, people did respect him for it. More than that, they were awed by the idea that a football game could mean so much.

As preparations continued in front of me, I turned away from the set, wandered out on the field. It was a balmy early February afternoon and physically, I knew where I was: I was in Miami, Florida, toeing the turf in the Orange Bowl, where Oliver Stone was shooting a film.

Yet my mind was occupying a different place. The fictitious black-clad Miami Sharks were reminiscent of the Oakland Raiders, for whom I played three complicated seasons late in my career. The words Pacino was speaking could have been the words of Fred Biletnikoff to his own young charges, after Fred became a Raider coach. Focus was key for Fred. Focus and fear.

The fact that Y. A. and I were playing coaches was also disorienting, particularly now that Stone had dressed Y. A. to look like Tom Landry. As a player, I detested Tom Landry, he was so mechanical and distant. He was military. An engineer. I left the Dallas Cowboys in 1974, after playing there for five years, in part to escape his suffocating ethic. Y. A. had no use for him either.

Yet here we were, Y. A. and I, dressed up like Landry and a top assistant. Were we to embody in this film an attitude we despised?

As the recorded crowd roared again, the Shark sidelines became a beehive of activity. But mentally I was too far away from it to be affected. However, now it was the Orange Bowl itself that had set me quivering.

I looked around the old stadium, with its fresh coat of paint and fluttering Sharks flags. Super Bowl VI was played here. Jim O'Brien won it for the Colts on a last-second field goal. I was a Cowboy rookie. Where was it, I wondered, that Bob Lilly, our great tackle, out of frustration, flung his helmet so high in the air? It seemed to stay up there forever. Hanging. Suspended. Before dropping like a bomb. The field was Astroturf then. Ragged. A faded green. Now the turf was lush and real. It was a shame nobody played here anymore.

Then I remembered that it was in Miami, after the game, while driving down Biscayne Boulevard, that I proposed to my ex-wife. Or rather asked my future ex-father-in-law for my future ex-wife's hand.

"Well, Rusty," I said, as we cruised along, "Becky and I have decided what we're going to do with our Super Bowl windfall."

"Oh? Let me guess," he said. "You're going to open a knit-shop."

We married anyway, divorcing 23 years later.

"Mr. Toomay?"

I turned to find myself facing one of the many young women working on the film as production assistants. Cute, in her early twenties, she was draped with communications gear. "You can go to lunch now," she said. "We'll be shooting your scene later this afternoon."

As she scurried off, I headed across the field for the open end of the stadium, where palm trees rustled in a gentle breeze. Beyond the trees was a big tent, the crew's dining area, with a catering truck parked next to it. I started in that direction, but once again memory of the place brought me to a halt.

This time it was of a late-season game against the Miami Dolphins, circa 1978. Wayne Moore, the Dolphins' aging left tackle, was hobbled by injuries, and the Raider coaches felt I could handle him. But for some reason one series was all I was allowed to play. After the game I was furious. In that one series, I had gotten to the quarterback twice. More playing time might have meant a victory.

In the locker room, I made a beeline for Al Davis. Al owned the team and controlled everything. He was in touch with the sidelines by walkie-talkie. He could dictate strategy, substitutions. He'd told the coaches I could handle Moore. He owed me an explanation.

"Hey. Great job, Pat," he said, as I hastened up. "You were the only one out there who did anything today." Then he walked away.

"So why didn't you play me!" I wanted to scream, but his compliment paralyzed me. Better, I thought, to leave it be.

At midfield now, I was tempted to drop into my stance. Stupid — a 50-year-old indulging some lost-youth fantasy. But then I did it anyway, I got down. Once again Wayne Moore was in front of me. I dug in my back foot. I was going to freeze him with an inside fake, then rocket by him to the quarterback. Bob Griese was calling the signals. "Blue, eighty-one! Blue, eighty-one!" I could hear him. It was Griese. But then I realized I was in the wrong game. Griese wasn't the Miami quarterback then, somebody else was. Griese was in another game. An earlier game. Jesus, I thought, and stood up. Wheeling, I faced the opposite sidelines. Then I was walking that way. There, I realized, peering ahead. It happened there. The play. That call.

The outrage was almost palpable. My Buffalo coach was screaming. I was screaming. Everybody was screaming. The fumble had bounced crazily toward our sidelines. I was stalking it when an official loomed in the periphery. Still focused on the football, I moved him aside. It was a crucial moment in a critical game. First place in the AFC East. Buffalo-Miami. A playoff berth . . . Tony Green, our left cornerback, scooped up the football. Six quick, I was thinking, as we bolted up the sidelines for the end zone.

But then, a whistle. We pulled up, turned around. The head linesman, whom I'd moved aside, was pointing at me. A yellow penalty flag was drifting across my face.

"What?" I shrieked. "A penalty? For what!"

Our sidelines were in hysterics. Players were yelling, screaming. Nothing made sense. The referee explained that the whistle had blown when Mercury Morris was dumped on his head. "Since he was down, there was no fumble."

"Then what's the flag for?" we wanted to know.

"Verbal abuse," said the referee, and pointed at me.

That triggered another explosion of outrage. I hadn't verbally abused anybody. Undeterred, the referee announced the penalty and stepped it off. Our players continued to protest even as Miami came out of their huddle: "What the fuck!" Then Griese, on a quick-count, took the snap. Players on both teams were not even set. Pivoting, Griese handed the football to his short-haul fullback, and before anybody knew what had happened, Don Nottingham was standing in the end zone 58 yards away. The officials signaled a touchdown. It stood. Our season went down the drain.

In the locker room after the game, reporters informed me that the league's publicity director had issued an official version of the call, that he was no longer saying it was for verbal abuse.

"Oh?"

"No," the reporters said. "What you're guilty of now, evidently, is 'Brushing an Official.'"

It was absurd. I knew there was no such penalty. So did the reporters.

Had that been the only controversial call that season, it might not have had the impact it had for me. But, in fact, it was the fifth such call. And it prompted me to look into the league, to research, as best I could, its owners and officials, to discover how what had seemed a noble endeavor had become such a mess. It was that play that gave me the idea for my novel. The idea that a referee could control the spread.

Across the field, the recorded crowd roared, as again Stone began to film the Shark sidelines. Wandering over, I sidled up to Y. A.

"You hungry?" I asked. "The girl said we could eat."

Y. A. nodded, but his eyes were locked on Al Pacino. The scene was a reaction shot to a Shark touchdown, and Pacino was shaking a fist as he prowled the sidelines in front of his cheering players. He was moving with a kind of stylized street swagger. The players towered above him.

"You know, I don't believe I've ever seen a head coach like that before. Have you?"

"I'm not sure I know what you mean."

"That guy from Notre Dame, maybe. He was small and wiry, too."

"Lou Holtz?"

"Yeah. Maybe Holtz."

As we watched Pacino, I tried to get a handle on what was troubling Y. A. Maybe it was that most head coaches were more contained, that they derived their authority from an internal conviction, rather than from external gestures. Pacino did seem uncomfortable, surrounded, as he was, by behemoths. But I couldn't think of many people who wouldn't be uncomfortable in such a situation. I wondered how he'd come across on film.

In the lunch tent, Y. A. and I grabbed trays and moved along food-laden tables before taking seats at the far end of the space. The food was good and I was gulping it down when Jim Brown pulled up a chair at the end of the table.

"Gentlemen, gentlemen," he said.

"Hey, Jim," said Y. A.

"Jim," I said.

After Y. A. had balked at understanding Jim's work with the troubled kids in South Central, Jim had retreated to a director's chair, where he sank deep into thought. Now, it felt like he'd figured something out.

"Y," said Jim, "bear with me for a minute, will you? I want to give you my impressions of the Giants, what you meant to them. Just hear me out and tell me if I'm wrong."

"Sure," said Y. A., edging forward in his chair.

"The Giants," said Jim, "before you got there, were mainly a defensive team. Huff. Robustelli. Running that Landry Umbrella. They were tough, sure. And the team was successful. But the offense was bullshit. Conerly might have been a good passer, but he wasn't great. Schnelker was about the best receiver they had. There were no McElhennys or Sayers. They couldn't score points."

He continued, "But then Allie picked you up from the 49ers and got Shofner from the Rams. You liked to throw deep and Shofner had speed, great hands. Finally, the Giants had an offensive spark. The rest is history. Records were broken. Titles rolled in. But it was you, Y. A., who pulled it together for them. You were key, because of the way you played. It inspired everybody. Not that you had the best physical tools. You didn't. But you gave 125 percent, always, in every game, no matter what. It was your greatest gift. Am I right or am I right?"

"You're right," Y. A. murmured.

Although it was clear to me that Jim had taken this tack in an attempt to connect with Y. A., to dispel old stereotypes, so that they could relate to each other in the present, as they were now, man-to-man, I was struck by other implications. As Y. A., having gathered his thoughts, began delivering the same kind of detailed analysis of Jim as a player, I waited for an opportunity, then jumped in with my own observations of the two of them.

"Excuse me, you guys, but it's mind-blowing, just listening to you. It really is. Not just now, but this whole trip. I mean, the kind of comprehensive knowledge you have of each other, and of your respective teams, of the league as a whole — when I was playing, that was the domain of coaches. Exclusively. Players weren't encouraged to think in those terms — it was almost like trespassing. Yet you guys speak of coaches as peers! And not only that. I mean, you seem to have had input on strategy, game plans, personnel decisions. You seem to have owned the game you played, to have possessed it in a way that for me is unimaginable. You were the game you played, it seems, and what's more, you knew you were the game. Sure, you didn't make much money, but you had something more valuable than money — you had autonomy. A sense of owning your own experience."

At that Y. A. gave a little start. "You know, I'll never understand it," he said. He grabbed a napkin, pulled out a pen. "I mean, it used to be that offensive linemen called all the blocking on the line of scrimmage." He drew up an offensive set, X's and O's. "The plays were simple. 'Sweep Left,' say. That's what the quarterback would call in the huddle. Then, on the line of scrimmage, the linemen would read the defense, make their calls. Doing it that way gave a team flexibility; you'd always have the best scheme for whatever defense you faced. But then Landry changed all that. He designed a system that determined the blocking when the play was called in the huddle. So, instead of saying 'Sweep Left,' you'd say, 'Power 28 Near-G-O.' Like a code. Right? With everything built in. Twenty-eight meant two back through the eight hole. G-O meant both the on- and off-guard pulled. So, in a way, he took the offensive linemen out of the game. Made them cogs in his wheel. And everybody thought it was 'Genius.'"

As the conversation continued, I slumped in my chair. Y. A. was 72, Jim was 63, I was 50. Together we represented three generations of professional football players, but I realized that the world they inhabited was gone by the time I got there. And I wanted that world. I knew it from watching them growing up. But it was gone, because people like Landry changed it. Landry, who played with the Giants in the fifties, who then went on to coach. Landry, who, for some reason, resented the autonomy of players. Who sought to appropriate their autonomy for himself.

"Mr. Tittle? Mr. Toomay?" One of the production assistants appeared, hovering over us. "I'm sorry to bother you," she said. "But it's getting hot outside, so I've been told to tell you guys that you should wait in your trailers after lunch. It'll be more comfortable there. We'll come and get you when we're ready."

"Thanks," we told her.

Jim, stretching, got to his feet. "I've got to get to the dentist," he said. "Later?"

"Sure," we said.

After bussing our trays, Y. A. and I returned to our respective trailers. Inside my trailer, I kicked off my shoes, flopped down on the floor.

It was gone by the time I got there. It was devastating to realize it. Certainly, there were residual pockets in Washington, under George Allen, and in Oakland, under John Madden, but when they left the game, it went with them. It was gone for good.

On the floor I took a deep breath, closed my eyes. It was my hope that the drone of the trailer's air conditioner would override the whirling in my head. But almost immediately the production assistant banged on my door.

"Mr. Toomay? Mr. Toomay, hurry."

As I sat up, the production assistant pulled open the door, and I could see the look of panic on her face.

"I thought they just wanted Mr. Tittle," she said, "but they want you, too. Hurry, please."

I pulled on my shoes, grabbed my Rhino cap, and followed her out to the field. We entered through the stadium's open end and immediately I saw two distinct hubs of activity: one to my left, at midfield, near the Shark bench; one to my right, across the field, near the Rhino bench. Y. A. was with the Rhino group, surrounded by technicians, and by green-clad Rhino players. One of the Rhino technicians was waving frantically at me.

I ran over. She thanked me for hurrying, then said they had to get us propped. It was late afternoon. "We're going to lose the light."

Headsets were produced. Y. A. refused a headset because he didn't think his character would wear one, but I grabbed one, slipped it on. "What about a play sheet?" someone asked. Again Y. A. refused, but I took one, thinking it'd be useful to have something in my hands.

Then I realized where we were, that we were assembling on the spot where the play occurred that inspired my novel. The novel whose title was being used for the film. That Oliver Stone intended to film us here.

I had two distinct memories of the event: one from participating in the play on the field during the game; one from watching film of the play after the game. The film had been shot from perches high in the stadium, from two angles: sideline and end zone. And now he was going to film us where everyone exploded with rage.

As another technician began taking Polaroids of us, for continuity, Stone hastened over from the opposite side of the field. I wanted to talk to him now, to point out the irony. If irony was what it was. Somehow it felt like more than irony.

I watched him closely as he conversed with the assistant director. Then he looked over at us. "I'll be right back," he said, smiling. And he turned to go. It was then that I blurted it out.

"Oliver?"

He stopped, turned, eyebrows arched. He was sunburned. Reading glasses dangled off his neck.

"Oliver, the events that inspired my novel happened right here. Right where we're standing," I said, pointing to the ground. "You're going to film us on the spot."

His eyes narrowed to slits. I studied him, wishing he would say something. But he wouldn't talk. I didn't know why. He just stood there, staring. Abruptly, he turned away.

"Are you all set?" asked the assistant director.

I nodded.

"Do you want to change your shirt? You're getting sweaty."

"No. I'm fine," I murmured. I felt like a fool.

A few minutes later, Stone was heading back across the field. With him was the Sharks offensive coordinator, a red-headed ex-jock who also seemed to be one of the production's football consultants. Behind them, at midfield, the Shark offense was huddling. A few Rhino defensive players were waiting along the line of scrimmage. The football had been spotted at the twenty yard line, on the near hashmark.

All business now, Stone approached Y. A., put his hands on Y. A.'s shoulders. "Okay," he said, taking a breath, but then broke off. He backed away from him. "Y. A., take off your glasses, please. I want to see your eyes."

Y. A. took off his glasses, stood there sweating in the late afternoon sun. Stone studied him, then hastened to his monitor.

"No wonder you were such a great quarterback," he gushed when he got back. "You gave them nothing! They couldn't read your eyes at all!"

Y. A. shrugged, put his glasses back on. He seemed tight. Sweat was trickling off the bridge of his nose.

"We're going to be shooting through that camera over there," Stone said. He pointed across the field to the Shark sidelines, where a camera was positioned low to the ground, on a squatty tripod. "First, they'll be focused on the Shark huddle, then, as the huddle breaks, they'll pick you up, doing whatever you're doing."

"What are we doing," Y. A. said.

"I'm sorry?" said Stone.

"What's the situation?" I asked.

Stone glanced at me, but addressed Y. A. "The Sharks have just broken a big play. So they're on the twelve yard line, going in. They're gonna score on the next play. But this is a cheat," he said, turning, gesturing at the twenty yard line where the ball was positioned. "It's a cheat, so we can get the right angle. You should be yelling stuff, I think." He turned to his consultant. "What should they be yelling? Tell them what they should be yelling."

I glanced at Y. A. In his fedora he looked like Tom Landry. And all at once, I knew what we should be yelling. We should be yelling what the Dallas staff sometimes yelled at their defensive players.

"Y. A., you yell, 'Watch the run.' I'll yell, 'Watch the pass.' That way, whatever happens, we can blame the idiot players."

Y. A. cracked a smile, but Stone was unamused. "Don't you say that," he snapped.

Recoiling, I was confused. How could he miss such an obvious joke? But then maybe he loved Landry. Or rather maybe he loved the image of Landry, having never known the man. Maybe he had taken Landry as the symbol of the old ways, now passing. Maybe Landry represented the very thing he wanted to honor.

"What you should be doing, I think," said the football consultant. "When the camera picks you up, you should be sending in your nickel package."

"Sending in our nickel package."

"Right."

"But that's a pass defense," I said.

"Of course."

"But it's first and ten on the twelve."

"Oh," he said.

Y. A. and I talked it over and decided we should blitz. Then the assistant director went over the blocking for the shot. It was determined that we should be looking over play sheets as the Shark huddle broke. Then Y. A. would tell me to blitz. I'd turn and call for one of our players, sending him in with the instructions.

We were about to run through our little scene when a technician hustled up to the assistant director. "Oliver wants them miked," he said. She nodded, as the technician wired us up, hiding microphones inside our shirts. When he was finished, one of the Rhino players gave me a nudge.

"That's an upgrade," he said. "You just got upgraded."

"Upgraded?"

"More money," he said. "Now you've got talking parts."

Wow. Great, I thought. But then I glanced at Stone. Was he miking us because he wanted the benefit of our experience? Or was he doing it because I'd made him afraid of what we might say?

"Okay," said the AD, "let's try it." She was backing off, as the recorded crowd began to roar. "And . . . ACTION!" somebody yelled.

We ran through the scene. But there was a problem. Something was wrong. The AD listened on her headphones, then turned to us. "Let's do it this way," she said. She told Y. A. that he should be looking over his play sheets with the coach to his left, rather than with me. Then, on her signal, he should turn to me and I should send in the substitute.

As we ran through the scene again, I studied the camera, the angles, and I realized I'd been eased out of the shot. I told myself it was because I was too tall. At 6'6", I was a full head taller than Y. A., and most of the Arena players who surrounded us. The coach to Y. A.'s left couldn't have been more than 5'5". Stone had seen it on his monitor. We looked like a circus act.

Oh, well, I thought. Just get through it and get home. That I'd pissed off Oliver Stone was too painful to admit.

We shot the scene three more times before we finally got it right. Then we were told to reassemble across the field to shoot one final scene: Y. A.'s close-up. None of us expected this.

"Did you know you had a close-up?" I asked Y. A., as we jogged over.

"No," he said.

On the opposite sidelines we were repositioned in front of a Panavision camera. Y. A. was in the middle, with me to his right, the other coaches to his left; the players were behind us, pressing in, gathering close. The camera was no more than ten feet away and I was struck by its size. It was huge. Maybe eight feet tall, with the cameraman mounted on it, riding it like an exotic beast, its rectangular lens protruding, big and black — a mouth, it seemed to me, intent on devouring its prey.

Then I noticed that a crowd was gathering around us. The Sharks, all the staff, the stars who were present — Jim, Pacino — everyone was there, circling up, and suddenly, an electric intensity was filling the air, a sort of concentrated excitement that was not present when the action was spread out across the field. The light

was changing, too. The sun had dipped below the rim of the stadium and now its rays were slanting in through the slit of the mez-
zanine, mingling with the artificial light, to bathe everything in an
eerie pink glow.

When Stone stepped out of his booth, all eyes were on him. He
spoke to Pacino, who was lingering behind the camera, then approached Y. A.

"The moment we want to capture," he said. "It could come anytime. During the game. Afterwards. It doesn't matter. But it's that
moment when two embattled warriors acknowledge each other,
when you look across the field at Al, and he looks at you . . . That's
what we want to get."

Y. A. nodded.

"Now, Al will be on the other side of the camera, prompting you,
so you won't be operating in a vacuum, you'll have him to look at.
Okay? Al?"

Still lingering behind the camera, Pacino nodded.

"So let's try it."

As Stone returned to his booth, Y. A. stiffened beside me. I wondered if he was thinking what I was thinking — that the moment
Stone wanted to capture never happened, that it was a sentimental
gloss of a code that, in its most extreme formulation, granted nothing to the opposition, least of all its existence. It had been seen a
thousand times. Those mechanical handshakes at the conclusion
of games. The perfunctory remarks. "Fuck you" under every word
and gesture.

"We're rolling," somebody said, and a hush fell over the group.
Y. A. stood there, peering into the camera. Then Pacino emerged
to prompt him. But it was confusing. Stone had defined a scenario
in which two coaches meet eyes across a field, but Pacino was pac-
ing behind the camera, delivering a kind of street rant reminiscent
of *Dog Day Afternoon*. But his words were out of Stone's scenario. It
took a minute to unravel the dissonance. But that was it, I thought.
The words were right, but the delivery was undermining them. An-
nihilating their meaning. Making it impossible for Y. A. to respond.

Beside me, Y. A. was getting rigid. When Pacino climbed up on
the camera and began mugging, giving Y. A. a goofy wave, Y. A.
seemed to fill with contempt. But still clinging to Stone's scenario,
he tipped his hat.

The camera continued to whir. As Pacino continued to mug, the interaction began to feel interminable. God, I thought. This is awful.

Suddenly, it happened. Pacino was gone. Jim Brown was in his place, ominous in his black outfit. Overwhelming in his hulking presence.

Instantly, Y. A. was alert. Standing behind the camera, but directly in front of Y. A., his arms folded across his chest, Jim seemed to be peering into him. It startled me when he took up our lunch conversation without missing a beat.

"You know, Y," Jim said, solemnly, an edge to his voice. "I don't believe you ever beat us."

Beside me, Y. A. gave a start. Then he was smoldering, radiating heat, about to burst into flames. "You got a bad memory," he hissed.

For an instant it seemed silly to me, that Y. A. would respond so forcefully to a comment that amounted to a schoolyard taunt. But then I realized that this was the core of Y. A.'s athletic self. Bucking up when challenged. Meeting it head on. Never flinching. It was what made him great.

Jim, too. He knew what he was saying. He knew the impact it would have for Y. A. He knew because he also embodied that reality.

Pacino couldn't touch it, because he didn't know it. He was an actor. It was alien to him. Acting, he could only evoke contempt. But now Jim had stepped in and was delivering the goods for Stone. He was delivering what Stone needed more than anything for his film. Authenticity.

"Well, I think my memory's pretty good," Jim was saying. "But that's all in the past. One thing's sure. You were a helluva player."

As Jim spoke these words, something inside of me gave a shuddering heave. It was too pat. The whole thing. Suddenly it felt like I was witnessing a robbery. They needed authenticity but the million-dollar actor couldn't deliver it. So they used Jim to steal it from Y. A. Was that what had happened? Was everything contrived, a set-up? It felt like a set-up, but was it? Was Jim's interest in us fake, a mere maneuver designed to deliver Y. A. to this moment? Who told him to step in for Pacino? Did he do it on his own, intuitively, or did Stone orchestrate the switch? I didn't know. I didn't see it happen.

But standing there, my arms began to itch. As if I was covered with cobwebs.

"That's it. That's a wrap," said Stone. He was beaming as he stepped out of his booth, headed straight for Y. A. Around us everybody relaxed, as Stone put his hands on Y. A.'s shoulders. For a long time he just looked up at him. Then, lamely, it seemed to me, he said, "I liked what you did with the hat. It was good," he said. Then: "We've got to get a picture of this."

Calling for the staff photographer, Stone grabbed Jim, Y. A., and Pacino, hooking his arms across their shoulders, pulling them close. "For my wall," he said. Everyone was beaming as the photographer snapped the shot.

As the group broke up, Y. A. was inundated with requests for autographs. People flocked around him, shaking his hand, patting his back. Finally, he seemed to relax. He was bantering with everyone, as he signed scraps of paper, T-shirts, an occasional football. I wondered, though, where these people had been. For two days Y. A. had been wandering around the set, watching, listening, an old guy in a silly hat. For the most part, nobody paid any attention to him. Now he was being swarmed. It was as if Y. A. didn't exist for them until he was put on camera. It was as if he wasn't real until Oliver Stone made him real.

A rash had broken out on my arms. Rubbing it, I hurried to my trailer, changed clothes, then grabbed the next van to the hotel. In my room, I turned on the shower, scalding hot. I soaked my arms until the itching stopped.

That night Y. A. and I ate dinner together in the hotel restaurant. We compared notes, Y. A. confirming his consternation when Pacino jumped up on the camera. He couldn't imagine why such a distinguished actor would behave like a monkey. When Y. A. mentioned he had an early flight, I got nervous.

"You mean you're leaving?" I asked.

"Yeah. Aren't you?"

"No," I said. "My ticket down was one way, with no return. I don't know what I'm doing."

"You mean you're staying here with these people?"

Oh, man, I thought.

The next morning I put in a call to Clayton Townsend. Clayton's secretary told me that he wouldn't be in for another hour, but that she was sure he'd get back to me. I told her I'd wait in my room for his call.

In the meantime, I started to pack. On the bureau was a copy of my novel and a pile of papers I'd collected from the production. I tossed the book into the suitcase, sorted through the papers. Since most of the pages were trash, I threw them away, but then I came across Tuesday's Call Sheet. A Call Sheet listed the cast by name and role, the scenes that were to be shot that day, but what I noticed about this one was the way they'd named the film. The heading said "Untitled Football Project."

I sat down on my bed. "Untitled Football Project." How odd, I thought.

I began to pace. Something must have happened. But what? I called my brother-in-law in California. He was a producer himself, mostly of cable movies. When I got him on the phone, I laid it all out for him. His opinion was that they got nailed by Errors and Omissions. "Those insurance company lawyers don't miss a thing," he said. "They probably turned up your book in a title search and told them to change it."

"But I thought titles couldn't be protected."

"They can't. But they don't want an Unfair Competition suit hanging out there." He explained what that was, then said, "That's probably why they brought you down there. You know, to butter you up. To establish a relationship so they can use your title without worrying about a lawsuit."

Right, I thought. At last something makes sense. "But should I get money for this?"

"Absolutely. But I wouldn't expect too much. If you try and hold them up, they'll probably drop it and move on."

"How much are we talking about?"

"Look at it this way, Pat. Right now you've got nothing. But if you get a few grand out of them, then get somebody to reissue the book in conjunction with the film, that could mean some real money."

After hanging up, I went downstairs for coffee, then came back up to wait for Clayton Townsend's call. When it came, I told him I'd had a great time, but if there was nothing else they wanted me to do, I was ready to go home.

"Well, I think you're done," he said.

"Then I need a return ticket," I replied. "Who do I see about that?"

"Are you sure you want to do that?"

I sat there with the phone pressed against my ear.

"Of course, if you do, it's not a problem. I'll put my secretary on it. You can probably get out of here this afternoon."

Now I was in a whirl. I didn't even know if my brother-in-law was right.

"Clayton, let me ask you something. What are the issues for you in terms of Errors and Omissions, the title, and all of that? I mean, everything you're doing looks great. The set. The players. What I've seen of the script. Why not just spend a few grand, lock up the title, and use it? I mean, it's perfect for what you're doing."

"Let me talk to the powers that be."

As I hung up the phone, my stomach flipped. It was business. It had been business all along. My brother-in-law had it nailed.

It was late that night before Clayton finally called. I'd gone out to eat. But he left a message. I was to meet him at the production office the next morning at 11:00.

When the cab pulled up in front of the building, it was 10:55, and Clayton was in the parking garage getting out of his car. "Hey. Perfect timing," he said, as I walked up. We shook hands and stepped into the elevator.

"Excuse me if I seem a little rushed, but I've got to grab a flight to Dallas. We're going to try to do some shooting there."

On the third floor the elevator ground to a halt and we stepped into a ragged suite of offices. He led me back to his office, gestured to a chair. I sat down. He opened a folder, slid a letter across the desk.

"They've agreed to pay you three thousand dollars," he said.

I stared at the letter. I didn't expect this. I thought we'd talk about it first.

February 5, 1999

Dear Pat,

Firstly, I wanted to thank you for your participation in our production. It was a pleasure working with you.

You raised the question of compensation for use of the title "ON ANY GIVEN SUNDAY" for our motion picture.

Though we are aware of your book entitled "ON ANY GIVEN SUN-

DAY," we have been advised that it is not necessary to obtain your permission for use of the title. Nevertheless, in view of our good relationship with you and our desire to avoid any hard feelings, we have agreed to pay you the sum of three thousand dollars in exchange for your consent to our use of either "ANY GIVEN SUNDAY" or "ON ANY GIVEN SUNDAY" as the title of our motion picture.

Sincerely,
Clayton Townsend
Producer
So Agreed
Pat Toomay

When I glanced up, a thin smile flitted across Clayton's face. "If you'll just sign at the bottom of the page, I'll give you your check." He slid a pen across the desk, then the check.

"Okay?"

I sighed, nodded. But it wasn't okay. I felt as though I'd been clotheslined. Part of me wished we were on the football field where I could crush him. It wasn't the amount of the check that was infuriating. It was his lack of respect for me. It was his disdain. It was his presumption that his world trumps my world. That I was a whore. That I could be had for whatever price he wanted to pay.

In my mind, as the pen found its way into my hand, Clayton was off his feet, sailing over backwards, my helmet planted in his chest. The image brought a smile to my face, as his body augured into the turf; he whimpered, like a quarterback, sacked. Clayton was smiling, too, as he took the letter, inspected my signature. Then we shook hands. I was pretending to be happy as I pocketed the check.

On the plane home, I tilted back in my chair, gazed out the window. Below me the suburban sprawl of Miami was receding, but my mind was elsewhere. I was thinking about the 1981 Academy Awards. I watched the program on television like everybody else, but it was an eerie evening, one I've never forgotten.

The theme of the show was "Movies are forever" and fittingly, it was Ronald Reagan who greeted the academy from the White House. "Film is forever," he told them. "It's the motion picture that shows all of us not only how we look and sound but — more important — how we feel." It was an eerie moment because, as everybody watched this image of a healthy president, the real president lay in a hospital bed, fighting for his life. He was in the hospital because

John W. Hinckley Jr., obsessed with the plot of the movie *Taxi Driver,* deliberately shot the president on the day of the Academy Awards. As scholar Michael Rogin put it: "Reagan was president because of film, hospitalized because of film, and present as an undamaged image because of film. The shooting climaxed film's ingestion of reality."

Film's ingestion of reality. Tom Landry, when Roger Staubach retired, said the game would miss Roger's image. Not Roger himself. His integrity, his drive. Not Roger the man. It would miss Roger's image.

Well, I thought, sipping a beer. They've got all of our images now. They've got my image. And Y. A.'s. And Y. A.'s image talking to Jim Brown but looking like he's talking to Al Pacino. We'll all be there.

I wondered how I'd feel if they cut me out.

MATT TEAGUE

The Return of the White Man

FROM ESQUIRE

IT'S DARK OUTSIDE, Super Cracker, so you keep playing even after
the blisters pop. You strap on your daddy's work gloves and keep
dribbling, slapping the ball up and down the floor, paddling it between your knees, over and over, until your hands float free, separate from you, and nothing hurts at all.

Inside the gym, rows of halogen lights buzz in the rafters, air
rushes between your crooked teeth, blood hums in your ears, and
the hardwood yelps under the soles of your shoes. Nonmarking
soles. Always nonmarking, because if you leave any evidence — if
anybody finds out you were here — they might change the locks
and take away your world.

Somewhere outside the gym, your parents are fighting, because
tonight your mother will sleep next to another man. Day will bring
no peace, because you will fall asleep in class — school is foolishness, you always say — and people who can teach you nothing will
raise their voices in frustration. But none of that matters, because
you are not outside now. You are in the gym, where you slip past an
invisible defender, pass the ball to yourself, drive to the hoop, and
send the ball up, rolling off the tips of four fingers, then three,
then two, then just the one loose-gloved middle finger, up toward
the halogen lights, up toward the basket . . . and off the rim, an ugly
embarrassment of a shot. You curse yourself like any fourteen-year-
old would — "Son-of-a!" — and watch the ball roll to a stop. You do
not curse the ball. The ball is perfect and without blame, and so
you pick it up and grip it tight.

Then the world turns, a decade walks by, and you find yourself standing with that ball still in your hands. Everything has changed and nothing has changed. You have failed life in every aspect but one, the one that matters to you most, here on the court. Without your daddy's gloves, you hardly have to dribble the ball at all — you just stroke it and it follows, like a faithful pet. The floor is the same, the goal is the same, but now thousands of people press in — and pay good money — to watch you, Super Cracker. Not that anybody uses that nickname anymore; now you're White Chocolate.

So you do it all again: slip past a defender, pass the ball between your legs, behind your back, into your own hands, and send it up — *whang!* — again. You curse yourself — "Bitch!" — and watch the ball roll to a stop. When the game is over, your mother cries like a siren in the crowd, "*Jaaaaason,*" as though you would suddenly forgive her and utter her rusted name, but you walk by without turning. You walk until you are alone, and when no one is around, you pull on the old work gloves and pick up the ball again. Because you love the ball, and, by God, it loves you back.

The sun is barely up, and Jason Williams already reeks. Although he is alone in the Sacramento Kings' weight room, he has tainted the air with buckets of sweat and deodorant. Wincing, he steps off the leg press and looks back at it: "Bitch."

A drop of sweat has dangled from the tip of his nose throughout the dumbbell sets and leg reps, but Williams seems too pressed for time to wipe it away. He takes long strides from machine to machine, checking off each exercise on a list he carries curled in his hand, unaware of the sweat drop, unaware of the stink, unaware of the world.

His appearance is so plain, so unremarkable, that he could be a composite of the average American man, a guy who could rob banks and never be picked out of a suspect lineup: a smidgen over six feet tall; hair the color of straw, not cut short or long; not muscular, not lanky, 190 pounds. White.

There are tattoos — a panther clings to his right shoulder, a dragon to his left, a fist-sized eyeball just above his right nipple, and the Chinese character for *crazy* on his right forearm — but they seem more helpful than rebellious; without them, he would be easily lost in a crowd.

As other players trickle into the weight room, they pick up golf clubs and practice their swings, compare handicaps, watch television. They cast aspersions on one another's sexual preferences and make fun of one another's wives. Throughout this, Williams squints straight ahead, lifting, rowing, pressing, careening through the room as though it were empty. He keeps his chin jutted out, almost even with his thin nose. His face would seem hawkish except for a touch of Howdy Doody around the ears. His hands and feet are huge, like a puppy's, as though he's still got a lot of growing to do.

Later, lying on a table in the rehab room, as Pete the trainer massages goop into his back, Williams loosens up and looks around the room. "I try to keep up with the golf stuff, handicaps or whatever," he says. His eyes are pale blue, like the hottest part of a flame, but right now they're half hidden under sleepy lids. Life seems to barely keep Williams awake, and golf does less. "It seems kinda slow. And it needs . . . I don't know, it needs defenders or something."

Williams's love for basketball is monogamous. He loves the running, the dribbling, the passing. He loves the ball itself. And why not? Without basketball, he would be slowly dying in a West Virginia coal mine right now instead of lying on a padded table in Sacramento while Pete gently attends to a "tweak" in his back. Thanks to basketball, Williams counts his money in the millions, travels the world, and plays on television before millions of pop-eyed viewers.

Williams is every sportscaster's dream. His jackrabbit quickness and abracadabra passes translate well into slo-mo, assuming an elegance and artistry formerly reserved for nature shows about cheetahs and antelopes. Like that made-for-TV moment in Seattle last year when a fast-breaking Williams found himself one-on-one with Gary "the Glove" Payton, a six-time member of the NBA all-defensive team. He dribbled straight at Payton, then pulled up short and hopped, as though winding up to shoot. Payton leaned in to block the shot, but Williams had somehow kept his dribble going and blew past him. All Payton could do was stick a leg out, as though to trip the baby-faced kid.

In Sacramento, Jason Williams jerseys sell for $130, twice as much as any other player's on the team, and the Kings say his number 55 sold more than any other player's number in the nation last year. Maybe it's because he averaged thirteen points, six assists, and a couple of steals per game. Maybe it's because he helped lead Sacramento to its first-ever winning record. Maybe it's because his team was the only team to average 100 points a game. Or maybe it's because of something harder to measure, like creativity, appearance, or a combination of both. Whatever it is, Williams stands at the intersection of two golden roads to basketball glory: otherworldly behavior on the court and hometown appeal everywhere else. That is to say, he's a white guy who plays as if he were black.

By the time Williams learned to dribble, the only remaining great white player was Larry Bird, by then a tower of brittle bones and sandpaper joints. As he crumbled away, Michael Jordan — a vibrant, tongue-wagging bald eagle of a man — burst onto the scene with a game that transcended race. But even so, no short, pimply white kid could ever match his dark, gold-flecked skin, could ever pull off his aerial feats, could ever *be* Michael Jordan. Now along comes Williams — a mop-headed corncob from rural West Virginia — with a street ball game that leaves veterans twitching. He is the perfect blank screen upon which millions of other hopeless wannabes can project their hoop daydreams: not transcendental, just common.

Williams may be a blue-eyed savior, but he's no flawless god. He is human. He makes mistakes. Public mistakes. He has screwed up so many times, actually, that the people around him wring their hands in fear that he will slip up again, waste his talent, squander the money, blow everything. "I don't like those tattoos," his father, Terry, says. "I mean, what if he needs to go to a job interview someday? Nobody will want to hire him."

Williams's handlers watch his every move. They have instructed him not to make any investments, strike any deals, or sign any contracts. They try to keep him out of the nearby big cities, like San Francisco, Los Angeles, and Las Vegas. They discourage interviews and public appearances, citing concern about disrupting their golden boy's daily "regimen." Ah, the regimen. It is a nose-to-the-grindstone schedule, a routine they hold sacred. And it goes like this: Work out from 8:00 A.M. to 10:00 A.M. Shower. Eat Chicken McNuggets. Play video games. Sleep.

Sometimes it seems the game has devoured Williams whole. When he is out of the shadow of the backboards, he gives the general impression of emptiness: detached from his surroundings, slack-jawed, mumbly. But with a ball in his hands, he is electric, aware, eyes humming back and forth, arms stretching and snapping like rubber hoses, feet always making space for the ball to fly between. Once, in a game against the Washington Wizards, he drove to the basket and missed, but the journey — the innovation of it — inspired the crowd to stand and cheer.

He is the flashiest, most riveting player in the game, perhaps the most promising point guard since Magic Johnson or Pete Maravich. People call him the white Michael Jordan, but that's backward. Jordan's gift was staying in the air while everybody else returned to earth. Williams sticks to the ground while everyone else leaps up to block shots that don't exist. Lots of guys can dribble behind their backs, transferring the ball from, say, the right hand to the left. But Williams can pass the ball to himself, wrapping either arm all the way around his back, as though disconnecting it at the shoulder, to deliver the ball to the same hand that it started from. Defenders can only swat at the ball and run around Williams, this punk, this kid, this human tetherball pole, and wonder where he got his game.

It's midnight in Belle, West Virginia, and you sneak your dad's keys off his dresser. You grab your ball and slip out the front door like a whisper.

Your eyes adjust to the dark as you walk, and, looking back, you can make out the house. It is painted beige but looks gray in the dark, and it is surrounded by nothing but empty space, a parking lot on one side and a football field on the other. What a dreary place to live, right smack in the middle of the DuPont High School campus. No neighborhood kids to ride bikes with, no doors to knock on at Halloween, no place to hide from boredom or anger or loneliness. But state troopers don't make much money in West Virginia, so your dad has to moonlight as an on-campus security guard. It's just part of the package.

Dad says your gift comes from heaven, but, boy, is he wrong. It bubbles up right here, a few dozen steps from home in an empty building with a locked door. As you feel the key go *snick*, something more powerful than electricity zaps your fingers, runs up your arm, and touches your brain: This is your sanctuary, your laboratory, your monastery. This is the gym.

Inside, you set to work, like every night. You make a two-by-two-foot square on the wall with black tape and pass the ball to it behind your back, between your legs, left-handed, right-handed, looking away, running full tilt.

Your brother is three years older than you, but you can kick his butt in basketball. That's because Shawn doesn't take time to practice like you do. He's always doing other stuff — cutting grass in the morning, working for that lawyer guy after school, taking tickets down at the movie theater every night. He bought his own car. Paid for it himself. That's cool. But he wants to go to college and all that. Be a cop like your dad, or whatever.

Not you. You pull on your father's work gloves, wrap ankle weights around your wrists, then dribble, pounding the ball until you can lace it through your legs as easy as a daydream. When you take off the gloves, your touch is a caress, and the ball is the object of your affections.

Affections. Your mom uses that word sometimes. She has affections for that Scott guy. Screw him. Screw her, too. Someday you're going to make it big, and when people open up their NBA programs to read about you, they're going to see it just the way it is: "Age twenty-three . . . son of Terry Williams . . . knew he wanted to play professional basketball at age seven." No mention of anybody named Delana Williams, formerly known as Dad's wife, formerly known as Mama.

It's so cool in here. No nagging teachers, no fighting parents, no sound at all, except for the sweet pock-pock-pocking of the ball against the floor.

It is a little odd to see legs like this, carved and pasty at the same time. Guys with this kind of definition tend to jump in a tanning bed once in a while or at least strut around in the sunshine.

Williams flicks his legs back and forth in the air, lying on his back while Al the conditioning coach barks out instructions: left, right, left, right. The legs are narrow at the ankle and wide at the thigh, like a horse's, but have the pallor of a hairless animal that has hidden in a dark place its entire life. The effect is heightened because Williams is lying on the floor next to second-team point guard Darrick Martin, who is black.

"Come on, ladies," Al growls. Al is a gray-haired guy with a Ph.D., and his motivational techniques lean heavily on emasculation. "Get 'em up," he says. "Faggots."

Williams has 'em up, way up straight. He is several days into his training and is used to the burn. But Martin, truth be told, is suffering. Today is his first day with the Kings after a year with the lowly L.A. Clippers.

"*Gah,*" he groans. Al is merciless, and he describes to Martin the various intricacies of the female anatomy, many of which he renames in Martin's honor.

There are televisions everywhere in the Kings' weight room, and they're always tuned to all-sports channels. Right now, football highlights are playing, and Randy Moss of the Minnesota Vikings is on the screen, sprinting down the sideline at the thirty . . . the twenty . . .

Williams stands up and looks alive. "Go, boy!" he shouts. "Dig!" And Moss does dig, at the fifteen . . . the ten . . . "Touchdown!" Williams shouts. "Where is that boy *from?*" he hollers. "If he can make it, anybody can."

Williams is a huge Moss fan, because Moss blew it in every possible way — he even did some jail time — yet he went on to silence critics and ignite professional football in his rookie year. And now here he is, a big shot, forgiven his transgressions and loved for his virtuosity.

"Let's do butts next," Al says. "Get 'em up." While Williams does the butt exercises, the equipment manager, a young guy named Rob, wanders over to watch. "Everything cool?" he asks. "*Mpff,*" Williams says, and Rob kneels down close. Politely, he begins to say something like, "Sorry, what?" but he is cut off by a great, suffocating fart. And then a second volley is launched before Rob can stagger up from the kneeling position. Williams cackles as Rob falls away, and Al laughs so hard he almost loses count of the exercises.

"Heh," Rob says, red-faced and sniffling. "Jason does stuff like that to keep it light, you know? It's cool."

If Williams had a motto, that would be it: Keep it light. People around him seem trained to dilute and deflect conversation, to keep it trivial, never serious. They talk about the funky shot he made in practice, or the new baseball cap he just bought, or Muhammad Ali versus Mike Tyson. They talk about women or cartoons or rap. But if anyone mentions Williams's ambitions, his money or his fame, his mother or his mistakes, he shuts down, retreats inside himself until everybody remembers to keep it light. "I just don't go there," says Troy Hanson, the Kings' media-relations director. "It's best to stick to basketball."

Sometimes people from the outside world forget to keep it light, and they accidentally acknowledge that Williams is wealthy or well-known. Like autograph seekers. "Restaurants are the worst," he says. "People have no respect. They bug you." To keep his profile low, he eats as often as possible at McDonald's. "Plus, I love Chicken McNuggets," he says. "My favorite."

McDonald's is the best because people there tend to keep it light. People there aren't nosy, because what are the chances of bumping into someone who's famous or rich? Williams is rich — six million over three years, plus a big-money shoe endorsement — but wealth is so uncomfortable, so unbearably heavy. His father once asked how big his paycheck is, and he answered, "I don't know." His bank balance? "I don't know."

Williams says he's thinking about buying a mountain bike, but he hears they're expensive. "What does a tuneup cost on one of those things?"

"Twelve bucks," somebody says.

Williams falls silent. "Man," he eventually mutters. "Twelve *dollars?*" That's almost as much as he paid for his sweet new purple-and-gold Minnesota Vikings hat. He's thinking about getting RANDY MOSS embroidered on the side, but Lord knows how much that'll cost.

This is high school, man, and this is the freaking *life.*

You are a DuPont Panther now, which means you get to hang out in the gym while the sun is still shining. And you get to pass to real people instead of a square on the wall, so you do it all the time: pass, pass, pass. Especially to your buddy Randy Moss. He can dunk, and that's so cool when you put it together with a trick pass. Like this one time, when you slung it behind your back, three-quarters court, and Randy caught it on stride and just stuffed it in the hoop like he was feeding a tiger. People love that crap, man. They'll be watching that game on tape ten years from now. Of course, by then you'll be playing in the NBA, if everything goes right.

Your dad gets all bent out of shape when you cut class. He says it takes "commitment" to make it through high school, but, hey, you graduate anyway. You sign to play with Providence, but the coach leaves, so you call it off. You enroll at Fork Union Military Academy, but that's no kind of life, man, so after a week you call that off, too. You sign with Marshall, but then coach Billy Donovan moves to the University of Florida, so you call it off at Marshall and follow Donovan down south.

What? You've gotta sit out a season if you switch schools? No hoops for a year? Just class? Screw that. You call it off at Florida. When you get home, your brother, Shawn, hits the roof. He goes on about how he graduated from college and took a job working as a cop down in Charleston and how you keep wasting opportunities. Maybe he's all uptight because he scraped and worked all this time while schools threw themselves at you, the guy who can bounce a stupid orange ball. And you screwed it up.

There's a 7-Eleven down the street where washed-up high school jocks hang out and drink beer. Every time you ride by the store with your dad, he glares at you and makes a crack: There they are, he says. The 7-Eleven All-Stars. You could be their captain.

That hurts, man. So after three weeks of pressure from your dad and brother, you give in and head back to Gainesville. There's a spot waiting for you on the team next time hoops season rolls around, but things fall apart fast: First, you fail a drug test for smoking pot and get suspended. Then you're suspended again for "behavior detrimental to the team," which means sulking on the bench.

There's no way you'll be tested a second time, though. You're a big-time athlete on a big-time campus, and the team is 13–8. They need you. So you keep hanging out with your boys, listening to their music, smoking their weed. And then — *bam!* — you get busted again. How much were you smoking? Too much. A lot. You can't even remember how much, but it was enough to get you booted from the team. And just like that, everything you ever wanted is gone.

Your dad is embarrassed to go to work. So is Coach Donovan, because without you the team goes 1–7. You feel yourself slipping down, down past your brother, past the All 7-Eleven team, past your love for the game. You swear to God that you will never again squander your gift — never smoke another joint, never tell another lie, never take another opportunity for granted — if only you can find a job coaching high school basketball. Four months later, something happens. The NBA draft rolls around, the scouts start talking about you, and despite all your screwups, you are the seventh pick of the first round. Somehow you are a pro, a millionaire, a star. And then you remember.

Basketball loves you back.

"Jump, fag!"

Al is working Williams hard. His black practice jersey is stuck to his chest, and his hair is plastered to his forehead. His nostrils flare when he breathes. He is tired.

When he finishes the workout, he shuffles down the hall to the elevator and rides all the way to the top floor of Arco Arena, to his secret place, a place you don't read about in the newspapers or see on television.

The top floor is unfinished, and it looks like a warehouse full of insulation, scrap metal, and dust. Williams ambles past rows of old stadium seats, outdated computers, and assorted junk to the back, where there is half a basketball court patched together with leftover wood flooring and a goal.

It is a Sacramento version of his gym back home, a place where he can lock himself away from the world, pull on the old work gloves, and caress the ball.

Williams steps on the court, and the blank mask falls from his face. His flame-blue eyes roll heavenward, and he pins the ball between his palms at his chest, elbows out. For a moment, he looks like a basketball saint, praying for grace. It doesn't come quickly, because his first few shots glance off the rim, sail wide, thud like bricks against the backboard.

"*Jason!*" he says. "*Bitch.*" Over and over, the ball flies up toward the hoop, until Williams's arm is calibrated and his vision is focused, and he strips the net every time.

He dribbles behind his back, between his legs, on and on, until his hands float free. He experiments with a move behind his back, one that will confound referees this year because he somehow arrests the motion of the ball without palming. He laughs to himself, like a little boy who knows a magic trick. There are no failing grades here, no quibbling parents, no contracts or autographs to sign, no endorsements, no drug tests. No disappointments. Everything here is light.

DAVID WHARTON

Soul Survivor

FROM THE LOS ANGELES TIMES

THE TRIP FROM New Mexico takes seven hours of driving, flying, then more driving. She comes every other week to watch a young and struggling USC basketball team.

"Her?" an usher at the Sports Arena asks. "That woman is in her own world."

Diane Taylor stands just under five feet tall. She is middle-aged and suitably dressed, a gold cross hanging from a gold chain around her neck. She always sits behind the bench and everyone knows her by the odd-looking stick she carries.

The size of a cane, it is covered with bells and bangles, and there is a cymbal attached on top. It is the kind of contraption a fan might rattle after dunks and three-point baskets.

"My boombah," she calls it. And once the game begins, Taylor *pounds* that stick.

She pounds it on the floor, hard enough to startle people sitting nearby. She pounds it for reasons that have little to do with basketball.

People wonder about that woman.

His voice settles between a whisper and a growl, his eyes half-lidded, as he tells his story. Elias Ayuso starts long ago, long before he became a sharpshooting guard for the Trojans, running the court with the jangle of the boombah in his ears. He was eight when he left Puerto Rico with his mother and brothers and sisters, on their way to becoming another immigrant family in the South Bronx.

"The guy who lived below us, he had some problems with drug stuff," Ayuso says. "I don't know if he owed money or what but they wanted to kill him. They threw a firebomb into his apartment."

It was late at night and Ayuso was watching television with his family.

"The hallway was nothing but smoke," he says. "We couldn't take the fire escape so we got everybody and we covered my little brother's mouth and we just ran down the steps."

They lost everything. People from the next building brought out old clothes but the best they could find for Ayuso was a blouse and baggy pants.

"They dressed me in girlie clothes," he says.

The next few years, as his family drifted through shelters and low-rent hotels, he was teased about his unusual name and his accent. One day he started calling himself Larry because it sounded more American.

Eventually, shame turned to anger, anger to recklessness. Ayuso stopped going to school. His mother, Socorro Carrillo, was too busy rearing four other children to stop him from hanging out on the corner of 137th and Cypress, amid the tenements and abandoned cars, a narrow strip of sky above.

"I'd go with my friends," he says. "Go do bad things."

They fought and stole and robbed.

What does it take to save a kid? What can salvage a child who learns to connive and brawl the way others learn to brush their teeth and do their homework? Before Taylor tries to answer the question, she has a story of her own to tell.

It goes back to a Pennsylvania mining town called Carbondale, where she was a little girl from an Irish-Italian family as big as it was poor. There wasn't money for a doctor's visit when she fell ill and she recalls coughing so loudly on the street that two well-dressed women stopped.

"Go home," one of them said. "You're disgusting."

Decades later, the 49-year-old woman clenches her fist and says, "I remember thinking that no one would ever treat me that way again."

The memory made her tough as nails, fiery as her red hair. It pushed her through college — neither of her parents made it past sixth grade — and into the hotel business in Los Angeles. Here,

Taylor met her husband, Dick, an accountant as calm as she was manic, and they moved to New Mexico when he was hired by a firm in Roswell. They worked hard enough and saved long enough to buy the firm.

Then the memory did something else for her.

"It's not something you plan to do," Taylor says. "I went to work for the Boys Club. I became a youth director and started working with abused and neglected kids.

"When they got in trouble, I'd bring them home."

Two thousand miles east, a world apart, Ayuso was unknowingly inching toward Taylor.

The strength and reflexes that made him a street fighter also made him a basketball player. Not the typical New York City guard with a quick dribble and flashy moves. No one mistook him for another Kenny Anderson or Tiny Archibald. Ayuso had something different. He had a natural jump shot, with a flick of the wrist at the end.

A friend dragged him to tryouts for a church league when he was 15 and he made the team.

"I was shocked," he says.

That pure shooting stroke got him noticed, got him a scholarship to St. Raymond's High School. The day Ayuso transferred, a cousin was wounded in a knife fight at their public school.

"If I was there, I would have gone down with him," he says, and he took his escape as a sign from God. Like so many kids in the projects, he saw basketball as a ticket out.

"He was raw but you could tell he had talent," St. Raymond's Coach Gary DeCesare says. "The game just came easily to him."

Schoolwork did not. In class, Ayuso had little more to offer than a street-wise sense of humor, the charm of his dark eyes and a half-grin. He would not do the homework and did not make the grades to play in a single game, so the school did not invite him back after his sophomore year.

That is how kids end up on street corners like 137th and Cypress.

Jeff Bryant, a youth director at the local Boys Club, calls it the process of "kids getting swallowed up." Bryant, a native of the Bronx, escaped to college in New Mexico, then returned to give others the same shot at redemption. The money he raised from raffles and car washes sent boys to foster families out West. First two, then two more.

In the summer of 1993, a new candidate for the program showed up at the club to shoot baskets.

"I don't want to say Larry was a slickster, but he was always looking out for himself," Bryant says. "If he could get one over on you, he would. If there was a shortcut, he would take it."

Ayuso was 16 and just desperate enough to wonder about New Mexico. His older brother and three friends had died on the streets. He had a long, tearful talk with his mother.

"I thought, 'Damn, I've got to get out of New York,'" he says. "I knew it was my last chance."

Two hundred miles of dirt separate Roswell and any major city. The place is undeniably oddball — a few too many locals insist a flying saucer crashed on a nearby ranch in 1947, a few too many shops peddle alien T-shirts and coffee mugs along Main Street.

Yet, in many respects, Roswell is a typical small town. Everyone knows everyone else and news travels fast when a transfer student starts a fight at Roswell High, or starts a gambling ring in the hallways, scamming his classmates out of their lunch money and Walkman radios.

Ayuso was living with a religious couple in the town's wealthiest neighborhood. Within a few weeks, they were on the telephone with Bryant, saying they could not handle the kid, but knew of someone who could. That's how Ayuso landed on Taylor's doorstep.

"You don't know what a jerk he was," Taylor says. "He thought he was *the man*. . . . Well, he ran into the wrong woman."

Other troubled kids had passed through her house, a cozy four bedrooms with a front lawn that turns brown in winter and an above-ground pool in back. They came one at a time, a boy here, a girl there, and Taylor treated them exactly as she had treated her own two sons. If they followed the rules, they got rewards.

The rules came first. No more misbehaving at school, no phone calls after 8 P.M. and no more baggy street clothes, which she confiscated one day. The next morning, Ayuso tore up his room looking for them, then ran from the house. She dragged him back by the shirt collar and made him clean up.

"She was the big dog," Ayuso says. "She wasn't going to cut the truth up in pieces and give me a little here and there. She gave it to me all at once."

Taylor overpowered the 6-foot-2 teenager with a single threat: "I can have you back in the Bronx by noon tomorrow."

That kept him out of trouble and kept him doing homework for two hours at the kitchen table each night. When he passed all his classes, she pushed him even harder, enrolling him in summer school and getting him a job on the 5 A.M. shift at a nearby Christmas ornament factory. He came home afternoons sweaty and covered with glitter.

But it was still a scam, the kid doing just enough to get by. Taylor could tell by the angry words he wrote in his notebook and left out for her to see. She could tell by the rap songs he performed in his room, loudly enough for her to hear: "Can't wait to get smart / I'll get rid of her and depart."

Taylor got the message: Ayuso had come West to escape but not to change. That wasn't good enough.

Life had dealt him so many broken promises. Ayuso says, "I realized Diane was trying to teach me a different way, but it was hard for me to trust her." He made Taylor prove herself.

That summer, they drove three hours to Albuquerque, where she wangled a meeting with two assistant coaches at the University of New Mexico. Ayuso followed them down a dark tunnel into their arena, "the Pit." Just as he stepped onto the court, overhead lights flickered on and they handed him a ball, told him to take a few shots.

"You should have seen him," Taylor says. "You have to hit a nerve with Larry. You have to shock him."

There, on the shining hardwood, he told her, "This is what I want to do. I want to play college basketball."

Every night after work and studies, they went to the Boys Club where he shot baskets for hours while she rebounded or waved a broom in his face, trying to imitate a defender. He did workouts she took from books on physical conditioning. When the school district declared him ineligible to play as a transfer student, Taylor became his legal guardian.

"She was showing me she was real," Ayuso says. "She was going to help me, no matter what it took."

No one on the playground had taught him to play zone defense or set screens away from the ball. As Roswell Coach Britt Cooper explains, "He was totally lacking in fundamentals." But once the high school season began, that sweet stroke translated to 28.8 points a game. Better than A. J. Bramlett, now a starting center at Arizona. Better than Kenny Thomas, who became a star for New Mexico at the Pit.

And every game, no matter where, Ayuso heard the clang of a cowbell — the first incarnation of the boombah — letting him know Taylor was in the stands. She faxed his statistics to universities across the nation and pestered coaches, though she knew nothing about the college game. At one point, she called North Carolina State and asked for Dean Smith, the coach at rival North Carolina.

"Is this a joke?" asked the voice at the other end of the line.

Recruiters eventually took notice, but no one believed Ayuso would graduate, let alone qualify for college. Needing to complete two years' worth of credits in his senior year, he took extra classes and correspondence courses. He spent nights and weekends at the kitchen table.

"It was real tough," Ayuso says. "Diane sat down with me and made sure I got down to it. She told me to be the first one in class, sit up front, get to know my teachers and turn in my papers *before* they were due."

Virginia Burton, an English teacher at Roswell High, saw a change in the kid who'd wandered the halls and flirted with girls.

"It was a whole new ballgame for Larry," she said. "He would listen better and he began to understand the concept of working for what you get academically."

On days when the grind became too much, Ayuso went to dinner with Dick Taylor, or they would play golf, anything to get out of the house for a few hours. Ayuso kept at it, earning a 3.67 grade-point average his senior year, and began taking the ACT in pursuit of a qualifying score.

"I took that test five times," he says. "I kept failing and feeling bad. When I passed, I was so happy you couldn't believe it."

But by that time, New Mexico had awarded all its basketball scholarships and Ayuso balked at leaving home for Fresno State or Brigham Young. He spent a year at New Mexico Junior College, an hour's drive from Roswell, close enough for weekend visits and for Taylor to clang her boombah at all his games.

The Thunderbirds won a regional championship that season. In the spring, USC Coach Henry Bibby visited to scout another player on the squad and noticed Ayuso draining one long jumper after another.

"I want *him,*" the coach said.

What does it take to save a kid?

Maybe it takes something inside the kid himself. Courage. Fear. The instinct to swim when others are sinking.

Maybe it takes a woman who has turned her pain around, who lives by one rule: "Never give up. Never, never, never." The more Ayuso fought her, the more committed she became.

Somewhere along the way, Taylor opened her heart to Ayuso. She stopped threatening to send him back to the Bronx, vowing instead that if he ever returned to his old life, she would track him down and drag him back by his shirt collar.

Somewhere along the way, Ayuso started telling people he had two mothers.

Maybe it takes a miracle.

"Just like you read in the Bible," Ayuso says. God works in mysterious ways, he says.

There is no more need for shame. Going into tonight's game at UCLA, Ayuso is averaging 11.7 points and is scheduled to graduate with a history degree in May. He has gone back to using his real name, Elias.

But this is no success story. Not yet.

"It's very tough living 16 years a certain way and then trying to change your whole life," Ayuso says.

Temptation persists. Soon after arriving at USC in the fall of 1996, Ayuso ran back to the Bronx, back to 137th and Cypress, where he did not have to prove himself to anyone. Taylor got him on the phone and gave him one day to reconsider, then she was coming to New York.

"I thought about it for a couple hours," Ayuso says. "The next day, I was back on the plane."

As recently as last spring, Ayuso cursed at Bibby in the weight room. Taylor found out and made Ayuso apologize before the entire team. A month ago, when he accumulated $1,000 in parking tickets, she flew to Los Angeles and confiscated the car she and Dick had given him.

Bibby chuckles about all this. The ups and downs have brought him closer to Ayuso, and he says what everyone says about the young man: "Larry is a great guy. He has come a long way, but he has a long way to go."

It gets no easier from here. The NBA is a pipe dream for a 21-year-old guard with only six years of organized basketball under his belt. Graduation means leaving school, the routine he once avoided, the structure to which he now clings.

"I've been having a good life, eating well and sleeping in a nice place," Ayuso says. "Maybe I'm not ready for the real world."

Maybe that is why Taylor has not brought any kids into her home since Ayuso left four years ago. She still meets regularly with his coaches and school counselors. She still devotes herself to Ayuso, though in darker moments, she wonders if he will ever love her as much as she loves him.

"I'm sure there are days he hates me," she says. "But I've only got a short window, a few years to teach him. I've got to stay in his face."

People wonder about that woman. They wonder why she travels so far to watch a mediocre basketball team. They wonder why she sits behind the bench every game, pounding that odd-looking stick.

She pounds it out of love and worry and sheer will. She pounds it to let him know she is still there.

GUY LAWSON

Merv Curls Lead

FROM SATURDAY NIGHT

Red Deer, Alberta, December 3

MERV BODNARCHUK PEELED a crisp new hundred-dollar bill from the wad of cash he kept tucked in the pocket of his curling pants and he ordered another round: two bottles of Pilsner for me, two cans of Coors Light and two glasses of Clamato juice for him. He poured the beer and juice, mixed half and half, into another glass to make a concoction he called a Clam's Eye. He took a long tug on the blood-red drink, and told me to hurry and down my Pilsners; he was ready to order another double round. It was late, nearing closing time on a Thursday night in early December, and JB's Lounge in the Black Knight Inn in Red Deer, Alberta, was packed with the world's finest curlers, in town for the Skyreach Curling Classic IV. Famous athletes, of a kind, they sat drinking Molson Canadian and rye and Cokes and Paralyzers, filling ashtrays with stubbed-out du Mauriers, discussing life on the bonspiel circuit. They were dressed in nylon sweatsuits and curling jackets with the names of hometown car dealerships and grain-supply companies stitched on the chest. The chubby, rosy-cheeked members of the Harris team, from Toronto, Olympic silver medal winners in 1998, stood propping up the bar in their red Nagano Team Canada winter jackets, which they insisted on wearing inside, despite the close, smoky warmth of JB's. The curlers had converged on Red Deer from small towns and cities across the prairies and Rockies and eastern provinces, just as curlers have come together to play almost since these parts were first settled.

Merv was forty-eight, older than most in JB's, a wealthy, barrel-chested Vancouver venture capitalist with a thick moustache and a booming voice and a surprisingly gentle handshake. He and I sat alone at a table, slightly apart from the rest. The other curlers in JB's had an easy familiarity with each other, their friendships and rivalries formed over thousands of hours spent on freezing curling rinks, watching each other slide a 40-pound slab of granite 150 feet down a sheet of ice. The curlers gathered in the bar were nearly all white, and most were in their thirties. They held down day jobs as farmers or accountants or teachers; they were in sales or trucking or government.

There generally isn't a great deal of money to be made in curling — for most teams, winnings don't exceed expenses — but what money there is is made in the first half of the season, in what is known as the World Curling Tour. The tour runs every weekend from late September until Christmas in curling clubs across the country. (The World, in this instance, is defined, for the most part, as Canada.) The Red Deer bonspiel was the second-richest event on the tour; the winning team would take home $40,000.

In the second half of the season, overseen by the Canadian Curling Association, the goal is to qualify for the Labatt Brier national finals in March, and the only rewards along the way are a trophy, face time on television, local-hero status, and the right to claim a corner of an antique mythology.

For Merv Bodnarchuk, though, the small-town traditions and ideals of curling held little appeal. He was going to make big bucks out of curling, upend the game, revolutionize the sport. Merv had a business plan. A concept. Curling is a major draw on Canadian television, he said, second only to hockey in ratings for sports. The Brier, he said, pulls in a bigger audience than the Super Bowl or the Grey Cup. In the United States, however, curling was next to nowhere. No cable deal, no Olympic medals, no Brier. But Merv was going to change all that. He had named his team the Anaheim Earthquake, and despite the fact that few people in that southern Californian city had ever heard of curling, let alone Merv's team, the Earthquake was, at least notionally, the pride of Anaheim. Merv said he was going to make curling big in California, as big as beach volleyball. Hell, Merv was going to create beach curling; the technology exists to make ice anywhere, he said. He would put in a rink at the corner of Hollywood and Vine and get Jay Leno and Arnold

Schwarzenegger to try the game. He was going to start a professional curling league, with the Anaheim Earthquake as the charter
member and franchises in half a dozen sunbelt cities. He would
package the games and sell them to American cable sports net-
works. Merv said he was getting a work visa for the States in the
next week or two; as soon as the curling season was done he was
moving to California. He said there weren't many entrepreneurial-
type people left in Canada because Canadians always sneered at
ambition, always found reasons why things couldn't be done. Like
the rest of the Earthquake — indeed, like every single man curling
in the Classic — Merv was Canadian, but before long, he said, he
was going to get citizenship in the United States, and then he was
going to hire a team of curlers to come down from Canada and
play for him. He would get his players citizenship, too. They would
curl for the U.S. at the 2002 Olympics in Salt Lake City and win the
gold medal.

"Imagine the publicity of winning a gold medal for America,"
Merv said. "I have to be up on that podium."

Paying for another double round of Clam's Eyes and Pilsners,
Merv explained that he had come late to the game: he had curled
as a boy in the prairie town of Binscarth, Manitoba, and socially in
the years since, but he had only taken it up in earnest in his forties.
He had spent more than half a million dollars on curling in the
past four years — half a million U.S., he said — and that was before
he had even launched his invasion of America. The sums Merv had
parted with were, of course, unheard of. No one spent half a million dollars on curling, and certainly not doing what Merv did: paying top players lucrative salaries to curl on his team. As a rule,
teams are formed out of local alliances and common ambition, but
not the Earthquake; to create the Earthquake, Merv recruited the
best players money could buy from across Canada. He offered
handsome wages and a quarter-share of all prize money, and he
covered all expenses: rent on the apartments in Vancouver he
leased for his players, airplane tickets, entry fees to bonspiels,
meals, hotels, drinks in the bar after a day at the rink. His curlers
would give up their day jobs and curl full-time. The Earthquake
would be the only professional franchise on the tour, and, of
course, they would be unbeatable. All this, with only one proviso —
Merv would curl lead.

Wayne Middaugh, the skip of the current Brier- and world-champion team, walked past our table, and Merv waved him over. "What's the most money you ever made in your life?" he asked Middaugh. "How much would it take to get you to come to California and play with me next year?" Middaugh was narrow-shouldered and soft-chinned, a Midland, Ontario, golf pro in his early thirties; he was arguably the single best curler in the world.

"I don't know, Merv," Middaugh said. "What are you offering?"

"A hundred grand," Merv said. "A hundred grand *American*."

Middaugh looked amazed. He didn't say yes, but he didn't say no; he whistled and he backed away from Merv and made for the lobby of the inn.

Merv asked me if I wanted a slice of pizza, and I said no. He bought us each two slices. C'mon, eat up, he said. The whole night, we'd been sitting on the far side of the bar from all the curlers. Now a drunken shout came from across the room, directed our way.

"There he is," a curler called. "Merv Bodnarchuk — Mr. Curling."

The curlers in JB's Lounge turned and laughed.

Merv lowered his gaze.

"Some people like me and others don't," he said quietly. "You have to take the good with the bad."

The next morning, the sky was slate-grey, and the parking lot outside the Red Deer Centrium Arena was slick with ice. Inside, the Plexiglas surrounding the hockey rink had been removed, and the relatively crude ice used for hockey had been covered with five perfectly level, perfectly white sheets of curling ice; the climate and relative humidities were carefully monitored by computer sensors, the surface shaved and shammied and sprinkled with tiny drops of purified warm water, which froze on contact and formed millions of pimple-sized pebbles. These served as the gliding surface for the rocks and created the low rumbling sound that envelops the game and is imprinted on every curler's unconscious.

To an outsider, curling can appear arcane, but the basics of the game are straightforward. There are four positions on a team — lead, second, third, skip — and they rise in the order in which they shoot and the degree of skill required. The skip is the most important; the lead, where Merv Bodnarchuk curled, the least. Each player delivers two rocks in each of the ten rounds, or ends, that make up a game, but each player has a specific role: the skip stays at the far end of the rink, directing the placement of shots; when everyone else has curled, the skip then shoots the last, usually decisive, two rocks. The other three curlers rotate through the shooting and sweeping positions, each delivery mounting in complexity and import.

Thirty-two teams had paid the $1,500 entry fee for the Skyreach Classic in the hope of qualifying for one of the eight places in the final rounds — the money rounds — and all five sheets in the arena were in use. The seeming inelegance of the curlers back in JB's Lounge — their stout bodies and skinny arms, their short legs and thick waists — was replaced, in the Centrium, by a preternatural grace, like a walrus finding its element as it slips into water. They slid down the ice and released their stones with the delicacy of a loving caress.

The Centrium resounded with shouts of curlers and the smack of granite colliding with granite. No! the skip would call to the sweepers once a stone was released and he could begin to assess the shot's prospects. No, Lay right of her, Never, Not ever. And then Yes! would suddenly be yelled, the voices as harsh as a pirate captain on the high seas: Yes! Yes! Don't stop. Hard! Harder! Harder! Every inch! Hurry! Hard! HURRY HURRY HURRRRRRY! The sweepers worked their brooms at a furious pace, trying to measure the speed and line of the rock against its objective, careful not to touch the rock with their brooms, not to "burn" a stone and disqualify it from play. The various uses of sweeping — to melt the ice for a split second and create a fine layer of water and train the rock to a straighter course, to clean the ice and make sure a rock doesn't "pick" on a piece of dirt or grit and stray from its appointed path — are fundamental to the game. It is sweeping, married with the ice conditions and the turn given to the handle of the stone as it is let go, that determines the amount of curl in curling. If delivery of the rock is taken to be Nature, then sweeping is Nurture: in a game of inches, and fractions of inches, sweeping can change the destiny of a thrown stone by as much as eight or ten feet.

It was still early in the draw in Red Deer, but things hadn't been going very well for the Earthquake so far: they had already lost twice and they faced elimination if they lost again. Things hadn't, in truth, gone very well for the Earthquake all season long. Despite their billing as a Dream Team, and all the money Merv was spending this year, they had yet to win a bonspiel. The $17,500 in prize money they had managed to collect placed them twentieth on the WCT rankings, the last qualifying place for the tour championship in March. At the Husky Oil bonspiel in Saskatoon, in one of only two games the Earthquake had played on television, Merv had misplayed a shot in sudden-death overtime and cost his team the game. Off the ice, too, there had been woes. Merv had fired the team's third, Bryan Derbowka, after a spiel in Portage La Prairie, Manitoba. Sharp words had been exchanged. In November, at the SGI Charity Classic in Regina, in the parking lot outside the Agri-dome arena, Merv had been punched in the face by a disgruntled investor in a car-rental company Merv had started in Vancouver. Merv's curlers had been called "mercenaries" in the *Winnipeg Free Press,* and other players had muttered that they were curling prostitutes and whores.

The Earthquake were scheduled to play next against the team, the "rink," of Mike Harris, the Olympic medallists. Before the match, Merv's team took their warm-up slides. Dale Duguid, the skip, went first. Last year the team Dale had skipped was the Manitoba champion and a semifinalist in the Brier. He was thirty-nine and being paid more than $50,000 by Merv, by far the largest amount on the team, in deference to his skill and to the central role of the skip. The money was enough to lure him into taking a leave of absence from his job as an auditor for Revenue Canada. Dale squatted low on the ice, an old cornstalk broom in his left hand, and he slid out compact and panther-like, his weight evenly poised on his front toes as he hissed along the ice. The two starting blocks, known as the hack, dug into the ice at either end of the rink and the beginning point for delivering the rock, were used by the rest of the team in descending rank: Mark Olson, a Winnipeg realtor and former Brier champion Merv had engaged for the weekend to play third, slid out steady and sure. Shane Park, twenty-seven, the former Alberta junior champion playing second (and, during the summer, a greenskeeper at a B.C. golf course), exploded from the hack, the stainless steel slider on the sole of his shoe lying flat on the ice and grating loudly. Merv, at lead, emerged from the hack more upright than the others. His balance held for eight, ten feet, and then he began to waver left and then right. He grabbed for the ice and he grimaced and rose unsteadily and went to wait for the game to start.

In Saskatoon, a commentator for The Sports Network had likened Merv to George Steinbrenner, the bloated and egomaniacal owner of the New York Yankees — only with Steinbrenner playing himself at shortstop. In JB's Lounge, Merv had told me that he was an excellent player, good enough to compete at the highest level. The function of the lead's rocks, like the opening gambits in a chess match, is largely to create a tactical advantage for later players, and Merv told me he knew his position well and had the skill to execute. But at the Classic, Merv's teammates hadn't even bothered to sweep his rocks. Some of his shots had come to rest in their intended place, but too many others had careened past the target. Shane had rolled his eyes heavenward with each of Merv's miscues.

Against the Harris rink, despite his earlier troubles, Merv curled nearly perfectly: he had flawless weight and line and his rocks arrived in the spots Dale signalled. Some of the other curlers watching in the stands, including former world champion Ed "The Wrench" Werenich, began to crack wise at Merv's fine play, but if Merv heard, he didn't seem to care. Between shots he stood in the middle of the rink, apart from the others, studying the proceedings on the other sheets. In the fifth end, the halfway point of the game, Harris was leading three points to one. The Earthquake had the final rock, the "hammer," and they were in a position to score two and tie the game. Merv and Shane swept as Dale yelled Yes! Hurry! HARD! Merv was working closest to the rock, following Dale's cues, his broom scouring the ice in a frantic jig . . . and then his broom touched the rock; Merv burned the rock. Shane slammed his broom on the ice in frustration. Dale turned away and gave his head a shake. Instead of the Earthquake picking up two points, Harris scored one and his team went ahead four to one. The Earthquake never recovered: they lost and were eliminated from the Classic; they shuttled back to the hotel and left Red Deer in angry haste. The next day Wayne Middaugh told me that he had decided how much Merv would have to pay him to play with him: a million dollars. Middaugh said he only wanted to play with his friends.

Yorkton, Saskatchewan, December 9

Bryan Derbowka sat in the back office of the City Limits Inn, the hotel and bar he owns and operates with his brother and father on

Yorkton's main drag, opposite the Dairy Queen. In September, Bryan had been hired by Merv to play third with the Earthquake for the season, with the promise of payment of $20,000 plus a quarter of any winnings. At the time Bryan had told the *Saskatoon Star-Phoenix* that he didn't have an opinion on the controversy raised by Merv staffing his team with "hired guns." "I'm not against it and I'm not for it," he had said. "I'm just in the middle of it." Six weeks later, he was fired. Bryan showed me the letter Merv had sent ending his contract, citing "sub-par" play and "irreconsilable differences." The letter demanded the return of Bryan's team jacket. The jacket, nylon slashes of purple and black and white in Merv's own design, had a crest depicting the world cracking at the seams, and above the globe, a stylized "Earthquake" logo. The word "Majik" was stitched on the opposite chest, a reference to Merv's childhood nickname of "Magic," but spelled in what Merv called "the French way," to avoid trademark hassles. Merv kept two sets of the jackets, one for the team to use when he wasn't with them, the other, "good" set, for use when he was. Bryan said he should never have given the jacket back, because the jackets meant everything to Merv.

When Bryan was dismissed, it was reported in the "Last Rock" column in the *Winnipeg Free Press* that "the firing actually came as a relief, after a brutal week that saw Bodnarchuk lambaste the Yorkton curler in the press for playing poorly and then humiliate him even further in Portage last weekend as Bodnarchuk openly recruited curlers" to take Bryan's place. Bryan told *Curler* ("Saskatchewan's only curling newspaper") that Merv shouldn't be pointing fingers; Merv wasn't capable of competing at the highest level. "If he feels I'm the problem," Merv replied in an interview with the *Winnipeg Sun*, "why does he want to play with me?" Bryan claimed that Merv still owed him half his contract fee. "If he honestly feels he deserves more money," Merv told the *Sun*, "good luck."

Sitting in his office in sweats and a windbreaker, Bryan described a swirl of conflicting emotions. It had been an honour to play on a team that Merv considered the best, but the Earthquake wasn't really a team. There hadn't been a single time that they had gotten together after a game, he said, bought a bottle of rye, and just talked and got to know each other. "When I was playing with Merv," he said, "I didn't go around saying bad things about him. I backed him 100 percent. The other guys on the team said things about Merv, but only to me; when Merv was around they'd say, 'Merv, you're playing great.'" Bryan had a stack of press clippings from his tenure with the Earthquake. One, which featured a prominent photograph of Merv Bodnarchuk, was annotated in the margin with the words "pariah" and "social outcast" and "bum" written in block letters. Bryan said the thing that hurt the most was that he had given his heart to Merv and Merv had stepped on it. He recalled the day Merv was attacked in the parking lot outside the Regina Agridome. The team arrived for their match, Bryan said, and there was a man waiting who demanded $50,000 from Merv. "Merv and the guy were nattering back and forth. Merv told us he could handle it, so we all went inside. But then I went back outside — Merv was my boss, I'm wearing his colours, I'm going to stick up for him. When I get outside, Merv's on his knees, halfway under the van, and the other guy's on top of Merv just giving it to him. My heart went out to him." Bryan said Merv played that day, despite a cut and bleeding lip, and Merv was humble and quiet, and the Earthquake won. The next day, during the semifinals of the spiel, a man in the stands stood up, Bryan said, and started screaming at Merv: "You cocksucker! You owe me fourteen thousand dollars! I want my money!" During the fifth end break, the man came out of the stands and went after Merv and had to be escorted from the arena. Merv, his lip stitched from the day before, slid out to the middle of the rink and watched as the man was removed. "Another investor," he said.

Bryan said it wasn't that he didn't like Merv. He wished there were more people like Merv in curling, more people who would invest in the game and have ideas to expand its horizons. He said he would play with Merv again, maybe. "I don't want to cut the son of a bitch down," he said.

North Battleford, Saskatchewan, December 11

"Thunder on Ice," the next stop on the tour, began on Thursday night at the Granite Curling Club in North Battleford, a Quonset hut–shaped building with arch-ribbed wooden rafters and signs advertising the likes of Con's Saw Sharpening and Green Acres Fertilizing. Merv was away on business in the Middle East, trying to convince investors in the United Arab Emirates to put money into the car-rental concern he was going to start in America in conjunction with his curling league, but he called the Granite Club from Dubai three and four times a day to check on how the Earthquake were doing. And the news, again, wasn't good.

Bryan's permanent replacement at third, Doran Johnson, had joined the team, and a friend of Shane's from Edmonton named Pat McCallum had signed on to curl lead for the weekend. The Earthquake had won their first two games without Merv, but they lost their next two and were forced to play at eight o'clock on Sunday morning to avoid elimination. Doran, who had taken a separate room with his girlfriend, visiting from Saskatoon, didn't drink and went to bed early on Saturday night. The others, though, were bunked together and they stayed out until late drinking rye and Blue and Paralyzers, first at the bar at the Tropical Inn, then at the box-like local casino, where a Native country and western outfit was playing Garth Brooks covers.

The next morning, standing in a freezing cold curling rink, bleary-eyed and pale, screaming at each other to sweep hard, hurry HARDER, tempers on the Earthquake were running short. Dale missed a shot and Shane slammed his broom, the game's signal gesture of disgust, and Pat kicked the cushioned barrier at the end of the rink. In the fifth end, Doran and Shane began to argue about tactics for sweeping rocks. Doran, pretending to rub some sleep from his eye, slyly flipped Shane the bird.

"You giving me the finger?" Shane asked.

"You bet ya," Doran said.

"Do that again, you'll be eating it," Shane said.

In the final end, the score tied at four points each, Dale had the last rock of the game — he had the hammer coming home. The other team's final rock was near the centre of the house, just off the bull's eye, and Dale had to clip his opponent's rock and stay in place to score one and win the game. Dale slid out of the hack and released the stone. It was moving on a perfect line. But in the time it takes a lightly thrown rock to curl toward its target — twenty-five seconds that can seem like a lifetime — chaos broke out. Shane and Pat were sliding beside the rock, their brooms poised, waiting for the yells to sweep or not, and the contradictions began quickly.

Dale, at the shooter's end of the ice, said No, Whoa, Lay off her. Doran, as the third and vice-skip, was at the other end. Yes! he screamed. Yes! Yes! On her! Hard! HURRRRRRRY!

No! from Dale; Yes! from Doran.

Shane and Pat hesitated, looked back and forth, and then began to sweep. The stone kept a straight path — too straight. Left to its own devices, left unswept and shaping its arc to the rind of frost on the ice, it might have curled enough, but as it was, Dale's shot just ticked the other stone; the other stone spun and stayed in place. The Earthquake had lost. They had failed to qualify for the final eight, again; they wouldn't win any money at Thunder on Ice; there would be another hasty, angry departure. Shane kicked a rock and almost fell over. Pat threw his broom. The crowd cheered their loss.

"I feel like I've been bent over and raped and pillaged," Shane said.

"Fuck," Pat yelled. "Fuck, fuck, fuck."

"Do you think Doran did it on purpose?" Dale asked Shane and Pat. "Do you think he *wanted* to lose?"

The Yellowhead Highway, December 12

Riding west on the Yellowhead that afternoon under a brilliant winter sun, passing barren, drought-plagued wheat farms and a herd of wild buffalo grazing in a nature reserve, Doran told me he had had the most unique curling life of anyone I would ever hear of. He said he had two suitcases full of newspaper stories about his exploits, and he was always referred to as "controversial" or the "bad boy" of curling. Doran was forty-one, plump, and dressed in tight blue jeans and cowboy boots. He had a fringe of thinning red hair and an easy, gap-tooth grin. Doran said he hadn't held a day job in nearly twenty years; he made his living as a professional gambler. He played a form of stud called Texas Hold 'Em, and he said he averaged fifty dollars an hour in winnings playing in casinos around western Canada. Like clockwork, he said: fifty dollars an hour, if no one was cheating and the table wasn't fixed. Doran said he was one of the sharpest knives in the drawer.

A few years ago, after more than a decade of disputes with the curling bureaucracy, Doran was banned from competition in southern Alberta for allegedly cursing and banging his broom and smashing up a locker room. He had been a curling nomad ever since. This season, at the spiel in Portage, Bryan's last with the Earthquake, the rink Doran was curling with had gone over the time limit imposed on teams to make their shots and had been disqualified. In protest, Doran had refused to leave the ice: the Sit-In on Sheet Seven, Doran's act of non-violent civil disobedience, had caused a stir in the curling press and furthered his reputation as a curling outlaw.

The loss in North Battleford was still fresh on Doran's mind, the feelings still raw, and he told me what he thought had gone wrong. It wasn't the sweeping crisis. "There was too much acrimony on our team throughout the game," he said. "We became four individuals instead of one team. That's why the rock didn't curl enough to make the shot. By the laws of physics, that rock should have curled enough to make the shot — it only needed another millimetre — but it didn't because we didn't collectively will it to happen. The only way a team does well with that last rock is if the team members keep each other safe from outside forces throughout a game so that there's a positive energy force going into the rock. I believe that men can move objects with their minds. If they are working together, they can will a rock to go to the right spot."

Jasper, Alberta, December 18

The weekend before Christmas, the streets of Jasper were covered with ice. The highway through the mountains into the national park was murderous, with strong, coursing winds, blinding drifts of snow, and mile after mile of black ice. In the Jasper Activity Centre, modern and tidy and alpine-fresh, like everything else in town, locals shrugged and effected indifference and said that the roads were fine, despite the deaths and pileups that had been in the news all week. It was thirty below outside, too cold for anyone except the wild elk grazing on the bushes along the main drag, but inside Blister's Curling Lounge, it was warm and cozy. On the curling rinks framed by the lounge's picture windows, the elements had been tamed, and curlers slid confidently down the ice.

Dale and Doran and Shane had come from Vancouver to Jasper on Thursday night, but Merv was still away on business somewhere, and they had no idea when, or if, he would turn up. In the past two weeks, the Earthquake had dropped to 23rd on the WCT money rankings, and if they didn't at least make the finals of the $25,000 Santa Spiel, they wouldn't qualify for the season-finale Tour Championship. The boys were in good spirits, though: it was the last weekend of the exhausting spiel season, and Shane had a thousand-dollar bill in his wallet, part of the proceeds from the $4,000 he had won in a single hand of Let-It-Ride poker during a team outing to a Vancouver casino. Doran had won $250 in five hours of gambling, precisely fifty bucks an hour.

Without Merv, Shane and Doran each threw an extra rock in every end, to make up for the two lead rocks, and the Earthquake won their first two games easily. In a match against the rink of Arnie Asham, from Winnipeg, the Earthquake took an early and commanding lead. The handles of the stones were marked with the names of some of the local sponsors — Chez François Hair Affair, Marmot Texaco Car Wash-Video-Rental; Shane had just played a pluperfect take-out with the Shovel Pass Home Hardware stone when one of the spiel's organizers handed me a telephone. It was Merv calling. He had returned from the Middle East and he was back in Vancouver and he had booked a flight. He could make it to Jasper by midnight. He wanted me to ask the others if they would let him play with them. He had missed a couple of games, he allowed, but he really wanted to play. He said he would call back in ten minutes. In between ends I passed along Merv's plea.

"Should we let him play?" Dale asked Doran and Shane.

"It's not right, him coming into a bonspiel cold like that," Shane said.

"He hasn't played much this month," Doran said. "We should make him sit out a game or two, make him practise before he plays."

"You can tell him that," Dale said to Doran. "I'm not telling Merv to sit."

"Ah, what the hell: let him play," Doran said.

"Tell him to bring his cheque book," Dale said to me.

The next morning Merv was in Jasper and he greeted me by waving the brand-new work visa for the United States that had been franked in his passport. It was a three-year investor's visa, made out to Merv Bodnarchuk of Curling International. The Earthquake had been winning, but with Merv curling lead they lost the next two games in quick succession. Merv's rocks were nearly always just a little off, his delivery too heavy one shot, too light the next. Forced, again, into playing at eight o'clock on Sunday morning in a sudden-death game to qualify for the round of eight, this time the Earthquake went to bed early, and this time they won. They were in the money.

As the Earthquake advanced through the quarter-finals and semifinals, the din of curlers on the ice gradually abated, the losing teams loading up their pick-ups and minivans and leaving town, some with eighteen-hour drives home ahead of them. In the parking lot outside the curling rink, CTV Sportsnet set up satellite trailers, and grandstands for the crowd were constructed next to the sheet of ice chosen for the cable network's broadcast of Monday night's final. Representatives of the International Management Group, the company that runs the world professional tennis and golf tours, arrived in Jasper; IMG owned the television rights to most of the World Curling Tour's bonspiels, and the Santa Spiel, as it was known locally, had been transformed by the power of commerce into the BellVu Express Classic. The final would be watched by nearly 100,000 viewers across the country.

Blister's Lounge, which had bristled all weekend with curlers downing Paralyzers and talking curling, had grown quiet. Alone with his fellow Earthquakes in the bar, Merv's enthusiasms took hold of him. He wanted to share his list of favourite things with me. His favourite colour was purple, he said, the dominant motif of the team jackets. Neil Diamond was his favourite singer — he loved his power music. *One Flew over the Cuckoo's Nest*, Donald Trump, Dolly Parton — Merv reeled off all his passions. He said his greatest regret in life was not pursuing a hockey career; he had once hired Gordie Howe and Bobby Hull to play in an exhibition game, with Merv playing centre on their line. Curling was a great sport, he said, and he thrived on the competition. He had convinced his Middle East investors to put money into his car-rental company, and he would get the Arabs to invest in curling, too, once they saw the operation he was going to create in California. The connection with the businessmen from Dubai had come from a chance encounter in an airport, he said. "I just meet people by destiny," Merv said. "Everyone has a plan set for them, and if everyone would learn to follow their own plan and their own intuitions, they'd get a lot more done in life."

The Monday night curling broadcast, the final of the Santa Spiel, began with the Jasper Highland Pipe Band and an honour guard of two Mounties in dress uniform parading the length of the ice. In the players' area next to the rink, Doran jogged on the spot and Dale and Shane had a last cigarette. Merv flipped through the pages of *The Joy of Curling*. The Earthquake were playing the rink of Kevin Martin, from Edmonton, former Brier and world champions who had won $50,045 in a spiel the weekend before. For the final, the Earthquake were wearing brand-new curling gloves and the special jackets that Merv kept in reserve. Each curler had groomed himself for TV, Doran brushing his prickles of hair, Shane shaving off his Vandyke and slicking his hair with gel, and they all wore looks of keen concentration. Merv won the coin toss, and so his rink had the advantage of throwing the last rock; they had the hammer. In the first end, Merv and Shane and Doran placed their rocks well, and the Earthquake were set to count two points, but Dale's hand appeared unsteady as he released the final rock and they only got a single point.

"Jesus," Dale muttered to himself.

"Sorry, guys," he said to the others. "I just overthrew it."

"That's okay," Doran said.

"Your weight was good," Shane said.

The recriminations of earlier bonspiels, the sullen silences and the thinly veiled contempt, had been vanquished in the white heat of the television lights. Merv, who had curled inconsistently in Jasper thus far, was superb, his accuracy the equal of the opposing lead, who was, by all reckonings, one of the best in the game. Merv's rocks were swept by his teammates, and when he squatted in the hack Doran and Shane encouraged him and reminded him of how to play the shot: Not too light, Keep her out of the house, Nice and easy. The strengths of the Earthquake came to the fore: Shane, fast out of the hack, deadly accurate at smacking into the other team's rocks and keeping them out of play; Doran, a leftie, slowly drawing back in the hack like a pool shark lining up an eight-

ball, playing soft touch shots and fine cuts; Dale, calm and sure after his early nerves, forcing difficult shots on Martin, moving the
game ever closer to a decisive moment. In the ninth end, with the
score tied at three and the Earthquake holding the hammer, Merv
played his two lead rocks to split to the left and the right sides of
the house. It was impossible for Martin's team to knock both of the
rocks out at once, and this tactical edge echoed through the shots
of the seconds and thirds: the Earthquake were in position to take
a commanding lead, with only the tenth and final end left to play.
With his final shot, Dale needed to draw his rock to the middle of
the target to score two points. Merv put Dale's rock next to the
hack, a gesture of respect for his skip, and Dale flipped the stone
over and shined the underbelly with his hand to make sure there
were no tiny pieces of grit on the granite riding surface. Dale's
hand was dead still as he released the stone.

"No," Dale yelled. "Right off her."

Merv and Shane carefully tracked the progress of the stone, waiting for a call to sweep.

"Yes!" Doran yelled from the far end of the rink. "Hurry!"

Merv and Shane waited for a moment.

"Yes," Dale joined in. "Hard. HURRRRRY!"

Merv and Shane leaned hard on their brooms, hurried their
broomheads across the ice. Five, ten, fifteen seconds passed. The
rock began to slow down: as if the Earthquake were willing a
thrown stone toward its fate; as if they had, for a fleeting moment,
kept each other safe from outside forces; as if there was such a
thing as destiny.

"It's right on the button," Shane said.

It was a piss-cutter, a real honey peach.

"Great shot," Doran said.

"Great shot," Merv said.

The Earthquake took up one of the tables in Blister's Lounge, the
beverage room now all but abandoned. Merv insisted on buying
drinks, though he finally relented and let me buy him a couple of
Clam's Eyes. The giant mock cheque for $10,000 presented to the
team was lying on the floor, and the trophy carvings of elk and deer
and grizzly bears were scattered on the table. Merv's quarter-share
of the winnings was $2,500, but there were airfares and hotel bills

and restaurant tabs to pay. Merv, it turned out, wouldn't get to keep any of the prize money; Merv, it turned out, still owed his curlers money. "C'mon, guys," he said. "Let me have five hundred bucks. I want to feel some of that money. I want to feel like I have something to show for it."

The curling rinks, visible through the picture windows of the lounge, were deserted, the lights dimmed and the television crew disappeared into the night. On the ice a few hours earlier, at the moment of victory, a moment now turning and arcing into memory, Merv and Shane and Doran and Dale had for the first time embraced each other.

"Look at us now, guys," Merv had said, draping his arms over the shoulders of the Earthquake. "Who says we're not a team?"

Biographical Notes

Notable Sports Writing of 1999

Biographical Notes

BURKHARD BILGER's work has appeared in the *Atlantic Monthly, Harper's,* the *New York Times,* and *Reader's Digest,* among other publications. A former deputy editor of *The Sciences* — where his work helped garner two National Magazine Awards — Bilger is currently a senior editor at *Discover,* an adjunct professor of science writing at New York University, and the author of *Noodling for Flatheads: Moonshine, Monster Catfish, and Other Southern Comforts.*

BRYAN BURROUGH is a special correspondent at *Vanity Fair,* where he has worked since 1992. He is the author of three books, *Barbarians at the Gate* (with John Helyar), *Vendetta: American Express and the Smearing of Edmond Safra,* and *Dragonfly: NASA and the Crisis Aboard Mir.*

DANIEL COYLE is the author of *Hardball: A Season in the Projects,* which was named best sports book of the year by *The Sporting News.* A contributing editor of *Outside,* he is a resident of Homer, Alaska.

MICHAEL FINKEL is a freelance writer and small-scale chicken farmer who lives in western Montana. His work has appeared in *National Geographic Adventure,* the *Atlantic Monthly, Sports Illustrated,* the *New York Times Magazine,* and *Audubon.* He is the author of *Alpine Circus,* a collection of wintertime adventure stories.

STEVE FRIEDMAN is a contributing editor at *Esquire* and also writes for *Outside* and other national publications. He is co-author of *Loose Balls: Easy Money, Hard Fouls, Cheap Laughs, and True Love in the NBA.*

ALLISON GLOCK, a writer-at-large for *GQ,* is at work on a book about her grandmother entitled *Beauty Before Comfort.*

DAVID HALBERSTAM is the author of *The Reckoning, The Summer of Forty-Nine, The Children,* and *Playing for Keeps: Michael Jordan and the World He Made.* He served as guest editor for the inaugural edition of *The Best American Sports Writing* and for *The Best American Sports Writing of the Century.*

JAMES HIBBERD is a staff writer at *Phoenix New Times.* His feature stories have appeared in *Salon, Playboy.com, Cosmopolitan,* and *Details.* He lives in Tempe, Arizona.

ROBERT HUBER's features and columns about marriage and other personal problems have appeared in *Esquire, GQ,* and *Men's Health.* He has also published short stories in *South Carolina Review, Hawaii Review,* and *Five Fingers Review.* Huber lives with his wife and two sons in the rural southwest corner of New Jersey, where he is writing a book about his marriage.

GARRISON KEILLOR is the host of the radio show *A Prairie Home Companion* and the author of a number of books, among them *Lake Wobegon Days, Wobegon Boy,* and *Me: By Jimmy (Big Boy) Valente, As Told to Garrison Keillor.*

JEANNE MARIE LASKAS is a contributing writer at *Esquire* and a columnist for the *Washington Post Magazine,* where her "Significant Others" essays appear weekly. She is the author of *The Balloon Lady and Other People I Know,* a collection of essays, and *We Remember,* profiles of old ladies. Her most recent book, *Fifty Acres and a Poodle,* is a memoir of life on her farm in Scenery Hill, Pennsylvania, with her husband, daughter, dogs, horses, and mule.

GUY LAWSON grew up in Australia and western Canada, and his story about junior league hockey, "Hockey Nights," appeared in *The Best American Sports Writing 1999.*

MARK LEVINE is an assistant professor at the University of Iowa's Writers' Project and the author of two collections of poetry, *Debt* and *Enola Gay.* He has received a Whiting Writer's Award and a fellowship from the National Endowment for the Arts. In 1994–95 he was the Hodder Fellow in the Humanities at Princeton. As a contributor to *The New Yorker* and *Outside,* Levine has reported on cultural, environmental, and social issues throughout the world.

JEFF MACGREGOR is a special contributor at *Sports Illustrated.* An MFA fellow from the Graduate Creative Writing Program at the Ohio State University, his short stories and essays appear frequently in *The New Yorker, Esquire, Story,* and the *New York Times.* Currently at work on a novel, he plays hockey twice a week near his home in Manhattan. He also teaches in the summer writing program at Yale University.

JONATHAN MILES was born in Cleveland in 1971 and educated at the University of Mississippi in Oxford, where he currently lives. His journalism, essays, and literary criticism have appeared in magazines such as *GQ, Salon.com*, the *New York Times Book Review, Food and Wine, Men's Journal*, and *Sports Afield*, where he is a contributing editor. His work was also included in *The Best American Sports Writing 1999*.

CHARLES P. PIERCE, a writer-at-large for *Esquire*, is the author of *Hard to Forget: An Alzheimer's Story*. This is his sixth appearance in *The Best American Sports Writing*.

STEPHEN RODRICK is a writer living in Boston. His work has appeared in *Esquire, GQ*, and *George*.

CHARLES SPRAWSON is the author of *Haunts of the Black Masseur: The Swimmer as Hero*.

MATT TEAGUE grew up in Vicksburg, Mississippi, and works at the *Raleigh* (N.C.) *News and Observer*. His work has appeared in *Men's Journal*, the *Oxford American, Esquire*, and *Harper's*.

RICK TELANDER is a sports columnist for the *Chicago Sun-Times* and a special contributor to *ESPN: The Magazine*. He has written five books, including *Heaven Is a Playground*, which has been in print for a quarter-century.

PAT TOOMAY played ten years in the National Football League. The author of *The Crunch* and *On Any Given Sunday*, he writes and lives in South Salem, New York.

CRAIG VETTER is a contributing editor of *Outside*.

DAVID WHARTON spent the first decade of his career at the *Los Angeles Times* as a news reporter before switching to sports writing. His work has appeared in publications ranging from *Surfer* magazine to literary journals. He is a graduate of the University of Southern California writing program.

Notable Sports Writing of 1999

SELECTED BY GLENN STOUT

KAREN ABBOTT
She Scared the Hell out of
Everybody. *Philadelphia Weekly,*
August 11

JOHN U. BACON
Puck-emon. *ESPN: The Magazine,*
June 14

ALLEN BARRA
The Legend in the Gray Flannel Suit.
The Village Voice, March 16

ERIC BATES
Jump! *Independent Weekly,* August 4–
10

MARY BATTIATA
A Perilous Beauty. *Washington Post
Magazine,* September 12

PHIL BERGER
How Reality Kicked Mike Tyson's Ass.
Men's Journal, February
When the Walls Come Tumbling
Down. *Sport,* May

RON BORGES
Ward A Warrior in Win. *Boston Globe,*
October 3

JASON BORTE
Surfing with the Enemy. *Surfer,* June

JACK BOULWARE
Rock 'Em! Sock 'Em! *SF Weekly,*
September 1–8

JOHN BRANT
Playing Dirty. *Outside,* July

ANDREW BUCHANEN
Voice from the Water. *Sailing,* April

PAUL BURKA
Savoring the Private Ryan. *Texas
Monthly,* April

TOM CHIARELLA
Blown Away. *Esquire,* December

BOB CHICK
Mystery Man Guarding the Gate.
Tampa Tribune, July 15

PAMELA COLOFF
The Outsiders. *Texas Monthly,*
November

CHRIS COLSTON
Revisiting Roto's Roots. *USA Today
Baseball Weekly,* December 8–14

ANDREW CORSELLO
Hallowed Be Thy Game. *GQ,*
September

FRANK DEFORD
The Ring Leader. *Sports Illustrated,*
May 10

BONNIE DESIMONE
In the Sport of Kings, Krone Was the
Undisputed Queen. *Chicago
Tribune,* April 19